Kweller Prep
New SHSAT Grammar and Reading
Fourth Edition

Douglas S. Kovel, Ed.M.

Copyright © 2025 Douglas S. Kovel

All rights reserved.

No part of this work may be reproduced, stored in a retrieval system, or transmitted in any form or by any means, including electronic, mechanical, photocopy, or recording, without the written permission of the author. For more information, please email info@kwellerprep.com.

ISBN- 9798284672808

Contents

Week 1: Detail and Purpose Questions 7
Week 2: Inference and Word Choice Questions 68
Week 3: Summary Questions 124
Week 4: Vocabulary Questions 160
Week 4B: Infographics 176
Week 5: Grammar Fundamentals 203
Week 6: Sentence Formation 218
Week 6B: Bonus Reading Passage 1 241
Week 7: Modifier Placement 245
Week 7B: Bonus Passage 2 253
Week 8: Pronoun Agreement 258
Week 8B: Bonus Reading Passage 3 269
Week 9: Verb Tense 273
Week 9B: Bonus Passage 4 278
Week 10: Subject Verb Agreement 283
Week 10B: Bonus Passage 5 288
Week 11: Punctuation 293
Week 11B: Bonus Passage 6 302
Week 12: Transitions 305
Week 12B: Bonus Passage 7 310
Week 13: Concise and Precise Language 315
Week 13B: Mixed Review 321
Week 14: Effective Writing in Paragraphs 335
Week 14 Bonus Drill: TEI (Technology Enhanced Items) 348
Key 382
   Week 1 382
   Week 2 392
   Week 3 401
   Week 4 406
   Week 4B 408

Week 5 411
Week 6 413
Week 6B: Bonus Reading Passage 1 417
Week 7 418
Week 7B: Bonus Reading Passage 2 420
Week 8 421
Week 8B: Bonus Passage 3 423
Week 9 424
Week 9B: Bonus Passage 4 425
Week 10 426
Week 10B: Bonus Passage 5 427
Week 11 428
Week 11B: Bonus Passage 6 430
Week 12 431
Week 12B: Bonus Passage 7 432
Week 13 433
Week 13B: Mixed Review 435
Week 14 438
Week 14B: TEI 440

Kweller Prep NEW SHSAT Grammar and Reading

Week 1

Week 1: Detail and Purpose Questions

Detail questions test your ability to locate and comprehend information that is directly stated in a passage.

Detail Questions Overview	
Common Question Phrasing	<ul><li>According to the passage…</li><li>The author indicates…</li></ul>
How to Answer	<ul><li>Locate the information needed to answer the question. Note that the correct answer will often use phrasing that is different than that of the passage.</li></ul>
Common Trap Wrong Answer Types	<ul><li>True details that are irrelevant to the question.</li><li>Illogical statements that are somewhat related to true details.</li><li>Inaccurate details that are contradicted by the passage.</li><li>Details that may or may not be true but are unsupported by the passage.</li></ul>

The excerpt below is from NASA's article, "NASA's Kepler Discovers First Earth-Size Planet In the 'Habitable Zone' of Another Star" (http://www.nasa.gov/ames/kepler/nasas-kepler-discovers-first-earth-size-planet-in-the-habitable-zone-of-another-star/).

Using NASA's Kepler Space Telescope, astronomers have discovered the first Earth-size planet orbiting a star in the "habitable zone" -- the range of distance from a star where liquid water might pool on the surface of an orbiting planet. The discovery of Kepler-186f confirms that planets the size of Earth exists in the habitable zone of stars
5   other than our sun. While planets have previously been found in the habitable zone, they are all at least 40 percent larger in size than Earth and understanding their makeup is challenging. Kepler-186f is more reminiscent of Earth. Although the size of Kepler-186f is known, its mass and composition are not. Previous research, however, suggests that a planet the size of Kepler-186f is likely to be rocky. Kepler-186f orbits its star once
10 every 130-days and receives one-third the energy from its star that Earth gets from the sun, placing it nearer the outer edge of the habitable zone. On the surface of Kepler-186f, the brightness of its star at high noon is only as bright as our sun appears to us about an hour before sunset. "Being in the habitable zone does not mean we know this planet is habitable. The temperature on the planet is strongly dependent on what kind of

15   atmosphere the planet has," said Thomas Barclay, research scientist at the Bay Area
     Environmental Research Institute at Ames, and co-author of the paper. "Kepler-186f can
     be thought of as an Earth-cousin rather than an Earth-twin. It has many properties that
     resemble Earth." The four companion planets, Kepler-186b, Kepler-186c, Kepler-186d,
     and Kepler-186e, whiz around their sun every four, seven, 13, and 22 days,
20   respectively, making them too hot for life as we know it. These four inner planets all
     measure less than 1.5 times the size of Earth.

Sample: In comparison to Earth, Kepler-186f is known to
   A. *be less rocky.*
   B. *have a longer revolution period.*
   C. *receive less energy from its respective star.*
   D. *be less massive.*

Kepler 186-f receives one third the light from its star that the Earth does from the sun (lines 9-11). Choice C is correct. Choice A is incorrect because the passage states that Kepler-186f is likely to be rocky, but no comparisons to Earth are made. Choice B is contradicted by the passage (the revolution period is only 130 days, less than Earth year). Choice D is incorrect because the mass is not known.

Sample: Scientists have concluded that Kepler-186f is likely rocky based on
   A. *previous research of similarly sized planets.*
   B. *data collected from direct sampling of soil.*
   C. *patterns of infrared radiation detected by satellites orbiting the planet.*
   D. *analysis of other planets in the habitable zone that are closer to Earth.*

Previous research of planets similar in size to Kepler-186f suggest that planet is rocky (lines 9-10). Choice A is correct. The other choices are not supported by the passage. Choice B is contradicted since scientists have not directly sampled any materials from the planet.

Sample: What is the relationship between the temperature of a planet and its atmosphere?
   A. *The temperature and the atmosphere are unrelated.*
   B. *The temperature of a planet determines the type of atmosphere it has.*
   C. *The temperature and the atmospheric conditions are determined by a planet's mass.*
   D. *The type of atmosphere a planet has influences its temperature.*

The temperature is dependent on the planet's atmosphere (lines 14-15). Choice D is correct. Choice B reverses the relationship, Choice A is contradicted by the passage, and Choice C is unsupported by the passage.

While detail questions focus on comprehending what the author says, **purpose questions** ask why the author includes certain details. You may need to analyze what function an excerpt from the passage, such as a paragraph, plays in the passage's overall structure.

Purpose Questions Overview	
Common Question Phrasing	- In order to…. - Serves to…. - Purpose of… - How does the _____ fit in the structure of the passage? - How does the _____ contribute to the plot of the passage?
How to Answer	- Locate and interpret the information needed to answer the question. - Consider how the information relates to other details or ideas in the passage. - Determine how the information provided helps the author make a particular point or affect the reader in a particular way.
Common Trap Wrong Answer Types	- True details that do not indicate WHY the author chose to include particular information.

Common Purposes

1. **Compare:** show similarities.
2. **Contrast:** show differences.
3. **Illustrate/Describe:** demonstrate through vivid details.
4. **Example:** a case study or specific instance.
5. **Explain:** to make plain or clear through reasoning.
6. **Suggest:** to imply.
7. **Emphasize:** to stress or highlight.
8. **Support:** evidence or examples that back up a claim or idea.
9. **Refute/Contradict:** evidence or reasoning that opposes or attempts to disprove a claim or idea.
10. **Chronology/Sequence:** to show the order of events, such as steps in a process or history of an event.
11. **Problem/Solution:** to explain a challenge and show how that challenge was overcome.

The article below is adapted from the National Institute of Health's article, "Brain May Flush Out Toxins During Sleep" (http://www.nih.gov/news/health/oct2013/ninds-17.htm).

A good night's rest may literally clear the mind. Using mice, researchers showed for the first time that the space between brain cells may increase during sleep, allowing the brain to flush out toxins that build up during waking hours. These results suggest a new role for sleep in health and disease. The study was funded by the National Institute of Neurological Disorders and Stroke (NINDS), part of the NIH. "Sleep changes the cellular structure of the brain. It appears to be a completely different state," said Maiken Nedergaard, M.D., D.M.Sc., co-director of the Center for Translational Neuromedicine at the University of Rochester Medical Center in New York, and a leader of the study.

For centuries, scientists and philosophers have wondered why people sleep and how it affects the brain. Only recently have scientists shown that sleep is important for storing memories. In this study, Dr. Nedergaard and her colleagues unexpectedly found that sleep may also be the period when the brain cleanses itself of toxic molecules. Their results, published in Science, show that during sleep a plumbing system called the glymphatic system may open, letting fluid flow rapidly through the brain. Dr. Nedergaard's lab recently discovered the glymphatic system helps control the flow of cerebrospinal fluid (CSF), a clear liquid surrounding the brain and spinal cord. Initially the researchers studied the system by injecting dye into the CSF of mice and watching it flow through their brains while simultaneously monitoring electrical brain activity. The dye flowed rapidly when the mice were unconscious, either asleep or anesthetized. In contrast, the dye barely flowed when the same mice were awake. "We were surprised by how little flow there was into the brain when the mice were awake," said Dr. Nedergaard. "It suggested that the space between brain cells changed greatly between conscious and unconscious states."

To test this idea, the researchers inserted electrodes into the brain to directly measure the space between brain cells. They found that the space inside the brains increased by 60 percent when the mice were asleep or anesthetized. "These are some dramatic changes in extracellular space," said Charles Nicholson, Ph.D., a professor at New York University's Langone Medical Center and an expert in measuring the dynamics of brain fluid flow and how it influences nerve cell communication. Certain brain cells, called glia, control flow through the glymphatic system by shrinking or swelling. Noradrenaline is an arousing hormone that is also known to control cell volume. Similar to using anesthesia, treating awake mice with drugs that block noradrenaline induced unconsciousness and increased brain fluid flow and the space between cells, further supporting the link between the glymphatic system and consciousness.

Previous studies suggest that toxic molecules involved in neurodegenerative disorders accumulate in the space between brain cells. In this study, the researchers tested whether the glymphatic system controls this by injecting mice with labeled beta-amyloid, a protein associated with Alzheimer's disease, and measuring how long it lasted in their brains when they were asleep or awake. Beta-amyloid disappeared faster in mice brains when the mice were asleep, suggesting sleep normally clears toxic molecules from the brain. "These results may have broad implications for multiple neurological disorders," said Jim Koenig, Ph.D., a program director at NINDS. "This means the cells regulating the glymphatic system may be new targets for treating a range of disorders." The results may also highlight the importance of sleep. "We need sleep. It cleans up the brain," said Dr. Nedergaard.

Sample: In context, "allowing the brain to flush out toxins that build up during waking hours" (lines 2-3) serves to
   A. *suggest an avenue for further research.*
   B. *explain a previous statement.*
   C. *debate an established belief.*
   D. *contrast the ways in which mice and humans sleep.*

The first statement states that sleep clears the mind, and the second explains how the brain does this. Choice B is correct.

Sample: The quote at the end of the second paragraph (lines 19-22) serves to
   A. *provide evidence for how sleep affects the brain.*
   B. *indicate that sleep plays the most important role in shaping brain circuitry.*
   C. *vividly describe how the structure of the brain changes shape.*
   D. *suggest that the role of sleep in diseases is exaggerated.*

The author provides a quote from an expert indicating that the brain is in a different state during sleep based on evidence of the flow of the dye. Choice A is correct. The quote does not describe in detail how the shape of the brain changes. The expert quoted simply posits that space between brain cells changes during sleep.

Sample: The first sentence of the second paragraph (line 9) is included to
   A. *contrast the perspectives from which scientists and philosophers study the brain.*
   B. *explain how the need for sleep has changed over the centuries.*
   C. *emphasize the enduring nature of a question.*
   D. *exemplify the ways in which scientists study the brain.*

The phrase "for centuries" suggests that questions over the role of sleep in the brain have been in existence for a long time. Choice C is correct.

Sample: The author's discussion of the dye is included to
   A. *compare the similarities between sleeping and conscious brains.*
   B. *illustrate the differences between the brain cells of sleeping and conscious brains.*
   C. *explain how dye alters the electrical activity of brains.*
   D. *exemplify organisms whose sleeping patterns are impacted by the dye.*

The author illustrates that the space between brain cells is larger in sleeping brains (hence, the faster flow of dye). Choice B is correct.

Week 1

These questions detail with purpose at the paragraph level.

The excerpt below is from the National Park Service website (http://www.nature.nps.gov/biology/biodiversity/).

The National Park Service began because people—explorers, artists, politicians, and everyday citizens—recognized something valuable in the vast wildlands of undeveloped America. Today, we recognize the value of not only our lands, but the biodiversity that thrives upon them, as well.

Biological diversity (or biodiversity) includes all the living organisms on earth, and in our parks,
5 *we are finding plants and animals that have disappeared in other parts of the world due to development, habitat fragmentation, climate change, invasive species, and other threats. National parks and other protected places are samples of the world's natural variety, often the last bastion of the earth's wild wealth. They are vital to our future well-being.*

The values of biodiversity in parks are legion: the value of nature for its own sake, a source of
10 *wonder and enjoyment; the value of learning about the workings of nature in places largely free of human influence, for comparison with landscapes dominated by humans; the survival value of multitudes of wild species that flourish as natural systems helping regulate climate, air quality, and cycles of carbon, nitrogen, oxygen, mineral elements, and water—all fundamental to life on Earth. There is economic value in these same plants and animals. They are potential sources of*
15 *food, medicine, and industrial products. Parks protect the species and their communities that underlie these values—serving if necessary as reservoirs of seed stock for restoring species lost elsewhere.*

To preserve biodiversity in parks for future generations, we must first discover the breadth of life forms that exist. In the past decade, numerous parks have teamed up with professional scientists,
20 *university students, school groups, volunteers and park partners for the purpose of biodiversity discovery. These efforts have identified species new to science, located species that have not been seen in parks in hundreds of years, and documented species that are able to survive in extreme conditions.*

Sample: One purpose of the first paragraph (lines 1-3) is to
   A. provide details supporting the importance of a concept.
   B. introduce the topic of a legal debate.
   C. present the importance of an issue to an organization.
   D. summarize the value of a method.

The purpose of this paragraph is to provide background information on the National Park Service (NPS) in relation to the topic of biodiversity. Specifically, the paragraph shows The NPS's commitment to diversity. Choice C is correct.

Sample: The main purpose of the second paragraph (lines 4-8) is to
   A. note the threats to biodiversity.
   B. summarize the benefits of biodiversity.
   C. question the merits of biodiversity.
   D. illustrate the controversial nature of biodiversity.

In this paragraph, the author lists the various threats to biodiversity throughout the world. Choice A is correct.

Sample: The main purpose of the third paragraph (lines 9-17) is to
   A. note the threats to biodiversity.
   B. summarize the benefits of biodiversity.
   C. question the merits of biodiversity.
   D. illustrate the controversial nature of biodiversity.

In this paragraph, the author mentions the environmental and economic importance of biodiversity. Choice B is correct.

Sample: One function of the fourth paragraph (lines 18-23) is to
   A. identify a problem facing a population.
   B. note actions that have advanced an objective.
   C. lament the impracticality of a solution.
   D. analyze the scientific knowledge gained from a study.

The author is describing efforts (actions) that have been done to advance the objective (meet the goal/serve the purpose) of protecting biodiversity. Choice B is correct.

Sample: The main function of this passage is to
   A. convey the importance of biodiversity.
   B. urge citizens to accept a proposal that protects biodiversity.
   C. argue against a destructive policy that harms biodiversity.
   D. warn against the dangers that invasive species pose to biodiversity.

All the paragraphs serve to illustrate or indicate that biodiversity is important and worth preserving. Choice A is correct. Choice D is only briefly discussed in the passage

Drill 1

The Grateful Dead is an iconic band known for its innovative music style. However, it is the band's unique business model that has recently been gaining attention from scholars. The band was ahead of its time in the ways it chose to do business. It was not afraid to improvise and shake up conventional norms to meet the needs of its clientele. For example, by touring year-round instead of focusing mostly
5   on record sales while only touring for a limited portion of the year, as most of its peers did, the band helped build a brand and a loyal base.

The tactics that the Grateful Dead adopted have had an influence on American businesses. For example, the band gave special treatment to its most loyal fans by giving them access to concert tickets across the country before announcing their concerts to the general public. In the 1980s, many American businesses
10 adopted this consumer-oriented model, focusing on providing their clients with quality products and services. Before that, "the customer comes first" mentality was not the norm. The band members also allowed people to record their concerts free of charge. Rather than suing people who recorded and distributed their recordings to others for free, they took advantage of the publicity that they gained by having their music spread. As a result of their increased popularity, they made more money in
15 merchandise and concert sales. Today, many companies embrace this principle. Clients who receive "free stuff" from companies are more inclined to give these companies their business.

In addition, the band's "in-sourcing" approach to management contrasted with the outsourcing model so common throughout corporate America. Many firms will hire contractors from other companies to perform certain business tasks, a practice that sometimes leads to conflict. The Grateful Dead preferred
20 to hire as many people as possible to work in-house for the band itself. Thus, the band had more control over its product and was able to better take care of its employees. As a result, it was better situated to meet the needs of its customers. Today, many companies hire in-house people when possible. For example, a company might hire a lawyer as a fulltime employee rather than make a contract with a separate law firm to do its legal work.

1. When a company hires a full-time lawyer to work on its staff, this is known as
    A. outsourcing.
    B. insourcing.
    C. the consumer-oriented model.
    D. a top-down economic model.

2. Which of the following is **not** mentioned as a characteristic of the Grateful Dead's business model?
    A. Outsourcing most major tasks.
    B. Challenging conventional norms.
    C. Rewarding loyal customers.
    D. Offering concerts year-round.

Week 1

3. According to the passage, the Grateful Dead may have influenced corporate America to be
   A. less innovative.
   B. afraid to improvise.
   C. resistant to insourcing.
   D. more focused on the needs of the consumer.

4. The passage states that the Grateful Dead
   A. copied business models of American businesses in the 1980s.
   B. gave away free concert tickets to its most loyal fans.
   C. profited from sales of merchandise.
   D. had a conventional musical style despite an innovative business model.

5. How does the third paragraph (lines 17-24) contribute to the structure of the passage?
   A. It explains one innovative business strategy employed by the Dead.
   B. It illustrates in detail the financial advantages of the customer-oriented model.
   C. It highlights the similarities between the Grateful Dead and other bands.
   D. It emphasizes the differences between outsourcing in the entertainment industry and in the legal industry.

Reread the sentence below from the first paragraph.

However, it is the band's unique business model that has recently been gaining attention from scholars.

6. What purpose does this sentence serve in the context of the first paragraph?
   A. It notes a change in priorities that typical Grateful Dead fans have had when analyzing the band's transformative impact.
   B. It marks a transition from a broad point about the significance of a musical group to a discussion of a different characteristic of the band on which the rest of the passage elaborates.
   C. It highlights the idea that studies on the innovative nature of Grateful Dead music have been rendered obsolete in light of more interesting recent scholarly discoveries.
   D. It conveys the idea that the Grateful Dead's success over rival bands whose music is similarly creative can be attributed to the business acumen of the Grateful Dead.

Mastodons, the now extinct relatives of the modern elephant, inhabited North and Central America until their extinction about 10,000 years ago. These mysterious animals have captured the attention of scientists and ordinary people alike. President Thomas Jefferson, a scientific expert in his own right, commissioned a team to collect mastodon fossils for him in order to learn more about these fascinating creatures.

The name "mastodon" means "breast tooth," in reference to the appearance of its molars. Mastodons had low-domed heads and large, long tusks. The tusks may have assisted the mastodons in feeding and competing with other animals. Mastodons were herbivorous creatures, whose diet was obtained mostly by browsing (feeding on high-growing plants). They also likely got some food by grazing (feeding on grass and low vegetation). Though they did not have many predators due to their large size, their predators included saber-toothed cats and lions. There is also evidence that humans hunted them. For example, an arrowhead was found among the bones of one American mastodon.

People sometimes confuse mastodons with their more famous cousin, the wooly mammoth, though modern reconstructions based on partial skeleton remains show that they are only distantly related. One notable difference between the two cousins was the shape of their teeth. While the mammoths had ridged molars suitable for eating grass, the mastodons had molars with cone-like cusps that were perfect for cutting trees, twigs, and shrubs. Carbon from the teeth of mastodons and mammoths provide scientists with a treasure trove of information, confirming their different dietary preferences.

Scientists speculate that mastodons may have been social creatures based on studies of their anatomical similarities to elephants, though scientists obviously cannot be sure about exactly how they behaved. Studies of mastodon bone sites suggest that they lived in mixed herds of adult females and young mastodons. The long maturation periods may indicate that mastodons required care for a long period of time. Although there is some speculation that mastodons were migratory creatures, some scientists now believe that many of them did not roam. Their habitats often had everything they needed to live comfortably.

There is still some debate over the primary cause of the mastodon's extinction. It has generally been thought that human pressures on their populations were the main culprit, though climate change may have been a more important factor. In 2016, a nearly complete mastodon skeleton preserved during the Ice Age, the most complete skeleton discovered in decades, was found in the Great Lakes region. Analysis of this skeleton revealed that many of the bones were in the same position relative to each other as when it was alive, suggesting that natural causes were not the cause of death. It is more likely that this mastodon's death served a more practical purpose. Specifically, it was probably stored by hunters as a source of meat under a pond that no longer exists.

7. Which of the following does the author indicate may provide evidence that mastodons required care from their mothers for a long time?
   A. Their anatomical similarities to elephants.
   B. The height of trees on which baby mastodons fed.
   C. The duration of the mastodon's maturation period.
   D. The variety of flora and fauna in mastodons' habitats.

8. Which of the following is **not** mentioned as a trait of mastodons?
   A. Cone-like cusps
   B. Low-domed heads
   C. Large, long tusks
   D. Ridged molars

9. The arrowhead is mentioned in order to
   A. prove that climate change played a minimal role in the mastodon's extinction.
   B. explain why the mastodon had few natural predators.
   C. provide an example of evidence suggesting that humans hunted mastodons.
   D. emphasize that the size of Clovis arrowheads was significantly bigger than the sizes of arrowheads from other cultures.

10. The debate over the primary cause of the mastodon's extinction
    A. has been wholly settled in recent years.
    B. will likely be settled within the next two to three years.
    C. has not been completely resolved.
    D. is hampered by a complete absence of scientific evidence.

11. The assertion that mastodons were social creatures is
    A. a fact that is entirely verifiable.
    B. a reasoned judgment based on scientific knowledge.
    C. complete conjecture based on wild speculation.
    D. a conclusion drawn from the study of mammoths.

12. What is the "treasure trove" referred to in the passage?
    A. Twigs and shrubs
    B. Carbon from mastodons' teeth
    C. The Great Lake region
    D. The shape of mastodons' teeth

Week 1

13. The author mentions the results from the carbon studies in order to
    A. suggest that studies of the structure of teeth are misleading.
    B. emphasize how accurate carbon studies are.
    C. highlight how carbon studies help us understand the nutritional preferences of animals.
    D. show that the pattern of carbon detected is unique to each individual mastodon.

14. How does the fourth paragraph (lines 19-25) contribute to the passage?
    A. It presents likely characteristics of mastodon behavior.
    B. It highlights the differences between mastodons and elephants.
    C. It presents theories about mastodon extinction.
    D. It explains how the migration habits of mastodons and mammoths differed.

15. The last sentence primarily serves to
    A. emphasize the extent to which humans depleted water resources.
    B. elaborate on an idea presented earlier in the paragraph.
    C. provide evidence that completely resolves a longstanding debate.
    D. explain why humans hunted mastodons.

Halloween has long been a popular holiday in many countries. It is typically celebrated on October 31st. To the modern person, this holiday frequently conjures up associations with trick or treating, costumes, and haunted houses. But the holiday as we know it today has a long and interesting history.

Halloween has its roots in the Irish festival Samhain, which was celebrated as far back as the 10th
5   century. Samhain was one of several holidays that signaled the end of the harvest season, as people began stocking up supplies for the winter. It was believed that on October 31st, the window between the worlds of the living and the dead opened. Thus, "scary" costumes and masks were often worn to prevent evil spirts from causing harm to people and their crops. People also made lanterns out of vegetables, such as turnips or pumpkins, to ward off evil spirits. These lanterns were the likely
10   inspiration behind modern-day jack-o-lanterns. It was also believed that spirits of the deceased would come visit their families, seeking hospitality. Thus, people often left out food and drinks for the spirits of their family members.

It was not until the 19th century that Samhain and the similar holiday All Hallows' Eve merged to become what is now known as Halloween. The holiday first came to America after a wave of Irish and Scottish
15   immigration. Though the holiday was originally confined to immigrant communities, it eventually became a mainstream holiday throughout the United States that is now associated with a variety of traditions, such as bonfires, apple bobbing, haunted houses, and scary movies. Halloween is largely a secular holiday with less of a religious dimension than the holidays from which it emerged.

Perhaps the most noteworthy Halloween tradition is "trick or treating." Children go to door to door
20   dressed in costumes saying "trick or treat" in expectation of receiving candy ("the treat"). Though not

usually done in practice, the alternative to a treat is for the children to play a "trick" on the owner of the house if no treat is given. Many countries expressly discourage or outlaw playing tricks due to the damage and disruption they cause. Trick or treating is loosely based on the medieval European practices of "guising" and "souling." Guising was a practice whereby children dressed in costumes would go from
25 door to door asking for coins or food in exchange for putting on entertaining performances. Similarly, "souling" involved beggars asking rich people for food ("soul cakes") on feast days such as All Hallows' Eve. By the 1950s, trick or treating was firmly established as a kid-friendly holiday in the United States. Today, adults are generally expected to go grocery shopping for treats in preparation for Halloween.

Interestingly, Halloween is not just a kid holiday anymore. While there aren't too many adults trick or
30 treating (unless they are accompanying children), many adults relish the opportunity to get dressed up. Some offices even encourage their staff to wear costumes on Halloween. The fun and fantastical holiday can give adults a needed escape from dwelling on the stresses of their lives.

16. According to the passage, what did celebrants of Samhain believe about October 31st?
    A. It was a day when the living must atone for their sins.
    B. It was a day when the barrier between the living and the dead was loosened.
    C. It was a day when good spirits and evil spirits engaged in public battles.
    D. It was a purely symbolic day when the living should light candles for their loved ones.

17. Based on the information provided in the passage, which was the first function of jack-o-lanterns?
    A. To provide light for reading on cold winter nights after the harvest.
    B. To serve as decorations adorning people's windows.
    C. To trap the spirits of loved ones.
    D. To ward off evil spirits.

18. Which of the following Halloween traditions was **not** mentioned as being specifically associated with Samhain?
    A. Apple bobbing
    B. Jack o' lanterns
    C. Masks
    D. Costumes

19. According to the passage, tricking has been outlawed in many countries because
    A. it can result in disturbances and harm to communities.
    B. it is inconsistent with the original practice of trick-or-treating.
    C. there are not enough resources to handle any negative consequences of tricking.
    D. the practice may encourage people to act criminally during the year.

20. How do lines 13-18 contribute to the passage?
    A. They show that Halloween traditions have remained fundamentally static over the centuries.
    B. They emphasize the religious elements undergirding popular Halloween practices.
    C. They provide an overview of some history of the origins of Halloween in the United States.
    D. They contrast Halloween practices between Irish and Scottish communities.

21. According to the passage, family members offered their deceased loved ones which of the following on Samhain?
    A. Clothing
    B. Costumes
    C. Entertainment
    D. Nourishment

In the past, scientists conceptualized taste as linked to taste buds in the mouth, which detect sweet, salty, sour, and bitter flavors. Now, it is clear that taste is an experience that also encompasses smell, touch, and even sight. The cortical workload of the brain processes the majority of information visually, so it makes sense that our eyes play a role in how we perceive food.

5   The appearance of food, including the color of the plates on which it is found, shapes our expectations. In one sense, this is protective. For example, we know not to eat food that looks like it can make us sick, like rotten apples or moldy bread. We may also avoid foods that look similar to those that have made us sick in the past. Visual cues can also assist us in identifying certain features of foods. For example, milk experts are better able to determine the fat content of milk when they can see it.

10 The appearance of food not only impacts expectations, but it can also affect how we actually experience certain flavors. If we try a food that looks disgusting, it may be "too late" to enjoy it because of our brain's expectation that it will taste bad affects how we actually perceive the food once it is in our mouths. Though sight is not technically part of taste, it can trigger our taste buds. The color of food also affects how we experience it. For example, if an apple-flavored drink is colored red, our brains may
15 perceive it to be sweeter than it actually is, since we associate red with sweetness.

In one study, subjects who tried an orange-flavored drink while blindfolded rarely identified the flavor correctly. When they could see that the color of the drink was orange, they almost always were correct. When the orange drink was dyed green, some subjects mistakenly identified it as lime-flavored. When it was not dyed green, no subjects made this mistake. Clearly, the color of food can influence how we
20 perceive taste.

The color of food can even trick so-called "experts." For instance, in a classic experiment, wine experts who tasted white wine that was secretly dyed red used descriptors characteristic of actual red wines. Their expectations for how red wine should taste may have triggered their brains to detect flavors that weren't actually present in the wine. When the wine was in opaque glasses, the experts were more
25 accurate in describing the wine.

The food industry is well aware of how our expectations shape how we taste food. For that reason, they alter the appearance of food and use colorimeters to make sure that foods are perfectly hued. For example, customers may be more inclined to purchase apples that have been colored red, believing them to be sweeter. Companies that make plant-based meat-like products often dye the food brown since customers are not "prepared" to eat green meat. People generally associate green meat with meat that has gone bad. Nevertheless, while we associate certain colors with certain foods, this learning happens from experience. Companies can effectively market flavors that counter our expectations to attract customers, as exemplified by green ketchup and blue lemonade.

Even though our eyes shape how we perceive taste, they don't tell the whole story. The brain and other senses, such as smell, can override the ugly appearance of certain foods. Many foods, such as chilies, sausages, and stews, are popular among people who do not necessarily find them visually appealing. For example, while a beef stew might look "gross" to someone, if it has a pleasant smell and one has positive memories associated with its taste, these factors take precedence. In other cases, a desire to be adventurous may override one's initial revulsion to a certain food's appearance. This is encouraging news to many people, including parents who want their kids to eat healthy foods that look less than appetizing.

22. According to the passage, people perceive bright red apple-flavored drink as tasting
    A. sweeter than it actually is.
    B. less sweet than it actually is.
    C. lime-flavored when consumed in a transparent glass.
    D. orange-flavored when consumed in an opaque glass.

23. What is one major goal of the research described in the third paragraph?
    A. To analyze consumer taste preferences.
    B. To determine how the color impacts flavor perception.
    C. To monitor the use of artificial dyes.
    D. To invent new flavors that will appeal to a diverse consumer base.

24. Which of the following is a conclusion from the studies described in the third paragraph?
    A. Visual cues affect how we perceive taste.
    B. Taste buds are present in the eyes.
    C. Vision is technically the most important aspect of taste.
    D. Odorless foods taste superior to ones with strong aromas.

25. What do food companies use colorimeters for?
    A. To alter the coloration of food with odorless dyes.
    B. To ensure that foods are perfectly hued.
    C. To add artificial flavors to products.
    D. To determine the optimal color at which foods can be frozen.

26. Blue lemonade is mentioned in order to
    A. provide an illustrative example of a commercially viable product that is colored unconventionally.
    B. emphasize the extent to which our expectations prevent us from being adventurous.
    C. support the idea that people associate certain colors with food that has gone bad.
    D. suggest that color is the primary determinant of food purchasing decisions.

27. The most likely reason that the author mentions the vegetable meat products is to
    A. provide evidence for how the food industry manipulates the appearance of products to drive sales.
    B. suggest that some people prefer food that counters their visual explanations.
    C. establish that experience can override visual cues when it comes to foods that are healthy.
    D. suggest that artificial meat products are more expensive than authentic meat products.

28. How does the final paragraph of the passage contribute to the overall structure of the passage?
    A. It highlights flaws in studies that suggest people prefer visually appealing foods by giving examples that contradict this finding.
    B. It argues that parents must have some basic competence in brain science in order to coax their children to consume healthful but unappetizing foods.
    C. It emphasizes that the ability of visual cues to influence nutritional preferences is limited.
    D. It explains why it is important to exercise cognitive control when making dietary decisions.

29. Which quote from the passage best supports the statement "The food industry is well aware of how our expectations shape how we taste food" (line 26)?
    A. "When the wine was in opaque glasses, the experts were more accurate in describing the wine."
    B. "For example, customers may be more inclined to purchase apples that have been colored red, believing them to be sweeter."
    C. "Companies that make plant-based meat-like products often dye the food brown since customers are not 'prepared' to eat green meat."
    D. "People generally associate green meat with meat that has gone bad."

Sea stars, or starfish, are known for their distinctive appearance. With their arms connected to their round body, giving them the appearance of stars, it is no wonder that many people are allured by these creatures. Beyond their dazzling features, sea stars play a particularly important role in maintaining the balance of ecosystems.

Despite their name and aquatic habitat, sea stars are not fish. Rather, they are echinoderms, closely related to other animals such as sea urchins and sand dollars. There are thousands of species of sea stars living in diverse habitats, from tropical waters to colder regions of the ocean.

Sea stars are carnivores, and their size is dependent on how much they eat. Sea stars eat prey outside their bodies. They use suction tubes on their feet to open up shells of shellfish, such as clams and mussels. Their stomachs then leave their bodies and secrete enzymes that break down the tissue of the shellfish. Then the stomachs return to the sea stars' bodies. The madreporite at the center of the star filters water through its body. The water that filters through their bodies acts similarly to "blood" in other animals. Most of the major organs of the sea star are located on the arms. For example, eyespots on the arm help them detect light. Interestingly, sea stars have no brain. Rather, their nervous system is spread throughout their arms. While most sea stars have five arms, there are some with more. Sea stars have calcified skin to protect them from predators, such as crabs and seagulls. Many come in color variations that allow them to hide among the coral reef, giving them another avenue of protection. The ridges and bumps on many starfish actually complement the spikes found in many coral reefs. Even when sea stars are attacked or are wounded, they do not necessarily die. Most sea stars can regenerate missing limbs. Thus, a sea star might sacrifice an arm to escape a predator, only to regrow it.

Sea stars are considered keystone species by scientists because of the role they play in maintaining the balance of ecosystems. They keep the population of their prey under control. For example, if sea stars are removed from an ecosystem, populations of mussels, urchins, and barnacles may grow uncontrollably, thus pushing out other organisms from the ecosystem. One danger posed by increased sea urchin populations is the destruction of kelp forests on which sea urchins feed. When sea stars keep the sea urchin population in check, kelp forests thrive. Kelp forests are vital to the health of marine ecosystems in part because they provide a habitat for many fish. Kelp forests also help the environment. Most scientists believe that excessive carbon dioxide in the atmosphere is responsible for global warming. Kelp forests absorb carbon dioxide from the atmosphere and release oxygen into the air.

Unfortunately, there are many threats to sea stars. Some companies harvest them for fertilizer and poultry feed. Another threat is sea star wasting syndrome, a disease whereby sea stars turn to goo. The disease is likely caused by a virus. It is believed that pollution and warmer waters associated with human-induced climate change may be contributing to the spread of this disease, which has affected as many as 98% of starfish in certain populations.

[6] Some people think that we need to treat sea stars like endangered species for their own protection. In some locations, there are laws restricting how many live sea stars that can be collected by humans from waters. Scientists are also trying to better understand the environmental factors that contribute to sea star viral infections so that we can better protect them. The discovery of young sea stars in areas

where adult populations had been thought to be wiped out brings renewed hope that their populations will rebound.

30. According to the passage, what advantage do coral reef provide for sea stars?
    A. A haven from violent storms.
    B. A place to sleep.
    C. A means to elude predators.
    D. A source of protection from pollution.

31. The third paragraph (lines 8-20) contributes to the passage mainly by
    A. contrasting sea stars with other aquatic species.
    B. highlighting interesting aspects of the anatomy of sea stars.
    C. emphasizing the importance of sea stars to the health of the environment.
    D. listing the threats to the stability of sea star populations.

32. Suction primarily plays a key role in sea stars'
    A. respiration.
    B. cognition.
    C. ingestion.
    D. locomotion.

33. Regeneration refers to sea stars' ability to
    A. detach their stomachs from their bodies.
    B. recover from sea star wasting syndrome.
    C. grow missing limbs.
    D. give up arms to predators.

34. Which of the following is **not** identified as a threat to sea stars?
    A. A virus
    B. Sea urchins
    C. Warming ocean waters
    D. Harvesting by humans

35. Which of the following best describes the function of a keystone organism?
    A. To provide other organisms with nutrition.
    B. To produce oxygen in the environment.
    C. To regulate the temperature of a system.
    D. To maintain stability in an ecosystem.

Week 1

If you've ever gone to a doctor's office or hospital, you've probably encountered nurses who often perform important medical tasks, such as taking blood, administering medicine, and monitoring patients' health. The jobs of nurses today reflect the deep influence of Florence Nightingale, who transformed the once-derided job into an honorable medical profession.

Born to a wealthy Italian family in 1820, Nightingale's mother encouraged her to marry someone in her station, as other upper-class women of her time did. However, Nightingale had different plans in mind. While on a tour of Europe, Nightingale connected with Mary Clarke. Clarke generally looked down on other upper-class women and instead spent most of her time with male intellectuals. Sensing that Nightingale was intelligent in her own right, Clarke took a liking to Nightingale, and the two remained in contact for decades. Clarke taught Nightingale that women can be regarded as equal to their male counterparts. When Nightingale decided to pursue a career in nursing, she did so despite the protests of her mother, who wanted Nightingale to instead focus on building a family of her own. At that time, taking on a job was seen as menial labor.

Nightingale gained prominence during the Crimean War when she treated soldiers. She was struck by the fact that more soldiers were dying of disease than of battle wounds. She noticed the poor hygiene practices of soldiers and unsanitary conditions of the wards and posited that they were making the soldiers sick and contributing to the spread of the disease. Nightingale improved sanitary conditions in the wards, having them scrubbed thoroughly and providing soldiers with clean linens. She also encouraged personal hygiene practices, such as handwashing. As a result of Nightingale's efforts, the death rate in the hospitals declined sharply. She became known as "the lady with the lamp" to the soldiers, as she frequently patrolled the wards with her lamp, checking on the soldiers, whom she reassured with her presence. Nightingale also argued to the Royal Commission that poor ventilation, overcrowding, and bad drainage systems contributed to the spread of infections. The Sanitary Commission fixed the ventilation and drainage systems, further contributing to reductions in death rates. Her influence on the sanitary design of hospitals and homes is still seen today.

Nightingale drew from ideas about nutrition and psychology when treating her patients. She believed that poor nutrition contributed to disease and a decline in overall health. She made sure that soldiers had diverse and appealing dietary options. Nightingale also recognized that mental health was closely linked to physical health. She had soldiers write letters so that they could express themselves emotionally. She provided them with books, classrooms, and libraries to stimulate their minds. Thus, Nightingale was innovative in her focus on treating the whole person.

Although Nightingale is most known for her contributions to nursing, she also has a somewhat underreported legacy in the field of statistics. Nightingale scrupulously collected data during her time as a nurse, and her statistical findings helped convince the Royal Commission on the Health of the Army to accept many of her policy recommendations. Her study of the sanitation system in India led to successful public health reforms that reduced deaths. Nightingale was one of the first people to make use of the pie chart, and she even helped developed the polar area diagram, a type of statistical chart. Nightingale was the first female elected to the Royal Statistical Society.

In 1860, Nightingale put her ideas into practice on a grander scale by establishing the Nightingale School for Nurses, the first school for nurses connected to a medical school program and hospital. Students would typically train for one year, taking classes and working with patients. The Nightingale school serves as a model for other nursing schools. Though the profession of nursing has evolved over the years, Nightingale's influence on the profession is enduring and she will continue to be regarded as a heroine for her contributions.

36. Nightingale believed that physical health and mental health
    A. were intertwined.
    B. were wholly distinct entities.
    C. had no relationship with one another.
    D. were less important than social health.

37. In 1860, Nightingale established a school for
    A. graduate students in statistics.
    B. people training to be nurses.
    C. doctors who oversaw the work of midwives.
    D. soldiers who suffered mental trauma during the Crimean War.

38. Which of the following was **not** identified by Nightingale as a factor for the high mortality rates among soldiers?
    A. Inadequate drainage systems.
    B. Poor personal hygiene.
    C. Unsanitary living quarters.
    D. Unusual military capabilities of enemy forces.

39. The information about Nightingale's family emphasizes that Nightingale
    A. valued her family's advice.
    B. defied the expectations of her family.
    C. pursued a career typical of other women in her class.
    D. had frequent altercations with her mother and sisters.

40. How were Nightingale and Mary Clarke alike?
    A. They only enjoyed the company of male intellectuals.
    B. They believed in the ability of women to be equal to men.
    C. They primarily made their livings by working as medical professionals.
    D. They rejected the principles of the Enlightenment.

Week 1

The poem below is "November" by Elizabeth Drew Stoddard.

Much have I spoken of the faded leaf;
   Long have I listened to the wailing wind,
And watched it ploughing through the heavy clouds,
   For autumn charms my melancholy mind.

5   When autumn comes, the poets sing a dirge:
   The year must perish; all the flowers are dead;
The sheaves are gathered; and the mottled quail
   Runs in the stubble, but the lark has fled!

Still, autumn ushers in the Christmas cheer,
10   The holly-berries and the ivy-tree:
They weave a chaplet for the Old Year's bier,
   These waiting mourners do not sing for me!

I find sweet peace in depths of autumn woods,
   Where grow the ragged ferns and roughened moss;
15   The naked, silent trees have taught me this,—
   The loss of beauty is not always loss!

41. The narrator indicates in the first stanza (lines 1-4) that she finds autumn to be
   A. captivating.
   B. irritating.
   C. depressing.
   D. unattractive.

42. The attitude of poets (line 5) towards the autumn can best be described as one of
   A. appreciation.
   B. fear.
   C. excitement.
   D. somberness.

43. The last stanza (lines 13-16) indicates that the autumn woods provide the narrator with a sense of
   A. tranquility.
   B. sadness.
   C. resignation.
   D. excitement.

Week 1

The poem below is "'Hope' is the Thing with Feathers" by Emily Dickinson.

"Hope" is the thing with feathers -
That perches in the soul -
And sings the tune without the words -
And never stops - at all -

5   And sweetest - in the Gale* - is heard -
And sore must be the storm -
That could abash the little Bird
That kept so many warm -

I've heard it in the chillest land -
10 And on the strangest Sea -
Yet - never - in Extremity,
It asked a crumb - of me.

*Gale: strong wind

44. The speaker directly compares hope to
    A. a feather.
    B. a song.
    C. a bird.
    D. the weather.

45. The song is described as lacking
    A. musicality.
    B. lyrics.
    C. soulfulness.
    D. warmth.

46. The speaker regards the tune described in the first stanza (lines 1-4) as
    A. a beautiful anomaly.
    B. a pleasant surprise.
    C. an unattainable ideal.
    D. a steady force.

47. The last two lines characterize hope as
    A. undemanding.
    B. tranquil.
    C. temperate.
    D. overbearing.

Week 1

The poem below is "When I Heard the Learn'd Astronomer" by Walt Whitman.

When I heard the learn'd astronomer,
When the proofs, the figures, were ranged in columns before me,
When I was shown the charts and diagrams, to add, divide, and measure them,
When I sitting heard the astronomer where he lectured with much applause in the lecture-room,
5 How soon unaccountable I became tired and sick,
Till rising and gliding out I wander'd off by myself,
In the mystical moist night-air, and from time to time,
Look'd up in perfect silence at the stars.

*unaccountable: unable to be explained

48. The speaker is unaccountable because he
    A. is not responsible for his behavior.
    B. cannot explain his subjective experience.
    C. is not capable of understanding the material presented.
    D. frequently suffers random spouts of illness.

49. The primary shift in the speaker's attitude is one from
    A. boredom to peacefulness.
    B. curiosity to resignation.
    C. regret to nostalgia.
    D. envy to relief.

50. The poem establishes a contrast between
    I. learned knowledge and sensory experience.
    II. indoors and outdoors.
    III. earth and sky.
      A. II only
      B. I and II only
      C. II and III
      D. I and III

The poem below is "We Wear the Mask" by Paul Laurence Dunbar.

We wear the mask that grins and lies,
It hides our cheeks and shades our eyes,—
This debt we pay to human guile;
With torn and bleeding hearts we smile,
5 And mouth with myriad subtleties.

Why should the world be over-wise,
In counting all our tears and sighs?
Nay, let them only see us, while
    We wear the mask.

10 We smile, but, O great Christ, our cries
To thee from tortured souls arise.
We sing, but oh the clay is vile
Beneath our feet, and long the mile;
But let the world dream otherwise,
15   We wear the mask!

    51. What primary function does the mask serve?
        A. It makes it possible for the wearers to feel joy.
        B. It makes it easier for the wearers to empathize with others.
        C. It annoys the people wearing it.
        D. It allows the wearers to hide their true feelings.

    52. The mask in the poem most directly represents
        A. sorrow.
        B. deception.
        C. piety.
        D. entertainment.

    53. The "we" in the poem feel
        A. tormented.
        B. scared.
        C. satisfied.
        D. cheerful.

    54. The "world" is portrayed as
        A. oblivious to people's true selves.
        B. sympathetic to the plight of a tortured group.
        C. wise to the problems endemic in a society.
        D. torn in heartache.

The poem below is "He Had His Dream" by Paul Laurence Dunbar.

    He had his dream, and all through life,
    Worked up to it through toil and strife.
    Afloat fore'er before his eyes,
    It colored for him all his skies:

5   The storm–cloud dark
    Above his bark,
    The calm and listless vault of blue
    Took on its hopeful hue,
    It tinctured every passing beam—
10   He had his dream.
    He labored hard and failed at last,
    His sails too weak to bear the blast,
    The raging tempests tore away
    And sent his beating bark astray.

15   But what cared he
    For wind or sea!
    He said, "The tempest will be short,
    My bark will come to port."
    He saw through every cloud a gleam—
20   He had his dream.

55. The man worked toward his dream
    A. with great effort.
    B. for a very short period of time.
    C. primarily while working at sea.
    D. in the face of few obstacles.

56. The man described in the poem can best be described as
    A. creative.
    B. resilient.
    C. pessimistic.
    D. successful.

57. "He saw through every cloud a gleam" (line 19) creates a sense of
    A. pride.
    B. gloominess.
    C. carefreeness.
    D. hopefulness.

Week 1

The excerpt below is from *The Story of My Life* by Helen Keller.

The most important day I remember in all my life is the one on which my teacher, Anne Mansfield Sullivan, came to me. I am filled with wonder when I consider the immeasurable contrasts between the two lives which it connects. It was the third of March, 1887, three months before I was seven years old. On the afternoon of that eventful day, I stood on the porch, dumb, expectant. I guessed vaguely from my mother's signs and from the hurrying to and fro in the house that something unusual was about to happen, so I went to the door and waited on the steps. The afternoon sun penetrated the mass of honeysuckle that covered the porch and fell on my upturned face. My fingers lingered almost unconsciously on the familiar leaves and blossoms which had just come forth to greet the sweet southern spring. I did not know what the future held of marvel or surprise for me. Anger and bitterness had preyed upon me continually for weeks and a deep languor had succeeded this passionate struggle.

Have you ever been at sea in a dense fog, when it seemed as if a tangible white darkness shut you in, and the great ship, tense and anxious, groped her way toward the shore with plummet and sounding-line, and you waited with beating heart for something to happen? I was like that ship before my education began, only I was without compass or sounding-line, and had no way of knowing how near the harbor was. "Light! give me light!" was the wordless cry of my soul, and the light of love shone on me in that very hour.

I felt approaching footsteps, I stretched out my hand as I supposed to my mother. Someone took it, and I was caught up and held close in the arms of her who had come to reveal all things to me, and, more than all things else, to love me. The morning after my teacher came she led me into her room and gave me a doll. The little blind children at the Perkins Institution had sent it and Laura Bridgman had dressed it; but I did not know this until afterward. When I had played with it a little while, Miss Sullivan slowly spelled into my hand the word "d-o-l-l." I was at once interested in this finger play and tried to imitate it. When I finally succeeded in making the letters correctly I was flushed with childish pleasure and pride. Running downstairs to my mother I held up my hand and made the letters for doll. I did not know that I was spelling a word or even that words existed; I was simply making my fingers go in monkey-like imitation. In the days that followed I learned to spell in this uncomprehending way a great many words, among them pin, hat, cup and a few verbs like sit, stand and walk. But my teacher had been with me several weeks before I understood that everything has a name.

One day, while I was playing with my new doll, Miss Sullivan put my big rag doll into my lap also, spelled "d-o-l-l" and tried to make me understand that "d-o-l-l" applied to both. Earlier in the day we had had a tussle over the words "m-u-g" and "w-a-t-e-r." Miss Sullivan had tried to impress it upon me that "m-u-g" is mug and that "w-a-t-e-r" is water, but I persisted in confounding the two. In despair she had dropped the subject for the time, only to renew it at the first opportunity. I became impatient at her repeated attempts and, seizing the new doll, I dashed it upon the floor. I was keenly delighted when I felt the fragments of the broken doll at my feet. Neither sorrow nor regret followed my passionate outburst. I had not loved the doll. In the still, dark world in which I lived there was no strong sentiment or tenderness. I felt my teacher sweep the fragments to one side of the hearth, and I had a sense of satisfaction that the cause of my discomfort was removed. She brought me my hat, and I knew I was going out into the warm sunshine. This thought, if a wordless sensation may be called a thought, made me hop and skip with pleasure.

We walked down the path to the well-house, attracted by the fragrance of the honeysuckle with which it was covered. Someone was drawing water and my teacher placed my hand under the spout. As the cool stream gushed over one hand she spelled into the other the word water, first slowly, then rapidly. I stood still, my whole attention fixed upon the motions of her fingers. Suddenly I felt a misty consciousness as of something forgotten—a thrill of returning thought; and somehow the mystery of language was revealed to me. I knew then that "w-a-t-e-r" meant the wonderful cool something that was flowing over my hand. That living word awakened my soul, gave it light, hope, joy, set it free! There were barriers still, it is true, but barriers that could in time be swept away.

I left the well-house eager to learn. Everything had a name, and each name gave birth to a new thought. As we returned to the house every object which I touched seemed to quiver with life. That was because I saw everything with the strange, new sight that had come to me. On entering the door, I remembered the doll I had broken. I felt my way to the hearth and picked up the pieces. I tried vainly to put them together. Then my eyes filled with tears; for I realized what I had done, and for the first time I felt repentance and sorrow.

I learned a great many new words that day. I do not remember what they all were; but I do know that mother, father, sister, teacher were among them—words that were to make the world blossom for me, "like Aaron's rod, with flowers." It would have been difficult to find a happier child than I was as I lay in my crib at the close of that eventful day and lived over the joys it had brought me, and for the first time longed for a new day to come.

58. How did Helen feel in the weeks prior to meeting Anne Sullivan?
    A. Energetic
    B. Complacent
    C. Irritated
    D. Puzzled

59. Helen compares herself prior to her education to a
    A. person at sea.
    B. directionless ship.
    C. malfunctioning compass.
    D. dense fog.

60. For Helen, the most important thing Anne did for her was
    A. teach her.
    B. love her.
    C. hold her hand.
    D. talk to her.

61. How did Helen first respond to learning how to spell "doll?"
    A. She was proud of her ability to learn new words.
    B. She did not realize she was learning a word.
    C. She immediately felt a profound love for Anne.
    D. She enjoyed saying and spelling the word aloud for her family.

Week 1

Below is "The Story of Prometheus" by James Baldwin.

In those old, old times, there lived two brothers who were not like other men, nor yet like those Mighty Ones who lived upon the mountain top. They were the sons of one of those Titans who had fought against Jupiter* and been sent in chains to the strong prison-house of the Lower World. The name of the elder of these brothers was Prometheus, or Forethought; for he was always thinking of the future and making things ready for what might happen to-morrow, or next week, or next year, or it may be in a hundred years to come. The younger was called Epimetheus, or Afterthought; for he was always so busy thinking of yesterday, or last year, or a hundred years ago, that he had no care at all for what might come to pass after a while. For some cause, Jupiter had not sent these brothers to prison with the rest of the Titans.

Prometheus did not care to live amid the clouds on the mountain top. He was too busy for that. While the Mighty Folk were spending their time in idleness, drinking nectar and eating ambrosia, he was intent upon plans for making the world wiser and better than it had ever been before. He went out amongst men to live with them and help them; for his heart was filled with sadness when he found that they were no longer happy as they had been during the golden days when Saturn was king. Ah, how very poor and wretched they were! He found them living in caves and in holes of the earth, shivering with the cold because there was no fire, dying of starvation, hunted by wild beasts and by one another–the most miserable of all living creatures.

"If they only had fire," said Prometheus to himself, "they could at least warm themselves and cook their food; and after a while they could learn to make tools and build themselves houses. Without fire, they are worse off than the beasts."

Then he went boldly to Jupiter and begged him to give fire to men, that so they might have a little comfort through the long, dreary months of winter.

"Not a spark will I give," said Jupiter. "No, indeed! Why, if men had fire they might become strong and wise like ourselves, and after a while they would drive us out of our kingdom. Let them shiver with cold, and let them live like the beasts. It is best for them to be poor and ignorant, that so we Mighty Ones may thrive and be happy."

Prometheus made no answer; but he had set his heart on helping mankind, and he did not give up. He turned away, and left Jupiter and his mighty company forever.

As he was walking by the shore of the sea he found a reed, or, as some say, a tall stalk of fennel, growing; and when he had broken it off he saw that its hollow center was filled with a dry, soft pith which would burn slowly and keep on fire a long time. He took the long stalk in his hands, and started with it towards the dwelling of the sun in the far east.

"Mankind shall have fire in spite of the tyrant who sits on the mountain top," he said.

He reached the place of the sun in the early morning just as the glowing, golden orb was rising from the earth and beginning his daily journey through the sky. He touched the end of the long reed to the flames, and the dry pith caught on fire and burned slowly. Then he turned and hastened back to his own land, carrying with him the precious spark hidden in the hollow center of the plant. He called some of the shivering men from their caves and built a fire for them, and showed them how to warm themselves by it and how to build other fires from the coals. Soon there was a cheerful blaze in every rude home in

40 the land, and men and women gathered round it and were warm and happy, and thankful to Prometheus for the wonderful gift which he had brought to them from the sun. It was not long until they learned to cook their food and so to eat like men instead of like beasts. They began at once to leave off their wild and savage habits; and instead of lurking in the dark places of the world, they came out into the open air and the bright sunlight, and were glad because life had been given to them.

45 After that, Prometheus taught them, little by little, a thousand things. He showed them how to build houses of wood and stone, and how to tame sheep and cattle and make them useful, and how to plow and sow and reap, and how to protect themselves from the storms of winter and the beasts of the woods. Then he showed them how to dig in the earth for copper and iron, and how to melt the ore, and how to hammer it into shape and fashion from it the tools and weapons which they needed in peace
50 and war; and when he saw how happy the world was becoming he cried out:

"A new Golden Age shall come, brighter and better by far than the old!"

*Jupiter: King of the gods in Roman mythology

62. The passage identifies all of the following as challenges humans faced when Prometheus visited them except
    A. inclement weather.
    B. food scarcity.
    C. predation from animals and each other.
    D. violent punishments from the Mighty Ones.

63. Prometheus wanted to give humans fire primarily so that they could
    A. refine their culinary tastes.
    B. be more powerful than Jupiter.
    C. live under dignified circumstances.
    D. enjoy the exact same pleasures as the Mighty Ones.

64. Why did Jupiter refuse Prometheus's request to give the humans fire?
    A. He did not want to jeopardize his own standing.
    B. He enjoyed watching the humans suffer.
    C. He was suspicious of Prometheus's motives.
    D. He did not believe humankind was prepared for the responsibility.

65. Prometheus did not teach people how to
    A. battle with other humans and the Mighty Folk.
    B. construct buildings.
    C. prepare their own food.
    D. domesticate animals.

Week 1

66. The Mighty Ones are
    A. human monarchs.
    B. Titans.
    C. divine beings.
    D. beasts.

The story below is "Hearts and Hands" by O'Henry.

At Denver there was an influx of passengers into the coaches on the eastbound B. & M. express. In one coach there sat a very pretty young woman dressed in elegant taste and surrounded by all the luxurious comforts of an experienced traveler. Among the newcomers were two young men, one of handsome presence with a bold, frank countenance and manner; the other a ruffled, glum-faced person, heavily
5 built and roughly dressed. The two were handcuffed together.

As they passed down the aisle of the coach the only vacant seat offered was a reversed one facing the attractive young woman. Here the linked couple seated themselves. The young woman's glance fell upon them with a distant, swift disinterest; then with a lovely smile brightening her countenance and a tender pink tingeing her rounded cheeks, she held out a little gray-gloved hand. When she spoke her
10 voice, full, sweet, and deliberate, proclaimed that its owner was accustomed to speak and be heard.

"Well, Mr. Easton, if you *will* make me speak first, I suppose I must. Don't you ever recognize old friends when you meet them in the West?"

The younger man roused himself sharply at the sound of her voice, seemed to struggle with a slight embarrassment which he threw off instantly, and then clasped her fingers with his left hand.

15 "It's Miss Fairchild," he said, with a smile. "I'll ask you to excuse the other hand; it's otherwise engaged just at present."

He slightly raised his right hand, bound at the wrist by the shining "bracelet" to the left one of his companion. The glad look in the girl's eyes slowly changed to a bewildered horror. The glow faded from her cheeks. Her lips parted in a vague, relaxing distress. Easton, with a little laugh, as if amused, was
20 about to speak again when the other forestalled him. The glum-faced man had been watching the girl's countenance with veiled glances from his keen, shrewd eyes.

"You'll excuse me for speaking, miss, but, I see you're acquainted with the marshal here. If you'll ask him to speak a word for me when we get to the pen he'll do it, and it'll make things easier for me there. He's taking me to Leavenworth prison. It's seven years for counterfeiting."

25 "Oh!" said the girl, with a deep breath and returning color. "So that is what you are doing out here? A marshal!"

"My dear Miss Fairchild," said Easton, calmly, "I had to do something. Money has a way of taking wings unto itself, and you know it takes money to keep step with our crowd in Washington. I saw this opening in the West, and—well, a marshalship isn't quite as high a position as that of ambassador, but—"

Week 1

"The ambassador," said the girl, warmly, "doesn't call any more. He needn't ever have done so. You ought to know that. And so now you are one of these dashing Western heroes, and you ride and shoot and go into all kinds of dangers. That's different from the Washington life. You have been missed from the old crowd."

The girl's eyes, fascinated, went back, widening a little, to rest upon the glittering handcuffs.

"Don't you worry about them, miss," said the other man. "All marshals handcuff themselves to their prisoners to keep them from getting away. Mr. Easton knows his business."

"Will we see you again soon in Washington?" asked the girl.

"Not soon, I think," said Easton. "My butterfly days are over, I fear."

"I love the West," said the girl irrelevantly. Her eyes were shining softly. She looked away out the car window. She began to speak truly and simply without the gloss of style and manner: "Mamma and I spent the summer in Denver. She went home a week ago because father was slightly ill. I could live and be happy in the West. I think the air here agrees with me. Money isn't everything. But people always misunderstand things and remain stupid—"

"Say, Mr. Marshal," growled the glum-faced man. "This isn't quite fair. I'm needing a drink, and haven't had a smoke all day. Haven't you talked long enough? Take me in the smoker now, won't you? I'm half dead for a pipe."

The bound travelers rose to their feet, Easton with the same slow smile on his face.

"I can't deny a petition for tobacco," he said, lightly. "It's the one friend of the unfortunate. Good-bye, Miss Fairchild. Duty calls, you know." He held out his hand for a farewell.

"It's too bad you are not going East," she said, reclothing herself with manner and style. "But you must go on to Leavenworth, I suppose?"

"Yes," said Easton, "I must go on to Leavenworth."

The two men sidled down the aisle into the smoker.

The two passengers in a seat nearby had heard most of the conversation. Said one of them: "That marshal's a good sort of chap. Some of these Western fellows are all right."

"Pretty young to hold an office like that, isn't he?" asked the other.

"Young!" exclaimed the first speaker, "why—Oh! didn't you catch on? Say—did you ever know an officer to handcuff a prisoner to his *right* hand?"

67. Compared to the younger man, the older man appears more
    A. confident.
    B. youthful.
    C. gloomy.
    D. engaging.

68. Miss Fairchild's initial reaction to seeing the handcuffs is one of
    A. amusement.
    B. horror.
    C. empathy.
    D. condescension.

69. What explanation does the older man give for Mr. Easton's current condition?
    A. Mr. Easton is serving a prison sentence.
    B. Mr. Easton is performing his occupational duties.
    C. Mr. Easton is protecting the older man.
    D. Mr. Easton is comforting the older man.

70. Which of the following details about Mr. Easton is true?
    A. He moved out West to become a marshal.
    B. He does not initially recognize Miss Fairchild.
    C. He is guarding the older man.
    D. He is headed to Leavenworth.

"An Obstacle" by Charlotte Perkins Gilman

    I was climbing up a mountain-path
    With many things to do,
    Important business of my own,
    And other people's too,
5   When I ran against a Prejudice
    That quite cut off the view.

    My work was such as could not wait,
    My path quite clearly showed,
    My strength and time were limited,
10 I carried quite a load;
    And there that hulking Prejudice
    Sat all across the road.

    So I spoke to him politely,
    For he was huge and high,
15 And begged that he would move a bit
    And let me travel by.
    He smiled, but as for moving! --
    He didn't even try.

           And then I reasoned quietly
20   With that colossal mule:
           My time was short -- no other path --
           The mountain winds were cool.
           I argued like a Solomon;*
           He sat there like a fool.

25   Then I flew into a passion,
           and I danced and howled and swore.
           I pelted and belabored him
           Till I was stiff and sore;
           He got as mad as I did --
30   But he sat there as before.

           And then I begged him on my knees;
           I might be kneeling still
           If so I hoped to move that mass
           Of obdurate ill-will --
35   As well invite the monument
           To vacate Bunker Hill!

           So I sat before him helpless,
           In an ecstasy of woe --
           The mountain mists were rising fast,
40   The sun was sinking slow --
           When a sudden inspiration came,
           As sudden winds do blow.

           I took my hat, I took my stick,
           My load I settled fair,
45   I approached that awful incubus
           With an absent-minded air --
           And I walked directly through him,
           As if he wasn't there!

           *Solomon: a wise person

71. The speaker's overall approach to her walk can best be described as
    A. purposeful.
    B. leisurely.
    C. frightened.
    D. amused.

Week 1

72. What effect does the statement "my strength and time were limited" (line 9) have on the poem?
    A. It conveys the speaker's impatience with an obstacle she encounters.
    B. It suggests that the speaker is too weak to fulfill her obligations.
    C. It implies that the speaker is not committed to the ideals she espouses.
    D. It underscores the unfairness the speaker encounters in all her endeavors.

73. The speaker compares Prejudice to a monument in order to
    A. foreshadow its defeat.
    B. highlight its stubborn refusal to move.
    C. marvel at its size.
    D. criticize the principles underlying a war.

74. The speaker ultimately gets around Prejudice by
    A. presenting it with compelling arguments.
    B. coercing it into submission.
    C. flattering it for its power.
    D. pretending it does not exist.

75. Prejudice's response to the speaker's screams can best be described as
    A. steadfast and enraged.
    B. violent and threatening.
    C. tickled and composed.
    D. compassionate but firm.

76. The last stanza shows that the speaker
    A. regrets trying to reason with Prejudice.
    B. knows she will never encounter Prejudice again.
    C. has adapted to an inconvenient truth.
    D. no longer must carry a heavy load.

77. The setting of the mountain-path most directly parallels the speaker's
    A. desire to help others as well as herself.
    B. uphill challenges she encounters on her journey.
    C. desire to dominate nature.
    D. confusion over what path she should take in life.

"To an Indifferent Woman" by Charlotte Perkins Gilman

1
You who are happy in a thousand homes,
Or overworked therein, to a dumb peace;
Whose souls are wholly centered in the life
Of that small group you personally love;
5 Who told you that you need not know or care
About the sin and sorrow of the world?

Do you believe the sorrow of the world
Does not concern you in your little homes? —
That you are licensed to avoid the care

Week 1

10 And toil for human progress, human peace,
And the enlargement of our power of love
Until it covers every field of life?

The one first duty of all human life
Is to promote the progress of the world
15 In righteousness, in wisdom, truth and love;
And you ignore it, hidden in your homes,
Content to keep them in uncertain peace,
Content to leave all else without your care.

Yet you are mothers! And a mother's care
20 Is the first step toward friendly human life.
Life where all nations in untroubled peace
Unite to raise the standard of the world
And make the happiness we seek in homes
Spread everywhere in strong and fruitful love.

25 You are content to keep that mighty love
In its first steps forever; the crude care
Of animals for mate and young and homes,
Instead of pouring it abroad in life,
Its mighty current feeding all the world
30 Till every human child can grow in peace.

You cannot keep your small domestic peace
Your little pool of undeveloped love,
While the neglected, starved, unmothered world
Struggles and fights for lack of mother's care,
35 And its tempestuous, bitter, broken life
Beats in upon you in your selfish homes.

We all may have our homes in joy and peace
When woman's life, in its rich power of love
Is joined with man's to care for all the world.

78. What does the speaker believe two types of women mentioned in the first stanza have in common?
   A. They are saddened by problems existing in thousands of homes.
   B. They live luxurious but disconnected lifestyles.
   C. They toil hard to meet the emotional needs of their loved ones.
   D. They have a generally insular attitude towards the world.

79. One way the speaker develops her argument is through
    A. supporting her point of view with a poignant anecdote.
    B. rhetorical questions with implicit positive answers.
    C. imagery about the suffering a specific group of people is enduring.
    D. showing that a universal human trait will make a certain promising outcome unlikely.

80. The exclamation point in line 19 serves to emphasize the speaker's
    A. outrage at the complacency of a class of individuals.
    B. anger over rampant inequality within domestic structures.
    C. excitement over possibilities to reform an unjust system.
    D. disappointment in certain parents for withholding affections from their children.

"Easter, 1916" by W.B. Yeats.

The poem below describes rebels of an Irish rebellion against England.

I have met them at close of day
Coming with vivid faces
From counter or desk among grey
Eighteenth-century houses.
5 I have passed with a nod of the head
Or polite meaningless words,
Or have lingered awhile and said
Polite meaningless words,
And thought before I had done
10 Of a mocking tale or a gibe
To please a companion
Around the fire at the club,
Being certain that they and I
But lived where motley is worn:
15 All changed, changed utterly:
A terrible beauty is born.

That woman's days were spent
In ignorant good-will,
Her nights in argument
20 Until her voice grew shrill.
What voice more sweet than hers
When, young and beautiful,
She rode to harriers?
This man had kept a school
25 And rode our wingèd horse;
This other his helper and friend
Was coming into his force;
He might have won fame in the end,

Week 1

    So sensitive his nature seemed,
30 So daring and sweet his thought.
    This other man I had dreamed
    A drunken, vainglorious lout.
    He had done most bitter wrong
    To some who are near my heart,
35 Yet I number him in the song;
    He, too, has resigned his part
    In the casual comedy;
    He, too, has been changed in his turn,
    Transformed utterly:
40 A terrible beauty is born.

    Hearts with one purpose alone
    Through summer and winter seem
    Enchanted to a stone
    To trouble the living stream.
45 The horse that comes from the road,
    The rider, the birds that range
    From cloud to tumbling cloud,
    Minute by minute they change;
    A shadow of cloud on the stream
50 Changes minute by minute;
    A horse-hoof slides on the brim,
    And a horse plashes within it;
    The long-legged moor-hens dive,
    And hens to moor-cocks call;
55 Minute by minute they live:
    The stone's in the midst of all.

    Too long a sacrifice
    Can make a stone of the heart.
    O when may it suffice?
60 That is Heaven's part, our part
    To murmur name upon name,
    As a mother names her child
    When sleep at last has come
    On limbs that had run wild.
65 What is it but nightfall?
    No, no, not night but death;
    Was it needless death after all?
    For England may keep faith
    For all that is done and said.
70 We know their dream; enough
    To know they dreamed and are dead;
    And what if excess of love
    Bewildered them till they died?
    I write it out in a verse—
75 MacDonagh and MacBride

And Connolly and Pearse
Now and in time to be,
Wherever green is worn,
Are changed, changed utterly:
80 A terrible beauty is born.

81. The first stanza indicates that the rebels were
    A. insignificant to the speaker.
    B. close friends of the speaker.
    C. people who looked up to the speaker for advice.
    D. business associates of the speaker.

82. Most of the speaker's interactions with the rebels happened
    A. in the early morning hours.
    B. at the end of the workday.
    C. during weekends.
    D. right before he went to sleep.

83. In the first stanza, what effect to the words "grey Eighteenth-century houses" and "polite meaningless words" have on the poem?
    A. They convey the snobbery of the speaker.
    B. They suggest the rebels' envy of the speaker's social status.
    C. They highlight the most important motive for an insurrection.
    D. They foreshadow a beautiful resolution to a violent conflict.

84. Before the rebellion, the speaker indicates that he sometimes
    A. made efforts to understand the rebels' political woes.
    B. ridiculed the rebels in private to his friends.
    C. lingered at the rebels' residences to try to convince them to not go through with the rebellion.
    D. chastised the rebels for their single-minded devotion to a harebrained cause.

85. The speaker's overall attitude toward the leaders of the rebellion can best be described as
    A. fearful.
    B. hateful.
    C. conflicted.
    D. apathetic.

86. The speaker regards the woman described in lines 17-20 as
    A. content with the status quo.
    B. uninformed and passionate.
    C. charming and honorable.
    D. levelheaded and influential.

Week 1

87. The speaker compares the hearts of the rebels to a stone in order to
    A. undermine the implication that the rebels were disciplined.
    B. convey that the rebels were attuned to their natural environment.
    C. underscore that the resolve of the rebels was unmovable.
    D. emphasize that the hearts of the rebels are cold and uncaring.

88. The speaker is most certain about
    A. whether the uprising was pointless.
    B. the extent to which the rebels' nationalism confused them.
    C. how historians will describe the rebellion in future generations.
    D. the ideals for which the rebels were willing to die.

89. The repetition of "a terrible beauty was born" conveys that
    A. the beauty of change and idealism often comes with violence.
    B. Ireland will continue to engage in armed conflicts for years to come.
    C. Ireland's physical beauty has been reinvigorated despite tragedy.
    D. a new government has ushered in an era of freedom following a tumultuous period.

The short story below is "Luck" by Mark Twain.

[Note—This is not a fancy sketch. I got it from a clergyman who was an instructor at Woolwich forty years ago, and who vouched for its truth.—M.T.]
It was at a banquet in London in honor of one of the two or three conspicuously illustrious English military names of this generation. For reasons which will presently appear, I will withhold his real name and titles, and call him Lieutenant General Lord Arthur Scoresby, V.C., K.C.B., etc., etc., etc. What a fascination there is in a renowned name! There sat the man, in actual flesh, whom I had heard of so many thousands of times since that day, thirty years before, when his name shot suddenly to the zenith from a Crimean battlefield, to remain forever celebrated. It was food and drink to me to look, and look, and look at that demigod; scanning, searching, noting: the quietness, the reserve, the noble gravity of his countenance; the simple honesty that expressed itself all over him; the sweet unconsciousness of his greatness—unconsciousness of the hundreds of admiring eyes fastened upon him, unconsciousness of the deep, loving, sincere worship welling out of the breasts of those people and flowing toward him. The clergyman at my left was an old acquaintance of mine—clergyman now, but had spent the first half of his life in the camp and field, and as an instructor in the military school at Woolwich. Just at the moment I have been talking about, a veiled and singular light glimmered in his eyes, and he leaned down and muttered confidentially to me—indicating the hero of the banquet with a gesture: "Privately—he's an absolute fool."
This verdict was a great surprise to me. If its subject had been Napoleon, or Socrates, or Solomon, my astonishment could not have been greater. Two things I was well aware of: that the Reverend was a man of strict veracity, and that his judgement of men was good. Therefore I knew, beyond doubt or question, that the world was mistaken about this hero: he *was* a fool. So I meant to find out, at a convenient moment, how the Reverend, all solitary and alone, had discovered the secret.
Some days later the opportunity came, and this is what the Reverend told me.
About forty years ago I was an instructor in the military academy at Woolwich. I was present in one of the sections when young Scoresby underwent his preliminary examination. I was touched to the quick with pity; for the rest of the class answered up brightly and handsomely, while he—why, dear me, he

didn't know *anything*, so to speak. He was evidently good, and sweet, and lovable, and guileless; and so it was exceedingly painful to see him stand there, as serene as a graven image, and deliver himself of answers which were veritably miraculous for stupidity and ignorance. All the compassion in me was aroused in his behalf. I said to myself, when he comes to be examined again, he will be flung over, of course; so it will be simply a harmless act of charity to ease his fall as much as I can. I took him aside, and found that he knew a little of Cæsar's history; and as he didn't know anything else, I went to work and drilled him like a galley slave on a certain line of stock questions concerning Cæsar which I knew would be used. If you'll believe me, he went through with flying colors on examination day! He went through on that purely superficial "cram," and got compliments too, while others, who knew a thousand times more than he, got plucked. By some strangely lucky accident—an accident not likely to happen twice in a century—he was asked no question outside of the narrow limits of his drill.

It was stupefying. Well, all through his course I stood by him, with something of the sentiment which a mother feels for a crippled child; and he always saved himself—just by miracle, apparently.

Now of course the thing that would expose him and kill him at last was mathematics. I resolved to make his death as easy as I could; so I drilled him and crammed him, and crammed him and drilled him, just on the line of questions which the examiners would be most likely to use, and then launching him on his fate. Well, sir, try to conceive of the result: to my consternation, he took the first prize! And with it he got a perfect ovation in the way of compliments.

Sleep? There was no more sleep for me for a week. My conscience tortured me day and night. What I had done I had done purely through charity, and only to ease the poor youth's fall—I never had dreamed of any such preposterous result as the thing that had happened. I felt as guilty and miserable as the creator of Frankenstein. Here was a woodenhead whom I had put in the way of glittering promotions and prodigious responsibilities, and but one thing could happen: he and his responsibilities would all go to ruin together at the first opportunity.

The Crimean war had just broken out. Of course there had to be a war, I said to myself: we couldn't have peace and give this donkey a chance to die before he is found out. I waited for the earthquake. It came. And it made me reel when it did come. He was actually gazetted to a captaincy in a marching regiment! Better men grow old and gray in the service before they climb to a sublimity like that. And who could ever have foreseen that they would go and put such a load of responsibility on such green and inadequate shoulders? I could just barely have stood it if they had made him a cornet; but a captain—think of it! I thought my hair would turn white.

Consider what I did—I who so loved repose and inaction. I said to myself, I am responsible to the country for this, and I must go along with him and protect the country against him as far as I can. So I took my poor little capital that I had saved up through years of work and grinding economy, and went with a sigh and bought a cornetcy in his regiment, and away we went to the field.

And there—oh dear, it was awful. Blunders? Why, he never did anything *but* blunder. But, you see, nobody was in the fellow's secret—everybody had him focused wrong, and necessarily misinterpreted his performance every time—consequently they took his idiotic blunders for inspirations of genius; they did, honestly! His mildest blunders were enough to make a man in his right mind cry; and they did make me cry—and rage and rave too, privately. And the thing that kept me always in a sweat of apprehension was the fact that every fresh blunder he made increased the luster of his reputation! I kept saying to myself, he'll get so high, that when discovery does finally come, it will be like the sun falling out of the sky.

He went right along up, from grade to grade, over the dead bodies of his superiors, until at last, in the hottest moment of the battle of ------- down went our colonel, and my heart jumped into my mouth, for Scoresby was next in rank! Now for it, said I; we'll all land in Sheol in ten minutes, sure.

The battle was awfully hot; the allies were steadily giving way all over the field. Our regiment occupied a position that was vital; a blunder now must be destruction. At this crucial moment, what does this immortal fool do but detach the regiment from its place and order a charge over a neighboring hill where there wasn't a suggestion of an enemy! "There you go!" I said to myself; "this *is* the end at last." And away we did go, and were over the shoulder of the hill before the insane movement could be discovered and stopped. And what did we find? An entire and unsuspected Russian army in reserve! And what happened? We were eaten up? That is necessarily what would have happened in ninety-nine cases out of a hundred. But no, those Russians argued that no single regiment would come browsing around there at such a time. It must be the entire English army, and that the sly Russian game was detected and blocked; so they turned tail, and away they went, pell-mell, over the hill and down into the field, in wild confusion, and we after them; they themselves broke the solid Russian center in the field, and tore through, and in no time there was the most tremendous rout you ever saw, and the defeat of the allies was turned into a sweeping and splendid victory! Marshal Canrobert looked on, dizzy with astonishment, admiration,and delight; and sent right off for Scoresby, and hugged him, and decorated him on the field, in presence of all the armies!

And what was Scoresby's blunder that time? Merely the mistaking his right hand for his left—that was all. An order had come to him to fall back and support our right; and instead, he fell *forward* and went over the hill to the left. But the name he won that day as a marvelous military genius filled the world with his glory, and that glory will never fade while history books last.

He is just as good and sweet and lovable and unpretending as a man can be, but he doesn't know enough to come in when it rains. Now that is absolutely true. He is the supremest donkey in the universe; and until half an hour ago nobody knew it but himself and me. He has been pursued, day by day and year by year, by a most phenomenal and astonishing luckiness. He has been a shining soldier in all our wars for a generation; he has littered his whole military life with blunders, and yet has never committed one that didn't make him a knight or a baronet or a lord or something. Look at his breast; why, he is just clothed in domestic and foreign decorations. Well, sir, every one of them is the record of some shouting stupidity or other; and taken together, they are proof that the very best thing in all this world that can befall a man is to be born lucky. I say again, as I said at the banquet, Scoresby's an absolute fool.

90. In lines 1-2, the narrator attempts to
   A. quell the reader of potential doubts about the authenticity of a story.
   B. argue that a course of events is too fanciful to be believed.
   C. question the testimony of a subject matter expert on a series of unusual events.
   D. acknowledge and refute a common counterargument to an unflattering assessment.

91. Reread the statement below (line 17).
    "Privately—he's an absolute fool."
    Within the plot, this line serves to
    A. transition from a gratuitous description of a subject's strengths to evidence that his remarkable abilities are counterbalanced by flaws of equal severity.
    B. transition from a discussion to the narrator's veneration of Scoresby to an account that conveys why this attitude is unjustified.
    C. mock the intelligence of a person who has worked harder than most of his contemporaries to overcome a stigma.
    D. cast aspersions at an unworthy beneficiary of accolades who relied on deception to advance his career.

92. On the preliminary examination, the reverend argues that Scoresby benefitted from
    A. knowing more about trivial topics than his classmates who failed despite having a smaller overall body knowledge.
    B. having a remarkable ability to memorize the entire curriculum in one night despite his under-preparation throughout the term.
    C. a fortunate sampling of test questions that coincided with his narrow scope of knowledge.
    D. a tendency for his instructors to misinterpret his objectively incorrect responses as evidence of creative thinking.

93. In the context of lines 62-69, what effect does the word choice of "rage and rave" and "sweat and apprehension" have on the poem?
    A. It underscores that a certain opinion of the clergyman is not shared by others.
    B. It highlights the envy the clergyman possesses of Scoresby's prowess.
    C. It suggests that the clergyman worries that Scoresby's failures have done irredeemable harm to the nation.
    D. It reveals why the clergyman has never gotten a good night of sleep since Scoresby's promotion.

94. The clergyman compares Scoresby to a donkey primarily to emphasize his supposed
    A. loyalty and industriousness.
    B. cowardliness and lethargy.
    C. optimism and pride.
    D. friendliness and dimness.

95. The fact that the clergyman helped Scoresby prepare for his exams most contradicts the clergyman's assertion that
    A. the clergyman cared about the wellbeing of his country.
    B. Scoresby regularly blundered.
    C. the clergyman was a man of repose and inaction.
    D. the clergyman could not sleep for a week after Scoresby got first prize.

"Human-Animal Interactions: Therapeutic and Surprising" (NIH)

[1] For most of my life, I've led an urban existence. Growing up in Manhattan and working for over 30 years in Boston, I rarely encountered wildlife, other than pigeons and squirrels. One evening, however, shortly after I arrived at NIH last fall, I was shocked to come face to face with a large buck as I headed toward my car. In subsequent conversations with colleagues, I learned that deer roam freely on the NIH campus. This was especially surprising because NIH isn't in the countryside, it's in a heavily populated suburb just outside of Washington, DC. This wildlife encounter startled me at first, but then I thought about how interactions with animals, particularly in the fast pace of modern life, help to calm us and give us perspective.

[2] Indeed, companion animals—the dogs, cats, birds, and other pets that share our homes and our lives—significantly affect our health and well-being. In fact, an important part of NICHD's research portfolio is the study of how these human-animal interactions influence child health and behavior, and impact our overall quality of life.

[3] For the past 10 years, NICHD's Child Development and Behavior Branch has had a partnership with the WALTHAM® Centre for Pet Nutrition, a division of Mars, Inc., to research the impact of animal interactions on child health and development. This partnership has led to several published works describing the therapeutic benefits of our companion animals.

[4] In a 2015 NICHD-funded study, a group of adolescents with type 1 diabetes each cared for a pet fish twice a day by feeding and checking water levels. The routine also included changing tank water each week, coupled with the children reviewing their glucose logs with parents. The researchers found that, when compared to teens who hadn't been given a fish to care for, the fishkeeping teens were more disciplined about checking their own blood glucose levels, which is essential for maintaining their health. Kids ages 10 to 13 years showed the greatest increase in self-monitoring following the pet fish intervention.

[5] That same year, **another study** found that children with autism spectrum disorder were calmer while playing with guinea pigs. Researchers gave each child a wristband that measured skin conductance—a measure for excitement and anxiety. A device inside the wristband sends an imperceptible electric current through the skin. The more anxious a person feels, the faster the current will travel through the skin. When the children with autism spent 10 minutes in a supervised group playtime with guinea pigs, their anxiety levels dropped. The children with autism also showed improved social functioning and were more engaged with their peers—an important benefit for children with autism. The researchers speculated that, because the animals offered unqualified acceptance, their presence comforted and calmed the children.

[6] Finally, dogs may prove to be an important addition to help kids cope with attention-deficit-hyperactivity disorder (ADHD). **Another NICHD study** enrolled two groups of children diagnosed with ADHD into a 12-week group therapy session. One group of kids read to a therapy dog once a week for 30 minutes, while the other group read to puppets that looked like dogs. Both groups showed improvements from the therapy sessions. However, the kids who read to the real animals performed better in measures of social skills, prosocial behaviors (such as sharing, cooperation, and volunteering), and behavioral problems. The researchers theorized that these interactions with dogs may help children focus their attention, thus improving their executive-functioning skills.

[7] As a scientist and a mother who has raised kids, fish, and cats, I understand and appreciate the importance that our furry and scaly friends have in our daily lives. **NICHD continues to support research** that examines the potential benefits of animals on our health and on the effectiveness of animal-assisted therapies in alleviating the symptoms of certain disorders and conditions, particularly in children. I have now grown accustomed to seeing the deer stroll undeterred around our bucolic campus, and I am even beginning to recognize some of the females by their numbered ear tags. On evenings when I am working late, I am grateful for a few moments of what I call the "NIH Safari," the view of a herd of deer eating grass and gracefully making their way down into the parking lot in front of our office building.

Reread the sentence below from paragraph 1

Growing up in Manhattan and working for over 30 years in Boston, I rarely encountered wildlife, other than pigeons and squirrels.

96. This sentence contributes to the overall structure of the excerpt by
    A. providing contextual information that clarifies the intensity of an emotional reaction described later in the passage.
    B. humanizing the writer by suggesting why she found her new work setting to be overwhelming.
    C. introducing critical autobiographical information that allows the reader to better understand the author's values.
    D. shifting the focus of the narrative from the author's beliefs about animals to the author's personal experiences working with and interacting with animals.

97. The studies included in this passage are important primarily because the findings
    A. highlight the author's opinion that there are individual differences in how children respond to companion animals.
    B. allow the author to make practical conclusions grounded in empirical evidence.
    C. clarify the theoretical underpinnings inspiring a line of innovative research.
    D. support the author's contention that more studies are needed to ascertain whether companion animals can improve children's health and well-being.

98. How does the overall structure of paragraphs 4 to 6 contribute to the development of ideas in the passage?
    A. The sequential structure illustrates the increasing importance of the value of animals in mitigating the effects of certain conditions in children.
    B. The descriptive structure presents distinct pieces of evidence that support a broader claim about the health benefits of animals on children.
    C. The chronological structure traces how research methodology in child-animal interactions has progressed from its inception to the present day.
    D. The compare and contrast structure evaluates which conditions in children are most and least successfully treated with animal interventions.

99. How does paragraph 2 fit within the overall structure of the excerpt?
   A. It segues from a broader point about human-animal interactions to a discussion about how animals affect a particular demographic of people.
   B. It highlights the rigorous challenges inherent in using research subjects who are children in the context of animal research.
   C. It introduces the methodologies that scientists use when studying human-animal interactions.
   D. It contrasts efforts to study human-animal interactions between people of different age groups.

100. The author conveys a point of view about the beneficial effects of animals on humans primarily by
   A. relating personal anecdotes that establish her credibility as both a scientist and a pet owner.
   B. describing a specific intervention that ameliorated the effects of a pathology.
   C. presenting the results of several research studies that examined the effects of animals on human behavior.
   D. critiquing experiments that aimed to show interactions with children and animals could promote healthful behaviors in children.

Reread the statement below from paragraph 1.

> **Indeed, companion animals—the dogs, cats, birds, and other pets that share our homes and our lives—significantly affect our health and well-being.**

101. Which statement from paragraph 5 provides the best evidence to support this claim?
   A. "Researchers gave each child a wristband that measured skin conductance—a measure for excitement and anxiety."
   B. "A device inside the wristband sends an imperceptible electric current through the skin."
   C. "The more anxious a person feels, the faster the current will travel through the skin."
   D. "When the children with autism spent 10 minutes in a supervised group playtime with guinea pigs, their anxiety levels dropped."

102. Which of the following provides the strongest evidence that children can experience health benefits from interacting with animals?
   A. Animals provide unqualified acceptance to children who experience social alienation.
   B. Children who read to puppets that looked like animals saw improvement in ADHD symptoms.
   C. The author grew to find the presence of wild animals relaxing on stressful work nights.
   D. Teens with diabetes who were assigned to care for fish were more watchful over their glucose levels than those in a control groups.

Reread the sentence below from paragraph 6.

The researchers theorized that these interactions with dogs may help children focus their attention, thus improving their executive-functioning skills.

103. How does this statement fit within the passage and contribute to the overall development of ideas?
    A. It concludes the description of the experiments, validating why their findings make intuitive scientific sense in light of previous research.
    B. It indicates that executive functioning skills are crucial to living a remote semblance of an organized life.
    C. It speculates a causal mechanism for an observed pattern in behavior within a specific research context.
    D. It establishes the superiority of dogs in mitigating certain ADHD symptoms relative to other service animals.

The excerpt below is adapted from *Song of the Lark* by Willa Cather.

[1] Mr. Kronborg considered Thea a remarkable child; but so were all his children remarkable. If one of the business men downtown remarked to him that he "had a mighty bright little girl, there," he admitted it, and at once began to explain what a "long head for business" his son Gus had, or that Charley was "a natural electrician," and had put in a telephone from the house to the preacher's study behind the church.

[2] Mrs. Kronborg watched her daughter thoughtfully. She found her more interesting than her other children, and she took her more seriously, without thinking much about why she did so. The other children had to be guided, directed, kept from conflicting with one another. Charley and Gus were likely to want the same thing, and to quarrel about it. Anna often demanded unreasonable service from her older brothers; that they should sit up until after midnight to bring her home from parties when she did not like the youth who had offered himself as her escort; or that they should drive twelve miles into the country, on a winter night, to take her to a ranch dance, after they had been working hard all day. Gunner often got bored with his own clothes or stilts or sled, and wanted Axel's. But Thea, from the time she was a little thing, had her own routine. She kept out of every one's way, and was hard to manage only when the other children interfered with her. Then there was trouble indeed: bursts of temper which used to alarm Mrs. Kronborg. "You ought to know enough to let Thea alone. She lets you alone," she often said to the other children.

[3] One may have staunch friends in one's own family, but one seldom has admirers. Thea, however, had one in the person of her addle-pated aunt, Tillie Kronborg. In older countries, where dress and opinions and manners are not so thoroughly standardized as in our own West, there is a belief that people who are foolish about the more obvious things of life are apt to have peculiar insight into what lies beyond the obvious. The old woman who can never learn not to put the kerosene can on the stove, may yet be able to tell fortunes, to persuade a backward child to grow, to cure warts, or to tell people what to do with a young girl who has gone melancholy. Tillie's mind was a curious machine; when she was awake it

went round like a wheel when the belt has slipped off, and when she was asleep she dreamed follies. But she had intuitions. She knew, for instance, that Thea was different from the other Kronborgs, worthy though they all were. Her romantic imagination found possibilities in her niece. When she was sweeping or ironing, or turning the ice-cream freezer at a furious rate, she often built up brilliant futures for Thea, adapting freely the latest novel she had read.

[4] Tillie made enemies for her niece among the church people because, at sewing societies and church suppers, she sometimes spoke vauntingly, with a toss of her head, just as if Thea's "wonderfulness" were an accepted fact in Moonstone, like Mrs. Archie's stinginess, or Mrs. Livery Johnson's duplicity. People declared that, on this subject, Tillie made them tired.

[5] Tillie belonged to a dramatic club that once a year performed in the Moonstone Opera House such plays as "Among the Breakers," and "The Veteran of 1812." Tillie played character parts, the flirtatious old maid or the spiteful *intrigante*. She used to study her parts up in the attic at home. While she was committing the lines, she got Gunner or Anna to hold the book for her, but when she began "to bring out the expression," as she said, she used, very timorously, to ask Thea to hold the book. Thea was usually—not always—agreeable about it. Her mother had told her that, since she had some influence with Tillie, it would be a good thing for them all if she could tone her down a shade and "keep her from taking on any worse than need be." Thea would sit on the foot of Tillie's bed, her feet tucked under her, and stare at the silly text. "I wouldn't make so much fuss, there, Tillie," she would remark occasionally; "I don't see the point in it"; or, "What do you pitch your voice so high for? It don't carry half as well."

[6] "I don't see how it comes Thea is so patient with Tillie," Mrs. Kronborg more than once remarked to her husband. "She ain't patient with most people, but it seems like she's got a peculiar patience for Tillie."

[7] Tillie always coaxed Thea to go "behind the scenes" with her when the club presented a play, and help her with her make-up. Thea hated it, but she always went. She felt as if she had to do it. There was something in Tillie's adoration of her that compelled her. There was no family impropriety that Thea was so much ashamed of as Tillie's "acting" and yet she was always being dragged in to assist her. Tillie simply had her, there. She didn't know why, but it was so. There was a string in her somewhere that Tillie could pull; a sense of obligation to Tillie's misguided aspirations. The saloon-keepers had some such feeling of responsibility toward Spanish Johnny.

[8] The dramatic club was the pride of Tillie's heart, and her enthusiasm was the principal factor in keeping it together. Sick or well, Tillie always attended rehearsals, and was always urging the young people, who took rehearsals lightly, to "stop fooling and begin now." The young men—bank clerks, grocery clerks, insurance agents—played tricks, laughed at Tillie, and "put it up on each other" about seeing her home; but they often went to tiresome rehearsals just to oblige her. They were good-natured young fellows.

[9] By one amazing indiscretion Tillie very nearly lost her hold upon the Moonstone Drama Club. The club had decided to put on "The Drummer Boy of Shiloh," a very ambitious undertaking because of the many supers needed and the scenic difficulties of the act which took place in Andersonville Prison. The members of the club consulted together in Tillie's absence as to who should play the part of the drummer boy. It must be taken by a very young person, and village boys of that age are self-conscious and are not

apt at memorizing. The part was a long one, and clearly it must be given to a girl. Some members of the club suggested Thea Kronborg, others advocated Lily Fisher. Lily's partisans urged that she was much prettier than Thea, and had a much "sweeter disposition." Nobody denied these facts. But there was nothing in the least boyish about Lily, and she sang all songs and played all parts alike. Lily's simper was popular, but it seemed not quite the right thing for the heroic drummer boy. Upping, the trainer, talked to one and another: "Lily's all right for girl parts," he insisted, "but you've got to get a girl with some ginger in her for this. Thea's got the voice, too. When she sings, 'Just Before the Battle, Mother,' she'll bring down the house."

[10] When all the members of the club had been privately consulted, they announced their decision to Tillie at the first regular meeting that was called to cast the parts. They expected Tillie to be overcome with joy, but, on the contrary, she seemed embarrassed. "I'm afraid Thea hasn't got time for that," she said jerkily. "She is always so busy with her music. Guess you'll have to get somebody else."

[11] The club lifted its eyebrows. Several of Lily Fisher's friends coughed. Mr. Upping flushed. The stout woman who always played the injured wife called Tillie's attention to the fact that this would be a fine opportunity for her niece to show what she could do. Her tone was condescending. The company broke up into groups and expressed their amazement. They confided to each other that Tillie was "just a little off, on the subject of her niece," and agreed that it would be as well not to excite her further. Tillie got a cold reception at rehearsals for a long while afterward, and Thea had a crop of new enemies without even knowing it.

104. In contrast to Tillie, Thea's father is portrayed as
  A. unimpressed with Thea's unique attributes.
  B. more critical of Thea's faults.
  C. less publicly boastful of Thea's talents.
  D. willing to spend time with Thea's siblings.

105. The contrast between Thea and her siblings is made clearest by
  A. dialogue between them highlighting their disagreements.
  B. descriptions of typical behaviors of Thea and her siblings.
  C. an account of the inner thoughts and feelings of Thea and those of her siblings.
  D. Thea's and her siblings' differing attitudes towards Tillie's theatrical aspirations.

106. Paragraph 7 primarily advances the plot by
  A. showing that the affection between two family members persists even when they are apart.
  B. describing the power of a familial bond in shaping a character's behavior.
  C. foreshadowing an altercation grounded in a toxic interpersonal dynamic.
  D. illustrating that Tillie takes perverse pleasure in manipulating Thea for her own personal gain.

Reread the lines below from paragraph 5.

Thea would sit on the foot of Tillie's bed, her feet tucked under her, and stare at the silly text. "I wouldn't make so much fuss, there, Tillie," she would remark occasionally; "I don't see the point in it"; or, "What do you pitch your voice so high for? It don't carry half as well."

107. How does the interaction contribute to the development of the plot?
    A. It reveals Thea's frustrations with Tillie's unwillingness to consider her feedback.
    B. It establishes a conflict between Tillie and Thea by casting doubt on both Thea's expertise in decoding a playwright's intent and Tillie's ability to give a believable performance.
    C. It illustrates the extent of Thea's sense of commitment to assisting her aunt while hinting at her frustration with this task.
    D. It shows the urgency that Thea feels in ensuring Tillie delivers a commendable performance.

108. In which line does a description of another character or characters most closely parallel the characterization of Thea in paragraph 7?
    A. "but they often went to tiresome rehearsals just to oblige her" (paragraph 8).
    B. "By one amazing indiscretion Tillie very nearly lost her hold upon the Moonstone Drama Club'" (paragraph 9).
    C. "When all the members of the club had been privately consulted, they announced their decision to Tillie at the first regular meeting that was called to cast the parts" (paragraph 10).
    D. "Tillie got a cold reception at rehearsals for a long while afterward" (paragraph 11).

Read the quote below from paragraph 10.

"I'm afraid Thea hasn't got time for that."

109. The line contributes to a conflict in the excerpt by
    A. shedding insight into Thea's desires to pursue other interests.
    B. causing tension between Tillie and the other theater members.
    C. prompting Thea to resent her aunt's interference in her affairs.
    D. leading to a verbal confrontation between Thea and her enemies.

"The Brain May Actively Forget During Sleep" (NIH)

[1] Rapid eye movement, or REM, sleep is a fascinating period when most of our dreams are made. Now, in a study of mice, a team of Japanese and U.S. researchers show that it may also be a time when the brain actively forgets. Their results suggest that forgetting during sleep may be controlled by neurons found deep inside the brain that were previously known for making an appetite stimulating hormone. The study was funded by the National Institute of Neurological Disorders and Stroke (NINDS), part of the National Institutes of Health.

[2] "Ever wonder why we forget many of our dreams?" said Thomas Kilduff, Ph.D., director of the Center for Neuroscience at SRI International, Menlo Park, California, and a senior author of the study published in Science. "Our results suggest that the firing of a particular group of neurons during REM sleep controls whether the brain remembers new information after a good night's sleep."

[3] REM is one of several sleep stages the body cycles through every night. It first occurs about 90 minutes after falling asleep and is characterized by darting eyes, raised heart rates, paralyzed limbs, awakened brain waves and dreaming.

[4] For more than a century, scientists have explored the role of sleep in storing memories. While many have shown that sleep helps the brain store new memories, others, including Francis Crick, the co-discoverer of the DNA double helix, have raised the possibility that sleep – in particular REM sleep – may be a time when the brain actively eliminates or forgets excess information. Moreover, recent studies in mice have shown that during sleep – including REM sleep – the brain selectively prunes synaptic connections made between neurons involved in certain types of learning. However, until this study, no one had shown how this might happen.

[5] "Understanding the role of sleep in forgetting may help researchers better understand a wide range of memory-related diseases like post-traumatic stress disorder and Alzheimer's," said Janet He, Ph.D., program director, at NINDS. "This study provides the most direct evidence that REM sleep may play a role in how the brain decides which memories to store."

[6] Dr. Kilduff's lab and that of his collaborator, Akihiro Yamanaka, Ph.D., at Nagoya University in Japan, have spent years examining the role of a hormone called hypocretin/orexin in controlling sleep and **narcolepsy**. Narcolepsy is a disorder that makes people feel excessively sleepy during the day and sometimes experience changes reminiscent of REM sleep, like loss of muscle tone in the limbs and hallucinations. Their labs and others have helped to show how narcolepsy may be linked to the loss of hypocretin/orexin-making neurons in the hypothalamus, a peanut-sized area found deep inside the brain.

[7] In this study, Dr. Kilduff worked with Dr. Yamanaka's lab and Akira Terao's, D.V.M., Ph.D., lab at Hokkaido University, Sapporo, Japan, to look at neighboring cells that produce melanin concentrating hormone (MCH), a molecule known to be involved in the control of both sleep and appetite. In agreement with previous studies, the researchers found that a majority (52.8%) of hypothalamic MCH cells fired when mice underwent REM sleep whereas about 35% fired only when the mice were awake and about 12% fired at both times.

[8] They also uncovered clues suggesting that these cells may play a role in learning and memory. Electrical recordings and tracing experiments showed that many of the hypothalamic MCH cells sent inhibitory messages, via long stringy axons, to the hippocampus, the brain's memory center.

[9] "From previous studies done in other labs, we already knew that MCH cells were active during REM sleep. After discovering this new circuit, we thought these cells might help the brain store memories," said Dr. Kilduff.

[10] To test this idea, the researchers used a variety of genetic tools to turn on and off MCH neurons in mice during memory tests. Specifically, they examined the role that MCH cells played in retention, the period after learning something new but before the new knowledge is stored, or consolidated, into long term memory. The scientists used several memory tests including one that assessed the ability of mice to distinguish between new and familiar objects.

[11] To their surprise, they found that "turning on" MCH cells during retention worsened memory whereas turning the cells off improved memories. For instance, activating the cells reduced the time mice spent sniffing around new objects compared to familiar ones, but turning the cells off had the opposite effect.

[12] Further experiments suggested that MCH neurons exclusively played this role during REM sleep. Mice performed better on memory tests when MCH neurons were turned off during REM sleep. In contrast, turning off the neurons while the mice were awake or in other sleep states had no effect on memory.

[13] "These results suggest that MCH neurons help the brain actively forget new, possibly, unimportant information," said Dr. Kilduff. "Since dreams are thought to primarily occur during REM sleep, the sleep stage when the MCH cells turn on, activation of these cells may prevent the content of a dream from being stored in the hippocampus – consequently, the dream is quickly forgotten."

[14] In the future, the researchers plan to explore whether this new circuit plays a role in sleep and memory disorders.

[15] This press release describes a basic research finding. Basic research increases our understanding of human behavior and biology, which is foundational to advancing new and better ways to prevent, diagnose, and treat disease. Science is an unpredictable and incremental process — each research advance builds on past discoveries, often in unexpected ways. Most clinical advances would not be possible without the knowledge of fundamental basic research.

110. The phrase "controlled by neurons" in paragraph 1 contributes to the overall structure of the passage by
    A. introducing a potential function of a particular class of neurons that research discussed later in the passage supports.
    B. shifting the focus away from the role of sleep in consolidating memories to its role in destroying them.
    C. suggesting that the long-standing belief that certain neurons were involved in appetite suppression is likely incorrect in light of surprising findings from a new study.
    D. revealing prevailing historical attitudes about the biological importance of MCH neurons.

111. Paragraph 3 primarily contributes to the ideas in the passage by
    A. noting features of REM sleep that recently piqued the interest of a class of researchers.
    B. providing descriptive information that contextualizes a broader scientific discussion.
    C. revealing why human physiology is especially vulnerable in REM sleep relative to other types of sleep.
    D. serving as a transition from a description of an experiment's methodology to an analysis of its findings.

112. The mention of Francis Crick in paragraph 4 contributes to the structure of the passage by
    A. indicating that the findings of the experiment had already been proven by earlier researchers.
    B. implying that sleep research should integrate findings from DNA research in order to better elucidate the function of dreams.
    C. suggesting that the study on which this passage focuses provides support for an existing hypothesis.
    D. revealing that the notion that dreaming promotes useful forgetting his highly contentious in a broader scientific context.

113. Paragraphs 5 and 6 contribute to the structure of the passage by
    A. highlighting personal and professional factors that motivated a research question.
    B. citing an expert authority that clarifies the need for improved technology to identify neural signatures associated with sleep-wake cycles.
    C. justifying the importance of experiments in terms of broadening scientists' understanding of various ailments.
    D. emphasizing that learning how sleep induces forgetting is crucial to treating a variety of human diseases.

114. The primary purpose of the information in paragraph 12 is to
    A. suggest an alternative interpretation to the conclusions of the researchers discussed in the preceding paragraph.
    B. prove that the neural circuit discussed in paragraph 8 is essential the maintenance of homeostasis.
    C. corroborate an unexpected finding by the scientists discussed in paragraph 11.
    D. contrast the effects on memory associated with suppressing MCH activity during non-REM sleep with doing so during wakefulness.

"Kansas: Fort Larned Historical Site" (National Park Service)

[1] Between 1822 and 1880, the Santa Fe Trail provided one of the most important overland transportation routes in America. The trail allowed millions of dollars of commercial traffic to flow between Independence, Missouri and Santa Fe, New Mexico. The flow of travelers, traders, and settlers moving west; the gold rushes of 1849 and 1858; and the acquisition of vast southwestern lands by the United States government after the Mexican War caused the American Indians of this region much turmoil. The great influx of people along the Santa Fe Trail disrupted their way of life and prompted them to retaliate. Fort Larned was established to protect travelers, trail commerce, and the mail because of the rising tensions between American Indians and those using the trail. Fort Larned National Historic Site preserves the buildings, stories, and historical themes associated with Fort Larned.

[2] By October of 1859, rising conflicts between American Indians and westward travelers along the Santa Fe Trail prompted the United States army to build a military post to protect and maintain peaceful relations with everyone on the trail. This first post, called "Camp on Pawnee Fork" and eventually called "Camp Alert," was set up near Lookout Hill (now Jenkins hill) on the bank of the Pawnee River about five miles from its junction with the Arkansas River. Less than a year later, in June 1860, the fort was moved three miles further west, near the confluence of the Pawnee and Arkansas Rivers.

[3] At this location, the army constructed sod and adobe buildings, including an officer's quarters, storehouse and barracks, a guardhouse, a hospital, soldier's quarters, a bakery, a meat house, and a building housing a blacksmith, carpenter, and saddler shops. Named Fort Larned for Col. Benjamin R. Larned, the US Army paymaster, this fort would serve as one of the most important defense posts along the Santa Fe Trail.

[4] Between 1866 and 1868, the government replaced the original sod and adobe buildings of Fort Larned with more durable stone and timber buildings. Visitors can see these buildings today at the Fort Larned National Historic Site. The fort complex of nine buildings arranged around a 400' square parade ground includes barracks, a post hospital, two company officer's quarters, commanding officer's quarters, quartermaster storehouse, the old commissary, the new commissary, and a shops building. Visitors may walk around and explore seven of the nine buildings at the fort to get a glimpse of what it was like to live on a western fort during the 19th century.

[5] As one of the most important defense posts along the Santa Fe Trail, Fort Larned served many purposes. One purpose was to protect the flow of commerce along the Kansas segment of the trail. After the Chivington Massacre at Sand Creek in 1864, the War Department forbade travel beyond Fort Larned without armed escort. Fort Larned prepared detachments for the protection of mail stages and wagon trains.

[6] By 1867, Fort Larned became the base for Maj. Gen. Winfield S. Hancock's unsuccessful campaign against Plains Indian tribes. This campaign intended to intimidate and pacify the Indians with US military strength; however, it had the reverse effect and only intensified their hostilities. Hancock's campaign

caused a general outbreak of raids by the Kiowa, Comanche, and Arapaho. To respond to these raids, Maj. Gen. Philip H. Sheridan ordered Lt. Col. George A. Custer into the area around Fort Larned. Eventually, Custer's campaign ended in the defeat of Black Kettle's Cheyenne at the Battle of the Washita on November 27, 1868. The Battle of the Washita ultimately ended American Indians' organized resistance around Fort Larned.

[7] While the military sought to prevent conflict along the trail, Fort Larned became the seat of other more peaceful efforts to reach out to the tribes throughout the 1860s. The fort served as the headquarters and principal annuity distribution point of the Indian Bureau. The Indian Bureau attempted to find peaceful solutions to conflicts between American Indians and travelers, settlers, and adventurers. The treaties of Fort Wise (1861), the Little Arkansas (1865), and Medicine Lodge (1867) supported these peaceful principles.

[8] In these treaties, the United States government agreed to pay annuities to the Cheyenne, Arapahos, Kiowa, Comanche, and the Plains Apache tribes in return for keeping peace along the trail and for staying on their reservations. Annuities included items like bacon, wheat, flour, coffee, sugar, fresh beef, tobacco, clothing, beads, blankets, metal tools, cooking utensils, gunpowder, and lead bullets. Presented with the great opportunities the Indian Bureau created for commerce, traders flocked to the area surrounding Fort Larned and established the fort as a major trading center. By 1868, with the movement of the tribes to new reservations in Indian Territory, Fort Larned's role as an agent for the Indian Bureau ended.

[9] Fort Larned's final function was to protect railroad construction crews. The building of the railroad ultimately led to the end of the use of the Santa Fe Trail, which the fort was originally constructed to protect. After the Civil War ended, Americans renewed their energetic push westward, laying thousands of miles of railroad track. The worn dirt-road ruts of the Santa Fe Trail could not compete with the high powered, fast, and efficient railroad. Fort Larned helped to protect the workers who completed laying the railroad line in Kansas by 1872. Nearly six years later, in July 1878, the military abandoned Fort Larned, because it was no longer necessary for protection and keeping peaceful relations along the Santa Fe Trail.

Reread this sentence from paragraph 1

The flow of travelers, traders, and settlers moving west; the gold rushes of 1849 and 1858; and the acquisition of vast southwestern lands by the United States government after the Mexican War caused the American Indians of this region much turmoil

115. The author most likely includes this detail in order to
    A. note that many factors contributed to the disruption of American Indians' way of life.
    B. suggest that Americans around the country were sympathetic with the Indians' plight.
    C. compare the commercial and political factors that flared up tensions between American Indians and the military.
    D. imply that the political ambitions of the United States government opened up commercial opportunities.

116. Which statement best conveys the idea that some miliary campaigns against the Plains Indians tribes were unsuccessful?
    A. "Fort Larned prepared detachments for the protection of mail stages and wagon trains" (paragraph 5).
    B. "This campaign intended to intimidate and pacify the Indians with US military strength" (paragraph 6).
    C. "Hancock's campaign caused a general outbreak of raids by the Kiowa, Comanche, and Arapaho" (paragraph 6).
    D. "Nearly six years later, in July 1878, the military abandoned Fort Larned, because it was no longer necessary for protection and keeping peaceful relations along the Santa Fe Trail" (paragraph 9).

117. What is one way that passage uses a problem and solution structure to contribute to the development of ideas in the passage?
    A. It explains why military campaigns to foster peaceful relations among American Indians and travelers along the Santa Fe Trail merely inflamed rather than tamped down hostilities, so the government adapted by engaging in peaceful negotiations in order to establish harmonious relations with American Indian tribes.
    B. It highlights how tensions between American Indians and the influx of traders and travelers heading West compromised important functions along a critical trade route, and it describes how Fort Larned served as both a military and diplomatic means of establishing peace.
    C. It explains that the original material used to build Fort Larned made residents vulnerable to outside attacks, and it states that trading could only resume once stronger materials were used.
    D. It explains that Fort Larned was too technologically unsophisticated to serve as a meaningful commercial and cultural hub, so the railroad was built in order to render this facility obsolete.

118. The use of chronological structure in paragraph 6 contributes to the development of the excerpt by
    A. showing how the United States military applied lessons learned from earlier military campaigns to foster a safe environment around Fort Larned.
    B. identifying the obstacles that had to be overcome to establish peaceful relations between travelers along the Santa Fe Trail and American Indian populations.
    C. demonstrating how Custer analyzed the failures of Hancock's campaign to suppress raids by American Indian tribes.
    D. providing a brief overview of a failed military effort to end hostilities with American Indian tribes and a subsequent successful effort to suppress organized incidents of violence in response to the first effort's shortcomings.

119. Which excerpt from the passage provides the best evidence that the United States government made physical adaptations to Fort Larned in direct response to safety concerns?
    A. "Fort Larned was established to protect travelers, trail commerce, and the mail because of the rising tensions between American Indians and those using the trail" (Paragraph 1).
    B. "Less than a year later, in June 1860, the fort was moved three miles further west, near the confluence of the Pawnee and Arkansas Rivers" (Paragraph 2).
    C. "Between 1866 and 1868, the government replaced the original sod and adobe buildings of Fort Larned with more durable stone and timber buildings" (Paragraph 4).
    D. "After the Chivington Massacre at Sand Creek in 1864, the War Department forbade travel beyond Fort Larned without armed escort" (Paragraph 5).

Read the excerpt below from paragraph 8.

In these treaties, the United States government agreed to pay annuities to the Cheyenne, Arapahos, Kiowa, Comanche, and the Plains Apache tribes in return for keeping peace along the trail and for staying on their reservations.

120. Which statement describes how this sentence fits into the overall structure of the passage?
    A. It introduces a shift in tone from a positive one to a negative one by noting efforts to quell tensions between American Indians and American settlers moving westward along the Santa Fe Trail.
    B. It marks a transition from a general discussion of efforts by the United States to establish peaceful relations with American Indian tribes to a more specific description of what the tribes were offered.
    C. It begins a comparison of the culture of American Indian tribes from the early nineteenth century to those from the late nineteenth century.
    D. It summarizes a piece of legislation that helped established feelings of affection among previously hostile groups.

121. One reason the Santa Fe Trail lost its status as an important overland transportation route is best illustrated through
   A. information comparing it to more popular transportation methods.
   B. a discussion of how armed conflicts with various American Indian tribes discouraged travel.
   C. a description of failed attempts at peaceful negotiations between the United States military and American Indian tribes.
   D. an explanation for why Americans embraced an energetic expansion westward.

The excerpt below is from "On a Mountain Trail" by Henry Perry Robinson.

[1] We had no warning. It was as if they had deliberately lain in ambush for us at the turn in the trail. They seemed suddenly and silently to rise on all sides of the sleigh at once. It is not often that the gray timber-wolves, or "black wolves," as the mountaineers call them, are seen hunting in packs, though the animal is plentiful enough among the foot-hills of the Rockies. As a general rule they are met with singly or in pairs. At the end of a long and severe winter, however, they sometimes come together in bands of fifteen or twenty; and every old mountaineer has a tale to tell perhaps of his own narrow escape from one of their fierce packs, perhaps of some friend of his who started one day in winter to travel alone from camp to camp, and whose clean-picked bones were found beside the trail long afterward.

[2] It was in February, and we, Gates and myself, were driving from Livingston, Montana, to Gulch City, fifty miles away, with a load of camp supplies — a barrel of flour and some bacon, coffee, and beans; a blanket or two, and some dynamite (or "giant powder," as the miners call it) for blasting; a few picks and shovels, and other odds and ends. We had started at daybreak. By five o'clock in the evening, with some ten miles more to travel, the worst of the trail was passed. There had been little snow that winter, so that even in the gulches and on the bottoms the exposed ground was barely covered; while, on the steep slopes, snow had almost entirely disappeared, leaving only ragged patches of white under overhanging boughs, and a thin coating of ice in the inequalities of the hard, frost-bound trail, making a treacherous footing for the horses' hoofs.

[3] The first forty miles of the road had lain entirely over hills — zigzagging up one side of a mountain only to zigzag down the other — with the dense growth of pine and tamarack and cedar on both sides, wreathed here and there in mist. But at last we were clear of the foot-hills and reached the level. The tall forest trees gave place to a wilderness of thick underbrush, lying black in the evening air, and the horses swung contentedly from the steep grade into the level trail, where at last they could let their legs move freely in a trot.

[4] Hardly had they settled into their stride, however, when both animals shied violently to the left side of the trail. A moment later they plunged back to the right side so suddenly as almost to throw me off into the brush.

[5] Then, out of the earth and the shadow of the bushes, the grim, dark forms seemed to rise on all sides of us. There was not a sound — not a snap nor a snarl; but in the gathering twilight of the February evening, we saw them moving noiselessly over the thin coat of snow which covered the ground. In the uncertain light, and moving as rapidly as we did, it was impossible to guess how many they were. An animal which was one moment in plain sight, running abreast of the horses, would, the next moment, be lost in the shadow of the bushes, while two more dark, silent forms would edge up to take its place. So, on both sides of us, they kept appearing and disappearing. In the rear, half a dozen jostled one another to push up nearer to the flying sleigh — a black mass that filled the whole width of the trail. Behind those again, others, less clearly visible, crossed and recrossed the roadway from side to side. They might be twenty in all — or thirty — or forty. It was impossible to tell.

[6] For a minute I did not think of danger. The individual wolf is the most skulking and cowardly of animals, and only by some such experience as we had that night does a hunter learn that wolves can be dangerous. But soon the stories of the old mountaineers came crowding into my mind, as the horses, terrified and snorting, plunged wildly along the narrow trail, while the ghostlike forms glided patiently alongside — appearing, disappearing, and reappearing. The silent pertinacity[1] with which, apparently making no effort, they kept pace beside the flying horses was horrible. Even a howl or a yelp or a growl would have been a relief. But not so much as the sound of their footfalls on the snow was to be heard.

[7] At the first sight of the wolves, I had drawn my revolver from the leather case in which it hung suspended from my belt. Gates, handling the reins, was entirely occupied with the horses; but I knew, without need of words, that he saw our pursuers and understood the peril as well as I.

[8] "Have you your gun?" I shouted in his ear.

---

[1] perseverance

122. The author mentions details about wolves traveling singly or in pairs in order to
    A. account for why the central conflict of the passage was somewhat unexpected from his perspective.
    B. reassure himself that the wolves likely did not pose a genuine danger during a moment of self-doubt.
    C. demonstrate that his knowledge of animal nature would prove fruitless in helping him navigate a life-threatening challenge.
    D. lament the cruelty of a situation that violated a fundamental law of nature.

123. How does paragraph 6 contribute to the plot of the excerpt?
    A. It reveals the narrator's biggest problems are in his own imagination.
    B. It suggests that the reality of the narrator's situation contradicts some assumptions he may have harbored.
    C. It shows the narrator experiences a perverse sense of excitement in the face of menacing situations.
    D. It underscores how the narrator usually behaves during moments of acute stress.

124. Which excerpt best suggests that the dilemma faced by the narrator had already possessed knowledge about the possibility of the dangerous encounter he experienced despite being caught off guard?
    A. "They seemed suddenly and silently to rise on all sides of the sleigh at once" (paragraph 1).
    B. "As a general rule they are met with singly or in pairs" (paragraph 1).
    C. "At the end of a long and severe winter, however, they sometimes come together in bands of fifteen or twenty" (paragraph 1).
    D. "By five o'clock in the evening, with some ten miles more to travel, the worst of the trail was passed" (paragraph 2).

125. According to paragraph 2, which of the following most directly presented a hazard to the horses?
    A. The overhanging boughs.
    B. The frosty trail.
    C. The uncovered gulches.
    D. The steep slopes.

Week 1

126. How does paragraph 3 convey one effect of the setting on the horses?
    A. It indicates that the zigzagging hills caused them to experience exhaustion.
    B. It describes how the darkness made it difficult for them to keep in the right direction.
    C. It shows how the steep terrain and thick underbrush reduced the freeness of their trots.
    D. It describes how the knowledge of wolves' presence created a tense and uncomfortable atmosphere.

127. How does paragraph 4 fit into the overall structure of the excerpt?
    A. It hints that a change in the horses' behavior caused the narrator to become alert to a danger.
    B. It foreshadows that the horses have the knowledge to take action to resolve an impending conflict.
    C. It presents the precise moment in which the narrator fully understood the nature of a looming threat.
    D. It shows the narrator was unprepared to avert a disaster by breaking a false sense of serenity.

128. Chronologically, paragraphs 2 and 3 serve to
    A. flashback to a period months ago of the dangerous situation described in paragraph 1.
    B. provide context for the events leading up to a confrontation alluded to in paragraph 1.
    C. show how the narrator has been affected by the encounter referenced in paragraph 1.
    D. establish when the narrator developed the skills needed to face an obstacle referenced in paragraph 1.

Reread the sentence from paragraph 6.
For a minute I did not think of danger. The individual wolf is the most skulking and cowardly of animals, and only by some such experience as we had that night does a hunter learn that wolves can be dangerous.

129. How does this sentence contribute to the paragraph?
    A. It details the needs for hunters to have quick reflexes to react to danger.
    B. It dispels the notion that wolves are capable of behaving cowardly by noting an experience that contradicts this idea.
    C. It presents the idea that common notions about certain animals' traits can provide a false sense of security that can be shaken by direct encounters with such animals.
    D. It provides an overview of a rite of passage faced by most hunters who underestimate wolves' capacity for violence.

*Kweller Prep NEW SHSAT Grammar and Reading*

Week 2

Week 2: Inference and Word Choice Questions

Inference questions require you to draw conclusions based on information that is heavily implied the authors.

Inference Questions Overview	
Common Question Phrasing	• The author implies…. • The author suggests… • It can be inferred that…
How to Approach	• Locate information needed to answer the question and determine which choice can be most reasonably concluded. • Predict the general ideas that relate to the right answer.
Common Trap Wrong Answer Types	• Answer choices that use extreme language, such as *never, always,* and *only*. • Details that are not supported by the passage.

A lawyer published a paper criticizing most law schools for hiring professors with little real-world experience in the legal field. He went on to say that while students do learn to develop logical thinking skills, they learn little about the realities of actually serving as competent practitioners.

Sample: It can be inferred that the lawyer mentioned in the passage would most likely agree that law schools should

    A. *eliminate all theoretical classes.*
    B. *recruit more applicants with interests in academia.*
    C. *expand course offerings in which practical legal skills are taught.*
    D. *teach logical reasoning skills more carefully.*

The lawyer criticizes law school professors for lacking experience in the legal field and complains that law students do not learn how to actually practice law. It can be logically inferred that the lawyer would approve if law schools taught more practical skills, so choice C is correct. Choice A is too extreme. While the lawyer would support less emphasis on purely theoretical classes, he likely would not support *completely* eliminating them. He even acknowledges that law school teaches logical reasoning skills, implying that he thinks law school has some good qualities. Choice B is opposite of what the lawyer wants. He wants law schools to focus less on academic skills and more on practical skills. The lawyer acknowledges that students do learn logical reasoning skills, so choice D is not true.

Sarah could not believe that the acclaimed public speaker had never heard of Pericles' Funeral Oration, a famous speech delivered in ancient Greece.

Sample: It can be inferred that Sarah believes that
   A. the general population enjoys the works of Pericles.
   B. reputable public speakers should be familiar with Pericles' Funeral Oration.
   C. Pericles is the most skilled rhetorician in human history.
   D. Pericles' wisdom is not relevant to the lives of people today.

Sarah was surprised that the public speaker had never heard of the speech. This suggests that Sarah believes that all reputable (respectable) public speakers should know about this speech. Choice B is correct. There is not enough information to support or refute choices A or C (the general population is not discussed, and there is no evidence that Pericles is Sarah's favorite speaker). Choice D is not supported by the statement because if Sarah thinks the speech is important, it likely contains ideas that have meaning today.

The excerpt below is from NASA's article, "NASA's Kepler Discovers First Earth-Size Planet In the 'Habitable Zone' of Another Star" (http://www.nasa.gov/ames/kepler/nasas-kepler-discovers-first-earth-size-planet-in-the-habitable-zone-of-another-star/).

Using NASA's Kepler Space Telescope, astronomers have discovered the first Earth-size planet orbiting a star in the "habitable zone" -- the range of distance from a star where liquid water might pool on the surface of an orbiting planet. The discovery of Kepler-186f confirms that planets the size of Earth exists in the habitable zone of stars other than our sun. While planets have previously been found in the habitable zone, they are all at least 40 percent larger in size than Earth and understanding their makeup is challenging. Kepler-186f is more reminiscent of Earth. Although the size of Kepler-186f is known, its mass and composition are not. Previous research, however, suggests that a planet the size of Kepler-186f is likely to be rocky. Kepler-186f orbits its star once every 130-days and receives one-third the energy from its star that Earth gets from the sun, placing it nearer the outer edge of the habitable zone. On the surface of Kepler-186f, the brightness of its star at high noon is only as bright as our sun appears to us about an hour before sunset. "Being in the habitable zone does not mean we know this planet is habitable. The temperature on the planet is strongly dependent on what kind of atmosphere the planet has," said Thomas Barclay, research scientist at the Bay Area Environmental Research Institute at Ames, and co-author of the paper. "Kepler-186f can be thought of as an Earth-cousin rather than an Earth-twin. It has many properties that resemble Earth." The four companion planets, Kepler-186b, Kepler-186c, Kepler-186d, and Kepler-186e, whiz around their sun every four, seven, 13, and 22 days, respectively, making them too hot for life as we know it. These four inner planets all measure less than 1.5 times the size of Earth.

Sample: What is the relationship between Kepler-186f and other planets that have been discovered in the habitable zone of stars?
   A. Kepler-186f was discovered earlier.
   B. Kepler-186f is larger.
   C. Kepler-186f is smaller.
   D. Kepler-186f is less like Earth.

The other planets in the habitable zone are 40% larger than Earth, while Kepler-186f is closer to the size of Earth (lines 5-7). Therefore, it can be inferred that Kepler 186-f is smaller than the other planets. Choice C is correct.

Sample: If Kepler-186f is in fact habitable, in comparison to its four companion planets, Kepler-186f is likely to have
   A. a larger size.
   B. a shorter period of revolution about its star.
   C. hotter surface temperatures.
   D. lower surface temperatures.

The four companion planets have shorter revolution periods and are too hot for life (lines 17-20). If Kepler 186- is in the habitable zone, it must have lower surface temperatures. Choice D is correct.

Inference skills can also be applied to **word choice questions.** Word choice refers to the author's selection of specific and accurate words to convey a certain meaning, image, and/or attitude. Words must be both precise and appropriate for the audience. Rhetoric is the way writers organize words to create a desired effect. When asked to analyze the rhetorical effect of specific words or an arrangement of words, pay attention to the following.

> ➢ Words or phrases that the author **repeats** to emphasize a particular point of view or detail.
> ➢ Language that has an **emotional effect**, such as to create tension, sadness, mystery, seriousness, or lightheartedness.
> ➢ Language that appeals to the audience's sense of **logic or reason.**
> ➢ Language that appeals to the audience's **morality.**
> ➢ Language that appeals to the **senses** (sight, hearing, taste, touch, and smell).
> ➢ Language that conveys humor or sarcasm.

- Reflect on why the author chose *these words* over others.
    - ➢ What does the reader learn from these words?
    - ➢ How do these words make the reader feel?
    - ➢ What point is the author better able to get across as a result of using these words?

Let's examine word choice in excerpt from Patrick Henry's "Give me Liberty or Give Me Death," in which he argues for the independence of the American colonies from Great Britain.

Mr. President it is natural to man to indulge in the illusions of hope. We are apt to shut our eyes against a painful truth ....Are we disposed to be of the number of those who, having eyes, see not, and having ears, hear not, the things which so nearly concern their temporal salvation? For my part, whatever anguish of spirit it may cost, I am willing to know the whole truth; to know the worst and to provide for it.

I have but one lamp by which my feet are guided; and that is the lamp of experience. I know of no way of judging of the future but by the past. And judging by the past, I wish to know what there has been in the conduct of the British ministry for the last ten years to justify those hopes with which gentlemen have been pleased to solace themselves and the house? Is it that insidious smile with which our petition has been lately received? Trust it not, sir; it will prove a snare to your feet. Suffer not yourselves to be betrayed with a kiss. Are fleets and armies necessary to a work of love and reconciliation? Have we shown ourselves so unwilling to be reconciled that force must be called in to win back our love? Let us not deceive ourselves, sir. These are the implements of war and subjugation - the last arguments to which kings resort. I ask gentlemen, sir, what means this martial array if its purpose be not to force us to submission? Can gentlemen assign any other possible motives for it? Has Great Britain any enemy, in this quarter of the world to call for all this accumulation of navies and armies? No, sir, she has none. They are meant for us: they can be meant for no other. They are sent over to bind and rivet upon us those chains which the British ministry have been so long forging.

Let us not, I beseech you, sir, deceive ourselves longer. Sir, we have done everything that could be done to avert the storm which is now coming on. We have petitioned - we have remonstrated - we have supplicated - we have prostrated ourselves before the throne, and have implored its interposition to arrest the tyrannical hands of the ministry and Parliament. Our petitions have been slighted; our remonstrances have produced additional violence and insult; our supplications have been disregarded; and we have been spurned, with contempt, from the foot of the throne. In vain, after these things, may we indulge the fond hope of peace and reconciliation. There is no longer any room for hope. If we wish to be free - if we mean to preserve inviolate those inestimable privileges for which we have been so long contending - if we mean not basely to abandon the noble struggle in which we have been so long engaged, and which we have pledged ourselves never to abandon until the glorious object of our contest shall be obtained - we must fight! I repeat it, sir, we must fight!

Sample: In context, the word "illusions" (line 1) implies that many colonists are
    A. *shrewdly perceptive.*
    B. *rightfully suspicious.*
    C. *naively ignorant.*
    D. *willfully deceptive*

The word "illusion" suggests that the colonists are ignoring reality. Their hope is misguided. Thus, the colonists can be described as "ignorant," or unaware of the truth. Choice C is correct.

Sample: Henry includes the word "natural" (line 1) in order to emphasize his
  A. understanding of a common sentiment.
  B. approval of a popular attitude.
  C. support for an extreme measure.
  D. optimistic outlook for the future.

In context, Henry says that it is "natural" to have illusions, or false ideas. Thus, he understands why many people are hopeful. Choice A is correct.

Sample: The phrase "anguish of spirit" (line 4) has what effect?
  A. It creates a somber tone, focusing on the pain associated with an impending revelation.
  B. It creates an optimistic tone, suggesting hope for the future in light of an initial setback.
  C. It creates a comforting tone, revealing the truth about a promising situation.
  D. It creates a ludicrous tone, poking fun at people who maintain hope in the face of adversity.

"Pain and anguish" are negative words that are "somber," or sad. Learning the "truth" will be "sad." Choice A is correct.

Sample: In the context of the second paragraph, "submission," "bind and rivet," and "chain" emphasize
  A. Britain's controlling influence over the colonies.
  B. Henry's respect for authority and desire for stability.
  C. the resistance that the British encounter in managing political affairs.
  D. the intricacy of locally run colonial assemblies.

Henry uses imagery of people being "tied up" to appeal to their emotions. Specifically, he asserts that the British are trying to put "chains" around (control) the colonists. Thus, choice A is correct.

Sample: What is the rhetorical effect of the questions in lines 7-17?
  A. To enlighten the audience about the reality of a predicament with increasing intensity.
  B. To draw attention to the complexity of an ambiguous moral issue.
  C. To provoke the audience into surrendering their freedoms to avoid further pain.
  D. To compel politicians to determine appropriate procedures for funding international wars.

Henry appeals to the audience's logic by making them realize that Britain is not trying to protect them but control them. He starts out by questioning if Britain's actions justify the colonists' assumption that Britain will change its ways. Henry ultimately asserts that Britain has no enemies on "this quarter of the world" (The Americas) and that the military presence is meant for the colonists. Choice A is correct.

Sample: Henry's use of repetition in lines 21 to 23 ("We have petitioned - we have remonstrated ... and Parliament") primarily has the effect of
- A. *emphasizing the understanding nature of the British.*
- B. *suggesting that war will be ineffective in resolving a conflict.*
- C. *implying that attempts at negotiation have been half-hearted.*
- D. *stressing that options for peaceful reconciliation have been exhausted.*

The repetition captures the audience's attention and powerfully emphasizes with increasing intensity that all peaceful means of getting the British to change their ways have been exhausted. War is the only solution left. Choice D is correct.

Sample: The repetition of the word "we" serves to
- A. *describe the differences among a group of people.*
- B. *establish solidarity among members of the audience.*
- C. *stress the individualistic nature of a fruitful endeavor.*
- D. *underscore the superiority of competition over cooperation.*

Henry tries to unite the people to fight against the British. He sought to establish solidarity, or unity, between the people. Choice B is correct.

Drill 1

The Grateful Dead is an iconic band known for its innovative music style. However, it is the band's unique business model that has recently been gaining attention from scholars. The band was ahead of its time in the ways it chose to do business. It was not afraid to improvise and shake up conventional norms to meet the needs of its clientele. For example, by touring year-round instead of focusing mostly on record sales while only touring for a limited portion of the year, as most of its peers did, the band helped build a brand and a loyal base.

The tactics that the Grateful Dead adopted have had an influence on American businesses. For example, the band gave special treatment to its most loyal fans by giving them access to concert tickets across the country before announcing their concerts to the general public. In the 1980s, many American businesses adopted this consumer-oriented model, focusing on providing their clients with quality products and services. Before that, "the customer comes first" mentality was not the norm. The band members also allowed people to record their concerts free of charge. Rather than suing people who recorded and distributed their recordings to others for free, they took advantage of the publicity that they gained by having their music spread. As a result of their increased popularity, they made more money in merchandise and concert sales. Today, many companies embrace this principle. Clients who receive "free stuff" from companies are more inclined to give these companies their business.

In addition, the band's "in-sourcing" approach to management contrasted with the outsourcing model so common throughout corporate America. Many firms will hire contractors from other companies to perform certain business tasks, a practice that sometimes leads to conflict. The Grateful Dead preferred to hire as many people as possible to work in-house for the band itself. Thus, the band had more control over its product and was able to better take care of its employees. As a result, it was better situated to meet the needs of its customers. Today, many companies hire in-house people when possible. For example, a company might hire a lawyer as a fulltime employee rather than make a contract with a separate law firm to do its legal work.

1. The author suggests that businesses often give away "free stuff" (line 15) because
   A. they are concerned that their services are too expensive.
   B. they hope that fans of the Grateful Dead will associate their own companies with the band.
   C. they believe that doing so will attract paying customers to their businesses.
   D. they need to get rid of extra inventory that takes up space in the workplace.

2. What did the author most nearly mean when he said the band was "ahead of its time? (lines 2-3)"
   A. They valued promptness at all performances.
   B. They anticipated that businesses would one day seek them out for advice.
   C. They were the only band of their generation to produce truly innovative music.
   D. They embraced sound business principles before they became popular on a wider scale.

3. It is implied that people who "give these companies their business" (line 16)
   A. become clients of these companies.
   B. tell these companies off.
   C. read about these companies in the newspaper.
   D. demand more free merchandise from these companies.

4. The passage implies that had the band relied on outsourcing instead of insourcing, the band members would have
   A. saved substantial costs.
   B. been better able to meet their customers' needs.
   C. had less control over their product.
   D. never gained substantial fame.

Mastodons, the now extinct relatives of the modern elephant, inhabited North and Central America until their extinction about 10,000 years ago. These mysterious animals have captured the attention of scientists and ordinary people alike. President Thomas Jefferson, a scientific expert in his own right, commissioned a team to collect mastodon fossils for him in order to learn more about these fascinating creatures.

The name "mastodon" means "breast tooth," in reference to the appearance of its molars. Mastodons had low-domed heads and large, long tusks. The tusks may have assisted the mastodons in feeding and competing with other animals. Mastodons were herbivorous creatures, whose diet was obtained mostly by browsing (feeding on high-growing plants). They also likely got some food by grazing (feeding on grass and low vegetation). Though they did not have many predators due to their large size, their predators included saber-toothed cats and lions. There is also evidence that humans hunted them. For example, an arrowhead was found among the bones of one American mastodon.

People sometimes confuse mastodons with their more famous cousin, the wooly mammoth, though modern reconstructions based on partial skeleton remains show that they are only distantly related. One notable difference between the two cousins was the shape of their teeth. While the mammoths had ridged molars suitable for eating grass, the mastodons had molars with cone-like cusps that were perfect for cutting trees, twigs, and shrubs. Carbon from the teeth of mastodons and mammoths provide scientists with a treasure trove of information, confirming their different dietary preferences.

Scientists speculate that mastodons may have been social creatures based on studies of their anatomical similarities to elephants, though scientists obviously cannot be sure about exactly how they behaved. Studies of mastodon bone sites suggest that they lived in mixed herds of adult females and young mastodons. The long maturation periods may indicate that mastodons required care for a long period of time. Although there is some speculation that mastodons were migratory creatures, some scientists now believe that many of them did not roam. Their habitats often had everything they needed to live comfortably.

There is still some debate over the primary cause of the mastodon's extinction. It has generally been thought that human pressures on their populations were the main culprit, though climate change may have been a more important factor. In 2016, a nearly complete mastodon skeleton preserved during the Ice Age, the most complete skeleton discovered in decades, was found in the Great Lakes region. Analysis of this skeleton revealed that many of the bones were in the same position relative to each other as when it was alive, suggesting that natural causes were not the cause of death. It is more likely that this mastodon's death served a more practical purpose. Specifically, it was probably stored by hunters as a source of meat under a pond that no longer exists.

5. Which of the following provides the best evidence that human pressures may have played a large role in the mastodon's extinction?
    A. Carbon studies of teeth found in mammoths and mastodons.
    B. The position of mastodon bones found in a recovered skeleton.
    C. The occurrence of the Ice Age around the time the mastodon is believed to have gone extinct.
    D. The discovery of an ancient pond known to be popular for hunters.

6. What does the author imply about mammoths?
    A. They somewhat resembled mastodons in appearance.
    B. They primarily ate twigs.
    C. They did not live during the same time as the mastodon.
    D. Their only predators were saber-toothed tigers.

7. What does the author imply was most unusual about the mastodon discovered in 2016?
    A. The location where it was found.
    B. The completeness of the skeleton.
    C. The age of the skeleton.
    D. The diet of the mastodon.

8. How would the author most likely respond to the belief that mastodons and mammoths are closely related?
    A. First impressions are usually accurate.
    B. Looks can be deceiving.
    C. The best way to learn about ancestors is to study their descendants.
    D. Direct observation trumps scientific analysis.

9. What did the author mean to imply about mastodons with the assertion that they "had everything they needed to live comfortably"?
    A. Their comfort with their surroundings limited their desire to travel.
    B. They never competed with other animals for food.
    C. Their habitats had unusually comfortable sleeping quarters.
    D. They never faced even the slightest of environmental challenges.

Week 2

Halloween has long been a popular holiday in many countries. It is typically celebrated on October 31st. To the modern person, this holiday frequently conjures up associations with trick or treating, costumes, and haunted houses. But the holiday as we know it today has a long and interesting history.

Halloween has its roots in the Irish festival Samhain, which was celebrated as far back as the 10th century. Samhain was one of several holidays that signaled the end of the harvest season, as people began stocking up supplies for the winter. It was believed that on October 31st, the window between the worlds of the living and the dead opened. Thus, "scary" costumes and masks were often worn to prevent evil spirts from causing harm to people and their crops. People also made lanterns out of vegetables, such as turnips or pumpkins, to ward off evil spirits. These lanterns were the likely inspiration behind modern-day jack-o-lanterns. It was also believed that spirits of the deceased would come visit their families, seeking hospitality. Thus, people often left out food and drinks for the spirits of their family members.

It was not until the 19th century that Samhain and the similar holiday All Hallows' Eve merged to become what is now known as Halloween. The holiday first came to America after a wave of Irish and Scottish immigration. Though the holiday was originally confined to immigrant communities, it eventually became a mainstream holiday throughout the United States that is now associated with a variety of traditions, such as bonfires, apple bobbing, haunted houses, and scary movies. Halloween is largely a secular holiday with less of a religious dimension than the holidays from which it emerged.

Perhaps the most noteworthy Halloween tradition is "trick or treating." Children go to door to door dressed in costumes saying "trick or treat" in expectation of receiving candy ("the treat"). Though not usually done in practice, the alternative to a treat is for the children to play a "trick" on the owner of the house if no treat is given. Many countries expressly discourage or outlaw playing tricks due to the damage and disruption they cause. Trick or treating is loosely based on the medieval European practices of "guising" and "souling." Guising was a practice whereby children dressed in costumes would go from door to door asking for coins or food in exchange for putting on entertaining performances. Similarly, "souling" involved beggars asking rich people for food ("soul cakes") on feast days such as All Hallows' Eve. By the 1950s, trick or treating was firmly established as a kid-friendly holiday in the United States. Today, adults are generally expected to go grocery shopping for treats in preparation for Halloween.

Interestingly, Halloween is not just a kid holiday anymore. While there aren't too many adults trick or treating (unless they are accompanying children), many adults relish the opportunity to get dressed up. Some offices even encourage their staff to wear costumes on Halloween. The fun and fantastical holiday can give adults a needed escape from dwelling on the stresses of their lives.

10. What does the passage suggest about the practice of dressing up in costumes in exchange for food?
    A. Its purpose was to protect people's homes from evil spirits.
    B. It was only done by beggars until the 1950s.
    C. Variations of this practice have occurred for centuries.
    D. It was considered selfish by the European nobility.

11. It is implied that when Halloween was originally brought to the United States,
    A. it served to preserve certain European traditions.
    B. it became increasingly focused on religious themes.
    C. it immediately became the most popular holiday behind Christmas.
    D. pranking was the most important component of the holiday.

12. The author's comments suggest that Halloween appeals to adults because
    A. the people first entering the workforce today were from the original generation of trick-or-treaters.
    B. they appreciate the opportunity to enjoy themselves and be less stressed.
    C. it gives them the chance to bond with the children in their lives.
    D. most employers will allow employees to take off work for the holidays.

In the past, scientists conceptualized taste as linked to taste buds in the mouth, which detect sweet, salty, sour, and bitter flavors. Now, it is clear that taste is an experience that also encompasses smell, touch, and even sight. The cortical workload of the brain processes the majority of information visually, so it makes sense that our eyes play a role in how we perceive food.

5   The appearance of food, including the color of the plates on which it is found, shapes our expectations. In one sense, this is protective. For example, we know not to eat food that looks like it can make us sick, like rotten apples or moldy bread. We may also avoid foods that look similar to those that have made us sick in the past. Visual cues can also assist us in identifying certain features of foods. For example, milk experts are better able to determine the fat content of milk when they can see it.

10 The appearance of food not only impacts expectations, but it can also affect how we actually experience certain flavors. If we try a food that looks disgusting, it may be "too late" to enjoy it because of our brain's expectation that it will taste bad affects how we actually perceive the food once it is in our mouths. Though sight is not technically part of taste, it can trigger our taste buds. The color of food also affects how we experience it. For example, if an apple-flavored drink is colored red, our brains may
15 perceive it to be sweeter than it actually is, since we associate red with sweetness.

In one study, subjects who tried an orange-flavored drink while blindfolded rarely identified the flavor correctly. When they could see that the color of the drink was orange, they almost always were correct. When the orange drink was dyed green, some subjects mistakenly identified it as lime-flavored. When it was not dyed green, no subjects made this mistake. Clearly, the color of food can influence how we
20 perceive taste.

The color of food can even trick so-called "experts." For instance, in a classic experiment, wine experts who tasted white wine that was secretly dyed red used descriptors characteristic of actual red wines. Their expectations for how red wine should taste may have triggered their brains to detect flavors that weren't actually present in the wine. When the wine was in opaque glasses, the experts were more
25 accurate in describing the wine.

The food industry is well aware of how our expectations shape how we taste food. For that reason, they alter the appearance of food and use colorimeters to make sure that foods are perfectly hued. For example, customers may be more inclined to purchase apples that have been colored red, believing them to be sweeter. Companies that make plant-based meat-like products often dye the food brown
30   since customers are not "prepared" to eat green meat. People generally associate green meat with meat that has gone bad. Nevertheless, while we associate certain colors with certain foods, this learning happens from experience. Companies can effectively market flavors that counter our expectations to attract customers, as exemplified by green ketchup and blue lemonade.

Even though our eyes shape how we perceive taste, they don't tell the whole story. The brain and other
35   senses, such as smell, can override the ugly appearance of certain foods. Many foods, such as chilies, sausages, and stews, are popular among people who do not necessarily find them visually appealing. For example, while a beef stew might look "gross" to someone, if it has a pleasant smell and one has positive memories associated with its taste, these factors take precedence. In other cases, a desire to be adventurous may override one's initial revulsion to a certain food's appearance. This is encouraging
40   news to many people, including parents who want their kids to eat healthy foods that look less than appetizing.

13. The studies involving white wine dyed red and fat content in milk are most likely mentioned in order to
    A. prove that only laymen can be deceived by transparent glasses.
    B. show that even experts' perception of taste is closely tied to color.
    C. suggest that people who sample drinks for a living are more likely to make errors than the general public when analyzing flavors.
    D. illustrate that people prefer the taste of milk to the taste of wine.

14. Jan believes that guacamole looks like slime, yet she eats it anyway. Which of the following is NOT a factor identified in the passage that might account for her behavior?
    A. She has memories about guacamole having a delicious taste.
    B. She is feeling adventurous and wants to try a new flavor.
    C. The fresh smell of the guacamole appeals to Jan.
    D. Jan believes that her health will be put in serious jeopardy if she does not eat the guacamole.

15. Based on the passage, what is a likely reason the author would give for why many people eat chilies that have an unpleasant appearance?
    A. Other sensory factors supersede the appearance.
    B. The concept of beauty is subjective.
    C. People tend to avoid new culinary experiences.
    D. They believe that the ugly appearance signals its healthy properties.

16. What is most likely meant by the statement that customers are not "prepared" for green meat?
    A. They are unlikely to accept meat that resembles meat that has gone bad.
    B. They are unable to explain why anyone would want to eat such products.
    C. They are incapable of learning that the green color comes from vegetables.
    D. They don't have the proper equipment for recoloring the meat themselves.

Sea stars, or starfish, are known for their distinctive appearance. With their arms connected to their round body, giving them the appearance of stars, it is no wonder that many people are allured by these creatures. Beyond their dazzling features, sea stars play a particularly important role in maintaining the balance of ecosystems.

5   Despite their name and aquatic habitat, sea stars are not fish. Rather, they are echinoderms, closely related to other animals such as sea urchins and sand dollars. There are thousands of species of sea stars living in diverse habitats, from tropical waters to colder regions of the ocean.

Sea stars are carnivores, and their size is dependent on how much they eat. Sea stars eat prey outside their bodies. They use suction tubes on their feet to open up shells of shellfish, such as clams and
10 mussels. Their stomachs then leave their bodies and secrete enzymes that break down the tissue of the shellfish. Then the stomachs return to the sea stars' bodies. The madreporite at the center of the star filters water through its body. The water that filters through their bodies acts similarly to "blood" in other animals. Most of the major organs of the sea star are located on the arms. For example, eyespots on the arm help them detect light. Interestingly, sea stars have no brain. Rather, their nervous system is
15 spread throughout their arms. While most sea stars have five arms, there are some with more. Sea stars have calcified skin to protect them from predators, such as crabs and seagulls. Many come in color variations that allow them to hide among the coral reef, giving them another avenue of protection. The ridges and bumps on many starfish actually complement the spikes found in many coral reefs. Even when sea stars are attacked or are wounded, they do not necessarily die. Most sea stars can regenerate
20 missing limbs. Thus, a sea star might sacrifice an arm to escape a predator, only to regrow it.

Sea stars are considered keystone species by scientists because of the role they play in maintaining the balance of ecosystems. They keep the population of their prey under control. For example, if sea stars are removed from an ecosystem, populations of mussels, urchins, and barnacles may grow uncontrollably, thus pushing out other organisms from the ecosystem. One danger posed by increased
25 sea urchin populations is the destruction of kelp forests on which sea urchins feed. When sea stars keep the sea urchin population in check, kelp forests thrive. Kelp forests are vital to the health of marine ecosystems in part because they provide a habitat for many fish. Kelp forests also help the environment. Most scientists believe that excessive carbon dioxide in the atmosphere is responsible for global warming. Kelp forests absorb carbon dioxide from the atmosphere and release oxygen into the air.

30 Unfortunately, there are many threats to sea stars. Some companies harvest them for fertilizer and poultry feed. Another threat is sea star wasting syndrome, a disease whereby sea stars turn to goo. The

disease is likely caused by a virus. It is believed that pollution and warmer waters associated with human-induced climate change may be contributing to the spread of this disease, which has affected as many as 98% of starfish in certain populations.

35 Some people think that we need to treat sea stars like endangered species for their own protection. In some locations, there are laws restricting how many live sea stars that can be collected by humans from waters. Scientists are also trying to better understand the environmental factors that contribute to sea star viral infections so that we can better protect them. The discovery of young sea stars in areas where adult populations had been thought to be wiped out brings renewed hope that their populations will
40 rebound.

17. Which of the following is most similar to the relationship between sea stars and mussels?
    A. An antibiotic that kills harmful bacteria responsible for an infection also kills beneficial bacteria, thus causing discomfort.
    B. The population of elk rises following the disappearance of the area's grizzly bear population.
    C. Flowers in a meadow survive only if bees are there to pollinate them.
    D. Humans use herbicides that cause the population of several insects to decrease.

18. Which of the following is most likely to result from increasing sea star populations in an ecosystem?
    A. A sharp decrease in coral reef populations.
    B. A moderate decline in kelp populations.
    C. Overfishing of shellfish populations.
    D. A decline in the mussel population.

19. The passage implies that many people want to treat sea stars like endangered species because
    A. rising kelp populations threaten sea stars' health.
    B. sea stars are regarded as the most beautiful creatures in the sea.
    C. sea stars face a variety of ecological and human threats.
    D. 98% of all sea star populations have been wiped out.

20. What is the most likely reason the author mentioned kelp?
    A. To give an example of an important plant that might die if there were no sea stars.
    B. To demonstrate the effect of global warming on rising sea levels.
    C. To illustrate why sea stars are able to camouflage themselves with great ease.
    D. To encourage farmers to use plant products for poultry feed.

21. What does the author suggest about kelp forests?
    A. They mostly grow in cold waters.
    B. Their only predators are sea urchins.
    C. Their survival may play a role in combatting global warming.
    D. Their natural beauty is the most important reason that they should be preserved.

22. The author implies that the term "starfish"
    A. is more scientifically accurate than "sea stars."
    B. does not accurately classify the types of organisms to which they refer.
    C. describes multiples species of fish.
    D. is used less often than "sea stars" by most laypeople.

If you've ever gone to a doctor's office or hospital, you've probably encountered nurses who often perform important medical tasks, such as taking blood, administering medicine, and monitoring patients' health. The jobs of nurses today reflect the deep influence of Florence Nightingale, who transformed the once-derided job into an honorable medical profession.

5   Born to a wealthy Italian family in 1820, Nightingale's mother encouraged her to marry someone in her station, as other upper-class women of her time did. However, Nightingale had different plans in mind. While on a tour of Europe, Nightingale connected with Mary Clarke. Clarke generally looked down on other upper-class women and instead spent most of her time with male intellectuals. Sensing that Nightingale was intelligent in her own right, Clarke took a liking to Nightingale, and the two remained in
10 contact for decades. Clarke taught Nightingale that women can be regarded as equal to their male counterparts. When Nightingale decided to pursue a career in nursing, she did so despite the protests of her mother, who wanted Nightingale to instead focus on building a family of her own. At that time, taking on a job was seen as menial labor.

    Nightingale gained prominence during the Crimean War when she treated soldiers. She was struck by
15 the fact that more soldiers were dying of disease than of battle wounds. She noticed the poor hygiene practices of soldiers and unsanitary conditions of the wards and posited that they were making the soldiers sick and contributing to the spread of the disease. Nightingale improved sanitary conditions in the wards, having them scrubbed thoroughly and providing soldiers with clean linens. She also encouraged personal hygiene practices, such as handwashing. As a result of Nightingale's efforts, the
20 death rate in the hospitals declined sharply. She became known as "the lady with the lamp" to the soldiers, as she frequently patrolled the wards with her lamp, checking on the soldiers, whom she reassured with her presence. Nightingale also argued to the Royal Commission that poor ventilation, overcrowding, and bad drainage systems contributed to the spread of infections. The Sanitary Commission fixed the ventilation and drainage systems, further contributing to reductions in death
25 rates. Her influence on the sanitary design of hospitals and homes is still seen today.

Nightingale drew from ideas about nutrition and psychology when treating her patients. She believed that poor nutrition contributed to disease and a decline in overall health. She made sure that soldiers had diverse and appealing dietary options. Nightingale also recognized that mental health was closely linked to physical health. She had soldiers write letters so that they could express themselves emotionally. She provided them with books, classrooms, and libraries to stimulate their minds. Thus, Nightingale was innovative in her focus on treating the whole person.

Although Nightingale is most known for her contributions to nursing, she also has a somewhat underreported legacy in the field of statistics. Nightingale scrupulously collected data during her time as a nurse, and her statistical findings helped convince the Royal Commission on the Health of the Army to accept many of her policy recommendations. Her study of the sanitation system in India led to successful public health reforms that reduced deaths. Nightingale was one of the first people to make use of the pie chart, and she even helped developed the polar area diagram, a type of statistical chart. Nightingale was the first female elected to the Royal Statistical Society.

In 1860, Nightingale put her ideas into practice on a grander scale by establishing the Nightingale School for Nurses, the first school for nurses connected to a medical school program and hospital. Students would typically train for one year, taking classes and working with patients. The Nightingale school serves as a model for other nursing schools. Though the profession of nursing has evolved over the years, Nightingale's influence on the profession is enduring and she will continue to be regarded as a heroine for her contributions.

23. The author implies that Nightingale's contributions to public health were most directly based on
    A. consultations with Indian doctors.
    B. data analysis and firsthand observation.
    C. her experiences fighting on the front lines of the Crimean War.
    D. books written by medical experts during the Enlightenment.

24. The passage most strongly implies that Nightingale's mother would most approve if Nightingale
    A. hosted a salon to discuss philosophical debates with other upper-class women.
    B. did not pursue a professional career.
    C. became a doctor instead of a nurse.
    D. taught children in a poor English neighborhood.

25. What is the most likely reason that the tasks of nurses were mentioned in the first paragraph?
    A. To demonstrate how Nightingale's practices influenced the modern nursing profession.
    B. To argue that techniques employed by Nightingale were outdated.
    C. To suggest that medical professionals act differently in hospitals than in other settings.
    D. To illustrate details about Nightingale's own schooling.

26. The nickname "the lady with the lamp" was most likely meant to convey
    A. condescension.
    B. respect.
    C. frustration.
    D. sympathy.

27. The words "although," "influence," and "regarding" in the last paragraph help most clearly convey the idea that
    A. while she was just one person and while the field of nursing has not remained static, Nightingale's impact was nonetheless important.
    B. Nightingale's relatively short time spent practicing nursing gave her hope that others would iterate on her accomplishments.
    C. though nursing was just of many fields in which Nightingale had a powerful impact, her legacy in nursing has been most compromised by changes to the field.
    D. even a field as ever-changing as nursing had to overcome many hurdles in order to be taken seriously, and Nightingale's efforts are to thank for that.

The poem below is "November" by Elizabeth Drew Stoddard.

Much have I spoken of the faded leaf;
   Long have I listened to the wailing wind,
And watched it ploughing through the heavy clouds,
   For autumn charms my melancholy mind.

5   When autumn comes, the poets sing a dirge:*
   The year must perish; all the flowers are dead;
The sheaves are gathered; and the mottled quail
   Runs in the stubble, but the lark has fled!

Still, autumn ushers in the Christmas cheer,
10   The holly-berries and the ivy-tree:
They weave a chaplet for the Old Year's bier,
   These waiting mourners do not sing for me!

I find sweet peace in depths of autumn woods,
   Where grow the ragged ferns and roughened moss;
15 The naked, silent trees have taught me this,—
   The loss of beauty is not always loss!

28. The first stanza (lines 1-4) suggests that that the narrator is a person who
    A. dislikes seasons other than autumn.
    B. is attuned to her natural surroundings.
    C. has a charming personality.
    D. seeks to better understand the natural forces governing seasonal changes.

29. It can be inferred that the "year must perish" (line 6) refers most literally to
    A. the narrator's personal connection to nature.
    B. the end of the calendar year.
    C. a destructive period of time.
    D. the death of sorrow.

30. The narrator seems to regard the views of the poets mentioned in line 5 as
    A. insightful.
    B. insincere.
    C. alarmist.
    D. unintelligible.

31. The statement "These waiting mourners do not sing for me!" (line 12) suggests that
    A. the mourners are inconsiderate of the narrator's feelings.
    B. the songs of the mourners do not reflect the narrator's emotions.
    C. the mourners choose not to perform for people with whom they disagree.
    D. the narrator is troubled by the mourners' selfishness.

32. The last line of the poem suggests that the narrator would most likely agree with which of the of the following statements about beauty?
    A. The absence of beauty during autumn is not problematic.
    B. Autumn is actually the most aesthetically pleasing time of year.
    C. Nature is the best teacher when it comes to all matters of beauty.
    D. Objective standards of beauty often prevent people from exploring nature.

The poem below is "'Hope' is the Thing with Feathers" by Emily Dickinson.

"Hope" is the thing with feathers -
That perches in the soul -
And sings the tune without the words -
And never stops - at all -

5   And sweetest - in the Gale* - is heard -
And sore must be the storm -
That could abash the little Bird
That kept so many warm -

I've heard it in the chillest land -
10   And on the strangest Sea -
Yet - never - in Extremity,
It asked a crumb - of me.

*Gale: strong wind

33. The second stanza (lines 5-8) implies that hope sounds the sweetest
    A. during difficult times.
    B. when the listener is open to hearing it.
    C. when one is feeling bashful.
    D. in the midst of natural scenery.

34. "And sore must be the storm/That could abash the little bird" (lines 6-7) most likely means
    A. there are no limits to hope's power.
    B. only a truly powerful force can dampen hope.
    C. perseverance is needed to overcome obstacles.
    D. humiliation is the biggest threat to hope.

35. The speaker most likely mentions to "chillest land" and "strangest sea" in order to imply that
    A. the speaker is well-traveled.
    B. the character of hope is fundamentally shaped by external conditional.
    C. hope is a pervasive force in difficult situations.
    D. hope is needed to endure strange circumstances.

The poem below is "When I Heard the Learn'd Astronomer" by Walt Whitman.

When I heard the learn'd astronomer;
When the proofs, the figures, were ranged in columns before me;
When I was shown the charts and the diagrams, to add, divide, and measure them;
When I, sitting, heard the astronomer, where he lectured with much applause in the lecture-room,
How soon, unaccountable,* I became tired and sick;
Till rising and gliding out, I wander'd off by myself,
In the mystical moist night-air, and from time to time,
Look'd up in perfect silence at the stars.

*unaccountable: unable to be explained

36. The speaker's feelings about the learn'd astronomer's lecture seem to
    A. be proof of his disdain for science.
    B. contrast with those of the other attendees.
    C. highlight his uneasiness with mathematical formulas.
    D. illustrate his anti-intellectual nature.

37. In context, the details in lines 2-3 suggest that the speaker
    A. is not educated enough to follow the presentation.
    B. has an unusual predilection for mathematics.
    C. is bored with the details presented to him.
    D. believes there are errors in the speaker's calculations.

38. It can be inferred that the speaker leaves the lecture hall
    A. before the lecture has officially ended.
    B. because he is suffering from a contagious illness.
    C. in a manner designed to attract attention.
    D. because he has no interest in astronomy.

39. Based on the information in the poem, the speaker would most likely agree that
    A. scientific data can obscure the deeper meaning of observed phenomena.
    B. charts and figures are of no use to anyone.
    C. the mysteries of the natural world can be fully understood.
    D. true happiness can only be experienced by those who defy social conventions.

The poem below is "We Wear the Mask" by Paul Laurence Dunbar.

We wear the mask that grins and lies,
It hides our cheeks and shades our eyes,—
This debt we pay to human guile;
With torn and bleeding hearts we smile
5   And mouth with myriad subtleties,

Why should the world be over-wise,
In counting all our tears and sighs?
Nay, let them only see us, while
    We wear the mask.

10 We smile, but oh great Christ, our cries
To thee from tortured souls arise.
We sing, but oh the clay is vile
Beneath our feet, and long the mile,
But let the world dream otherwise,
15   We wear the mask!

40. The "them" in the poem most likely refers to people who
    A. physically and emotionally torture the speaker.
    B. avoid the speaker in daily life.
    C. do not accept the speaker's authentic self.
    D. have a close personal relationship with the speaker.

41. "With torn and bleeding hearts we smile" (line 4) most directly suggests that the people who wear the mask
    A. are free to express their frustration with their lot in life.
    B. keep their suffering private from the rest of the world.
    C. hide their pity for those less fortunate than them.
    D. regularly undergo transformative experiences.

42. The "mask" most likely refers most literally to
    A. protective decorative gear.
    B. official standards of conduct.
    C. superficial expressions.
    D. a reflection of people's authentic selves.

The poem below is "He Had His Dream" by Paul Laurence Dunbar.

He had his dream, and all through life,
Worked up to it through toil and strife.
Afloat fore'er before his eyes,
It colored for him all his skies:

5   The storm–cloud dark
    Above his bark,
    The calm and listless vault of blue
    Took on its hopeful hue,
    It tinctured every passing beam—
10 He had his dream.
    He labored hard and failed at last,
    His sails too weak to bear the blast,
    The raging tempests tore away
    And sent his beating bark astray.

15 But what cared he
    For wind or sea!
    He said, "The tempest will be short,
    My bark will come to port."
    He saw through every cloud a gleam—
20 He had his dream.

43. The phrase "colored for him all his skies" (line 4) suggests that the speaker's dream
    A. shaped his perception.
    B. caused him anguish and turmoil.
    C. guided his moral compass.
    D. was unusually complex in nature.

44. The "raging tempests" (lie 13) most likely refer to
    A. weather on an unusually cloudy day.
    B. obstacles facing the man with the dream.
    C. people who doubt the man with the dream.
    D. work required to achieve success.

45. It can be inferred that the man with the dream
    A. has not yet achieved it.
    B. was never all that invested in his dream.
    C. refused to put in the hard work needed to make his dream come true.
    D. was oblivious to the challenges facing him along the way to achieving his dream.

46. The quotation (lines 17-18) from the man with the dream most directly suggests that he believes
    A. the journey is more valuable than the destination.
    B. failure is an inevitable part of personal growth.
    C. difficult times are temporary and manageable.
    D. sailing is an enjoyable pastime.

The excerpt below is from *The Story of My Life* by Helen Keller.

The most important day I remember in all my life is the one on which my teacher, Anne Mansfield Sullivan, came to me. I am filled with wonder when I consider the immeasurable contrasts between the two lives which it connects. It was the third of March, 1887, three months before I was seven years old. On the afternoon of that eventful day, I stood on the porch, dumb, expectant. I guessed vaguely from
5   my mother's signs and from the hurrying to and fro in the house that something unusual was about to happen, so I went to the door and waited on the steps. The afternoon sun penetrated the mass of honeysuckle that covered the porch, and fell on my upturned face. My fingers lingered almost unconsciously on the familiar leaves and blossoms which had just come forth to greet the sweet southern spring. I did not know what the future held of marvel or surprise for me. Anger and bitterness
10 had preyed upon me continually for weeks and a deep languor had succeeded this passionate struggle.

Have you ever been at sea in a dense fog, when it seemed as if a tangible white darkness shut you in, and the great ship, tense and anxious, groped her way toward the shore with plummet and sounding-line, and you waited with beating heart for something to happen? I was like that ship before my education began, only I was without compass or sounding-line, and had no way of knowing how near
15 the harbor was. "Light! give me light!" was the wordless cry of my soul, and the light of love shone on me in that very hour.

I felt approaching footsteps, I stretched out my hand as I supposed to my mother. Someone took it, and I was caught up and held close in the arms of her who had come to reveal all things to me, and, more than all things else, to love me. The morning after my teacher came she led me into her room and gave me a doll. The little blind children at the Perkins Institution had sent it and Laura Bridgman had dressed it; but I did not know this until afterward. When I had played with it a little while, Miss Sullivan slowly spelled into my hand the word "d-o-l-l." I was at once interested in this finger play and tried to imitate it. When I finally succeeded in making the letters correctly I was flushed with childish pleasure and pride. Running downstairs to my mother I held up my hand and made the letters for doll. I did not know that I was spelling a word or even that words existed; I was simply making my fingers go in monkey-like imitation. In the days that followed I learned to spell in this uncomprehending way a great many words, among them pin, hat, cup and a few verbs like sit, stand and walk. But my teacher had been with me several weeks before I understood that everything has a name.

One day, while I was playing with my new doll, Miss Sullivan put my big rag doll into my lap also, spelled "d-o-l-l" and tried to make me understand that "d-o-l-l" applied to both. Earlier in the day we had had a tussle over the words "m-u-g" and "w-a-t-e-r." Miss Sullivan had tried to impress it upon me that "m-u-g" is mug and that "w-a-t-e-r" is water, but I persisted in confounding the two. In despair she had dropped the subject for the time, only to renew it at the first opportunity. I became impatient at her repeated attempts and, seizing the new doll, I dashed it upon the floor. I was keenly delighted when I felt the fragments of the broken doll at my feet. Neither sorrow nor regret followed my passionate outburst. I had not loved the doll. In the still, dark world in which I lived there was no strong sentiment or tenderness. I felt my teacher sweep the fragments to one side of the hearth, and I had a sense of satisfaction that the cause of my discomfort was removed. She brought me my hat, and I knew I was going out into the warm sunshine. This thought, if a wordless sensation may be called a thought, made me hop and skip with pleasure.

We walked down the path to the well-house, attracted by the fragrance of the honeysuckle with which it was covered. Someone was drawing water and my teacher placed my hand under the spout. As the cool stream gushed over one hand she spelled into the other the word water, first slowly, then rapidly. I stood still, my whole attention fixed upon the motions of her fingers. Suddenly I felt a misty consciousness as of something forgotten—a thrill of returning thought; and somehow the mystery of language was revealed to me. I knew then that "w-a-t-e-r" meant the wonderful cool something that was flowing over my hand. That living word awakened my soul, gave it light, hope, joy, set it free! There were barriers still, it is true, but barriers that could in time be swept away.

I left the well-house eager to learn. Everything had a name, and each name gave birth to a new thought. As we returned to the house every object which I touched seemed to quiver with life. That was because I saw everything with the strange, new sight that had come to me. On entering the door, I remembered the doll I had broken. I felt my way to the hearth and picked up the pieces. I tried vainly to put them together. Then my eyes filled with tears; for I realized what I had done, and for the first time I felt repentance and sorrow.

I learned a great many new words that day. I do not remember what they all were; but I do know that mother, father, sister, teacher were among them—words that were to make the world blossom for me, "like Aaron's rod, with flowers." It would have been difficult to find a happier child than I was as I lay in my crib at the close of that eventful day and lived over the joys it had brought me, and for the first time longed for a new day to come.

47. Helen most likely asks the reader a question in the second paragraph in order to
    A. help the reader visualize the struggles she faced.
    B. tell an amusing anecdote about an important episode in her life.
    C. boast about the significance of her accomplishments in light of her initial struggles.
    D. make clear to the reader her fascination with the sea.

48. Why was Helen's cry for light "wordless"?
    A. She never experienced light.
    B. She had no concept of language.
    C. She could not register emotions normally.
    D. She could not produce sounds.

49. In the context of the passage as a whole, it can be inferred that for Helen, light represented
    A. knowledge.
    B. friendship.
    C. innocence.
    D. compassion.

50. Why did Helen most likely break the doll?
    A. She never liked the doll.
    B. She no longer was interested in mimicking Miss Sullivan's gestures.
    C. She was frustrated by her struggle to comprehend a certain lesson.
    D. She wanted to make Miss Sullivan clean up her mess as punishment for teaching her.

51. Why did the objects Helen encountered seem to "quiver with life?"
    A. They now took on a new meaning for her.
    B. They seemed to feel happy for her accomplishments.
    C. She had never noticed them before.
    D. She grew to appreciate their unique attributes that made them beautiful.

52. Why was the episode at the well-house life changing for Helen?
    A. She realized that Miss Sullivan truly loved her.
    B. She learned that everything has a name.
    C. She understood that there would be necessary but conquerable barriers in her education.
    D. She knew the joy of immersing herself in refreshing water.

53. It can be inferred that Helen attempted to fix the doll because
    A. she realized that she actually loved the doll.
    B. the doll was symbolic of her childhood.
    C. she felt guilty for breaking it.
    D. Miss Sullivan told her to do so.

Week 2

Below is "The Story of Prometheus" by James Baldwin.

In those old, old times, there lived two brothers who were not like other men, nor yet like those Mighty Ones who lived upon the mountain top. They were the sons of one of those Titans who had fought against Jupiter* and been sent in chains to the strong prison-house of the Lower World. The name of the elder of these brothers was Prometheus, or Forethought; for he was always thinking of the future and making things ready for what might happen to-morrow, or next week, or next year, or it may be in a hundred years to come. The younger was called Epimetheus, or Afterthought; for he was always so busy thinking of yesterday, or last year, or a hundred years ago, that he had no care at all for what might come to pass after a while. For some cause, Jupiter had not sent these brothers to prison with the rest of the Titans.

Prometheus did not care to live amid the clouds on the mountain top. He was too busy for that. While the Mighty Folk were spending their time in idleness, drinking nectar and eating ambrosia, he was intent upon plans for making the world wiser and better than it had ever been before. He went out amongst men to live with them and help them; for his heart was filled with sadness when he found that they were no longer happy as they had been during the golden days when Saturn was king. Ah, how very poor and wretched they were! He found them living in caves and in holes of the earth, shivering with the cold because there was no fire, dying of starvation, hunted by wild beasts and by one another–the most miserable of all living creatures.

"If they only had fire," said Prometheus to himself, "they could at least warm themselves and cook their food; and after a while they could learn to make tools and build themselves houses. Without fire, they are worse off than the beasts."

Then he went boldly to Jupiter and begged him to give fire to men, that so they might have a little comfort through the long, dreary months of winter.

"Not a spark will I give," said Jupiter. "No, indeed! Why, if men had fire they might become strong and wise like ourselves, and after a while they would drive us out of our kingdom. Let them shiver with cold, and let them live like the beasts. It is best for them to be poor and ignorant, that so we Mighty Ones may thrive and be happy."

Prometheus made no answer; but he had set his heart on helping mankind, and he did not give up. He turned away, and left Jupiter and his mighty company forever.

As he was walking by the shore of the sea he found a reed, or, as some say, a tall stalk of fennel, growing; and when he had broken it off he saw that its hollow center was filled with a dry, soft pith which would burn slowly and keep on fire a long time. He took the long stalk in his hands, and started with it towards the dwelling of the sun in the far east.

"Mankind shall have fire in spite of the tyrant who sits on the mountain top," he said.

He reached the place of the sun in the early morning just as the glowing, golden orb was rising from the earth and beginning his daily journey through the sky. He touched the end of the long reed to the flames, and the dry pith caught on fire and burned slowly. Then he turned and hastened back to his own land, carrying with him the precious spark hidden in the hollow center of the plant. He called some of

the shivering men from their caves and built a fire for them, and showed them how to warm themselves by it and how to build other fires from the coals. Soon there was a cheerful blaze in every rude home in
40 the land, and men and women gathered round it and were warm and happy, and thankful to Prometheus for the wonderful gift which he had brought to them from the sun. It was not long until they learned to cook their food and so to eat like men instead of like beasts. They began at once to leave off their wild and savage habits; and instead of lurking in the dark places of the world, they came out into the open air and the bright sunlight, and were glad because life had been given to them.

45 After that, Prometheus taught them, little by little, a thousand things. He showed them how to build houses of wood and stone, and how to tame sheep and cattle and make them useful, and how to plow and sow and reap, and how to protect themselves from the storms of winter and the beasts of the woods. Then he showed them how to dig in the earth for copper and iron, and how to melt the ore, and how to hammer it into shape and fashion from it the tools and weapons which they needed in peace
50 and war; and when he saw how happy the world was becoming he cried out:

"A new Golden Age shall come, brighter and better by far than the old!"

*Jupiter: King of the gods in Roman mythology

54. It can be inferred that compared to Prometheus, Hephaestus would be
    A. more likely to analyze the ramifications of his actions.
    B. less likely to think longingly about past accomplishments.
    C. more likely to forget fond memories.
    D. more likely to dwell on painful past experiences.

55. It can be inferred that the attitude of the Mighty Folk towards the tribulations of the humans was primarily one of
    A. sadistic amusement.
    B. feigned concern.
    C. crass indifference.
    D. genuine compassion.

56. It can be inferred that Prometheus uses the term "Golden Age" to refer to an era of
    A. high production of precious metals.
    B. civilizational advancement.
    C. no armed conflicts.
    D. divine intervention.

The story below is "Hearts and Hands" by O'Henry.

At Denver there was an influx of passengers into the coaches on the eastbound B. & M. express. In one coach there sat a very pretty young woman dressed in elegant taste and surrounded by all the luxurious comforts of an experienced traveler. Among the newcomers were two young men, one of handsome presence with a bold, frank countenance and manner; the other a ruffled, glum-faced person, heavily built and roughly dressed. The two were handcuffed together.

As they passed down the aisle of the coach the only vacant seat offered was a reversed one facing the attractive young woman. Here the linked couple seated themselves. The young woman's glance fell upon them with a distant, swift disinterest; then with a lovely smile brightening her countenance and a tender pink tingeing her rounded cheeks, she held out a little gray-gloved hand. When she spoke her voice, full, sweet, and deliberate, proclaimed that its owner was accustomed to speak and be heard.

"Well, Mr. Easton, if you *will* make me speak first, I suppose I must. Don't you ever recognize old friends when you meet them in the West?"

The younger man roused himself sharply at the sound of her voice, seemed to struggle with a slight embarrassment which he threw off instantly, and then clasped her fingers with his left hand.

"It's Miss Fairchild," he said, with a smile. "I'll ask you to excuse the other hand; it's otherwise engaged just at present."

He slightly raised his right hand, bound at the wrist by the shining "bracelet" to the left one of his companion. The glad look in the girl's eyes slowly changed to a bewildered horror. The glow faded from her cheeks. Her lips parted in a vague, relaxing distress. Easton, with a little laugh, as if amused, was about to speak again when the other forestalled him. The glum-faced man had been watching the girl's countenance with veiled glances from his keen, shrewd eyes.

"You'll excuse me for speaking, miss, but, I see you're acquainted with the marshal here. If you'll ask him to speak a word for me when we get to the pen he'll do it, and it'll make things easier for me there. He's taking me to Leavenworth prison. It's seven years for counterfeiting."

"Oh!" said the girl, with a deep breath and returning color. "So that is what you are doing out here? A marshal!"

"My dear Miss Fairchild," said Easton, calmly, "I had to do something. Money has a way of taking wings unto itself, and you know it takes money to keep step with our crowd in Washington. I saw this opening in the West, and—well, a marshalship isn't quite as high a position as that of ambassador, but—"

"The ambassador," said the girl, warmly, "doesn't call any more. He needn't ever have done so. You ought to know that. And so now you are one of these dashing Western heroes, and you ride and shoot and go into all kinds of dangers. That's different from the Washington life. You have been missed from the old crowd."

The girl's eyes, fascinated, went back, widening a little, to rest upon the glittering handcuffs.

"Don't you worry about them, miss," said the other man. "All marshals handcuff themselves to their prisoners to keep them from getting away. Mr. Easton knows his business."

"Will we see you again soon in Washington?" asked the girl.

"Not soon, I think," said Easton. "My butterfly days are over, I fear."

"I love the West," said the girl irrelevantly. Her eyes were shining softly. She looked away out the car window. She began to speak truly and simply without the gloss of style and manner: "Mamma and I spent the summer in Denver. She went home a week ago because father was slightly ill. I could live and be happy in the West. I think the air here agrees with me. Money isn't everything. But people always misunderstand things and remain stupid—"

"Say, Mr. Marshal," growled the glum-faced man. "This isn't quite fair. I'm needing a drink, and haven't had a smoke all day. Haven't you talked long enough? Take me in the smoker now, won't you? I'm half dead for a pipe."

The bound travelers rose to their feet, Easton with the same slow smile on his face.

"I can't deny a petition for tobacco," he said, lightly. "It's the one friend of the unfortunate. Good-bye, Miss Fairchild. Duty calls, you know." He held out his hand for a farewell.

"It's too bad you are not going East," she said, reclothing herself with manner and style. "But you must go on to Leavenworth, I suppose?"

"Yes," said Easton, "I must go on to Leavenworth."

The two men sidled down the aisle into the smoker.

The two passengers in a seat nearby had heard most of the conversation. Said one of them: "That marshal's a good sort of chap. Some of these Western fellows are all right."

"Pretty young to hold an office like that, isn't he?" asked the other.

"Young!" exclaimed the first speaker, "why—Oh! didn't you catch on? Say—did you ever know an officer to handcuff a prisoner to his *right* hand?"

57. What does the passenger who speaks at the very end of the story likely realize?
    A. Mr. Easton is actually the criminal.
    B. Mr. Easton is a relatively inexperienced marshal.
    C. Mr. Easton intentionally broke protocol.
    D. Mr. Easton came up with a plan to deceive his love interest.

58. What is the most likely reason Mr. Easton felt embarrassed when Miss Fairchild greeted him?
    A. He did not recognize her.
    B. She had become engaged to another man.
    C. He no longer had any money.
    D. He was handcuffed to another man.

59. It can be inferred that the older man is actually
    A. stern and callous.
    B. sensitive and perceptive.
    C. cruel and rebellious.
    D. cultured and charismatic.

60. Why does the older man most likely speak to Miss Fairchild?
    A. He is in love with Miss Fairchild.
    B. He wants to spare Mr. Easton from humiliation.
    C. He does not want Miss Fairchild to get the wrong impression of Mr. Easton.
    D. He enjoys playing pranks on people.

61. Miss Fairchild's feelings for Mr. Easton seem to be those of
    A. pity.
    B. admiration.
    C. indifference.
    D. disgust.

62. What can be inferred about Mr. Easton?
    A. He is creative because he roped the older man into a story he concocted.
    B. He is still hopelessly in love with Miss Fairchild.
    C. He likely got into trouble because he values money.
    D. He has a close friendship with the older man.

63. The description of Miss Fairchild when she first enters with the influx of passengers suggests that she values
    A. modesty.
    B. authority.
    C. honesty.
    D. sophistication.

64. Mr. Easton implies that he was part of a culture in Washington, D.C. that
    A. discouraged him from being social.
    B. made him feel compelled to travel often.
    C. placed a premium on extravagance.
    D. made him feel alienated and depressed.

65. It can be inferred that the ambassador
    A. is engaged to Miss Fairchild.
    B. once had a romantic interest in Miss Fairchild.
    C. was a close friend with Mr. Easton in Washington, D.C.
    D. feels arrogantly superior to those who are marshals.

The poem below is "The Chimney Sweeper: A Little Black Thing Among the Snow" by William Blake

A little black thing among the snow,
Crying "weep! 'weep!" in notes of woe!
"Where are thy father and mother? say?"
"They are both gone up to the church to pray.

5   Because I was happy upon the heath,
And smil'd among the winter's snow,
They clothed me in the clothes of death,
And taught me to sing the notes of woe.

And because I am happy and dance and sing,
10 They think they have done me no injury,
And are gone to praise God and his Priest and King,
Who make up a heaven of our misery."

66. It can be inferred that the child described
A. is only given black clothing.
B. harbors sinister thoughts.
C. is covered in soot.
D. stays indoors during the winter to avoid the white snow.

67. The cries of the child in the first stanza (lines 1-4) are described as
A. religious.
B. melancholy.
C. hopeful.
D. painful.

68. It can be inferred that the speaker regards the child with
A. reverence.
B. concern.
C. envy.
D. pride.

69. The child's answer to the speaker of the poem (lines 4-12) implies that
A. appearances can be deceiving.
B. industrialization and nature are in irreconcilable conflict.
C. child labor regulations must be loosened.
D. suffering is essential to living a truly human life.

Week 2

70. The passage suggests that the child's outward behaviors
   A. belie his authentic emotions.
   B. reflect his pious nature.
   C. are primarily driven by a desire to please his parents.
   D. reveal his musical talent.

71. The child's parents are portrayed as
   A. indifferent to their child's claims that he is suffering.
   B. completely unconcerned about the safety of their child.
   C. resentful of the misery that has been inflicted on them.
   D. oblivious to the impact of their actions.

The poem below is "The Factory Bell" and was published in *The Factory Girl's Garland* in 1844.

Sisters, haste, the bell is tolling,
Soon will close the dreadful gate;
Then, alas! We must go strolling,
Through the counting room, too late.

5   Now the sun is upward climbing,
    And the breakfast hour has come;
    Ding, dong, ding, the bell is chiming,
    Hasten, sisters, hasten home.

    Quickly now we take our ration,
10 For the bell will babble soon;
    Each must hurry to her station,
    There to toil till weary noon.

    Mid-day sun is heaven is shining,
    Merrily now the clear bell rings,
15 And the grateful hour of dining
    To us weary sisters brings.

    Now we give a welcome greeting
    To these viands cooked so well;
    Horror! Oh! Not half done eating -
20 Rattle, rattle goes the bell.

    Sol behind the hills descend,
    Upwards throws his ruby light;
    Ding dong ding, - our toil is ended,
    Joyous bell, good night, good nig

72. The narrator of the poem is most likely
    A. the factory owner.
    B. one of the factory workers.
    C. the bell.
    D. the kitchen staff at the factory.

73. The meals in the factory are portrayed as
    A. extravagant.
    B. rushed.
    C. unhealthy.
    D. poorly cooked.

74. Throughout the poem, the bell seems to
    A. overrule all other standards of time.
    B. sound sporadically at random times.
    C. listen to the voices of the factory workers.
    D. provide feedback to the factory girls about their daily progress.

75. The factory girls regard their hours of dining with
    A. dread.
    B. confusion.
    C. appreciation.
    D. boredom.

76. The word "sisters" is most likely intended to establish that a certain group of people
    A. are biologically related.
    B. are friendly and talkative with each other during working hours.
    C. work primarily to help their families.
    D. have a sense of solidarity over a shared experience.

77. The bell functions in which contrasting roles at different points in the poem?
    A. A demanding taskmaster and a welcome respite.
    B. A cruel tyrant and a sympathetic ally.
    C. A source of nourishment and a drainer of energy.
    D. A marker of orderliness and a sign of chaos.

78. Why is the bell most likely called "joyous" in the last stanza?
    A. It signifies the end of the workday.
    B. Its sound is exceptionally clear.
    C. It appears to take on a ruby hue.
    D. It corresponds with the beauty of sunset.

Week 2

79. The word "toil" as used throughout the poem most directly suggests that
    A. the workday is highly structured.
    B. the factory work is physically demanding.
    C. the factory girls are intellectually engaged with their assignments.
    D. conditions in the factory are unsafe and unsanitary.

"The Raven" by Edgar Allan Poe.

Once upon a midnight dreary, while I pondered, weak and weary,
Over many a quaint and curious volume of forgotten lore—
   While I nodded, nearly napping, suddenly there came a tapping,
As of some one gently rapping, rapping at my chamber door.
5 "'Tis some visitor," I muttered, "tapping at my chamber door—
   Only this and nothing more."

   Ah, distinctly I remember it was in the bleak December;
And each separate dying ember wrought its ghost upon the floor.
   Eagerly I wished the morrow*;—vainly I had sought to borrow
10 From my books surcease of sorrow—sorrow for the lost Lenore—
For the rare and radiant maiden whom the angels name Lenore—
   Nameless *here* for evermore.

   And the silken, sad, uncertain rustling of each purple curtain
Thrilled me—filled me with fantastic terrors never felt before;
15   So that now, to still the beating of my heart, I stood repeating
   "'Tis some visitor entreating entrance at my chamber door—
Some late visitor entreating entrance at my chamber door;—
   This it is and nothing more."

   Presently my soul grew stronger; hesitating then no longer,
20 "Sir," said I, "or Madam, truly your forgiveness I implore;
   But the fact is I was napping, and so gently you came rapping,
And so faintly you came tapping, tapping at my chamber door,
That I scarce was sure I heard you"—here I opened wide the door;—
   Darkness there and nothing more.

25   Deep into that darkness peering, long I stood there wondering, fearing,
Doubting, dreaming dreams no mortal ever dared to dream before;
   But the silence was unbroken, and the stillness gave no token,
And the only word there spoken was the whispered word, "Lenore?"
This I whispered, and an echo murmured back the word, "Lenore!"—
30   Merely this and nothing more.

   Back into the chamber turning, all my soul within me burning,
Soon again I heard a tapping somewhat louder than before.
   "Surely," said I, "surely that is something at my window lattice;
Let me see, then, what thereat is, and this mystery explore—
35 Let my heart be still a moment and this mystery explore;—
   'Tis the wind and nothing more!"

Open here I flung the shutter, when, with many a flirt and flutter,
In there stepped a stately Raven of the saintly days of yore;
   Not the least obeisance made he; not a minute stopped or stayed he;
40   But, with mien of lord or lady, perched above my chamber door—
Perched upon a bust of Pallas just above my chamber door—
      Perched, and sat, and nothing more.

Then this ebony bird beguiling my sad fancy into smiling,
By the grave and stern decorum of the countenance it wore,
45 "Though thy crest be shorn and shaven, thou," I said, "art sure no craven,
Ghastly grim and ancient Raven wandering from the Nightly shore—
Tell me what thy lordly name is on the Night's Plutonian shore!"
      Quoth the Raven "Nevermore."
Much I marvelled this ungainly fowl to hear discourse so plainly,
50 Though its answer little meaning—little relevancy bore;
   For we cannot help agreeing that no living human being
   Ever yet was blessed with seeing bird above his chamber door—
Bird or beast upon the sculptured bust above his chamber door,
      With such name as "Nevermore."

55   But the Raven, sitting lonely on the placid bust, spoke only
That one word, as if his soul in that one word he did outpour.
   Nothing farther then he uttered—not a feather then he fluttered—
   Till I scarcely more than muttered "Other friends have flown before—
On the morrow *he* will leave me, as my Hopes have flown before."
60   Then the bird said "Nevermore."
Startled at the stillness broken by reply so aptly spoken,

"Doubtless," said I, "what it utters is its only stock and store
   Caught from some unhappy master whom unmerciful Disaster
   Followed fast and followed faster till his songs one burden bore—
65 Till the dirges of his Hope that melancholy burden bore
      Of 'Never—nevermore'."

   But the Raven still beguiling all my fancy into smiling,
Straight I wheeled a cushioned seat in front of bird, and bust and door;
   Then, upon the velvet sinking, I betook myself to linking
70   Fancy unto fancy, thinking what this ominous bird of yore—
What this grim, ungainly, ghastly, gaunt, and ominous bird of yore
      Meant in croaking "Nevermore."

   This I sat engaged in guessing, but no syllable expressing
To the fowl whose fiery eyes now burned into my bosom's core;
75   This and more I sat divining, with my head at ease reclining
   On the cushion's velvet lining that the lamp-light gloated o'er,
But whose velvet-violet lining with the lamp-light gloating o'er,
      She shall press, ah, nevermore!

   Then, methought, the air grew denser, perfumed from an unseen censer
80 Swung by Seraphim whose foot-falls tinkled on the tufted floor.
   "Wretch," I cried, "thy God hath lent thee—by these angels he hath sent thee

Respite—respite and nepenthe from thy memories of Lenore;
Quaff, oh quaff this kind nepenthe and forget this lost Lenore!"
      Quoth the Raven "Nevermore."
85   "Prophet!" said I, "thing of evil!—prophet still, if bird or devil!—
Whether Tempter sent, or whether tempest tossed thee here ashore,
Desolate yet all undaunted, on this desert land enchanted—
On this home by Horror haunted—tell me truly, I implore—
Is there—*is* there balm in Gilead?—tell me—tell me, I implore!"
90   Quoth the Raven "Nevermore."
"Prophet!" said I, "thing of evil!—prophet still, if bird or devil!
By that Heaven that bends above us—by that God we both adore—
Tell this soul with sorrow laden if, within the distant Aidenn,
It shall clasp a sainted maiden whom the angels name Lenore—
95 Clasp a rare and radiant maiden whom the angels name Lenore."
      Quoth the Raven "Nevermore."

"Be that word our sign of parting, bird or fiend!" I shrieked, upstarting—
"Get thee back into the tempest and the Night's Plutonian shore!
Leave no black plume as a token of that lie thy soul hath spoken!
100   Leave my loneliness unbroken!—quit the bust above my door!
Take thy beak from out my heart, and take thy form from off my door!"
      Quoth the Raven "Nevermore."

And the Raven, never flitting, still is sitting, *still* is sitting
On the pallid bust of Pallas just above my chamber door;
105   And his eyes have all the seeming of a demon's that is dreaming,
And the lamp-light o'er him streaming throws his shadow on the floor;
And my soul from out that shadow that lies floating on the floor
      Shall be lifted—nevermore!

*morrow: morning

80. The mood of the entire poem can best be described as
A. suspenseful.
B. lighthearted.
C. threatening.
D. humorous.

81. The first two lines of the poem give the impression that the speaker is
A. anxious about an upcoming reunion.
B. lost in thought on an otherwise boring evening.
C. tense because an unusual event is about to happen.
D. plotting an ill-conceived gambit.

82. It can be inferred that the speaker is reading in order to
A. make the time pass more slowly.
B. discover a way to reunite with Lenore.
C. help him fall asleep.
D. stop feeling sadness for a lost love.

83. The speaker repeats "nothing more" in lines 6,18, and 24
A. out of resignation that he will not be reunited with Lenore.
B. when he remembers that he planned on having visitors.
C. to comfort himself during a moment of tension.
D. in despair while feeling dismal about his future.

84. The speaker's attitude towards the raven is initially one of
A. terror.
B. intrigue.
C. reverence.
D. pity.

85. When the speaker says that "other friends have flown here before" (line 58), he implies that
A. he prefers solitude to the company of others.
B. he frequently cuts people out of his life who do not meet his emotional needs.
C. other people have abandoned him in the past.
D. other birds have entered through his chamber door.

86. What does the sentence in line 78 intend to convey?
A. The speaker will never feel pressured by Lenore's memory again.
B. The speaker will never hallucinate seeing Lenore again.
C. Lenore will never sit on the cushion again.
D. The couch will forever bring the speaker painful associations.

87. The raven is most likely symbolic of
A. the permanence of grief.
B. the pain of unrequited love.
C. the impossibility of sleep.
D. the power of madness.

88. The speaker most likely grows angry with the raven because
A. it refuses to speak to him.
B. it repeats lies its former master has told him.
C. he does not like what the raven tells him.
D. the raven foreshadows his own death.

The short story below is "Luck" by Mark Twain.

[Note—This is not a fancy sketch. I got it from a clergyman who was an instructor at Woolwich forty years ago, and who vouched for its truth.—M.T.]

It was at a banquet in London in honor of one of the two or three conspicuously illustrious English military names of this generation. For reasons which will presently appear, I will withhold his real name and titles, and call him Lieutenant General Lord Arthur Scoresby, V.C., K.C.B., etc., etc., etc. What a fascination there is in a renowned name! There sat the man, in actual flesh, whom I had heard of so many thousands of times since that day, thirty years before, when his name shot suddenly to the zenith from a Crimean battlefield, to remain forever celebrated. It was food and drink to me to look, and look, and look at that demigod; scanning, searching, noting: the quietness, the reserve, the noble gravity of his countenance; the simple honesty that expressed itself all over him; the sweet unconsciousness of his greatness—unconsciousness of the hundreds of admiring eyes fastened upon him, unconsciousness of the deep, loving, sincere worship welling out of the breasts of those people and flowing toward him.

The clergyman at my left was an old acquaintance of mine—clergyman now, but had spent the first half of his life in the camp and field, and as an instructor in the military school at Woolwich. Just at the moment I have been talking about, a veiled and singular light glimmered in his eyes, and he leaned down and muttered confidentially to me—indicating the hero of the banquet with a gesture: "Privately—he's an absolute fool."

This verdict was a great surprise to me. If its subject had been Napoleon, or Socrates, or Solomon, my astonishment could not have been greater. Two things I was well aware of: that the Reverend was a man of strict veracity, and that his judgement of men was good. Therefore I knew, beyond doubt or question, that the world was mistaken about this hero: he *was* a fool. So I meant to find out, at a convenient moment, how the Reverend, all solitary and alone, had discovered the secret.

Some days later the opportunity came, and this is what the Reverend told me.

About forty years ago I was an instructor in the military academy at Woolwich. I was present in one of the sections when young Scoresby underwent his preliminary examination. I was touched to the quick with pity; for the rest of the class answered up brightly and handsomely, while he—why, dear me, he didn't know *anything*, so to speak. He was evidently good, and sweet, and lovable, and guileless; and so it was exceedingly painful to see him stand there, as serene as a graven image, and deliver himself of answers which were veritably miraculous for stupidity and ignorance. All the compassion in me was aroused in his behalf. I said to myself, when he comes to be examined again, he will be flung over, of course; so it will be simply a harmless act of charity to ease his fall as much as I can. I took him aside, and found that he knew a little of Cæsar's history; and as he didn't know anything else, I went to work and drilled him like a galley slave on a certain line of stock questions concerning Cæsar which I knew would be used. If you'll believe me, he went through with flying colors on examination day! He went through on that purely superficial "cram," and got compliments too, while others, who knew a thousand times more than he, got plucked. By some strangely lucky accident—an accident not likely to happen twice in a century—he was asked no question outside of the narrow limits of his drill.

It was stupefying. Well, all through his course I stood by him, with something of the sentiment which a mother feels for a crippled child; and he always saved himself—just by miracle, apparently.

Now of course the thing that would expose him and kill him at last was mathematics. I resolved to make his death as easy as I could; so I drilled him and crammed him, and crammed him and drilled him, just on the line of questions which the examiners would be most likely to use, and then launching him on his fate. Well, sir, try to conceive of the result: to my consternation, he took the first prize! And with it he got a perfect ovation in the way of compliments.

Sleep? There was no more sleep for me for a week. My conscience tortured me day and night. What I had done I had done purely through charity, and only to ease the poor youth's fall—I never had dreamed of any such preposterous result as the thing that had happened. I felt as guilty and miserable as the creator of Frankenstein. Here was a woodenhead whom I had put in the way of glittering promotions and prodigious responsibilities, and but one thing could happen: he and his responsibilities would all go to ruin together at the first opportunity.

The Crimean war had just broken out. Of course there had to be a war, I said to myself: we couldn't have peace and give this donkey a chance to die before he is found out. I waited for the earthquake. It came. And it made me reel when it did come. He was actually gazetted to a captaincy in a marching regiment! Better men grow old and gray in the service before they climb to a sublimity like that. And who could ever have foreseen that they would go and put such a load of responsibility on such green and inadequate shoulders? I could just barely have stood it if they had made him a cornet; but a captain—think of it! I thought my hair would turn white.

Consider what I did—I who so loved repose and inaction. I said to myself, I am responsible to the country for this, and I must go along with him and protect the country against him as far as I can. So I took my poor little capital that I had saved up through years of work and grinding economy, and went with a sigh and bought a cornetcy in his regiment, and away we went to the field.

And there—oh dear, it was awful. Blunders? Why, he never did anything *but* blunder. But, you see, nobody was in the fellow's secret—everybody had him focused wrong, and necessarily misinterpreted his performance every time—consequently they took his idiotic blunders for inspirations of genius; they did, honestly! His mildest blunders were enough to make a man in his right mind cry; and they did make me cry—and rage and rave too, privately. And the thing that kept me always in a sweat of apprehension was the fact that every fresh blunder he made increased the luster of his reputation! I kept saying to myself, he'll get so high, that when discovery does finally come, it will be like the sun falling out of the sky.

He went right along up, from grade to grade, over the dead bodies of his superiors, until at last, in the hottest moment of the battle of ------- down went our colonel, and my heart jumped into my mouth, for Scoresby was next in rank! Now for it, said I; we'll all land in Sheol in ten minutes, sure.

The battle was awfully hot; the allies were steadily giving way all over the field. Our regiment occupied a position that was vital; a blunder now must be destruction. At this crucial moment, what does this immortal fool do but detach the regiment from its place and order a charge over a neighboring hill where there wasn't a suggestion of an enemy! "There you go!" I said to myself; "this *is* the end at last." And away we did go, and were over the shoulder of the hill before the insane movement could be discovered and stopped. And what did we find? An entire and unsuspected Russian army in reserve! And what happened? We were eaten up? That is necessarily what would have happened in ninety-nine cases out of a hundred. But no, those Russians argued that no single regiment would come browsing around there at such a time. It must be the entire English army, and that the sly Russian game was detected and blocked; so they turned tail, and away they went, pell-mell, over the hill and down into the field, in wild confusion, and we after them; they themselves broke the solid Russian center in the field, and tore through, and in no time there was the most tremendous rout you ever saw, and the defeat of the allies was turned into a sweeping and splendid victory! Marshal Canrobert looked on, dizzy with astonishment, admiration,and delight; and sent right off for Scoresby, and hugged him, and decorated him on the field, in presence of all the armies!

And what was Scoresby's blunder that time? Merely the mistaking his right hand for his left—that was all. An order had come to him to fall back and support our right; and instead, he fell *forward* and went over the hill to the left. But the name he won that day as a marvelous military genius filled the world with his glory, and that glory will never fade while history books last.

He is just as good and sweet and lovable and unpretending as a man can be, but he doesn't know enough to come in when it rains. Now that is absolutely true. He is the supremest donkey in the universe; and until half an hour ago nobody knew it but himself and me. He has been pursued, day by day and year by year, by a most phenomenal and astonishing luckiness. He has been a shining soldier in all our wars for a generation; he has littered his whole military life with blunders, and yet has never committed one that didn't make him a knight or a baronet or a lord or something. Look at his breast; why, he is just clothed in domestic and foreign decorations. Well, sir, every one of them is the record of some shouting stupidity or other; and taken together, they are proof that the very best thing in all this world that can befall a man is to be born lucky. I say again, as I said at the banquet, Scoresby's an absolute fool.

89. The fact that nobody else shared the clergyman's opinion of Scoresby allows the reader to infer the possibility that
    A. the clergyman might have undervalued Scoresby's worth.
    B. the public should celebrate heroes merely for their bravery regardless of their foibles.
    C. the clergyman's help is responsible for Scoresby's success.
    D. the clergyman is anxious to expose Scoresby for his fraudulence.

90. The clergyman's assertion that "Everybody had him focused wrong" implies that, from his perspective,
    A. people intentionally overlooked Scoresby's flaws because they craved an idol to provide them with hope for the future.
    B. Scoresby formed many superficial relationships but few genuine ones.
    C. Scoresby's seeming superiority in a certain endeavor was merely illusory.
    D. most people were not invested enough in military strategy to carefully analyze the granular details of Scoresby's plans.

91. Reread the line below
    Well, all through his course I stood by him, with something of the sentiment which a mother feels for a crippled child; and he always saved himself—just by miracle, apparently.
    This paragraph helps establish the plot by implying that the clergyman
    A. secretly wished for Scoresby to fail his exams.
    B. had compassion for Scoresby yet perceived himself as superior to him.
    C. nurtured Scoresby when he suffered ailments but doubted his ability to survive.
    D. admired Scoresby's resilience yet admonished him for his laziness.

92. In context, the sentence "And what was Scoresby's blunder that time? Merely the mistaking his right hand for his left—that was all. An order had come to him to fall back and support our right; and instead, he fell *forward* and went over the hill to the left" suggests that the clergyman believes Scoresby
    A. benefitted without relying on any discernible skills.
    B. luckily anticipated that a creative approach would fool his enemies.
    C. deliberately disobeyed an order by following his keen instincts.
    D. was overconfident in his abilities despite his lack of concrete knowledge.

93. Which excerpt most directly suggests that clergyman believes Scoresby's reputation was unwarranted?
    A. "An entire and unsuspected Russian army in reserve! And what happened? We were eaten up? That is necessarily what would have happened in ninety-nine cases out of a hundred."
    B. "Marshal Canrobert looked on, dizzy with astonishment, admiration, and delight".
    C. "He has been a shining soldier in all our wars for a generation."
    D. "So I took my poor little capital that I had saved up through years of work and grinding economy, and went with a sigh and bought a cornetcy in his regiment, and away we went to the field."

94. The clergyman would likely agree with the statement that
    A. intellectualism is essential to all pragmatic endeavors.
    B. a person's reputation can overshadow his or her true character.
    C. kindness is often mistaken for foolishness.
    D. creative approaches to practical endeavors should always be regarded suspiciously.

95. Reread the excerpt below.
    I drilled him and crammed him, and crammed him and drilled him, just on the line of questions which the examiners would be most likely to use, and then launching him on his fate. Well, sir, try to conceive of the result: to my consternation, he took the first prize!
    It can be inferred from this excerpt that
    A. the clergyman was envious that Scoresby was better at math than he was.
    B. the clergyman's plan to sabotage Scoresby's study session backfired.
    C. the clergyman resented that Scoresby did not acknowledge his help.
    D. Scoresby was more diligent than the clergyman gave him credit for.

"Human-Animal Interactions: Therapeutic and Surprising" (NIH)

[1] For most of my life, I've led an urban existence. Growing up in Manhattan and working for over 30 years in Boston, I rarely encountered wildlife, other than pigeons and squirrels. One evening, however, shortly after I arrived at NIH last fall, I was shocked to come face to face with a large buck as I headed toward my car. In subsequent conversations with colleagues, I learned that deer roam freely on the NIH campus. This was especially surprising because NIH isn't in the countryside, it's in a heavily populated suburb just outside of Washington, DC. This wildlife encounter startled me at first, but then I thought about how interactions with animals, particularly in the fast pace of modern life, help to calm us and give us perspective.

[2] Indeed, companion animals—the dogs, cats, birds, and other pets that share our homes and our lives—significantly affect our health and well-being. In fact, an important part of NICHD's research portfolio is the study of how these human-animal interactions influence child health and behavior, and impact our overall quality of life.

[3] For the past 10 years, NICHD's Child Development and Behavior Branch has had a partnership with the WALTHAM® Centre for Pet Nutrition, a division of Mars, Inc., to research the impact of animal interactions on child health and development. This partnership has led to several published works describing the therapeutic benefits of our companion animals.

[4] In a 2015 NICHD-funded study, a group of adolescents with type 1 diabetes each cared for a pet fish twice a day by feeding and checking water levels. The routine also included changing tank water each week, coupled with the children reviewing their glucose logs with parents. The researchers found that, when compared to teens who hadn't been given a fish to care for, the fishkeeping teens were more disciplined about checking their own blood glucose levels, which is essential for maintaining their health. Kids ages 10 to 13 years showed the greatest increase in self-monitoring following the pet fish intervention.

[5] That same year, **another study** found that children with autism spectrum disorder were calmer while playing with guinea pigs. Researchers gave each child a wristband that measured skin conductance—a measure for excitement and anxiety. A device inside the wristband sends an imperceptible electric current through the skin. The more anxious a person feels, the faster the current will travel through the skin. When the children with autism spent 10 minutes in a supervised group playtime with guinea pigs, their anxiety levels dropped. The children with autism also showed improved social functioning and were more engaged with their peers—an important benefit for children with autism. The researchers speculated that, because the animals offered unqualified acceptance, their presence comforted and calmed the children.

[6] Finally, dogs may prove to be an important addition to help kids cope with attention-deficit-hyperactivity disorder (ADHD). **Another NICHD study** enrolled two groups of children diagnosed with ADHD into a 12-week group therapy session. One group of kids read to a therapy dog once a week for 30 minutes, while the other group read to puppets that looked like dogs. Both groups showed improvements from the therapy sessions. However, the kids who read to the real animals performed better in measures of social skills, prosocial behaviors (such as sharing, cooperation, and volunteering), and behavioral problems. The researchers theorized that these interactions with dogs may help children focus their attention, thus improving their executive-functioning skills.

[7] As a scientist and a mother who has raised kids, fish, and cats, I understand and appreciate the importance that our furry and scaly friends have in our daily lives. **NICHD continues to support research** that examines the potential benefits of animals on our health and on the effectiveness of animal-assisted therapies in alleviating the symptoms of certain disorders and conditions, particularly in children. I have now grown accustomed to seeing the deer stroll undeterred around our bucolic campus, and I am even beginning to recognize some of the females by their numbered ear tags. On evenings when I am working late, I am grateful for a few moments of what I call the "NIH Safari," the view of a herd of deer eating grass and gracefully making their way down into the parking lot in front of our office building.

96. Which evidence from the passage best allows us to infer that human-animal interactions can help provide children with an enhanced sense of personal responsibility?
    A. "Indeed, companion animals—the dogs, cats, birds, and other pets that share our homes and our lives—significantly affect our health and well-being" (paragraph 2).
    B. "Kids ages 10 to 13 years showed the greatest increase in self-monitoring following the pet fish intervention" (paragraph 4).
    C. "When the children with autism spent 10 minutes in a supervised group playtime with guinea pigs, their anxiety levels dropped" (paragraph 5).
    D. "Finally, dogs may prove to be an important addition to help kids cope with attention-deficit-hyperactivity disorder (ADHD)" (paragraph 6).

97. It can be inferred that the author's initial encounter with the deer on the NIH campus
    A. inspired her to pursue research on the positive health effects of animals on humans.
    B. caused her to feel an intense and long-lasting feeling of terror.
    C. caught her off guard in the moment but made intuitive sense to her upon later introspection.
    D. surprised her until she discovered research that elucidated the usefulness of woodland creatures in urban locales.

Reread this sentence from paragraph 5

The researchers **speculated** that, because the animals offered unqualified acceptance, their presence comforted and calmed the children.

98. What is the main effect of the word "speculated" in context?
    A. It suggests that a flaw in the design of the study prevented scientists from drawing definitive conclusions about the impact of guinea pigs on the mental states of children with autism.
    B. It implies the researchers have no way of ascertaining if the health impacts of the intervention they studied were genuine.
    C. It emphasizes the somewhat tentative nature of the researchers' conclusions about the causal mechanism underlying their findings.
    D. It creates a critical tone that suggests the author regrets that the researchers employed an approach that was not definitive.

99. The use of the word "accustomed" in paragraph 7 is most likely used to show that
    A. the author has established bonds with some of the animals whose tags she recognizes.
    B. a type of incident that the author initially found shocking is now commonplace.
    C. the author's research has caused her to reevaluate her assumptions about human-animal interactions.
    D. the author's encounters with animals during the workday provide her with a needed respite from professional stressors.

100. The author would most likely agree with which of the following statements?
    A. Future research is unlikely to establish whether animals actually do improve health outcomes in children.
    B. Scientists should continue researching the nature and extent of the salutatory benefits of human-animal interactions.
    C. Scientists should take care to avoid drawing conclusions about the impact of animals on humans when the animals have been trained.
    D. To elucidate the unique benefits of interspecies interactions human health, scientists must repeat the studies in the passage with plants.

The excerpt below is adapted from *Song of the Lark* by Willa Cather.

[1] Mr. Kronborg considered Thea a remarkable child; but so were all his children remarkable. If one of the business men downtown remarked to him that he "had a mighty bright little girl, there," he admitted it, and at once began to explain what a "long head for business" his son Gus had, or that Charley was "a natural electrician," and had put in a telephone from the house to the preacher's study behind the church.

Week 2

[2] Mrs. Kronborg watched her daughter thoughtfully. She found her more interesting than her other children, and she took her more seriously, without thinking much about why she did so. The other children had to be guided, directed, kept from conflicting with one another. Charley and Gus were likely to want the same thing, and to quarrel about it. Anna often demanded unreasonable service from her older brothers; that they should sit up until after midnight to bring her home from parties when she did not like the youth who had offered himself as her escort; or that they should drive twelve miles into the country, on a winter night, to take her to a ranch dance, after they had been working hard all day. Gunner often got bored with his own clothes or stilts or sled, and wanted Axel's. But Thea, from the time she was a little thing, had her own routine. She kept out of every one's way, and was hard to manage only when the other children interfered with her. Then there was trouble indeed: bursts of temper which used to alarm Mrs. Kronborg. "You ought to know enough to let Thea alone. She lets you alone," she often said to the other children.

[3] One may have staunch friends in one's own family, but one seldom has admirers. Thea, however, had one in the person of her addle-pated aunt, Tillie Kronborg. In older countries, where dress and opinions and manners are not so thoroughly standardized as in our own West, there is a belief that people who are foolish about the more obvious things of life are apt to have peculiar insight into what lies beyond the obvious. The old woman who can never learn not to put the kerosene can on the stove, may yet be able to tell fortunes, to persuade a backward child to grow, to cure warts, or to tell people what to do with a young girl who has gone melancholy. Tillie's mind was a curious machine; when she was awake it went round like a wheel when the belt has slipped off, and when she was asleep she dreamed follies. But she had intuitions. She knew, for instance, that Thea was different from the other Kronborgs, worthy though they all were. Her romantic imagination found possibilities in her niece. When she was sweeping or ironing, or turning the ice-cream freezer at a furious rate, she often built up brilliant futures for Thea, adapting freely the latest novel she had read.

[4] Tillie made enemies for her niece among the church people because, at sewing societies and church suppers, she sometimes spoke vauntingly, with a toss of her head, just as if Thea's "wonderfulness" were an accepted fact in Moonstone, like Mrs. Archie's stinginess, or Mrs. Livery Johnson's duplicity. People declared that, on this subject, Tillie made them tired.

[5] Tillie belonged to a dramatic club that once a year performed in the Moonstone Opera House such plays as "Among the Breakers," and "The Veteran of 1812." Tillie played character parts, the flirtatious old maid or the spiteful *intrigante*. She used to study her parts up in the attic at home. While she was committing the lines, she got Gunner or Anna to hold the book for her, but when she began "to bring out the expression," as she said, she used, very timorously, to ask Thea to hold the book. Thea was usually—not always—agreeable about it. Her mother had told her that, since she had some influence with Tillie, it would be a good thing for them all if she could tone her down a shade and "keep her from taking on any worse than need be." Thea would sit on the foot of Tillie's bed, her feet tucked under her, and stare at the silly text. "I wouldn't make so much fuss, there, Tillie," she would remark occasionally; "I don't see the point in it"; or, "What do you pitch your voice so high for? It don't carry half as well."

[6] "I don't see how it comes Thea is so patient with Tillie," Mrs. Kronborg more than once remarked to her husband. "She ain't patient with most people, but it seems like she's got a peculiar patience for Tillie."

[7] Tillie always coaxed Thea to go "behind the scenes" with her when the club presented a play, and help her with her make-up. Thea hated it, but she always went. She felt as if she had to do it. There was something in Tillie's adoration of her that compelled her. There was no family impropriety that Thea was so much ashamed of as Tillie's "acting" and yet she was always being dragged in to assist her. Tillie simply had her, there. She didn't know why, but it was so. There was a string in her somewhere that Tillie could pull; a sense of obligation to Tillie's misguided aspirations. The saloon-keepers had some such feeling of responsibility toward Spanish Johnny.

[8] The dramatic club was the pride of Tillie's heart, and her enthusiasm was the principal factor in keeping it together. Sick or well, Tillie always attended rehearsals, and was always urging the young people, who took rehearsals lightly, to "stop fooling and begin now." The young men—bank clerks, grocery clerks, insurance agents—played tricks, laughed at Tillie, and "put it up on each other" about seeing her home; but they often went to tiresome rehearsals just to oblige her. They were good-natured young fellows.

[9] By one amazing indiscretion Tillie very nearly lost her hold upon the Moonstone Drama Club. The club had decided to put on "The Drummer Boy of Shiloh," a very ambitious undertaking because of the many supers needed and the scenic difficulties of the act which took place in Andersonville Prison. The members of the club consulted together in Tillie's absence as to who should play the part of the drummer boy. It must be taken by a very young person, and village boys of that age are self-conscious and are not apt at memorizing. The part was a long one, and clearly it must be given to a girl. Some members of the club suggested Thea Kronborg, others advocated Lily Fisher. Lily's partisans urged that she was much prettier than Thea, and had a much "sweeter disposition." Nobody denied these facts. But there was nothing in the least boyish about Lily, and she sang all songs and played all parts alike. Lily's simper was popular, but it seemed not quite the right thing for the heroic drummer boy. Upping, the trainer, talked to one and another: "Lily's all right for girl parts," he insisted, "but you've got to get a girl with some ginger in her for this. Thea's got the voice, too. When she sings, 'Just Before the Battle, Mother,' she'll bring down the house."

[10] When all the members of the club had been privately consulted, they announced their decision to Tillie at the first regular meeting that was called to cast the parts. They expected Tillie to be overcome with joy, but, on the contrary, she seemed embarrassed. "I'm afraid Thea hasn't got time for that," she said jerkily. "She is always so busy with her music. Guess you'll have to get somebody else."

[11] The club lifted its eyebrows. Several of Lily Fisher's friends coughed. Mr. Upping flushed. The stout woman who always played the injured wife called Tillie's attention to the fact that this would be a fine opportunity for her niece to show what she could do. Her tone was condescending. The company broke up into groups and expressed their amazement. They confided to each other that Tillie was "just a little off, on the subject of her niece," and agreed that it would be as well not to excite her further. Tillie got a cold reception at rehearsals for a long while afterward, and Thea had a crop of new enemies without even knowing it.

101. How does paragraph 5 introduce the idea that Tillie is not a talented actor?
    A. Tillie only allows Thea to watch her practice once she has moved beyond memorizing lines and to emoting.
    B. Thea's mother hints she wants her to make sure Tillie delivers a relatively subdued performance.
    C. Thea's mother laments that Tillie will inevitably bring the family great shame and embarrassment.
    D. Thea presents a general philosophy on quality acting that clashes with Tillie's style.

Reread the sentence below from paragraph 3.

She knew, for instance, that Thea was different from the other Kronborgs, worthy though they all were.

102. What effect does "worthy though they all were" have at this point in the passage?
    A. It shows that Tillie feels guilty for favoring Thea over her other family members, so she convinces herself that they also have admirable traits.
    B. It magnifies the extent to which Tillie finds Thea special by noting that she stands out even among other individuals with positive attributes.
    C. It concedes that Thea might not be so special after all given how remarkable her family is as a whole.
    D. It creates a vaguely uncomfortable tone that suggests Thea will never be able to achieve her aunt's expectations despite coming from a respectable family.

Reread the sentences below from paragraph 2.

Then there was trouble indeed: bursts of temper which used to alarm Mrs. Kronborg. "You ought to know enough to let Thea alone. She lets you alone," she often said to the other children.

103. In context, lines above suggest that Mrs. Kronborg
    A. feared for the physical safety of Thea's siblings during Thea's bouts of anger.
    B. was surprised that Thea's siblings seemed to take delight in provoking her.
    C. would admonish her other children frequently for disturbing Thea.
    D. found certain generally uncharacteristic displays of behavior from Thea jarring.

104. Mr. Kronborg's response to his neighbors' compliments towards Thea suggests that he
    A. consciously avoids appearing partial to Thea over his other children.
    B. feels remorseful for agreeing with praises of Thea.
    C. believes the skills Thea's siblings possess are more valuable than those Thea possesses.
    D. is insecure about how precocious Thea is relative to her siblings.

"The Brain May Actively Forget During Sleep" (NIH)

[1] Rapid eye movement, or REM, sleep is a fascinating period when most of our dreams are made. Now, in a study of mice, a team of Japanese and U.S. researchers show that it may also be a time when the brain actively forgets. Their results suggest that forgetting during sleep may be controlled by neurons found deep inside the brain that were previously known for making an appetite stimulating hormone. The study was funded by the National Institute of Neurological Disorders and Stroke (NINDS), part of the National Institutes of Health.

[2] "Ever wonder why we forget many of our dreams?" said Thomas Kilduff, Ph.D., director of the Center for Neuroscience at SRI International, Menlo Park, California, and a senior author of the study published in Science. "Our results suggest that the firing of a particular group of neurons during REM sleep controls whether the brain remembers new information after a good night's sleep."

[3] REM is one of several sleep stages the body cycles through every night. It first occurs about 90 minutes after falling asleep and is characterized by darting eyes, raised heart rates, paralyzed limbs, awakened brain waves and dreaming.

[4] For more than a century, scientists have explored the role of sleep in storing memories. While many have shown that sleep helps the brain store new memories, others, including Francis Crick, the co-discoverer of the DNA double helix, have raised the possibility that sleep – in particular REM sleep – may be a time when the brain actively eliminates or forgets excess information. Moreover, recent studies in mice have shown that during sleep – including REM sleep – the brain selectively prunes synaptic connections made between neurons involved in certain types of learning. However, until this study, no one had shown how this might happen.

[5] "Understanding the role of sleep in forgetting may help researchers better understand a wide range of memory-related diseases like post-traumatic stress disorder and Alzheimer's," said Janet He, Ph.D., program director, at NINDS. "This study provides the most direct evidence that REM sleep may play a role in how the brain decides which memories to store."

[6] Dr. Kilduff's lab and that of his collaborator, Akihiro Yamanaka, Ph.D., at Nagoya University in Japan, have spent years examining the role of a hormone called hypocretin/orexin in controlling sleep and **narcolepsy**. Narcolepsy is a disorder that makes people feel excessively sleepy during the day and sometimes experience changes reminiscent of REM sleep, like loss of muscle tone in the limbs and hallucinations. Their labs and others have helped to show how narcolepsy may be linked to the loss of hypocretin/orexin-making neurons in the hypothalamus, a peanut-sized area found deep inside the brain.

[7] In this study, Dr. Kilduff worked with Dr. Yamanaka's lab and Akira Terao's, D.V.M., Ph.D., lab at Hokkaido University, Sapporo, Japan, to look at neighboring cells that produce melanin concentrating hormone (MCH), a molecule known to be involved in the control of both sleep and appetite. In agreement with previous studies, the researchers found that a majority (52.8%) of hypothalamic MCH cells fired when mice underwent REM sleep whereas about 35% fired only when the mice were awake and about 12% fired at both times.

[8] They also uncovered clues suggesting that these cells may play a role in learning and memory. Electrical recordings and tracing experiments showed that many of the hypothalamic MCH cells sent inhibitory messages, via long stringy axons, to the hippocampus, the brain's memory center.

[9] "From previous studies done in other labs, we already knew that MCH cells were active during REM sleep. After discovering this new circuit, we thought these cells might help the brain store memories," said Dr. Kilduff.

[10] To test this idea, the researchers used a variety of genetic tools to turn on and off MCH neurons in mice during memory tests. Specifically, they examined the role that MCH cells played in retention, the period after learning something new but before the new knowledge is stored, or consolidated, into long term memory. The scientists used several memory tests including one that assessed the ability of mice to distinguish between new and familiar objects.

[11] To their surprise, they found that "turning on" MCH cells during retention worsened memory whereas turning the cells off improved memories. For instance, activating the cells reduced the time mice spent sniffing around new objects compared to familiar ones, but turning the cells off had the opposite effect.

[12] Further experiments suggested that MCH neurons exclusively played this role during REM sleep. Mice performed better on memory tests when MCH neurons were turned off during REM sleep. In contrast, turning off the neurons while the mice were awake or in other sleep states had no effect on memory.

[13] "These results suggest that MCH neurons help the brain actively forget new, possibly, unimportant information," said Dr. Kilduff. "Since dreams are thought to primarily occur during REM sleep, the sleep stage when the MCH cells turn on, activation of these cells may prevent the content of a dream from being stored in the hippocampus – consequently, the dream is quickly forgotten."

[14] In the future, the researchers plan to explore whether this new circuit plays a role in sleep and memory disorders.

[15] This press release describes a basic research finding. Basic research increases our understanding of human behavior and biology, which is foundational to advancing new and better ways to prevent, diagnose, and treat disease. Science is an unpredictable and incremental process — each research advance builds on past discoveries, often in unexpected ways. Most clinical advances would not be possible without the knowledge of fundamental basic research.

105. The passage suggests that the researchers were interested in how much time mice spent sniffing new and familiar objects primarily because such information would allow them to
    A. identify the precise neural pathways that govern memory storage and retrieval.
    B. gauge how familiar the objects subjectively feel to mice whose neural activity had been manipulated.
    C. compare patterns of brain activation when the mice examine each object to when they are experiencing REM sleep.
    D. draw conclusions about the usefulness of forgetting to mice's homeostasis.

106. Based on the details in paragraphs 8 and 13, it can most reasonably be inferred that damage to the hippocampus would most likely result in which of the following symptoms?
    A. Excessive sleepiness.
    B. Difficulty forgetting traumatic experiences.
    C. Superior memory for insignificant details.
    D. Forgetfulness of episodic details of one's life.

107. What does the passage suggest about the relationship between sleep and learning?
    A. Sleep seems to primarily function to help people strategically forget useless information.
    B. Sleep may play an important role in the delicate interplay between enhancing memories for some new information and inducing forgetting for other pieces of information.
    C. Sleep's role in strengthening or diminishing memories is the primary factor influencing the severity of certain sleep disorders.
    D. Sleep only actively diminishes memory for information that is harmful to an organism's emotional state.

108. The phrase "direct evidence" in paragraph 5 most clearly conveys that a central goal of the research team was to
    A. develop a procedure that would yield bountiful data about the changes the memory circuits in the brain undergo during and following REM sleep.
    B. identify indications of a relationship between a phase of sleep and memory for learned information.
    C. discover new data that would directly rebut previous studies on the association between sleep and forgetting.
    D. design a novel model that could juxtapose multiple theories about the important role that sleep plays in storing and discarding memories.

109. Which statement provides the best evidence that MCH neuron's impact on memory is limited by the timing of when such neurons are activated or suppressed?
    A. "For instance, activating the cells reduced the time mice spent sniffing around new objects compared to familiar ones, but turning the cells off had the opposite effect" (paragraph 11).
    B. "Mice performed better on memory tests when MCH neurons were turned off during REM sleep" (paragraph 12).
    C. "In contrast, turning off the neurons while the mice were awake or in other sleep states had no effect on memory" (paragraph 12).
    D. "In the future, the researchers plan to explore whether this new circuit plays a role in sleep and memory disorders" (paragraph 13).

110. Based on the passage, how can studies of mice enhance knowledge of sleep's role in humans?
    A. Understanding the roles of certain neuron types common to both mice and humans during sleep in mice can shed insight into the effects that the activity of such neurons might have in humans.
    B. Genetically manipulating mice's activation or suppression of certain neurons allows scientists to pinpoint the precise evolutionary function of dreaming in humans.
    C. Observing activation of hippocampal and thalamic regions during sleep and memory exams in mice allows scientists to draw causal inferences about conditions under which sleep enhances or inhibits memory in humans.
    D. Finding neurons that are common to both mice and humans helps researchers determine signals that govern sleep-wake cycles and their corresponding correlations with performance on memory exams.

111. With which statement about basic research would the author most likely agree?
    A. In the context of studying biological systems, it is best to engage in this research without any hope or expectation that its findings might be used in a more practical context.
    B. Its findings can often spur unanticipated lines of research that have more obviously practical implications for human health.
    C. It is primarily concerned with increasing foundational knowledge about topics that are not already well-studied.
    D. Its main objective is to study interventions that directly improve lives of biological entities.

"Kansas: Fort Larned Historical Site" (National Park Service).

[1] Between 1822 and 1880, the Santa Fe Trail provided one of the most important overland transportation routes in America. The trail allowed millions of dollars of commercial traffic to flow between Independence, Missouri and Santa Fe, New Mexico. The flow of travelers, traders, and settlers moving west; the gold rushes of 1849 and 1858; and the acquisition of vast southwestern lands by the United States government after the Mexican War caused the American Indians of this region much turmoil. The great influx of people along the Santa Fe Trail disrupted their way of life and prompted them to retaliate. Fort Larned was established to protect travelers, trail commerce, and the mail because of the rising tensions between American Indians and those using the trail. Fort Larned National Historic Site preserves the buildings, stories, and historical themes associated with Fort Larned.

[2] By October of 1859, rising conflicts between American Indians and westward travelers along the Santa Fe Trail prompted the United States army to build a military post to protect and maintain peaceful relations with everyone on the trail. This first post, called "Camp on Pawnee Fork" and eventually called "Camp Alert," was set up near Lookout Hill (now Jenkins hill) on the bank of the Pawnee River about five miles from its junction with the Arkansas River. Less than a year later, in June 1860, the fort was moved three miles further west, near the confluence of the Pawnee and Arkansas Rivers.

[3] At this location, the army constructed sod and adobe buildings, including an officer's quarters, storehouse and barracks, a guardhouse, a hospital, soldier's quarters, a bakery, a meat house, and a building housing a blacksmith, carpenter, and saddler shops. Named Fort Larned for Col. Benjamin R.

Larned, the US Army paymaster, this fort would serve as one of the most important defense posts along the Santa Fe Trail.

[4] Between 1866 and 1868, the government replaced the original sod and adobe buildings of Fort Larned with more durable stone and timber buildings. Visitors can see these buildings today at the Fort Larned National Historic Site. The fort complex of nine buildings arranged around a 400' square parade ground includes barracks, a post hospital, two company officer's quarters, commanding officer's quarters, quartermaster storehouse, the old commissary, the new commissary, and a shops building. Visitors may walk around and explore seven of the nine buildings at the fort to get a glimpse of what it was like to live on a western fort during the 19th century.

[5] As one of the most important defense posts along the Santa Fe Trail, Fort Larned served many purposes. One purpose was to protect the flow of commerce along the Kansas segment of the trail. After the Chivington Massacre at Sand Creek in 1864, the War Department forbade travel beyond Fort Larned without armed escort. Fort Larned prepared detachments for the protection of mail stages and wagon trains.

[6] By 1867, Fort Larned became the base for Maj. Gen. Winfield S. Hancock's unsuccessful campaign against Plains Indian tribes. This campaign intended to intimidate and pacify the Indians with US military strength; however, it had the reverse effect and only intensified their hostilities. Hancock's campaign caused a general outbreak of raids by the Kiowa, Comanche, and Arapaho. To respond to these raids, Maj. Gen. Philip H. Sheridan ordered Lt. Col. George A. Custer into the area around Fort Larned. Eventually, Custer's campaign ended in the defeat of Black Kettle's Cheyenne at the Battle of the Washita on November 27, 1868. The Battle of the Washita ultimately ended American Indians' organized resistance around Fort Larned.

[7] While the military sought to prevent conflict along the trail, Fort Larned became the seat of other more peaceful efforts to reach out to the tribes throughout the 1860s. The fort served as the headquarters and principal annuity distribution point of the Indian Bureau. The Indian Bureau attempted to find peaceful solutions to conflicts between American Indians and travelers, settlers, and adventurers. The treaties of Fort Wise (1861), the Little Arkansas (1865), and Medicine Lodge (1867) supported these peaceful principles.

[8] In these treaties, the United States government agreed to pay annuities to the Cheyenne, Arapahos, Kiowa, Comanche, and the Plains Apache tribes in return for keeping peace along the trail and for staying on their reservations. Annuities included items like bacon, wheat, flour, coffee, sugar, fresh beef, tobacco, clothing, beads, blankets, metal tools, cooking utensils, gunpowder, and lead bullets. Presented with the great opportunities the Indian Bureau created for commerce, traders flocked to the area surrounding Fort Larned and established the fort as a major trading center. By 1868, with the movement of the tribes to new reservations in Indian Territory, Fort Larned's role as an agent for the Indian Bureau ended.

[9] Fort Larned's final function was to protect railroad construction crews. The building of the railroad ultimately led to the end of the use of the Santa Fe Trail, which the fort was originally constructed to protect. After the Civil War ended, Americans renewed their energetic push westward, laying thousands of miles of railroad track. The worn dirt-road ruts of the Santa Fe Trail could not compete with the high powered, fast, and efficient railroad. Fort Larned helped to protect the workers who completed laying the railroad line in Kansas by 1872. Nearly six years later, in July 1878, the military abandoned Fort Larned, because it was no longer necessary for protection and keeping peaceful relations along the Santa Fe Trail.

Reread this sentence from paragraph 7.

While the military sought to prevent conflict along the trail, Fort Larned became the seat of other more peaceful efforts to reach out to the tribes throughout the 1860s.

112. In context, the words "while" and "other" suggest that
    A. the military underestimated the capabilities of American Indian tribes.
    B. violence should never be met with more violence if the goal is to establish harmonious relations.
    C. a multipronged approach was needed to address a pressing challenge.
    D. the government employed diplomacy as a last resort since it would involve making economic concessions.

113. It is implied that the buildings at Fort Larned as described in paragraph 4
    A. have largely maintained the character of how they were in the nineteenth century.
    B. are primarily appealing to those with a firm understanding of American history.
    C. continue to serve the same functions today as they did when they were originally constructed.
    D. allow visitors to understand the survival challenges and intercultural tensions of the nineteenth century.

114. With which statement would the author most likely agree?
    A. Fort Larned was intended to serve a temporary military base until more efficient forms of transportation could be perfected.
    B. Fort Larned is the most significant relic of historical themes associated with overland transportation from the 1820s to 1860s.
    C. Despite no longer functioning as a major cultural hub, Fort Larned's preservation is of great historical importance.
    D. Military leaders of the United States were wise to employ armed retaliation against American Indian tribes before considering more peaceful alternatives.

The excerpt below is from "On a Mountain Trail" by Henry Perry Robinson.

[1] We had no warning. It was as if they had deliberately lain in ambush for us at the turn in the trail. They seemed suddenly and silently to rise on all sides of the sleigh at once. It is not often that the gray timber-wolves, or "black wolves," as the mountaineers call them, are seen hunting in packs, though the animal is plentiful enough among the foot-hills of the Rockies. As a general rule they are met with singly or in pairs. At the end of a long and severe winter, however, they sometimes come together in bands of fifteen or twenty; and every old mountaineer has a tale to tell perhaps of his own narrow escape from one of their fierce packs, perhaps of some friend of his who started one day in winter to travel alone from camp to camp, and whose clean-picked bones were found beside the trail long afterward.

[2] It was in February, and we, Gates and myself, were driving from Livingston, Montana, to Gulch City, fifty miles away, with a load of camp supplies — a barrel of flour and some bacon, coffee, and beans; a blanket or two, and some dynamite (or "giant powder," as the miners call it) for blasting; a few picks and shovels, and other odds and ends. We had started at daybreak. By five o'clock in the evening, with some ten miles more to travel, the worst of the trail was passed. There had been little snow that winter, so that even in the gulches and on the bottoms the exposed ground was barely covered; while, on the steep slopes, snow had almost entirely disappeared, leaving only ragged patches of white under overhanging boughs, and a thin coating of ice in the inequalities of the hard, frost-bound trail, making a treacherous footing for the horses' hoofs.

[3] The first forty miles of the road had lain entirely over hills — zigzagging up one side of a mountain only to zigzag down the other — with the dense growth of pine and tamarack and cedar on both sides, wreathed here and there in mist. But at last we were clear of the foot-hills and reached the level. The tall forest trees gave place to a wilderness of thick underbrush, lying black in the evening air, and the horses swung contentedly from the steep grade into the level trail, where at last they could let their legs move freely in a trot.

[4] Hardly had they settled into their stride, however, when both animals shied violently to the left side of the trail. A moment later they plunged back to the right side so suddenly as almost to throw me off into the brush.

[5] Then, out of the earth and the shadow of the bushes, the grim, dark forms seemed to rise on all sides of us. There was not a sound — not a snap nor a snarl; but in the gathering twilight of the February evening, we saw them moving noiselessly over the thin coat of snow which covered the ground. In the uncertain light, and moving as rapidly as we did, it was impossible to guess how many they were. An animal which was one moment in plain sight, running abreast of the horses, would, the next moment, be lost in the shadow of the bushes, while

two more dark, silent forms would edge up to take its place. So, on both sides of us, they kept appearing and disappearing. In the rear, half a dozen jostled one another to push up nearer to the flying sleigh — a black mass that filled the whole width of the trail. Behind those again, others, less clearly visible, crossed and recrossed the roadway from side to side. They might be twenty in all — or thirty — or forty. It was impossible to tell.

[6] For a minute I did not think of danger. The individual wolf is the most skulking and cowardly of animals, and only by some such experience as we had that night does a hunter learn that wolves can be dangerous. But soon the stories of the old mountaineers came crowding into my mind, as the horses, terrified and snorting, plunged wildly along the narrow trail, while the ghostlike forms glided patiently alongside — appearing, disappearing, and reappearing. The silent pertinacity[2] with which, apparently making no effort, they kept pace beside the flying horses was horrible. Even a howl or a yelp or a growl would have been a relief. But not so much as the sound of their footfalls on the snow was to be heard.

[7] At the first sight of the wolves, I had drawn my revolver from the leather case in which it hung suspended from my belt. Gates, handling the reins, was entirely occupied with the horses; but I knew, without need of words, that he saw our pursuers and understood the peril as well as I.

[8] "Have you your gun?" I shouted in his ear.

115. The question that the narrator asks his companion in paragraph 8 suggests that he
    A. has much experienced operating firearms.
    B. knows imminent action must be taken to neutralize a threat.
    C. prefers his companion stave off the wolves so he doesn't have to.
    D. doubts his own abilities to handle a confrontation.

---

[2] perseverance

116. Which quote most clearly reveals the mood of the excerpt before the narrator drew his gun?
    A. "In the rear, half a dozen jostled one another to push up nearer to the flying sleigh" (paragraph 5).
    B. "They might be twenty in all — or thirty — or forty. It was impossible to tell." (paragraph 5).
    C. "But soon the stories of the old mountaineers came crowding into my mind, as the horses, terrified and snorting, plunged wildly along the narrow trail, while the ghostlike forms glided patiently alongside — appearing, disappearing, and reappearing" (paragraph 6).
    D. "But not so much as the sound of their footfalls on the snow was to be heard." (paragraph 6).

Reread this sentence from paragraph 6.

> But soon the stories of the old mountaineers came crowding into my mind, as the horses, terrified and snorting, plunged wildly along the narrow trail, while the ghostlike forms glided patiently alongside — appearing, disappearing, and reappearing.

117. The figurative language in this excerpt serves to emphasize the narrator's
    A. growing unease that the narrator feels as the wolves stealthily keep pace with him and his companion.
    B. anger that the wolves have decided to toy with him instead of launch their attack outright.
    C. realization that he is helpless to defend himself against the intelligent pack of wolves.
    D. embarrassment that he did not heed the warnings of old mountaineers before embarking on his journey.

118. The mood of paragraph 5 can best be described as
    A. menacing and tense.
    B. playful and energetic.
    C. somber and reverential.
    D. hostile and violent.

Week 2

Reread the sentence below from paragraph 5.

There was not a sound — not a snap nor a snarl; but in the gathering twilight of the February evening, we saw them moving noiselessly over the thin coat of snow which covered the ground.

119. This quote affects the tone of the paragraph by emphasizing a
    A. comforting feeling as the narrator connects the quietness of the wolves to their benign intentions.
    B. sense of confusion as the narrator is caught off guard that the wolves have yet to launch their attack.
    C. sense of unease as the narrator is unsettled by the silent perseverance of the wolves.
    D. feeling of dread with regards to the bleakness of the landscape.

120. The phrase "a black mass that filled the whole width of the trail" (paragraph 5) most directly conveys the idea that the wolves
    A. crossed back and forth to confuse the horses.
    B. were impossible to perceive because they blended in with the night.
    C. were present in large numbers near the narrator's path.
    D. needed to run very fast to keep pace with the horses.

Kweller Prep NEW SHSAT Grammar and Reading

Week 3

Week 3: Summary Questions

Summary questions test your ability to sum up what the passage is about. The very first question of each passage will always be the summary question. Relatedly, main idea questions will test your ability to understand the major points the author is trying to make. Being able to summarize what happened in a passage is key to determining big picture ideas versus more granular details.

Summary and Main Idea Questions Overview	
Common Question Phrasing	<ul><li>Which of the following best tells what this passage is about?</li><li>What is the central idea of the passage?</li></ul>
How to Answer	<ul><li>Before looking at the choices, try to recap the passage briefly in your own words. Ask yourself<ol><li>What is the **topic,** or concept being discussed in the passage?</li><li>What main points does the author make about the topic? For example, does the author express any opinions or make any broad claims supported by evidence?</li><li>What big ideas does reader learn from this passage?</li></ol></li><li>Pay attention to ideas that recur throughout the **entirety of the passage or paragraph.** For example, a central idea about a paragraph should not be too specific to minor details, but it should also not be so broad that it is unclear what the passage is about.</li><li>When applicable, you may find it useful to answer the summary question last. The answers to the detail and inference questions may give you clues about the main idea.</li></ul>

| **Common Trap Wrong Answer Types** | - Statements that are too general and only vaguely relate to what is actually discussed in the passage.
- Statements that are too specific or that focus on minor points from the passage.
- Statements that provide inaccurate information contradicting what is in the passage.
- Statements providing information that is beyond the scope of the passage. |
|---|---|

Ostriches are one of the few species of birds that cannot fly. Instead, they have powerful legs that allow them to run at great speeds, and they can sprint up to 43 miles per hour. If ostriches can't fly, why do they have wings? For one, the wings help the ostriches stabilize their bodies when they run. This ability is useful when ostriches have to make more complicated maneuvers and change directions. Furthermore, ostriches use their wings to communicate with one another. For instance, they can use their wings to either establish dominance or demonstrate submission to other ostriches.

Sample: What is the central idea of the passage?
  A. *Ostriches can run at speeds up to 43 miles per hour.*
  B. *Flightless birds take various measures to survive without wings.*
  C. *Ostriches' wings serve practical and social functions.*
  D. *Communication between ostriches can signal dominance or submission.*

The passage primarily discusses how ostriches use their wings. Choice C is correct. Choices A and D are too specific. The speed at which ostriches run is only briefly discussed. Communication between ostriches is only briefly mentioned in the context of ostriches' wings. Choice B is too broad. The paragraph is focused on ostriches, not flightless birds in general. Also, the paragraph focuses on how wings assist with locomotion and communication, not survival in general.

The excerpt below is from NASA's article, "NASA's Kepler Discovers First Earth-Size Planet In the 'Habitable Zone' of Another Star" (http://www.nasa.gov/ames/kepler/nasas-kepler-discovers-first-earth-size-planet-in-the-habitable-zone-of-another-star/).

Using NASA's Kepler Space Telescope, astronomers have discovered the first Earth-size planet orbiting a star in the "habitable zone" -- the range of distance from a star where liquid water might pool on the surface of an orbiting planet. The discovery of Kepler-186f confirms that planets the size of Earth exists in the habitable zone of stars other than our sun. While planets have previously been found in the habitable zone, they are all at least 40 percent larger in size than Earth and understanding their makeup is challenging. Kepler-186f is more reminiscent of Earth. Although the size of Kepler-186f is known, its mass and composition are not. Previous research, however, suggests that a planet the size of Kepler-186f is likely to be rocky. Kepler-186f orbits its star once every 130-days and receives one-third the energy from its star that Earth gets from the sun, placing it nearer the outer edge of the habitable zone. On the surface of Kepler-186f, the brightness of its star at high noon is only as bright as our sun appears to us about an hour before sunset. "Being in the habitable zone does not mean we know this planet is habitable. The temperature on the planet is strongly dependent on what kind of atmosphere the planet has," said Thomas Barclay, research scientist at the Bay Area Environmental Research Institute at Ames, and co-author of the paper. "Kepler-186f can be thought of as an Earth-cousin rather than an Earth-twin. It has many properties that resemble Earth." The four companion planets, Kepler-186b, Kepler-186c, Kepler-186d, and Kepler-186e, whiz around their sun every four, seven, 13, and 22 days, respectively, making them too hot for life as we know it. These four inner planets all measure less than 1.5 times the size of Earth.

Sample: Which of the following best tells what this passage is about?
   A. *The significant discovery of a planet in the habitable zone of its star.*
   B. *The short revolution periods of the companion planets of Kepler 186-b.*
   C. *The size of most exoplanets in habitable zones.*
   D. *The history of exoplanet discoveries.*

The passage of focuses on the discovery of Kepler-186b, the first Earth-like planet lying in a habitable zone of its star. Choice A is correct. Choice B is an important detail, but it does not identify the main topic (the discovery of the Kepler 186-b). Choice C is also an important detail, but it does not identify the main topic. Choice D is too broad. Though other exoplanets are mentioned, the passage does not give an overall history of exoplanet discoveries. Rather, it primarily mentions other exoplanets in relation to how they compare to Kepler-186 b.

Drill 1

When Darla moved to a new town due to her dad's new job, she struggled to make new friends for the first month. She spent most of her time keeping in touch with friends from her hometown. Eventually, she found her niche when she joined the art club and connected with like-minded students who appreciated art history.

1. What is the central idea of the paragraph?
    A. A character ultimately fails to adapt to a novel situation.
    B. A shared interest helps a character overcome an initial struggle to embrace a new situation.
    C. A parent is responsible for a character's interest in a new hobby.
    D. The discovery of a passion strains a girl's connections with her existing friends.

Amy's mother hoped that her daughter would grow up to be a doctor or a lawyer. Although life as a writer was not materially rewarding at first, Amy was always content because she knew that she was following her calling. This was no comfort to her mother, who avoided talking about her daughter with her own friends during the early years of the author's writing career. When Amy first published a novel that had significant financial success, only then could her mother bring herself to brag about her daughter's talents.

2. What is the central idea of the paragraph?
    A. A mother who struggles to accept her daughter's life choices eventually comes to accept them.
    B. An author harbors guilt about the anxiety her career causes for her mother.
    C. An author's legal and medical aspirations never fully diminish, but her mother is relieved that she has finally received external validation for her writings.
    D. A mother does not believe that her daughter has any talent but is relieved to be proven wrong.

In an era of electronic communication and mass entertainment, reading has seemingly fallen by the wayside. This has prompted a panic amongst people concerned about the endangerment of an important pastime that provides people with intellectual and personal enrichment. However, many people do read high-quality newspaper articles, blogs, and magazines, even if they do not read fiction very often. While there are some unique benefits associated with reading novels and short stories, fears about the end of reading are greatly exaggerated.

3. What is the central idea of the paragraph?
    A. A once prevalent diversion is in serious jeopardy.
    B. Alarm about a certain societal trend is misguided.
    C. Reading fiction is superior to reading nonfiction.
    D. A certain practice is needed to unlock society's creative potential.

A common staple of the American diet is wheat. However, overconsumption of wheat is associated with certain health problems, such as obesity and heart disease. Researchers are working to produce wheat with resistant starch that contains important dietary fibers that reduce cholesterol and blood glucose levels as well as improve gastrointestinal health.

4. What is the central idea of the paragraph?
    A. A new invention will serve as a universal panacea.
    B. Heart disease is primarily linked to wheat consumption habits.
    C. An innovative development is associated with many health benefits.
    D. Many health conditions can be prevented by cutting all grains from one's diet.

First Lady Dolley Madison, wife of President James Madison, took charge of a White House renovation project that created public spaces that could accommodate citizens and members of government. At her famous weekly drawing room parties, she was a charming and gracious host who welcomed guests from all social classes. These parties advanced her husband's goal of promoting social and political unity. Politicians with opposing political ideologies socialized at these parties and strengthened their bonds. As a result, they were able to work together more effectively, setting a precedent for the importance of cooperation amongst government officials with different political beliefs.

5. Which of the following best tells what this passage is about?
   A. How Dolley Madison tempered her husband's political ambitions.
   B. The indirect but important role that Dolley Madison had on political affairs.
   C. How Dolley Madison's social skills compared to those of other First Ladies.
   D. The beauty of the White House under the supervision of Dolley Madison.

Geothermal energy is usually obtained from hot spots on the Earth's surface, such as volcanoes. Unlike energy derived from fossil fuels, geothermal energy does not cause significant amounts of pollution. Geothermal energy is also renewable, meaning its supply cannot be exhausted. In addition, unlike with other forms of clean energy, such as solar energy and wind energy, the effectiveness of geothermal energy is not limited by weather conditions. Despite the large initial investment, geothermal energy can save people thousands of dollars each year.

6. Which of the following best tells what this paragraph is about?
   A. Volcanoes as a major source of geothermal energy.
   B. The importance of different energy sources.
   C. The limitations of solar energy.
   D. The environmental and economic advantages of geothermal energy.

Artists prior to the Renaissance* did not generally focus on presenting subjects realistically. For example, they often used rigid lines that made their subjects appear flat. By contrast, Renaissance artists made use of light, shadows, and perspective** to give their art the appearance of depth. Furthermore, Renaissance artists paid more attention to balance and proportion than did their predecessors. For instance, items were depicted at their proper sizes relative to one another. Humans painted in natural settings were also scaled properly relative to the background of the paintings. Lastly, unlike many artists during the Middle Ages, Renaissance artists portrayed the emotions of human subjects, as seen in Leonardo da Vinci's *Last Supper*.

*Renaissance: a period from the 14th to 17th centuries following the Middle Ages, which began as a cultural movement in Italy.

**perspective: an artistic technique that creates an effect of depth and distance.

7. What is the central idea of the paragraph?
   A. The most significant aspect of art during the Renaissance was its use of perspective.
   B. During the Renaissance, there was a notable shift to producing art that depicted people and scenery realistically.
   C. Art immediately prior to the Renaissance accurately depicted human emotions.
   D. The most famous Renaissance painting was Leonardo da Vinci's *Last Supper*.

Theodore Roosevelt believed that large corporations improved the standard of living, yet he also criticized businesses for abusing their powers and believing they were superior to the law of the land. Many companies held monopolies over entire industries, thereby limiting trade and competition. Under the Roosevelt administration, Congress passed the Sherman Antitrust Act, which made various practices that reduced competition between businesses illegal. In addition, the act allowed the federal government to investigate the practices of big businesses. For example, Roosevelt used this act to sue the Northern Securities Company, which controlled the vast majority of the railroad trade. The court voted 5 to 4 to dissolve the company for its illegal practices that limited trade, a decision that was seen as a victory for ordinary people.

8. What is the central idea of the paragraph?
    A. Roosevelt worked closely with big businesses to help them strengthen their hold over the industries they controlled.
    B. Big businesses valued the interests of the common people.
    C. Roosevelt was a reformer who worked to combat abusive practices of big businesses.
    D. The Northern Securities Company limited railroad competition.

In his plays, Aeschylus depicted various monarchical forms of government dominated by arrogant leaders who made unwise decisions. He thought that only in democratic governments, which had mechanisms for thoughtful deliberation amongst the citizenry, could the abusive power of individual leaders be limited. On the contrary, Euripides' plays depicted dangerous democratic governments in which majorities often made decisions that contributed to war and political tragedies within the state. The rulers themselves were often portrayed as weak leaders constrained by the imperfect will of the majority.

9. What is the central idea of the paragraph?
    A. Democracy was the cornerstone of ancient Greek society.
    B. Greek playwrights' differing political philosophies were evident in their portrayal of characters and events.
    C. Imperfect leaders often ignore the will of the majority.
    D. Weak leaders were a common important feature of Greek tragedies.

In the past, anthropologists focused on studying isolated populations in order to gain a more purified understanding of culture. Today, many anthropologists see cultures as fluid and interactive units that are situated within a global context. For example, some anthropologists study how certain global products, such as coffee, take on different meanings in different societies. Because culture is not something "shared" equally by all members of a population, dimensions such as power and struggle have also grown in importance to anthropologists. For example, some anthropologists study how the culture of a workplace is experienced differently by employees at different levels in an organization's hierarchy. Clearly, the field of anthropology has come a long way since the days of observing and interacting with people in remote areas.

10. What is the central idea of the paragraph?
    A. Power dynamics in the workplace are important.
    B. Anthropologists have lost interest in academic analysis.
    C. It is common to study populations in which power is distributed evenly between its members.
    D. Modern anthropologists have adopted a more complex view of culture.

The Grateful Dead is an iconic band known for its innovative music style. However, it is the band's unique business model that has recently been gaining attention from scholars. The band was ahead of its time in the ways it chose to do business. It was not afraid to improvise and shake up conventional norms to meet the needs of its clientele. For example, by touring year-round instead of focusing mostly on record sales while only touring for a limited portion of the year, as most of its peers did, the band helped build a brand and a loyal base.

The tactics that the Grateful Dead adopted have had an influence on American businesses. For example, the band gave special treatment to its most loyal fans by giving them access to concert tickets across the country before announcing their concerts to the general public. In the 1980s, many American businesses adopted this consumer-oriented model, focusing on providing their clients with quality products and services. Before that, "the customer comes first" mentality was not the norm. The band members also allowed people to record their concerts free of charge. Rather than suing people who recorded and distributed their recordings to others for free, they took advantage of the publicity that they gained by having their music spread. As a result of their increased popularity, they made more money in merchandise and concert sales. Today, many companies embrace this principle. Clients who receive "free stuff" from companies are more inclined to give these companies their business.

In addition, the band's "in-sourcing" approach to management contrasted with the outsourcing model so common throughout corporate America. Many firms will hire contractors from other companies to perform certain business tasks, a practice that sometimes leads to conflict. The Grateful Dead preferred to hire as many people as possible to work in-house for the band itself. Thus, the band had more control over its product and was able to better take care of its employees. As a result, it was better situated to meet the needs of its customers. Today, many companies hire in-house people when possible. For example, a company might hire a lawyer as a fulltime employee rather than make a contract with a separate law firm to do its legal work.

11. What is the central idea of the passage?
    A. A successful band uses a groundbreaking business model.
    B. A band has musical talent unmatched by its contemporaries.
    C. Outsourcing causes problems for many businesses.
    D. A band allows its fans to record its content for free.

Mastodons, the now extinct relatives of the modern elephant, inhabited North and Central America until their extinction about 10,000 years ago. These mysterious animals have captured the attention of scientists and ordinary people alike. President Thomas Jefferson, a scientific expert in his own right, commissioned a team to collect mastodon fossils for him in order to learn more about these fascinating creatures.

The name "mastodon" means "breast tooth," in reference to the appearance of its molars. Mastodons had low-domed heads and large, long tusks. The tusks may have assisted the mastodons in feeding and competing with other animals. Mastodons were herbivorous creatures, whose diet was obtained mostly by browsing (feeding on high-growing plants). They also likely got some food by grazing (feeding on grass and low vegetation). Though they did not have many predators due to their large size, their predators included saber-toothed cats and lions. There is also evidence that humans hunted them. For example, an arrowhead was found among the bones of one American mastodon.

People sometimes confuse mastodons with their more famous cousin, the wooly mammoth, though modern reconstructions based on partial skeleton remains show that they are only distantly related. One notable difference between the two cousins was the shape of their teeth. While the mammoths had ridged molars suitable for eating grass, the mastodons had molars with cone-like cusps that were perfect for cutting trees, twigs, and shrubs. Carbon from the teeth of mastodons and mammoths provide scientists with a treasure trove of information, confirming their different dietary preferences.

Scientists speculate that mastodons may have been social creatures based on studies of their anatomical similarities to elephants, though scientists obviously cannot be sure about exactly how they behaved. Studies of mastodon bone sites suggest that they lived in mixed herds of adult females and young mastodons. The long maturation periods may indicate that mastodons required care for a long period of time. Although there is some speculation that mastodons were migratory creatures, some scientists now believe that many of them did not roam. Their habitats often had everything they needed to live comfortably.

There is still some debate over the primary cause of the mastodon's extinction. It has generally been thought that human pressures on their populations were the main culprit, though climate change may have been a more important factor. In 2016, a nearly complete mastodon skeleton preserved during the Ice Age, the most complete skeleton discovered in decades, was found in the Great Lakes region. Analysis of this skeleton revealed that many of the bones were in the same position relative to each other as when it was alive, suggesting that natural causes were not the cause of death. It is more likely that this mastodon's death served a more practical purpose. Specifically, it was probably stored by hunters as a source of meat under a pond that no longer exists.

12. Which of the following best tells what this passage is about?
    A. The traits of a long-extinct animal.
    B. Future research projects on how environmental pressures affect certain animals.
    C. How scientists discovered a mastodon skeleton.
    D. The methods scientists use to analyze bones.

Halloween has long been a popular holiday in many countries. It is typically celebrated on October 31st. To the modern person, this holiday frequently conjures up associations with trick or treating, costumes, and haunted houses. But the holiday as we know it today has a long and interesting history.

Halloween has its roots in the Irish festival Samhain, which was celebrated as far back as the 10th century. Samhain was one of several holidays that signaled the end of the harvest season, as people began stocking up supplies for the winter. It was believed that on October 31st, the window between the worlds of the living and the dead opened. Thus, "scary" costumes and masks were often worn to prevent evil spirts from causing harm to people and their crops. People also made lanterns out of vegetables, such as turnips or pumpkins, to ward off evil spirits. These lanterns were the likely inspiration behind modern-day jack-o-lanterns. It was also believed that spirits of the deceased would come visit their families, seeking hospitality. Thus, people often left out food and drinks for the spirits of their family members.

It was not until the 19th century that Samhain and the similar holiday All Hallows' Eve merged to become what is now known as Halloween. The holiday first came to America after a wave of Irish and Scottish immigration. Though the holiday was originally confined to immigrant communities, it eventually became a mainstream holiday throughout the United States that is now associated with a variety of traditions, such as bonfires, apple bobbing, haunted houses, and scary movies. Halloween is largely a secular holiday with less of a religious dimension than the holidays from which it emerged.

Perhaps the most noteworthy Halloween tradition is "trick or treating." Children go to door to door dressed in costumes saying "trick or treat" in expectation of receiving candy ("the treat"). Though not usually done in practice, the alternative to a treat is for the children to play a "trick" on the owner of the house if no treat is given. Many countries expressly discourage or outlaw playing tricks due to the damage and disruption they cause. Trick or treating is loosely based on the medieval European practices of "guising" and "souling." Guising was a practice whereby children dressed in costumes would go from door to door asking for coins or food in exchange for putting on entertaining performances. Similarly, "souling" involved beggars asking rich people for food ("soul cakes") on feast days such as All Hallows' Eve. By the 1950s, trick or treating was firmly established as a kid-friendly holiday in the United States. Today, adults are generally expected to go grocery shopping for treats in preparation for Halloween.

Interestingly, Halloween is not just a kid holiday anymore. While there aren't too many adults trick or treating (unless they are accompanying children), many adults relish the opportunity to get dressed up. Some offices even encourage their staff to wear costumes on Halloween. The fun and fantastical holiday can give adults a needed escape from dwelling on the stresses of their lives.

13. Which of the following best tells what this passage is about?
    A. The influence of Europeans on American religions.
    B. The historical context for Halloween.
    C. A contrast between Halloween in modern Ireland and the United States.
    D. Celebrations of Halloween around the world.

In the past, scientists conceptualized taste as linked to taste buds in the mouth, which detect sweet, salty, sour, and bitter flavors. Now, it is clear that taste is an experience that also encompasses smell, touch, and even sight. The cortical workload of the brain processes the majority of information visually, so it makes sense that our eyes play a role in how we perceive food.

The appearance of food, including the color of the plates on which it is found, shapes our expectations. In one sense, this is protective. For example, we know not to eat food that looks like it can make us sick, like rotten apples or moldy bread. We may also avoid foods that look similar to those that have made us sick in the past. Visual cues can also assist us in identifying certain features of foods. For example, milk experts are better able to determine the fat content of milk when they can see it.

The appearance of food not only impacts expectations, but it can also affect how we actually experience certain flavors. If we try a food that looks disgusting, it may be "too late" to enjoy it because of our brain's expectation that it will taste bad affects how we actually perceive the food once it is in our mouths. Though sight is not technically part of taste, it can trigger our taste buds. The color of food also affects how we experience it. For example, if an apple-flavored drink is colored red, our brains may perceive it to be sweeter than it actually is, since we associate red with sweetness.

In one study, subjects who tried an orange-flavored drink while blindfolded rarely identified the flavor correctly. When they could see that the color of the drink was orange, they almost always were correct. When the orange drink was dyed green, some subjects mistakenly identified it as lime-flavored. When it was not dyed green, no subjects made this mistake. Clearly, the color of food can influence how we perceive taste.

The color of food can even trick so-called "experts." For instance, in a classic experiment, wine experts who tasted white wine that was secretly dyed red used descriptors characteristic of actual red wines. Their expectations for how red wine should taste may have triggered their brains to detect flavors that weren't actually present in the wine. When the wine was in opaque glasses, the experts were more accurate in describing the wine.

The food industry is well aware of how our expectations shape how we taste food. For that reason, they alter the appearance of food and use colorimeters to make sure that foods are perfectly hued. For example, customers may be more inclined to purchase apples that have been colored red, believing them to be sweeter. Companies that make plant-based meat-like products often dye the food brown since customers are not "prepared" to eat green meat. People generally associate green meat with meat that has gone bad. Nevertheless, while we associate certain colors with certain foods, this learning happens from experience. Companies can effectively market flavors that counter our expectations to attract customers, as exemplified by green ketchup and blue lemonade.

Even though our eyes shape how we perceive taste, they don't tell the whole story. The brain and other senses, such as smell, can override the ugly appearance of certain foods. Many foods, such as chilies, sausages, and stews, are popular among people who do not necessarily find them visually appealing. For example, while a beef stew might look "gross" to someone, if it has a pleasant smell and one has positive memories associated with its taste, these factors take precedence. In other cases, a desire to be adventurous may override one's initial revulsion to a certain food's appearance. This is encouraging news to many people, including parents who want their kids to eat healthy foods that look less than appetizing.

14. Which of the following best tells what this passage is about?
    A. How the color of wine can fool expert wine testers.
    B. How eyes process visual information in the brain.
    C. The relationship between vision and taste.
    D. The role that smell can play in overpowering sight when judging food.

Sea stars, or starfish, are known for their distinctive appearance. With their arms connected to their round body, giving them the appearance of stars, it is no wonder that many people are allured by these creatures. Beyond their dazzling features, sea stars play a particularly important role in maintaining the balance of ecosystems.

Despite their name and aquatic habitat, sea stars are not fish. Rather, they are echinoderms, closely related to other animals such as sea urchins and sand dollars. There are thousands of species of sea stars living in diverse habitats, from tropical waters to colder regions of the ocean.

Sea stars are carnivores, and their size is dependent on how much they eat. Sea stars eat prey outside their bodies. They use suction tubes on their feet to open up shells of shellfish, such as clams and mussels. Their stomachs then leave their bodies and secrete enzymes that break down the tissue of the shellfish. Then the stomachs return to the sea stars' bodies. The madreporite at the center of the star filters water through its body. The water that filters through their bodies acts similarly to "blood" in other animals. Most of the major organs of the sea star are located on the arms. For example, eyespots on the arm help them detect light. Interestingly, sea stars have no brain. Rather, their nervous system is spread throughout their arms. While most sea stars have five arms, there are some with more. Sea stars have calcified skin to protect them from predators, such as crabs and seagulls. Many come in color variations that allow them to hide among the coral reef, giving them another avenue of protection. The ridges and bumps on many starfish actually complement the spikes found in many coral reefs. Even when sea stars are attacked or are wounded, they do not necessarily die. Most sea stars can regenerate missing limbs. Thus, a sea star might sacrifice an arm to escape a predator, only to regrow it.

Sea stars are considered keystone species by scientists because of the role they play in maintaining the balance of ecosystems. They keep the population of their prey under control. For example, if sea stars are removed from an ecosystem, populations of mussels, urchins, and barnacles may grow uncontrollably, thus pushing out other organisms from the ecosystem. One danger posed by increased sea urchin populations is the destruction of kelp forests on which sea urchins feed. When sea stars keep the sea urchin population in check, kelp forests thrive. Kelp forests are vital to the health of marine ecosystems in part because they provide a habitat for many fish. Kelp forests also help the environment. Most scientists believe that excessive carbon dioxide in the atmosphere is responsible for global warming. Kelp forests absorb carbon dioxide from the atmosphere and release oxygen into the air.

Unfortunately, there are many threats to sea stars. Some companies harvest them for fertilizer and poultry feed. Another threat is sea star wasting syndrome, a disease whereby sea stars turn to goo. The disease is likely caused by a virus. It is believed that pollution and warmer waters associated with human-induced climate change may be contributing to the spread of this disease, which has affected as many as 98% of starfish in certain populations.

Some people think that we need to treat sea stars like endangered species for their own protection. In some locations, there are laws restricting how many live sea stars that can be collected by humans from waters. Scientists are also trying to better understand the environmental factors that contribute to sea star viral infections so that we can better protect them. The discovery of young sea stars in areas where adult populations had been thought to be wiped out brings renewed hope that their populations will rebound.

15. Which of the following best tells what this passage is about?
    A. An organism that plays an important role in the environment.
    B. The origin of sea star wasting syndrome.
    C. Legislation designed to protect sea stars.
    D. The relationship between mussels and sea urchins.

If you've ever gone to a doctor's office or hospital, you've probably encountered nurses who often perform important medical tasks, such as taking blood, administering medicine, and monitoring patients' health. The jobs of nurses today reflect the deep influence of Florence Nightingale, who transformed the once-derided job into an honorable medical profession.

Born to a wealthy Italian family in 1820, Nightingale's mother encouraged her to marry someone in her station, as other upper-class women of her time did. However, Nightingale had different plans in mind. While on a tour of Europe, Nightingale connected with Mary Clarke. Clarke generally looked down on other upper-class women and instead spent most of her time with male intellectuals. Sensing that Nightingale was intelligent in her own right, Clarke took a liking to Nightingale, and the two remained in contact for decades. Clarke taught Nightingale that women can be regarded as equal to their male counterparts. When Nightingale decided to pursue a career in nursing, she did so despite the protests of her mother, who wanted Nightingale to instead focus on building a family of her own. At that time, taking on a job was seen as menial labor for upper class women.

Nightingale gained prominence during the Crimean War when she treated soldiers. She was struck by the fact that more soldiers were dying of disease than battle wounds. She noticed the unsanitary conditions of the wards and posited that they were making the soldiers sick and contributing to the spread of the disease. Nightingale improved sanitary conditions in the wards, having them scrubbed thoroughly and providing soldiers with clean linens. She also encouraged personal hygiene practices, such as handwashing. As a result of Nightingale's efforts, the death rate in the hospitals declined sharply. She became known as "the lady with the lamp" to the soldiers, as she frequently patrolled the wards with her lamp, checking on the soldiers, whom she reassured with her presence. Nightingale also argued to the Royal Commission that poor ventilation, overcrowding, and bad drainage systems contributed to the spread of infections. The Sanitary Commission fixed the ventilation and drainage systems, further contributing to reductions in death rates. Her influence on the sanitary design of hospitals and homes is still seen today.

Nightingale drew from ideas about nutrition and psychology when treating her patients. She believed that poor nutrition contributed to disease and a decline in overall health. She made sure that soldiers had diverse and appealing dietary options. Nightingale also recognized that mental health was closely linked to physical health. She had soldiers write letters so that they could express themselves emotionally. She provided them with books, classrooms, and libraries to stimulate their minds. Thus, Nightingale was innovative in her focus on treating the whole person.

Although Nightingale is most known for her contributions to nursing, she also has a somewhat underreported legacy in the field of statistics. Nightingale scrupulously collected data during her time as a nurse, and her statistical findings helped convince the Royal Commission on the Health of the Army to accept many of her policy recommendations. Her study of the sanitation system in India led to successful public health reforms that reduced deaths. Nightingale was one of the first people to make use of the pie chart, and she even helped developed the polar area diagram, a type of statistical chart. Nightingale was the first female elected to the Royal Statistical Society.

In 1860, Nightingale put her ideas into practice on a grander scale by establishing the Nightingale School for Nurses, the first school for nurses connected to a medical school program and hospital. Students would typically train for one year, taking classes and working with patients. The Nightingale school serves as a model for other nursing schools. Though the profession of nursing has evolved over the years, Nightingale's influence on the profession is enduring and she will continue to be regarded as a heroine for her contributions.

16. Which of the following best tells what this passage is about?
    A. An important historical figure and her influence on the nursing profession.
    B. How nutrition, psychology, and physiology interact in synergistic ways.
    C. How attitudes towards the role of upper-class women in society have evolved.
    D. The history of modern medicine in Europe.

The excerpt below is from *The Story of My Life* by Helen Keller.

The most important day I remember in all my life is the one on which my teacher, Anne Mansfield Sullivan, came to me. I am filled with wonder when I consider the immeasurable contrasts between the two lives which it connects. It was the third of March, 1887, three months before I was seven years old. On the afternoon of that eventful day, I stood on the porch, dumb, expectant. I guessed vaguely from my mother's signs and from the hurrying to and fro in the house that something unusual was about to happen, so I went to the door and waited on the steps. The afternoon sun penetrated the mass of honeysuckle that covered the porch, and fell on my upturned face. My fingers lingered almost unconsciously on the familiar leaves and blossoms which had just come forth to greet the sweet southern spring. I did not know what the future held of marvel or surprise for me. Anger and bitterness had preyed upon me continually for weeks and a deep languor had succeeded this passionate struggle.

Have you ever been at sea in a dense fog, when it seemed as if a tangible white darkness shut you in, and the great ship, tense and anxious, groped her way toward the shore with plummet and sounding-line, and you waited with beating heart for something to happen? I was like that ship before my education began, only I was without compass or sounding-line, and had no way of knowing how near the harbor was. "Light! give me light!" was the wordless cry of my soul, and the light of love shone on me in that very hour.

I felt approaching footsteps, I stretched out my hand as I supposed to my mother. Someone took it, and I was caught up and held close in the arms of her who had come to reveal all things to me, and, more than all things else, to love me. The morning after my teacher came she led me into her room and gave me a doll. The little blind children at the Perkins Institution had sent it and Laura Bridgman had dressed it; but I did not know this until afterward. When I had played with it a little while, Miss Sullivan slowly spelled into my hand the word "d-o-l-l." I was at once interested in this finger play and tried to imitate it. When I finally succeeded in making the letters correctly I was flushed with childish pleasure and pride. Running downstairs to my mother I held up my hand and made the letters for doll. I did not know that I was spelling a word or even that words existed; I was simply making my fingers go in monkey-like imitation. In the days that followed I learned to spell in this uncomprehending way a great many words, among them pin, hat, cup and a few verbs like sit, stand and walk. But my teacher had been with me several weeks before I understood that everything has a name.

One day, while I was playing with my new doll, Miss Sullivan put my big rag doll into my lap also, spelled "d-o-l-l" and tried to make me understand that "d-o-l-l" applied to both. Earlier in the day we had had a tussle over the words "m-u-g" and "w-a-t-e-r." Miss Sullivan had tried to impress it upon me that "m-u-g" is mug and that "w-a-t-e-r" is water, but I persisted in confounding the two. In despair she had dropped the subject for the time, only to renew it at the first opportunity. I became impatient at her repeated attempts and, seizing the new doll, I dashed it upon the floor. I was keenly delighted when I felt the fragments of the broken doll at my feet. Neither sorrow nor regret followed my passionate outburst. I had not loved the doll. In the still, dark world in which I lived there was no strong sentiment or tenderness. I felt my teacher sweep the fragments to one side of the hearth, and I had a sense of satisfaction that the cause of my discomfort was removed. She brought me my hat, and I knew I was going out into the warm sunshine. This thought, if a wordless sensation may be called a thought, made me hop and skip with pleasure.

We walked down the path to the well-house, attracted by the fragrance of the honeysuckle with which it was covered. Someone was drawing water and my teacher placed my hand under the spout. As the cool stream gushed over one hand she spelled into the other the word water, first slowly, then rapidly. I stood still, my whole attention fixed upon the motions of her fingers. Suddenly I felt a misty consciousness as of something forgotten—a thrill of returning thought; and somehow the mystery of language was revealed to me. I knew then that "w-a-t-e-r" meant the wonderful cool something that was flowing over my hand. That living word awakened my soul, gave it light, hope, joy, set it free! There were barriers still, it is true, but barriers that could in time be swept away.

I left the well-house eager to learn. Everything had a name, and each name gave birth to a new thought. As we returned to the house every object which I touched seemed to quiver with life. That was because I saw everything with the strange, new sight that had come to me. On entering the door, I remembered the doll I had broken. I felt my way to the hearth and picked up the pieces. I tried vainly to put them together. Then my eyes filled with tears; for I realized what I had done, and for the first time I felt repentance and sorrow.

I learned a great many new words that day. I do not remember what they all were; but I do know that mother, father, sister, teacher were among them—words that were to make the world blossom for me, "like Aaron's rod, with flowers." It would have been difficult to find a happier child than I was as I lay in my crib at the close of that eventful day and lived over the joys it had brought me, and for the first time longed for a new day to come.

17. Which of the following best tells what this passage is about?
    A. A woman reflects on a transformative episode in her life.
    B. A woman ponders deep moral and philosophical theories.
    C. A woman recounts a time she taught someone an important lesson.
    D. A woman traces the development of her career.

Below is "The Story of Prometheus" by James Baldwin.

In those old, old times, there lived two brothers who were not like other men, nor yet like those Mighty Ones who lived upon the mountain top. They were the sons of one of those Titans who had fought against Jupiter* and been sent in chains to the strong prison-house of the Lower World. The name of the elder of these brothers was Prometheus, or Forethought; for he was always thinking of the future and making things ready for what might happen to-morrow, or next week, or next year, or it may be in a hundred years to come. The younger was called Epimetheus, or Afterthought; for he was always so busy thinking of yesterday, or last year, or a hundred years ago, that he had no care at all for what might come to pass after a while. For some cause, Jupiter had not sent these brothers to prison with the rest of the Titans.

Prometheus did not care to live amid the clouds on the mountain top. He was too busy for that. While the Mighty Folk were spending their time in idleness, drinking nectar and eating ambrosia, he was intent upon plans for making the world wiser and better than it had ever been before. He went out amongst men to live with them and help them; for his heart was filled with sadness when he found that they were no longer happy as they had been during the golden days when Saturn was king. Ah, how very poor and wretched they were! He found them living in caves and in holes of the earth, shivering with the cold because there was no fire, dying of starvation, hunted by wild beasts and by one another—the most miserable of all living creatures.

"If they only had fire," said Prometheus to himself, "they could at least warm themselves and cook their food; and after a while they could learn to make tools and build themselves houses. Without fire, they are worse off than the beasts."

Then he went boldly to Jupiter and begged him to give fire to men, that so they might have a little comfort through the long, dreary months of winter.

"Not a spark will I give," said Jupiter. "No, indeed! Why, if men had fire they might become strong and wise like ourselves, and after a while they would drive us out of our kingdom. Let them shiver with cold, and let them live like the beasts. It is best for them to be poor and ignorant, that so we Mighty Ones may thrive and be happy."

Prometheus made no answer; but he had set his heart on helping mankind, and he did not give up. He turned away, and left Jupiter and his mighty company forever.

As he was walking by the shore of the sea he found a reed, or, as some say, a tall stalk of fennel, growing; and when he had broken it off he saw that its hollow center was filled with a dry, soft pith which would burn slowly and keep on fire a long time. He took the long stalk in his hands, and started with it towards the dwelling of the sun in the far east.

"Mankind shall have fire in spite of the tyrant who sits on the mountain top," he said.

He reached the place of the sun in the early morning just as the glowing, golden orb was rising from the earth and beginning his daily journey through the sky. He touched the end of the long reed to the flames, and the dry pith caught on fire and burned slowly. Then he turned and hastened back to his own land, carrying with him the precious spark hidden in the hollow center of the plant. He called some of the shivering men from their caves and built a fire for them, and showed them how to warm themselves by it and how to build other fires from the coals. Soon there was a cheerful blaze in every rude home in the land, and men and women gathered round it and were warm and happy, and thankful to Prometheus for the wonderful gift which he had brought to them from the sun. It was not long until they learned to cook their food and so to eat like men instead of like beasts. They began at once to leave off their wild and savage habits; and instead of lurking in the dark places of the world, they came out into the open air and the bright sunlight, and were glad because life had been given to them.

After that, Prometheus taught them, little by little, a thousand things. He showed them how to build houses of wood and stone, and how to tame sheep and cattle and make them useful, and how to plow and sow and reap, and how to protect themselves from the storms of winter and the beasts of the woods. Then he showed them how to dig in the earth for copper and iron, and how to melt the ore, and how to hammer it into shape and fashion from it the tools and weapons which they needed in peace and war; and when he saw how happy the world was becoming he cried out:

"A new Golden Age shall come, brighter and better by far than the old!"

*Jupiter: King of the gods in Roman mythology

18. The story as a whole can best be described as
    A. a myth that portrays the vast mysteries of nature.
    B. a folktale that explains an element of the human condition.
    C. a legend that delves into the complex relationship between two prominent figures.
    D. a work of fantasy that traces the history of a divine race.

The story below is "Hearts and Hands" by O'Henry.

At Denver there was an influx of passengers into the coaches on the eastbound B. & M. express. In one coach there sat a very pretty young woman dressed in elegant taste and surrounded by all the luxurious comforts of an experienced traveler. Among the newcomers were two young men, one of handsome presence with a bold, frank countenance and manner; the other a ruffled, glum-faced person, heavily built and roughly dressed. The two were handcuffed together.

As they passed down the aisle of the coach the only vacant seat offered was a reversed one facing the attractive young woman. Here the linked couple seated themselves. The young woman's glance fell upon them with a distant, swift disinterest; then with a lovely smile brightening her countenance and a tender pink tingeing her rounded cheeks, she held out a little gray-gloved hand. When she spoke her voice, full, sweet, and deliberate, proclaimed that its owner was accustomed to speak and be heard.

"Well, Mr. Easton, if you *will* make me speak first, I suppose I must. Don't you ever recognize old friends when you meet them in the West?"

The younger man roused himself sharply at the sound of her voice, seemed to struggle with a slight embarrassment which he threw off instantly, and then clasped her fingers with his left hand.

"It's Miss Fairchild," he said, with a smile. "I'll ask you to excuse the other hand; it's otherwise engaged just at present."

He slightly raised his right hand, bound at the wrist by the shining "bracelet" to the left one of his companion. The glad look in the girl's eyes slowly changed to a bewildered horror. The glow faded from her cheeks. Her lips parted in a vague, relaxing distress. Easton, with a little laugh, as if amused, was about to speak again when the other forestalled him. The glum-faced man had been watching the girl's countenance with veiled glances from his keen, shrewd eyes.

"You'll excuse me for speaking, miss, but, I see you're acquainted with the marshal here. If you'll ask him to speak a word for me when we get to the pen he'll do it, and it'll make things easier for me there. He's taking me to Leavenworth prison. It's seven years for counterfeiting."

"Oh!" said the girl, with a deep breath and returning color. "So that is what you are doing out here? A marshal!"

"My dear Miss Fairchild," said Easton, calmly, "I had to do something. Money has a way of taking wings unto itself, and you know it takes money to keep step with our crowd in Washington. I saw this opening in the West, and—well, a marshalship isn't quite as high a position as that of ambassador, but—"

"The ambassador," said the girl, warmly, "doesn't call any more. He needn't ever have done so. You ought to know that. And so now you are one of these dashing Western heroes, and you ride and shoot and go into all kinds of dangers. That's different from the Washington life. You have been missed from the old crowd."

The girl's eyes, fascinated, went back, widening a little, to rest upon the glittering handcuffs.

"Don't you worry about them, miss," said the other man. "All marshals handcuff themselves to their prisoners to keep them from getting away. Mr. Easton knows his business."

"Will we see you again soon in Washington?" asked the girl.

"Not soon, I think," said Easton. "My butterfly days are over, I fear."

"I love the West," said the girl irrelevantly. Her eyes were shining softly. She looked away out the car window. She began to speak truly and simply without the gloss of style and manner: "Mamma and I spent the summer in Denver. She went home a week ago because father was slightly ill. I could live and be happy in the West. I think the air here agrees with me. Money isn't everything. But people always misunderstand things and remain stupid—"

"Say, Mr. Marshal," growled the glum-faced man. "This isn't quite fair. I'm needing a drink, and haven't had a smoke all day. Haven't you talked long enough? Take me in the smoker now, won't you? I'm half dead for a pipe."

The bound travelers rose to their feet, Easton with the same slow smile on his face.

"I can't deny a petition for tobacco," he said, lightly. "It's the one friend of the unfortunate. Good-bye, Miss Fairchild. Duty calls, you know." He held out his hand for a farewell.

"It's too bad you are not going East," she said, reclothing herself with manner and style. "But you must go on to Leavenworth, I suppose?"

"Yes," said Easton, "I must go on to Leavenworth."

The two men sidled down the aisle into the smoker.

The two passengers in a seat nearby had heard most of the conversation. Said one of them: "That marshal's a good sort of chap. Some of these Western fellows are all right."

"Pretty young to hold an office like that, isn't he?" asked the other.

"Young!" exclaimed the first speaker, "why—Oh! didn't you catch on? Say—did you ever know an officer to handcuff a prisoner to his *right* hand?"

19. What best tells what this story is about?
    A. A man navigates a potentially awkward encounter with a person from his past.
    B. A law enforcement officer plays a sinister trick on an unsuspecting stranger.
    C. A criminal repents for his sins after being reminded of the life he could have had.
    D. A woman is charmed by the accomplishments of her old friend.

The short story below is "Luck" by Mark Twain.

[Note—This is not a fancy sketch. I got it from a clergyman who was an instructor at Woolwich forty years ago, and who vouched for its truth.—M.T.]
It was at a banquet in London in honor of one of the two or three conspicuously illustrious English military names of this generation. For reasons which will presently appear, I will withhold his real name
5   and titles, and call him Lieutenant General Lord Arthur Scoresby, V.C., K.C.B., etc., etc., etc. What a fascination there is in a renowned name! There sat the man, in actual flesh, whom I had heard of so many thousands of times since that day, thirty years before, when his name shot suddenly to the zenith from a Crimean battlefield, to remain forever celebrated. It was food and drink to me to look, and look, and look at that demigod; scanning, searching, noting: the quietness, the reserve, the noble gravity of
10 his countenance; the simple honesty that expressed itself all over him; the sweet unconsciousness of his greatness—unconsciousness of the hundreds of admiring eyes fastened upon him, unconsciousness of the deep, loving, sincere worship welling out of the breasts of those people and flowing toward him. The clergyman at my left was an old acquaintance of mine—clergyman now, but had spent the first half of his life in the camp and field, and as an instructor in the military school at Woolwich. Just at the
15 moment I have been talking about, a veiled and singular light glimmered in his eyes, and he leaned down and muttered confidentially to me—indicating the hero of the banquet with a gesture: "Privately—he's an absolute fool."
This verdict was a great surprise to me. If its subject had been Napoleon, or Socrates, or Solomon, my astonishment could not have been greater. Two things I was well aware of: that the Reverend was a
20 man of strict veracity, and that his judgement of men was good. Therefore I knew, beyond doubt or

question, that the world was mistaken about this hero: he *was* a fool. So I meant to find out, at a convenient moment, how the Reverend, all solitary and alone, had discovered the secret.

Some days later the opportunity came, and this is what the Reverend told me.

About forty years ago I was an instructor in the military academy at Woolwich. I was present in one of the sections when young Scoresby underwent his preliminary examination. I was touched to the quick with pity; for the rest of the class answered up brightly and handsomely, while he—why, dear me, he didn't know *anything*, so to speak. He was evidently good, and sweet, and lovable, and guileless; and so it was exceedingly painful to see him stand there, as serene as a graven image, and deliver himself of answers which were veritably miraculous for stupidity and ignorance. All the compassion in me was aroused in his behalf. I said to myself, when he comes to be examined again, he will be flung over, of course; so it will be simply a harmless act of charity to ease his fall as much as I can. I took him aside, and found that he knew a little of Cæsar's history; and as he didn't know anything else, I went to work and drilled him like a galley slave on a certain line of stock questions concerning Cæsar which I knew would be used. If you'll believe me, he went through with flying colors on examination day! He went through on that purely superficial "cram," and got compliments too, while others, who knew a thousand times more than he, got plucked. By some strangely lucky accident—an accident not likely to happen twice in a century—he was asked no question outside of the narrow limits of his drill.

It was stupefying. Well, all through his course I stood by him, with something of the sentiment which a mother feels for a crippled child; and he always saved himself—just by miracle, apparently.

Now of course the thing that would expose him and kill him at last was mathematics. I resolved to make his death as easy as I could; so I drilled him and crammed him, and crammed him and drilled him, just on the line of questions which the examiners would be most likely to use, and then launching him on his fate. Well, sir, try to conceive of the result: to my consternation, he took the first prize! And with it he got a perfect ovation in the way of compliments.

Sleep? There was no more sleep for me for a week. My conscience tortured me day and night. What I had done I had done purely through charity, and only to ease the poor youth's fall—I never had dreamed of any such preposterous result as the thing that had happened. I felt as guilty and miserable as the creator of Frankenstein. Here was a woodenhead whom I had put in the way of glittering promotions and prodigious responsibilities, and but one thing could happen: he and his responsibilities would all go to ruin together at the first opportunity.

The Crimean war had just broken out. Of course there had to be a war, I said to myself: we couldn't have peace and give this donkey a chance to die before he is found out. I waited for the earthquake. It came. And it made me reel when it did come. He was actually gazetted to a captaincy in a marching regiment! Better men grow old and gray in the service before they climb to a sublimity like that. And who could ever have foreseen that they would go and put such a load of responsibility on such green and inadequate shoulders? I could just barely have stood it if they had made him a cornet; but a captain—think of it! I thought my hair would turn white.

Consider what I did—I who so loved repose and inaction. I said to myself, I am responsible to the country for this, and I must go along with him and protect the country against him as far as I can. So I took my poor little capital that I had saved up through years of work and grinding economy, and went with a sigh and bought a cornetcy in his regiment, and away we went to the field.

And there—oh dear, it was awful. Blunders? Why, he never did anything *but* blunder. But, you see, nobody was in the fellow's secret—everybody had him focused wrong, and necessarily misinterpreted his performance every time—consequently they took his idiotic blunders for inspirations of genius; they did, honestly! His mildest blunders were enough to make a man in his right mind cry; and they did make me cry—and rage and rave too, privately. And the thing that kept me always in a sweat of apprehension was the fact that every fresh blunder he made increased the luster of his reputation! I kept saying to myself, he'll get so high, that when discovery does finally come, it will be like the sun falling out of the sky.

70 He went right along up, from grade to grade, over the dead bodies of his superiors, until at last, in the hottest moment of the battle of ------- down went our colonel, and my heart jumped into my mouth, for Scoresby was next in rank! Now for it, said I; we'll all land in Sheol in ten minutes, sure.

The battle was awfully hot; the allies were steadily giving way all over the field. Our regiment occupied a position that was vital; a blunder now must be destruction. At this crucial moment, what does this
75 immortal fool do but detach the regiment from its place and order a charge over a neighboring hill where there wasn't a suggestion of an enemy! "There you go!" I said to myself; "this *is* the end at last." And away we did go, and were over the shoulder of the hill before the insane movement could be discovered and stopped. And what did we find? An entire and unsuspected Russian army in reserve! And what happened? We were eaten up? That is necessarily what would have happened in ninety-nine cases
80 out of a hundred. But no, those Russians argued that no single regiment would come browsing around there at such a time. It must be the entire English army, and that the sly Russian game was detected and blocked; so they turned tail, and away they went, pell-mell, over the hill and down into the field, in wild confusion, and we after them; they themselves broke the solid Russian center in the field, and tore through, and in no time there was the most tremendous rout you ever saw, and the defeat of the allies
85 was turned into a sweeping and splendid victory! Marshal Canrobert looked on, dizzy with astonishment, admiration,and delight; and sent right off for Scoresby, and hugged him, and decorated him on the field, in presence of all the armies!

And what was Scoresby's blunder that time? Merely the mistaking his right hand for his left—that was all. An order had come to him to fall back and support our right; and instead, he fell *forward* and went
90 over the hill to the left. But the name he won that day as a marvelous military genius filled the world with his glory, and that glory will never fade while history books last.

He is just as good and sweet and lovable and unpretending as a man can be, but he doesn't know enough to come in when it rains. Now that is absolutely true. He is the supremest donkey in the universe; and until half an hour ago nobody knew it but himself and me. He has been pursued, day by
95 day and year by year, by a most phenomenal and astonishing luckiness. He has been a shining soldier in all our wars for a generation; he has littered his whole military life with blunders, and yet has never committed one that didn't make him a knight or a baronet or a lord or something. Look at his breast; why, he is just clothed in domestic and foreign decorations. Well, sir, every one of them is the record of some shouting stupidity or other; and taken together, they are proof that the very best thing in all this
100 world that can befall a man is to be born lucky. I say again, as I said at the banquet, Scoresby's an absolute fool.

20. What is the one way that the first paragraph (lines 1-16) contributes to the plot?
    A. It provides context for why a subsequent recounting of events may seem incongruous.
    B. It underscores a point of contention in an argument between the narrator and the clergyman.
    C. It establishes important information about the clergyman's upbringing.
    D. It reveals that the narrator does not trust the clergyman's assessment.

21. The idea that Scoresby is a fool is most directly expressed through
    A. gossip and rumor.
    B. comical descriptions through melodramatic anecdotes.
    C. hyperbolic comparisons to historical figures.
    D. psychological of analysis of internal traits.

22. Reread the excerpt below.
    But the name he won that day as a marvelous military genius filled the world with his glory, and that glory will never fade while history books last.
    This sentence conveys the central idea that
    A. impact often overrides intention in matters of public perception.
    B. many people are motivated by a desire for fame even if that fame is based on little genuine talent.
    C. the motives of people should be disregarded when assessing their abilities.
    D. history only remembers those who have contributed meaningfully and flashily.

23. Which statement conveys a central idea of the passage?
    A. Teachers will sometimes sabotage their students who outshine them.
    B. Capable leadership skills are developed through trial and error rather than through diligent preparation.
    C. Success can be attributed to chance rather than merit.
    D. It is important to be proud of the accomplishments of one's friends, no matter how undeserved one might feel they are.

24. The passage can best be described as
    A. a satirical commentary on the shallowness of hero worship.
    B. a psychological profile of a deceptive individual.
    C. the psychotic rantings of an arrogant character.
    D. a playful melodrama about a rivalry between a student and his mentor.

"To An Indifferent Woman" by Charlotte Perkins Gilman

1
You who are happy in a thousand homes,
Or overworked therein, to a dumb peace;
Whose souls are wholly centered in the life
Of that small group you personally love;
5 Who told you that you need not know or care
About the sin and sorrow of the world?

Do you believe the sorrow of the world
Does not concern you in your little homes? —
That you are licensed to avoid the care
10 And toil for human progress, human peace,
And the enlargement of our power of love
Until it covers every field of life?

The one first duty of all human life
Is to promote the progress of the world
15 In righteousness, in wisdom, truth and love;
And you ignore it, hidden in your homes,
Content to keep them in uncertain peace,
Content to leave all else without your care.

Yet you are mothers! And a mother's care
20 Is the first step toward friendly human life.
Life where all nations in untroubled peace
Unite to raise the standard of the world
And make the happiness we seek in homes
Spread everywhere in strong and fruitful love.

25 You are content to keep that mighty love
In its first steps forever; the crude care
Of animals for mate and young and homes,
Instead of pouring it abroad in life,
Its mighty current feeding all the world
30 Till every human child can grow in peace.

You cannot keep your small domestic peace
Your little pool of undeveloped love,
While the neglected, starved, unmothered world
Struggles and fights for lack of mother's care,
35 And its tempestuous, bitter, broken life
Beats in upon you in your selfish homes.

We all may have our homes in joy and peace
When woman's life, in its rich power of love
Is joined with man's to care for all the world.

25. Reread the lines below.
And its tempestuous, bitter, broken life
Beats in upon you in your selfish homes.

What effect do these lines have on the poem?
A. They suggest that those who do not care for those in need may ultimately lose their own domestic happiness.
B. They suggest that those who do not open their hearts to others will experience stormy weather.
C. They suggest that those who suffer will personally shame those who have ignored their plights.
D. They suggest that the houses of those who engage in selfish behaviors are in imminent danger of being irreparably destroyed.

26. One central idea of the poem is that
A. women should see their roles in promoting world progress as just and important.
B. women can only have a positive influence on society if they work cooperatively with men.
C. awareness of the problems of others is more important than the resolution these problems.
D. love is completely meaningless if there are some people who suffer.

Week 3

27. The speaker's assertion that "a mother's care/Is the first step toward friendly human life" (lines 19-20) helps convey the central idea that
   A. men are not nurturing enough to participate in peacemaking ventures.
   B. politeness is the foundation of modern civilization.
   C. the duties of motherhood are not inconsistent with humanitarian principles.
   D. children inevitably elicit nurturing emotions in those who know them.

28. The tone of the poem can best be described as
   A. bittersweet.
   B. critical.
   C. amused.
   D. histrionic.

"Human-Animal Interactions: Therapeutic and Surprising" (NIH)

[1] For most of my life, I've led an urban existence. Growing up in Manhattan and working for over 30 years in Boston, I rarely encountered wildlife, other than pigeons and squirrels. One evening, however, shortly after I arrived at NIH last fall, I was shocked to come face to face with a large buck as I headed toward my car. In subsequent conversations with colleagues, I learned that deer roam freely on the NIH campus. This was especially surprising because NIH isn't in the countryside, it's in a heavily populated suburb just outside of Washington, DC. This wildlife encounter startled me at first, but then I thought about how interactions with animals, particularly in the fast pace of modern life, help to calm us and give us perspective.

[2] Indeed, companion animals—the dogs, cats, birds, and other pets that share our homes and our lives—significantly affect our health and well-being. In fact, an important part of NICHD's research portfolio is the study of how these human-animal interactions influence child health and behavior, and impact our overall quality of life.

[3] For the past 10 years, NICHD's Child Development and Behavior Branch has had a partnership with the WALTHAM® Centre for Pet Nutrition, a division of Mars, Inc., to research the impact of animal interactions on child health and development. This partnership has led to several published works describing the therapeutic benefits of our companion animals.

[4] In a 2015 NICHD-funded study, a group of adolescents with type 1 diabetes each cared for a pet fish twice a day by feeding and checking water levels. The routine also included changing tank water each week, coupled with the children reviewing their glucose logs with parents. The researchers found that, when compared to teens who hadn't been given a fish to care for, the fishkeeping teens were more disciplined about checking their own blood glucose levels, which is essential for maintaining their health. Kids ages 10 to 13 years showed the greatest increase in self-monitoring following the pet fish intervention.

[5] That same year, **another study** found that children with autism spectrum disorder were calmer while playing with guinea pigs. Researchers gave each child a wristband that measured skin conductance—a measure for excitement and anxiety. A device inside the wristband sends an imperceptible electric current through the skin. The more anxious a person feels, the faster the current will travel through the skin. When the children with autism spent 10 minutes in a supervised group playtime with guinea pigs, their anxiety levels dropped. The children with autism also showed improved social functioning and

were more engaged with their peers—an important benefit for children with autism. The researchers speculated that, because the animals offered unqualified acceptance, their presence comforted and calmed the children.

[6] Finally, dogs may prove to be an important addition to help kids cope with attention-deficit-hyperactivity disorder (ADHD). **Another NICHD study** enrolled two groups of children diagnosed with ADHD into a 12-week group therapy session. One group of kids read to a therapy dog once a week for 30 minutes, while the other group read to puppets that looked like dogs. Both groups showed improvements from the therapy sessions. However, the kids who read to the real animals performed better in measures of social skills, prosocial behaviors (such as sharing, cooperation, and volunteering), and behavioral problems. The researchers theorized that these interactions with dogs may help children focus their attention, thus improving their executive-functioning skills.

[7] As a scientist and a mother who has raised kids, fish, and cats, I understand and appreciate the importance that our furry and scaly friends have in our daily lives. **NICHD continues to support research** that examines the potential benefits of animals on our health and on the effectiveness of animal-assisted therapies in alleviating the symptoms of certain disorders and conditions, particularly in children. I have now grown accustomed to seeing the deer stroll undeterred around our bucolic campus, and I am even beginning to recognize some of the females by their numbered ear tags. On evenings when I am working late, I am grateful for a few moments of what I call the "NIH Safari," the view of a herd of deer eating grass and gracefully making their way down into the parking lot in front of our office building.

29. What is the best summary of the research presented in paragraphs 4, 5, and 6 about companion animals?
    A. Interventions requiring children to take personal responsibility for animals seems to lead them to take better care of themselves.
    B. Caring for and interacting with companion animals can provide therapeutic benefits for several conditions that impact children, such as by enhancing their self-monitoring, social functioning, and executive functioning skills.
    C. Children see greater health benefits when interacting with companion animals relative to engaging in similar control tasks that do not involve interactions with animals.
    D. The main benefit of companion animals for children with diabetes is helping them become more independent, while the main benefit for children with autism and ADHD is enhanced prosocial behaviors.

30. Which sentence best captures the author's perspective on the clinical value of human-animal interactions?
    A. "Indeed, companion animals—the dogs, cats, birds, and other pets that share our homes and our lives—significantly affect our health and well-being." (paragraph 2)
    B. "For the past 10 years, NICHD's Child Development and Behavior Branch has had a partnership with the WALTHAM® Centre for Pet Nutrition, a division of Mars, Inc., to research the impact of animal interactions on child health and development." (paragraph 3)
    C. "The researchers theorized that these interactions with dogs may help children focus their attention, thus improving their executive-functioning skills." (paragraph 6).
    D. "I am grateful for a few moments of what I call the "NIH Safari," the view of a herd of deer eating grass and gracefully making their way down into the parking lot in front of our office building." (paragraph 7)

The excerpt below is adapted from *Song of the Lark* by Willa Cather.

[1] Mr. Kronborg considered Thea a remarkable child; but so were all his children remarkable. If one of the business men downtown remarked to him that he "had a mighty bright little girl, there," he admitted it, and at once began to explain what a "long head for business" his son Gus had, or that Charley was "a natural electrician," and had put in a telephone from the house to the preacher's study behind the church.

[2] Mrs. Kronborg watched her daughter thoughtfully. She found her more interesting than her other children, and she took her more seriously, without thinking much about why she did so. The other children had to be guided, directed, kept from conflicting with one another. Charley and Gus were likely to want the same thing, and to quarrel about it. Anna often demanded unreasonable service from her older brothers; that they should sit up until after midnight to bring her home from parties when she did not like the youth who had offered himself as her escort; or that they should drive twelve miles into the country, on a winter night, to take her to a ranch dance, after they had been working hard all day. Gunner often got bored with his own clothes or stilts or sled, and wanted Axel's. But Thea, from the time she was a little thing, had her own routine. She kept out of every one's way, and was hard to manage only when the other children interfered with her. Then there was trouble indeed: bursts of temper which used to alarm Mrs. Kronborg. "You ought to know enough to let Thea alone. She lets you alone," she often said to the other children.

[3] One may have staunch friends in one's own family, but one seldom has admirers. Thea, however, had one in the person of her addle-pated aunt, Tillie Kronborg. In older countries, where dress and opinions and manners are not so thoroughly standardized as in our own West, there is a belief that people who are foolish about the more obvious things of life are apt to have peculiar insight into what lies beyond the obvious. The old woman who can never learn not to put the kerosene can on the stove, may yet be able to tell fortunes, to persuade a backward child to grow, to cure warts, or to tell people what to do with a young girl who has gone melancholy. Tillie's mind was a curious machine; when she was awake it went round like a wheel when the belt has slipped off, and when she was asleep she dreamed follies. But she had intuitions. She knew, for instance, that Thea was different from the other Kronborgs, worthy though they all were. Her romantic imagination found possibilities in her niece. When she was sweeping or ironing, or turning the ice-cream freezer at a furious rate, she often built up brilliant futures for Thea, adapting freely the latest novel she had read.

[4] Tillie made enemies for her niece among the church people because, at sewing societies and church suppers, she sometimes spoke vauntingly, with a toss of her head, just as if Thea's "wonderfulness" were an accepted fact in Moonstone, like Mrs. Archie's stinginess, or Mrs. Livery Johnson's duplicity. People declared that, on this subject, Tillie made them tired.

[5] Tillie belonged to a dramatic club that once a year performed in the Moonstone Opera House such plays as "Among the Breakers," and "The Veteran of 1812." Tillie played character parts, the flirtatious old maid or the spiteful *intrigante*. She used to study her parts up in the attic at home. While she was committing the lines, she got Gunner or Anna to hold the book for her, but when she began "to bring out the expression," as she said, she used, very timorously, to ask Thea to hold the book. Thea was usually—not always—agreeable about it. Her mother had told her that, since she had some influence with Tillie, it would be a good thing for them all if she could tone her down a shade and "keep her from taking on any

worse than need be." Thea would sit on the foot of Tillie's bed, her feet tucked under her, and stare at the silly text. "I wouldn't make so much fuss, there, Tillie," she would remark occasionally; "I don't see the point in it"; or, "What do you pitch your voice so high for? It don't carry half as well."

[6] "I don't see how it comes Thea is so patient with Tillie," Mrs. Kronborg more than once remarked to her husband. "She ain't patient with most people, but it seems like she's got a peculiar patience for Tillie."

[7] Tillie always coaxed Thea to go "behind the scenes" with her when the club presented a play, and help her with her make-up. Thea hated it, but she always went. She felt as if she had to do it. There was something in Tillie's adoration of her that compelled her. There was no family impropriety that Thea was so much ashamed of as Tillie's "acting" and yet she was always being dragged in to assist her. Tillie simply had her, there. She didn't know why, but it was so. There was a string in her somewhere that Tillie could pull; a sense of obligation to Tillie's misguided aspirations. The saloon-keepers had some such feeling of responsibility toward Spanish Johnny.

[8] The dramatic club was the pride of Tillie's heart, and her enthusiasm was the principal factor in keeping it together. Sick or well, Tillie always attended rehearsals, and was always urging the young people, who took rehearsals lightly, to "stop fooling and begin now." The young men—bank clerks, grocery clerks, insurance agents—played tricks, laughed at Tillie, and "put it up on each other" about seeing her home; but they often went to tiresome rehearsals just to oblige her. They were good-natured young fellows.

[9] By one amazing indiscretion Tillie very nearly lost her hold upon the Moonstone Drama Club. The club had decided to put on "The Drummer Boy of Shiloh," a very ambitious undertaking because of the many supers needed and the scenic difficulties of the act which took place in Andersonville Prison. The members of the club consulted together in Tillie's absence as to who should play the part of the drummer boy. It must be taken by a very young person, and village boys of that age are self-conscious and are not apt at memorizing. The part was a long one, and clearly it must be given to a girl. Some members of the club suggested Thea Kronborg, others advocated Lily Fisher. Lily's partisans urged that she was much prettier than Thea, and had a much "sweeter disposition." Nobody denied these facts. But there was nothing in the least boyish about Lily, and she sang all songs and played all parts alike. Lily's simper was popular, but it seemed not quite the right thing for the heroic drummer boy. Upping, the trainer, talked to one and another: "Lily's all right for girl parts," he insisted, "but you've got to get a girl with some ginger in her for this. Thea's got the voice, too. When she sings, 'Just Before the Battle, Mother,' she'll bring down the house."

[10] When all the members of the club had been privately consulted, they announced their decision to Tillie at the first regular meeting that was called to cast the parts. They expected Tillie to be overcome with joy, but, on the contrary, she seemed embarrassed. "I'm afraid Thea hasn't got time for that," she said jerkily. "She is always so busy with her music. Guess you'll have to get somebody else."

[11] The club lifted its eyebrows. Several of Lily Fisher's friends coughed. Mr. Upping flushed. The stout woman who always played the injured wife called Tillie's attention to the fact that this would be a fine opportunity for her niece to show what she could do. Her tone was condescending. The company broke up into groups and expressed their amazement. They confided to each other that Tillie was "just a little

off, on the subject of her niece," and agreed that it would be as well not to excite her further. Tillie got a cold reception at rehearsals for a long while afterward, and Thea had a crop of new enemies without even knowing it.

Read this except from paragraph 3.

She knew, for instance, that Thea was different from the other Kronborgs, worthy though they all were. Her romantic imagination found possibilities in her niece. When she was sweeping or ironing, or turning the ice-cream freezer at a furious rate, she often built up brilliant futures for Thea, adapting freely the latest novel she had read.

31. One way this excerpt contributes to a central idea of the passage is by
    A. revealing the respect Tillie has for Thea.
    B. introducing that Tillie has a contrary personality.
    C. indicating that Tillie has high expectations for herself in guiding Thea to achieve her potential.
    D. showing that Tillie knows what lies in store for Thea's future.

Reread the sentences below from paragraph 3.
Tillie's mind was a curious machine; when she was awake it went round like a wheel when the belt has slipped off, and when she was asleep she dreamed follies. But she had intuitions.
32. Which theme from the passage is best supported by these sentences?
    A. Possessing factual knowledge is less important than having a realistic appreciation of interpersonal situations.
    B. A seeming lack of certain basic abilities in some domains may belie a talent for understanding in others.
    C. Most people who display intuitive talents cannot also think logically.
    D. The mind is a wondrous entity that frequently embroils people in inner turmoil.

33. In context, which sentence from the passage provides the best support for the theme that many people find boastfulness unsettling?
    A. "She found her more interesting than her other children, and she took her more seriously, without thinking much about why she did so." (paragraph 2)
    B. "One may have staunch friends in one's own family, but one seldom has admirers." (paragraph 3)
    C. "People declared that, on this subject, Tillie made them tired." (paragraph 4)
    D. "Thea hated it, but she always went." (paragraph 7)

Reread the sentence below from paragraph 8.
The dramatic club was the pride of Tillie's heart, and her enthusiasm was the principal factor in keeping it together.

34. This sentence helps develop a central idea of this except by
    A. suggesting that people with misguided aspirations should be practical about their limitations.
    B. illustrating that individuals who are dedicated to an endeavor can be impactful even if their talents for the endeavors themselves are limited.
    C. showing that organizations whose success depends on the work of an ensemble will fail in the absence of a singular committed leader.
    D. revealing that it is important to never give up on one's dreams even if they seem unrealistic to others.

"The Brain May Actively Forget During Sleep" (NIH)

[1] Rapid eye movement, or REM, sleep is a fascinating period when most of our dreams are made. Now, in a study of mice, a team of Japanese and U.S. researchers show that it may also be a time when the brain actively forgets. Their results suggest that forgetting during sleep may be controlled by neurons found deep inside the brain that were previously known for making an appetite stimulating hormone. The study was funded by the National Institute of Neurological Disorders and Stroke (NINDS), part of the National Institutes of Health.

[2] "Ever wonder why we forget many of our dreams?" said Thomas Kilduff, Ph.D., director of the Center for Neuroscience at SRI International, Menlo Park, California, and a senior author of the study published in Science. "Our results suggest that the firing of a particular group of neurons during REM sleep controls whether the brain remembers new information after a good night's sleep."

[3] REM is one of several sleep stages the body cycles through every night. It first occurs about 90 minutes after falling asleep and is characterized by darting eyes, raised heart rates, paralyzed limbs, awakened brain waves and dreaming.

[4] For more than a century, scientists have explored the role of sleep in storing memories. While many have shown that sleep helps the brain store new memories, others, including Francis Crick, the co-discoverer of the DNA double helix, have raised the possibility that sleep – in particular REM sleep – may be a time when the brain actively eliminates or forgets excess information. Moreover, recent studies in mice have shown that during sleep – including REM sleep – the brain selectively prunes synaptic connections made between neurons involved in certain types of learning. However, until this study, no one had shown how this might happen.

[5] "Understanding the role of sleep in forgetting may help researchers better understand a wide range of memory-related diseases like post-traumatic stress disorder and Alzheimer's," said Janet He, Ph.D., program director, at NINDS. "This study provides the most direct evidence that REM sleep may play a role in how the brain decides which memories to store."

[6] Dr. Kilduff's lab and that of his collaborator, Akihiro Yamanaka, Ph.D., at Nagoya University in Japan, have spent years examining the role of a hormone called hypocretin/orexin in controlling sleep

and **narcolepsy**. Narcolepsy is a disorder that makes people feel excessively sleepy during the day and sometimes experience changes reminiscent of REM sleep, like loss of muscle tone in the limbs and hallucinations. Their labs and others have helped to show how narcolepsy may be linked to the loss of hypocretin/orexin-making neurons in the hypothalamus, a peanut-sized area found deep inside the brain.

[7] In this study, Dr. Kilduff worked with Dr. Yamanaka's lab and Akira Terao's, D.V.M., Ph.D., lab at Hokkaido University, Sapporo, Japan, to look at neighboring cells that produce melanin concentrating hormone (MCH), a molecule known to be involved in the control of both sleep and appetite. In agreement with previous studies, the researchers found that a majority (52.8%) of hypothalamic MCH cells fired when mice underwent REM sleep whereas about 35% fired only when the mice were awake and about 12% fired at both times.

[8] They also uncovered clues suggesting that these cells may play a role in learning and memory. Electrical recordings and tracing experiments showed that many of the hypothalamic MCH cells sent inhibitory messages, via long stringy axons, to the hippocampus, the brain's memory center.

[9] "From previous studies done in other labs, we already knew that MCH cells were active during REM sleep. After discovering this new circuit, we thought these cells might help the brain store memories," said Dr. Kilduff.

[10] To test this idea, the researchers used a variety of genetic tools to turn on and off MCH neurons in mice during memory tests. Specifically, they examined the role that MCH cells played in retention, the period after learning something new but before the new knowledge is stored, or consolidated, into long term memory. The scientists used several memory tests including one that assessed the ability of mice to distinguish between new and familiar objects.

[11] To their surprise, they found that "turning on" MCH cells during retention worsened memory whereas turning the cells off improved memories. For instance, activating the cells reduced the time mice spent sniffing around new objects compared to familiar ones, but turning the cells off had the opposite effect.

[12] Further experiments suggested that MCH neurons exclusively played this role during REM sleep. Mice performed better on memory tests when MCH neurons were turned off during REM sleep. In contrast, turning off the neurons while the mice were awake or in other sleep states had no effect on memory.

[13] "These results suggest that MCH neurons help the brain actively forget new, possibly, unimportant information," said Dr. Kilduff. "Since dreams are thought to primarily occur during REM sleep, the sleep stage when the MCH cells turn on, activation of these cells may prevent the content of a dream from being stored in the hippocampus – consequently, the dream is quickly forgotten."

[14] In the future, the researchers plan to explore whether this new circuit plays a role in sleep and memory disorders.

[15] This press release describes a basic research finding. Basic research increases our understanding of human behavior and biology, which is foundational to advancing new and better ways to prevent, diagnose, and treat disease. Science is an unpredictable and incremental process — each research advance builds on past discoveries, often in unexpected ways. Most clinical advances would not be possible without the knowledge of fundamental basic research.

35. The phrases "actively eliminates or forgets" (paragraph 4) and "actively forgets" (paragraph 13) convey a central idea of the passage in part by
    A. suggesting that people effortfully forget information they rather not remember, and this process is aided by sleep.
    B. explaining qualities that differentiate important information that is retained from more trivial information that is forgotten.
    C. implying that sleep discards information that is not vital to an organism's well-being.
    D. demonstrating that biological circuits to store and remove information have become more refined over time.

36. Which of the following is the best summary of the information in paragraph 4?
    A. It was always known that sleep helps consolidate memories, but it was only recently found that sleep can help play a role in forgetting excess information.
    B. A new study found compelling evidence of mechanisms that might underlie how sleep prunes synaptic connections associated with active forgetting.
    C. Though scientists have long studied sleep's role in enhancing memories, and later studies have shown its role in forgetting memories, a more recent study finally provided clues into the mechanisms by which the brain might induce forgetting during sleep.
    D. Sleep is usually thought of as helping people retain new information, but Francis Crick countered that sleep might actually help people forget trivial information instead, and a new study employed a novel methodology to explain why sleep promotes forgetting.

37. Which of the following best expresses a central idea of the scientists' findings in paragraphs 11 to 13?
    A. Suppressing MCH cell activity seems to reduce forgetfulness during all stages of sleep, but not wakefulness.
    B. Stimulation of MCH cells during REM sleep seems to weaken consolidation of new memories.
    C. Activation of MCH neurons during wakefulness seems to enhance retrieval-induced forgetting.
    D. MCH neurons are the only neurons modulating the extent to which new memories are forgotten or consolidated during REM sleep.

"Kansas: Fort Larned Historical Site" (National Park Service).

[1] Between 1822 and 1880, the Santa Fe Trail provided one of the most important overland transportation routes in America. The trail allowed millions of dollars of commercial traffic to flow between Independence, Missouri and Santa Fe, New Mexico. The flow of travelers, traders, and settlers moving west; the gold rushes of 1849 and 1858; and the acquisition of vast southwestern lands by the United States government after the Mexican War caused the American Indians of this region much turmoil. The great influx of people along the Santa Fe Trail disrupted their way of life and prompted

them to retaliate. Fort Larned was established to protect travelers, trail commerce, and the mail because of the rising tensions between American Indians and those using the trail. Fort Larned National Historic Site preserves the buildings, stories, and historical themes associated with Fort Larned.

[2] By October of 1859, rising conflicts between American Indians and westward travelers along the Santa Fe Trail prompted the United States army to build a military post to protect and maintain peaceful relations with everyone on the trail. This first post, called "Camp on Pawnee Fork" and eventually called "Camp Alert," was set up near Lookout Hill (now Jenkins hill) on the bank of the Pawnee River about five miles from its junction with the Arkansas River. Less than a year later, in June 1860, the fort was moved three miles further west, near the confluence of the Pawnee and Arkansas Rivers.

[3] At this location, the army constructed sod and adobe buildings, including an officer's quarters, storehouse and barracks, a guardhouse, a hospital, soldier's quarters, a bakery, a meat house, and a building housing a blacksmith, carpenter, and saddler shops. Named Fort Larned for Col. Benjamin R. Larned, the US Army paymaster, this fort would serve as one of the most important defense posts along the Santa Fe Trail.

[4] Between 1866 and 1868, the government replaced the original sod and adobe buildings of Fort Larned with more durable stone and timber buildings. Visitors can see these buildings today at the Fort Larned National Historic Site. The fort complex of nine buildings arranged around a 400' square parade ground includes barracks, a post hospital, two company officer's quarters, commanding officer's quarters, quartermaster storehouse, the old commissary, the new commissary, and a shops building. Visitors may walk around and explore seven of the nine buildings at the fort to get a glimpse of what it was like to live on a western fort during the 19th century.

[5] As one of the most important defense posts along the Santa Fe Trail, Fort Larned served many purposes. One purpose was to protect the flow of commerce along the Kansas segment of the trail. After the Chivington Massacre at Sand Creek in 1864, the War Department forbade travel beyond Fort Larned without armed escort. Fort Larned prepared detachments for the protection of mail stages and wagon trains.

[6] By 1867, Fort Larned became the base for Maj. Gen. Winfield S. Hancock's unsuccessful campaign against Plains Indian tribes. This campaign intended to intimidate and pacify the Indians with US military strength; however, it had the reverse effect and only intensified their hostilities. Hancock's campaign caused a general outbreak of raids by the Kiowa, Comanche, and Arapaho. To respond to these raids, Maj. Gen. Philip H. Sheridan ordered Lt. Col. George A. Custer into the area around Fort Larned. Eventually, Custer's campaign ended in the defeat of Black Kettle's Cheyenne at the Battle of the Washita on November 27, 1868. The Battle of the Washita ultimately ended American Indians' organized resistance around Fort Larned.

[7] While the military sought to prevent conflict along the trail, Fort Larned became the seat of other more peaceful efforts to reach out to the tribes throughout the 1860s. The fort served as the

headquarters and principal annuity distribution point of the Indian Bureau. The Indian Bureau attempted to find peaceful solutions to conflicts between American Indians and travelers, settlers, and adventurers. The treaties of Fort Wise (1861), the Little Arkansas (1865), and Medicine Lodge (1867) supported these peaceful principles.

[8] In these treaties, the United States government agreed to pay annuities to the Cheyenne, Arapahos, Kiowa, Comanche, and the Plains Apache tribes in return for keeping peace along the trail and for staying on their reservations. Annuities included items like bacon, wheat, flour, coffee, sugar, fresh beef, tobacco, clothing, beads, blankets, metal tools, cooking utensils, gunpowder, and lead bullets. Presented with the great opportunities the Indian Bureau created for commerce, traders flocked to the area surrounding Fort Larned and established the fort as a major trading center. By 1868, with the movement of the tribes to new reservations in Indian Territory, Fort Larned's role as an agent for the Indian Bureau ended.

[9] Fort Larned's final function was to protect railroad construction crews. The building of the railroad ultimately led to the end of the use of the Santa Fe Trail, which the fort was originally constructed to protect. After the Civil War ended, Americans renewed their energetic push westward, laying thousands of miles of railroad track. The worn dirt-road ruts of the Santa Fe Trail could not compete with the high powered, fast, and efficient railroad. Fort Larned helped to protect the workers who completed laying the railroad line in Kansas by 1872. Nearly six years later, in July 1878, the military abandoned Fort Larned, because it was no longer necessary for protection and keeping peaceful relations along the Santa Fe Trail.

38. Which statement best captures the author's point of view about Fort Larned's historical significance?
    A. "Visitors may walk around and explore seven of the nine buildings at the fort to get a glimpse of what it was like to live on a western fort during the 19th century." (paragraph 4).
    B. "As one of the most important defense posts along the Santa Fe Trail, Fort Larned served many purposes." (paragraph 5)
    C. "While the military sought to prevent conflict along the trail, Fort Larned became the seat of other more peaceful efforts to reach out to the tribes throughout the 1860s." (paragraph 7)
    D. "Nearly six years later, in July 1878, the military abandoned Fort Larned, because it was no longer necessary for protection and keeping peaceful relations along the Santa Fe Trail." (paragraph 9)

39. The central idea that the Santa Fe Trail contributed to "rising tensions between American Indians and those using the trail" is best conveyed through a description of
    A. the diverse functions of the trail.
    B. specific ways that the trail disrupted the daily lives of American Indians.
    C. armed conflicts along the trail and efforts by the United States government to minimize them.
    D. chilly negotiations between the military and representatives of the American Indians.

40. Which of the following summarizes the experience of the Indian Bureau at Fort Larned?
    A. Discouraged by the failure of military efforts to establish peace along the Santa Fe Trail, the Indian Bureau was established to provide more peaceful solutions.
    B. The Indian Bureau at Fort Larned successfully negotiated treaties with various American Indian tribes in which the United States agreed to pay them annuities in exchange for maintaining peaceful relations along the Santa Fe Trail, and, when many of the tribes settled on reservations, the fort no longer needed to function as an agent of the Indian Bureau.
    C. The Plains Indians tribes negotiated with the Indian Bureau at Fort Larned for annuities such as food, clothing, and tools in exchange for staying on their reservations and not attacking travelers along the Santa Fe Trail.
    D. The Indian Bureau came to Fort Larned in the wake of military conflicts between American Indians and traders along the Santa Fe Trail, and it left when the violence was no longer a threat.

41. The details in paragraphs 7 and 8 contribute to a central idea of the passage by showing that the United States government
    A. believed that Fort Larned's central location made it an ideal commercial trading center.
    B. valued the input of Indigenous tribes because it allowed tribes to dictate the terms by which they would agree to end military hostilities.
    C. attempted to instill American Indian tribes with Western values through the exchange of goods and ideas.
    D. understood military tactics designed to end hostilities between American Indian tribes and others using the trail were insufficient.

The excerpt below is from "On a Mountain Trail" by Henry Perry Robinson

[1] We had no warning. It was as if they had deliberately lain in ambush for us at the turn in the trail. They seemed suddenly and silently to rise on all sides of the sleigh at once. It is not often that the gray timber-wolves, or "black wolves," as the mountaineers call them, are seen hunting in packs, though the animal is plentiful enough among the foot-hills of the Rockies. As a general rule they are met with singly or in pairs. At the end of a long and severe winter, however, they sometimes come together in bands of fifteen or twenty; and every old mountaineer has a tale to tell perhaps of his own narrow escape from one of their fierce packs, perhaps of some friend of his who started one day in winter to travel alone from camp to camp, and whose clean-picked bones were found beside the trail long afterward.

[2] It was in February, and we, Gates and myself, were driving from Livingston, Montana, to Gulch City, fifty miles away, with a load of camp supplies — a barrel of flour and some bacon, coffee, and beans; a blanket or two, and some dynamite (or "giant powder," as the miners call it) for blasting; a few picks and shovels, and other odds and ends. We had started at daybreak. By five o'clock in the evening, with some ten miles more to travel, the worst of the trail was passed. There had been little snow that winter, so that even in the gulches and on the bottoms

the exposed ground was barely covered; while, on the steep slopes, snow had almost entirely disappeared, leaving only ragged patches of white under overhanging boughs, and a thin coating of ice in the inequalities of the hard, frost-bound trail, making a treacherous footing for the horses' hoofs.

[3] The first forty miles of the road had lain entirely over hills — zigzagging up one side of a mountain only to zigzag down the other — with the dense growth of pine and tamarack and cedar on both sides, wreathed here and there in mist. But at last we were clear of the foothills and reached the level. The tall forest trees gave place to a wilderness of thick underbrush, lying black in the evening air, and the horses swung contentedly from the steep grade into the level trail, where at last they could let their legs move freely in a trot.

[4] Hardly had they settled into their stride, however, when both animals shied violently to the left side of the trail. A moment later they plunged back to the right side so suddenly as almost to throw me off into the brush.

[5] Then, out of the earth and the shadow of the bushes, the grim, dark forms seemed to rise on all sides of us. There was not a sound — not a snap nor a snarl; but in the gathering twilight of the February evening, we saw them moving noiselessly over the thin coat of snow which covered the ground. In the uncertain light, and moving as rapidly as we did, it was impossible to guess how many they were. An animal which was one moment in plain sight, running abreast of the horses, would, the next moment, be lost in the shadow of the bushes, while two more dark, silent forms would edge up to take its place. So, on both sides of us, they kept appearing and disappearing. In the rear, half a dozen jostled one another to push up nearer to the flying sleigh — a black mass that filled the whole width of the trail. Behind those again, others, less clearly visible, crossed and recrossed the roadway from side to side. They might be twenty in all — or thirty — or forty. It was impossible to tell.

[6] For a minute I did not think of danger. The individual wolf is the most skulking and cowardly of animals, and only by some such experience as we had that night does a hunter learn that wolves can be dangerous. But soon the stories of the old mountaineers came crowding into my mind, as the horses, terrified and snorting, plunged wildly along the narrow trail, while the ghostlike forms glided patiently alongside — appearing, disappearing, and reappearing. The silent pertinacity[3] with which, apparently making no effort, they kept pace beside the flying horses was horrible. Even a howl or a yelp or a growl would have been a relief. But not so much as the sound of their footfalls on the snow was to be heard.

[7] At the first sight of the wolves, I had drawn my revolver from the leather case in which it hung suspended from my belt. Gates, handling the reins, was entirely occupied with the

---

[3] perseverance

horses; but I knew, without need of words, that he saw our pursuers and understood the peril as well as I.

[8] "Have you your gun?" I shouted in his ear.

Reread the excerpt below from paragraph 6.

Even a howl or a yelp or a growl would have been a relief. But not so much as the sound of their footfalls on the snow was to be heard.

42. How does this sentence reveal the narrator's perspective about his first encounter with a wolf pack?
    A. It emphasizes that the stealth of the wolves magnified the severity of an already tense situation.
    B. It suggests he was frustrated by the weather conditions that made for poor visibility that day.
    C. It provides a comparison between different methods by which wolves make their presence known.
    D. It highlights the importance of understanding one's enemies' tactics in order to lob an effective defense

43. Which of the following is the best summary of paragraph 3?
    A. The narrator's horse and his companion's horse each experienced a great deal of fear on the forested steep foothills during the first 40 miles of the trek because they could not see where they were going, but they experienced welcome relief at the end of the trail when the large trees no longer occluded their view.
    B. The first four fifths of the road from Livingston to Gulch City included treacherous ice, but conditions were more manageable after the narrator and his companion made it past the thick underbrush.
    C. The first forty miles of the narrator and his companion's trip from Livingston to Gulch City was on a zigzagging, steep, forested hill, presenting challenges for the horses, but the horses could finally trot freely once they reached the level part of the trail.
    D. The zigzagging pine growth on a hill made it difficult for the narrator and his companion's horses to settle into a trot, but the lack of ice and improved visibility at the end of the trail broke the tension and improved their mood.

44. Which of the following is the best summary of the wolves' actions in paragraph 5?
    A. The wolves launched a stealth attack on the horses, alternately biting them and retreating into the bushes.
    B. The wolves kept pace with the horses, snarling at them at random intervals, causing the horses to experience fear.
    C. The wolves remained completely invisible in the darkness of the night and the protection of the bushes, watching the narrator and his companion intently as they followed them along the trail.
    D. The wolves moved silently as a large pack, appearing and disappearing around the riders and their horses, keeping pace with their movements.

Kweller Prep NEW SHSAT Grammar and Reading

Week 4

Week 4: Vocabulary Questions

Some questions will ask you to determine the meaning of a particular word. To answer these questions, use the context of the entire sentence or the sentences surrounding it to determine its meaning. Note that more than one choice will probably be a correct meaning of the word in some context.

Consider the following sentences.

1) **Cause-and-Effect Clue:** The judge has a reputation for making **fair** rulings. He is thus regarded as a beacon of justice.

In this case, fair means "just" or "equitable." We are given the effect of his rulings (he is seen as a beacon, or model, of justice), and the word "fair" is the cause for why he is viewed that way.

2) **Definition/Synonym Clue:** It will take a **fair** amount of time to complete the essay: it requires *considerable* thought and planning.

In this case fair means "considerable," or "moderately large." It will take an appreciable amount of time to plan the essay before writing it.

3) **Contrast Clue:** His project was **fair**, but it was not exceptional enough to qualify him for a raise.

In this case "fair" means "adequate" or "**not** excellent or poor." The project was not or excellent enough to earn him a raise.

The organization should eagerly embrace reforms that minimize the negative environmental impacts of its production methods.

Sample: In the sentence above, the word "embrace" means
  A. hug affectionately.
  B. adopt readily.
  C. enclose tightly.
  D. comprise partially.

In context, reforms can be adopted (taken up). Choice B is correct. Choice A is the most common meaning of embrace, but it is incorrect because reforms are abstract ideas that cannot be physically hugged in the way people hug each other.

Drill 1

Part 1: Select the choice that most nearly has the same meaning as the bolded word.

1. The company faced **critical** financial problems after it lost one of its biggest customers.
   A. serious
   B. essential
   C. judgmental
   D. monetary

2. The **element** of surprise undoubtedly gave the small army a tactical advantage over its unsuspecting enemies.
   A. ingredient
   B. factor
   C. hodgepodge
   D. qualification

3. Because the Broadway show is so popular, one must **book** seats two years in advance.
   A. distinguish
   B. reserve
   C. read
   D. entertain

4. What was supposed to be a peaceful protest **approached** the level of a violent riot.
   A. approximated
   B. loomed
   C. contacted
   D. handled

5. The actress is often complimented for her **fine** sense of comedic timing.
   A. delicate
   B. adequate
   C. keen
   D. overelaborate

6. After a **clear** pattern of corrupt activity was noted by the press, the politician was forced to resign.
   A. cloudless
   B. flawless
   C. obvious
   D. pleasant

7. The forensic evidence **allows** the detectives to draw firm conclusions.
   A. tolerates
   B. enables
   C. endures
   D. grants

Week 4

8. It is not in Finley's **nature** to get into arguments with people she barely knows. She prefers to avoid drama at all costs.
    A. environment
    B. capability
    C. description
    D. character

9. Many people criticized the leader for his rash behavior, arguing it was not **becoming** of someone who is expected to act calmly and rationally.
    A. fitting
    B. developing
    C. growing
    D. occurring

10. We avoided disaster by **sheer** luck; there was no skill on our part.
    A. fierce
    B. pure
    C. sudden
    D. precipitous

Part 2: Select the best answer to each question.

The Grateful Dead is an iconic band known for its innovative music style. However, it is the band's unique business model that has recently been gaining attention from scholars. The band was ahead of its time in the ways it chose to do business. It was not afraid to improvise and shake up conventional norms to meet the needs of its clientele. For example, by touring year-round instead of focusing mostly
5   on record sales while only touring for a limited portion of the year, as most of its peers did, the band helped build a brand and a loyal base.

The tactics that the Grateful Dead adopted have had an influence on American businesses. For example, the band gave special treatment to its most loyal fans by giving them access to concert tickets across the country before announcing their concerts to the general public. In the 1980s, many American businesses
10   adopted this consumer-oriented model, focusing on providing their clients with quality products and services. Before that, "the customer comes first" mentality was not the norm. The band members also allowed people to record their concerts free of charge. Rather than suing people who recorded and distributed their recordings to others for free, they took advantage of the publicity that they gained by having their music spread. As a result of their increased popularity, they made more money in
15   merchandise and concert sales. Today, many companies embrace this principle. Clients who receive "free stuff" from companies are more inclined to give these companies their business.

In addition, the band's "in-sourcing" approach to management contrasted with the outsourcing model so common throughout corporate America. Many firms will hire contractors from other companies to perform certain business tasks, a practice that sometimes leads to conflict. The Grateful Dead preferred to hire as many people as possible to work in-house for the band itself. Thus, the band had more control over its product and was able to better take care of its employees. As a result, it was better situated to meet the needs of its customers. Today, many companies hire in-house people when possible. For example, a company might hire a lawyer as a fulltime employee rather than make a contract with a separate law firm to do its legal work.

11. Which of the following phrases has the same meaning or most nearly has the same meaning as the word "base" in line 6?
    A. group of followers
    B. bottom layer
    C. pedestal
    D. center of operations

12. Which of the following phrases has the same meaning or most nearly has the same meaning as the word "adopted" in lines 7 and 10?
    A. legally take
    B. accept responsibility for
    C. formally notified
    D. implemented

13. Which of the following phrases has the same meaning or most nearly has the same meaning as the word "inclined" in line 16?
    A. sloped
    B. prone
    C. tilting
    D. put off

Mastodons, the now extinct relatives of the modern elephant, inhabited North and Central America until their extinction about 10,000 years ago. These mysterious animals have captured the attention of scientists and ordinary people alike. President Thomas Jefferson, a scientific expert in his own right, commissioned a team to collect mastodon fossils for him in order to learn more about these fascinating creatures.

The name "mastodon" means "breast tooth," in reference to the appearance of its molars. Mastodons had low-domed heads and large, long tusks. The tusks may have assisted the mastodons in feeding and competing with other animals. Mastodons were herbivorous creatures, whose diet was obtained mostly by browsing (feeding on high-growing plants). They also likely got some food by grazing (feeding on grass and low vegetation). Though they did not have many predators due to their large size, their

Week 4   163 predators included saber-toothed cats and lions. There is also evidence that humans hunted them. For example, an arrowhead was found among the bones of one American mastodon.

People sometimes confuse mastodons with their more famous cousin, the wooly mammoth, though modern reconstructions based on partial skeleton remains show that they are only distantly related. One notable difference between the two cousins was the shape of their teeth. While the mammoths had ridged molars suitable for eating grass, the mastodons had molars with cone-like cusps that were perfect for cutting trees, twigs, and shrubs. Carbon from the teeth of mastodons and mammoths provide scientists with a treasure trove of information, confirming their different dietary preferences.

Scientists speculate that mastodons may have been social creatures based on studies of their anatomical similarities to elephants, though scientists obviously cannot be sure about exactly how they behaved. Studies of mastodon bone sites suggest that they lived in mixed herds of adult females and young mastodons. The long maturation periods may indicate that mastodons required care for a long period of time. Although there is some speculation that mastodons were migratory creatures, some scientists now believe that many of them did not roam. Their habitats often had everything they needed to live comfortably.

There is still some debate over the primary cause of the mastodon's extinction. It has generally been thought that human pressures on their populations were the main culprit, though climate change may have been a more important factor. In 2016, a nearly complete mastodon skeleton preserved during the Ice Age, the most complete skeleton discovered in decades, was found in the Great Lakes region. Analysis of this skeleton revealed that many of the bones were in the same position relative to each other as when it was alive, suggesting that natural causes were not the cause of death. It is more likely that this mastodon's death served a more practical purpose. Specifically, it was probably stored by hunters as a source of meat under a pond that no longer exists.

14. Which of the following phrases has the same meaning or most nearly has the same meaning as the word "captured" in line 2?
    A. take over
    B. depict
    C. grab hold of
    D. trap

15. Which of the following phrases has the same meaning or most nearly has the same meaning as the word "primary" in line 26?
    A. first
    B. main
    C. exclusive
    D. initial

Halloween has long been a popular holiday in many countries. It is typically celebrated on October 31st. To the modern person, this holiday frequently conjures up associations with trick or treating, costumes, and haunted houses. But the holiday as we know it today has a long and interesting history.

Halloween has its roots in the Irish festival Samhain, which was celebrated as far back as the 10th century. Samhain was one of several holidays that signaled the end of the harvest season, as people began stocking up supplies for the winter. It was believed that on October 31st, the window between the worlds of the living and the dead opened. Thus, "scary" costumes and masks were often worn to prevent evil spirts from causing harm to people and their crops. People also made lanterns out of vegetables, such as turnips or pumpkins, to ward off evil spirits. These lanterns were the likely inspiration behind modern-day jack-o-lanterns. It was also believed that spirits of the deceased would come visit their families, seeking hospitality. Thus, people often left out food and drinks for the spirits of their family members.

It was not until the 19th century that Samhain and the similar holiday All Hallows' Eve merged to become what is now known as Halloween. The holiday first came to America after a wave of Irish and Scottish immigration. Though the holiday was originally confined to immigrant communities, it eventually became a mainstream holiday throughout the United States that is now associated with a variety of traditions, such as bonfires, apple bobbing, haunted houses, and scary movies. Halloween is largely a secular holiday with less of a religious dimension than the holidays from which it emerged.

Perhaps the most noteworthy Halloween tradition is "trick or treating." Children go to door to door dressed in costumes saying "trick or treat" in expectation of receiving candy ("the treat"). Though not usually done in practice, the alternative to a treat is for the children to play a "trick" on the owner of the house if no treat is given. Many countries expressly discourage or outlaw playing tricks due to the damage and disruption they cause. Trick or treating is loosely based on the medieval European practices of "guising" and "souling." Guising was a practice whereby children dressed in costumes would go from door to door asking for coins or food in exchange for putting on entertaining performances. Similarly, "souling" involved beggars asking rich people for food ("soul cakes") on feast days such as All Hallows' Eve. By the 1950s, trick or treating was firmly established as a kid-friendly holiday in the United States. Today, adults are generally expected to go grocery shopping for treats in preparation for Halloween.

Interestingly, Halloween is not just a kid holiday anymore. While there aren't too many adults trick or treating (unless they are accompanying children), many adults relish the opportunity to get dressed up. Some offices even encourage their staff to wear costumes on Halloween. The fun and fantastical holiday can give adults a needed escape from dwelling on the stresses of their lives.

16. Which of the following phrases has the same meaning or most nearly has the same meaning as the word "conjures" in line 2?
    A. mesmerize
    B. charms
    C. brings to mind
    D. perform tricks

17. Which of the following phrases has the same meaning or most nearly has the same meaning as the word "wave" in line 14?
    A. upsurge
    B. gesture
    C. curl
    D. flutter

18. Which of the following phrases has the same meaning or most nearly has the same meaning as the word "dimension" in line 18?
    A. heaviness
    B. measurement
    C. aspect
    D. location

In the past, scientists conceptualized taste as linked to taste buds in the mouth, which detect sweet, salty, sour, and bitter flavors. Now, it is clear that taste is an experience that also encompasses smell, touch, and even sight. The cortical workload of the brain processes the majority of information visually, so it makes sense that our eyes play a role in how we perceive food.

5   The appearance of food, including the color of the plates on which it is found, shapes our expectations. In one sense, this is protective. For example, we know not to eat food that looks like it can make us sick, like rotten apples or moldy bread. We may also avoid foods that look similar to those that have made us sick in the past. Visual cues can also assist us in identifying certain features of foods. For example, milk experts are better able to determine the fat content of milk when they can see it.

10 The appearance of food not only impacts expectations, but it can also affect how we actually experience certain flavors. If we try a food that looks disgusting, it may be "too late" to enjoy it because of our brain's expectation that it will taste bad affects how we actually perceive the food once it is in our mouths. Though sight is not technically part of taste, it can trigger our taste buds. The color of food also affects how we experience it. For example, if an apple-flavored drink is colored red, our brains may
15 perceive it to be sweeter than it actually is, since we associate red with sweetness.

In one study, subjects who tried an orange-flavored drink while blindfolded rarely identified the flavor correctly. When they could see that the color of the drink was orange, they almost always were correct. When the orange drink was dyed green, some subjects mistakenly identified it as lime-flavored. When it was not dyed green, no subjects made this mistake. Clearly, the color of food can influence how we
20 perceive taste.

The color of food can even trick so-called "experts." For instance, in a classic experiment, wine experts who tasted white wine that was secretly dyed red used descriptors characteristic of actual red wines. Their expectations for how red wine should taste may have triggered their brains to detect flavors that

Week 4

weren't actually present in the wine. When the wine was in opaque glasses, the experts were more accurate in describing the wine.

The food industry is well aware of how our expectations shape how we taste food. For that reason, they alter the appearance of food and use colorimeters to make sure that foods are perfectly hued. For example, customers may be more inclined to purchase apples that have been colored red, believing them to be sweeter. Companies that make plant-based meat-like products often dye the food brown since customers are not "prepared" to eat green meat. People generally associate green meat with meat that has gone bad. Nevertheless, while we associate certain colors with certain foods, this learning happens from experience. Companies can effectively market flavors that counter our expectations to attract customers, as exemplified by green ketchup and blue lemonade.

Even though our eyes shape how we perceive taste, they don't tell the whole story. The brain and other senses, such as smell, can override the ugly appearance of certain foods. Many foods, such as chilies, sausages, and stews, are popular among people who do not necessarily find them visually appealing. For example, while a beef stew might look "gross" to someone, if it has a pleasant smell and one has positive memories associated with its taste, these factors take precedence. In other cases, a desire to be adventurous may override one's initial revulsion to a certain food's appearance. This is encouraging news to many people, including parents who want their kids to eat healthy foods that look less than appetizing.

19. Which of the following phrases has the same meaning or most nearly has the same meaning as the word "encompasses" in line 2?
    A. grapples
    B. determines
    C. rejects
    D. includes

20. Which of the following phrases has the same meaning or most nearly has the same meaning as the word "associate" in line 31?
    A. mix
    B. connect
    C. sever
    D. assort

21. Which of the following phrases has the same meaning or most nearly has the same meaning as the word "counter" in line 32?
    A. oppose
    B. determine
    C. frustrate
    D. respond to

Sea stars, or starfish, are known for their distinctive appearance. With their arms connected to their round body, giving them the appearance of stars, it is no wonder that many people are allured by these creatures. Beyond their dazzling features, sea stars play a particularly important role in maintaining the balance of ecosystems.

Despite their name and aquatic habitat, sea stars are not fish. Rather, they are echinoderms, closely related to other animals such as sea urchins and sand dollars. There are thousands of species of sea stars living in diverse habitats, from tropical waters to colder regions of the ocean.

Sea stars are carnivores, and their size is dependent on how much they eat. Sea stars eat prey outside their bodies. They use suction tubes on their feet to open up shells of shellfish, such as clams and mussels. Their stomachs then leave their bodies and secrete enzymes that break down the tissue of the shellfish. Then the stomachs return to the sea stars' bodies. The madreporite at the center of the star filters water through its body. The water that filters through their bodies acts similarly to "blood" in other animals. Most of the major organs of the sea star are located on the arms. For example, eyespots on the arm help them detect light. Interestingly, sea stars have no brain. Rather, their nervous system is spread throughout their arms. While most sea stars have five arms, there are some with more. Sea stars have calcified skin to protect them from predators, such as crabs and seagulls. Many come in color variations that allow them to hide among the coral reef, giving them another avenue of protection. The ridges and bumps on many starfish actually complement the spikes found in many coral reefs. Even when sea stars are attacked or are wounded, they do not necessarily die. Most sea stars can regenerate missing limbs. Thus, a sea star might sacrifice an arm to escape a predator, only to regrow it.

Sea stars are considered keystone species by scientists because of the role they play in maintaining the balance of ecosystems. They keep the population of their prey under control. For example, if sea stars are removed from an ecosystem, populations of mussels, urchins, and barnacles may grow uncontrollably, thus pushing out other organisms from the ecosystem. One danger posed by increased sea urchin populations is the destruction of kelp forests on which sea urchins feed. When sea stars keep the sea urchin population in check, kelp forests thrive. Kelp forests are vital to the health of marine ecosystems in part because they provide a habitat for many fish. Kelp forests also help the environment. Most scientists believe that excessive carbon dioxide in the atmosphere is responsible for global warming. Kelp forests absorb carbon dioxide from the atmosphere and release oxygen into the air.

Unfortunately, there are many threats to sea stars. Some companies harvest them for fertilizer and poultry feed. Another threat is sea star wasting syndrome, a disease whereby sea stars turn to goo. The disease is likely caused by a virus. It is believed that pollution and warmer waters associated with human-induced climate change may be contributing to the spread of this disease, which has affected as many as 98% of starfish in certain populations.

Some people think that we need to treat sea stars like endangered species for their own protection. In some locations, there are laws restricting how many live sea stars that can be collected by humans from waters. Scientists are also trying to better understand the environmental factors that contribute to sea star viral infections so that we can better protect them. The discovery of young sea stars in areas where adult populations had been thought to be wiped out brings renewed hope that their populations will rebound.

22. Which of the following phrases has the same meaning or most nearly has the same meaning as the word "allured" in line 2?
    A. shocked
    B. horrified
    C. charmed
    D. confused

23. Which of the following phrases has the same meaning or most nearly has the same meaning as the word "avenue" in line 17?
    A. street
    B. means
    C. hole
    D. obstacle

24. Which of the following phrases has the same meaning or most nearly has the same meaning as the word "rebound" in line 40?
    A. reflect
    B. recover
    C. diminish
    D. stabilize

If you've ever gone to a doctor's office or hospital, you've probably encountered nurses who often perform important medical tasks, such as taking blood, administering medicine, and monitoring patients' health. The jobs of nurses today reflect the deep influence of Florence Nightingale, who transformed the once-derided job into an honorable medical profession.

Born to a wealthy Italian family in 1820, Nightingale's mother encouraged her to marry someone in her station, as other upper-class women of her time did. However, Nightingale had different plans in mind. While on a tour of Europe, Nightingale connected with Mary Clarke. Clarke generally looked down on other upper-class women and instead spent most of her time with male intellectuals. Sensing that Nightingale was intelligent in her own right, Clarke took a liking to Nightingale, and the two remained in contact for decades. Clarke taught Nightingale that women can be regarded as equal to their male counterparts. When Nightingale decided to pursue a career in nursing, she did so despite the protests of her mother, who wanted Nightingale to instead focus on building a family of her own. At that time, taking on a job was seen as menial labor for upper class women.

Nightingale gained prominence during the Crimean War when she treated soldiers. She was struck by the fact that more soldiers were dying of disease than battle wounds. She noticed the unsanitary

conditions of the wards and posited that they were making the soldiers the sick and contributing to the spread of the disease. Nightingale improved sanitary conditions in the wards, having them scrubbed thoroughly and providing soldiers with clean linens. She also encouraged personal hygiene practices, such as handwashing. As a result of Nightingale's efforts, the death rate in the hospitals declined
20 sharply. She became known as "the lady with the lamp" to the soldiers, as she frequently patrolled the wards with her lamp, checking on the soldiers, whom she reassured with her presence. Nightingale also argued to the Royal Commission that poor ventilation, overcrowding, and bad drainage systems contributed to the spread of infections. The Sanitary Commission fixed the ventilation and drainage systems, further contributing to reductions in death rates. Her influence on the sanitary design of
25 hospitals and homes is still seen today.

Nightingale drew from ideas about nutrition and psychology when treating her patients. She believed that poor nutrition contributed to disease and a decline in overall health. She made sure that soldiers had diverse and appealing dietary options. Nightingale also recognized that mental health was closely linked to physical health. She had soldiers write letters so that they could express themselves
30 emotionally. She provided them with books, classrooms, and libraries to stimulate their minds. Thus, Nightingale was innovative in her focus on treating the whole person.

Although Nightingale is most known for her contributions to nursing, she also has a somewhat underreported legacy in the field of statistics. Nightingale scrupulously collected data during her time as a nurse, and her statistical findings helped convince the Royal Commission on the Health of the Army to
35 accept many of her policy recommendations. Her study of the sanitation system in India led to successful public health reforms that reduced deaths. Nightingale was one of the first people to make use of the pie chart, and she even helped developed the polar area diagram, a type of statistical chart. Nightingale was the first female elected to the Royal Statistical Society.

In 1860, Nightingale put her ideas into practice on a grander scale by establishing the Nightingale School
40 for Nurses, the first school for nurses connected to a medical school program and hospital. Students would typically train for one year, taking classes and working with patients. The Nightingale school serves as a model for other nursing schools. Though the profession of nursing has evolved over the years, Nightingale's influence on the profession is enduring and she will continue to be regarded as a heroine for her contributions.

25. Which of the following phrases has the same meaning or most nearly has the same meaning as the word "derided" in line 4?
    A. coveted
    B. disdained
    C. lauded
    D. obsolete

26. Which of the following phrases has the same meaning or most nearly has the same meaning as the word "station" in line 6?
    A. social class
    B. location
    C. desire
    D. profession

27. Which of the following phrases has the same meaning or most nearly has the same meaning as the word "scale" in line 39?
    A. calibration
    B. level
    C. balance
    D. covering

The excerpt below is from *The Story of My Life* by Helen Keller.

The most important day I remember in all my life is the one on which my teacher, Anne Mansfield Sullivan, came to me. I am filled with wonder when I consider the immeasurable contrasts between the two lives which it connects. It was the third of March, 1887, three months before I was seven years old. On the afternoon of that eventful day, I stood on the porch, dumb, expectant. I guessed vaguely from
5   my mother's signs and from the hurrying to and fro in the house that something unusual was about to happen, so I went to the door and waited on the steps. The afternoon sun penetrated the mass of honeysuckle that covered the porch, and fell on my upturned face. My fingers lingered almost unconsciously on the familiar leaves and blossoms which had just come forth to greet the sweet southern spring. I did not know what the future held of marvel or surprise for me. Anger and bitterness
10 had preyed upon me continually for weeks and a deep languor had succeeded this passionate struggle.

Have you ever been at sea in a dense fog, when it seemed as if a tangible white darkness shut you in, and the great ship, tense and anxious, groped her way toward the shore with plummet and sounding-line, and you waited with beating heart for something to happen? I was like that ship before my education began, only I was without compass or sounding-line, and had no way of knowing how near
15 the harbor was. "Light! give me light!" was the wordless cry of my soul, and the light of love shone on me in that very hour.

I felt approaching footsteps, I stretched out my hand as I supposed to my mother. Someone took it, and I was caught up and held close in the arms of her who had come to reveal all things to me, and, more than all things else, to love me. The morning after my teacher came she led me into her room and gave
20 me a doll. The little blind children at the Perkins Institution had sent it and Laura Bridgman had dressed it; but I did not know this until afterward. When I had played with it a little while, Miss Sullivan slowly spelled into my hand the word "d-o-l-l." I was at once interested in this finger play and tried to imitate it. When I finally succeeded in making the letters correctly I was flushed with childish pleasure and pride. Running downstairs to my mother I held up my hand and made the letters for doll. I did not know that I
25 was spelling a word or even that words existed; I was simply making my fingers go in monkey-like imitation. In the days that followed I learned to spell in this uncomprehending way a great many words, among them pin, hat, cup and a few verbs like sit, stand and walk. But my teacher had been with me several weeks before I understood that everything has a name.

Week 4

One day, while I was playing with my new doll, Miss Sullivan put my big rag doll into my lap also, spelled "d-o-l-l" and tried to make me understand that "d-o-l-l" applied to both. Earlier in the day we had had a tussle over the words "m-u-g" and "w-a-t-e-r." Miss Sullivan had tried to impress it upon me that "m-u-g" is mug and that "w-a-t-e-r" is water, but I persisted in confounding the two. In despair she had dropped the subject for the time, only to renew it at the first opportunity. I became impatient at her repeated attempts and, seizing the new doll, I dashed it upon the floor. I was keenly delighted when I felt the fragments of the broken doll at my feet. Neither sorrow nor regret followed my passionate outburst. I had not loved the doll. In the still, dark world in which I lived there was no strong sentiment or tenderness. I felt my teacher sweep the fragments to one side of the hearth, and I had a sense of satisfaction that the cause of my discomfort was removed. She brought me my hat, and I knew I was going out into the warm sunshine. This thought, if a wordless sensation may be called a thought, made me hop and skip with pleasure.

We walked down the path to the well-house, attracted by the fragrance of the honeysuckle with which it was covered. Someone was drawing water and my teacher placed my hand under the spout. As the cool stream gushed over one hand she spelled into the other the word water, first slowly, then rapidly. I stood still, my whole attention fixed upon the motions of her fingers. Suddenly I felt a misty consciousness as of something forgotten—a thrill of returning thought; and somehow the mystery of language was revealed to me. I knew then that "w-a-t-e-r" meant the wonderful cool something that was flowing over my hand. That living word awakened my soul, gave it light, hope, joy, set it free! There were barriers still, it is true, but barriers that could in time be swept away.

I left the well-house eager to learn. Everything had a name, and each name gave birth to a new thought. As we returned to the house every object which I touched seemed to quiver with life. That was because I saw everything with the strange, new sight that had come to me. On entering the door, I remembered the doll I had broken. I felt my way to the hearth and picked up the pieces. I tried vainly to put them together. Then my eyes filled with tears; for I realized what I had done, and for the first time I felt repentance and sorrow.

I learned a great many new words that day. I do not remember what they all were; but I do know that mother, father, sister, teacher were among them—words that were to make the world blossom for me, "like Aaron's rod, with flowers." It would have been difficult to find a happier child than I was as I lay in my crib at the close of that eventful day and lived over the joys it had brought me, and for the first time longed for a new day to come.

28. Which of the following phrases has the same meaning or most nearly has the same meaning as the word "confounding" in line 32?
    A. imitating
    B. comparing
    C. confusing
    D. asserting

29. Which of the following phrases has the same meaning or most nearly has the same meaning as the word "sensation" in line 39?
    A. spectacle
    B. perception
    C. commotion
    D. smash

30. Which of the following phrases has the same meaning or most nearly has the same meaning as the word "vainly" in line 52?
    A. ineffectively
    B. hollowly
    C. arrogantly
    D. casually

The story below is "Hearts and Hands" by O'Henry.

At Denver there was an influx of passengers into the coaches on the eastbound B. & M. express. In one coach there sat a very pretty young woman dressed in elegant taste and surrounded by all the luxurious comforts of an experienced traveler. Among the newcomers were two young men, one of handsome presence with a bold, frank countenance and manner; the other a ruffled, glum-faced person, heavily
5   built and roughly dressed. The two were handcuffed together.

As they passed down the aisle of the coach the only vacant seat offered was a reversed one facing the attractive young woman. Here the linked couple seated themselves. The young woman's glance fell upon them with a distant, swift disinterest; then with a lovely smile brightening her countenance and a tender pink tingeing her rounded cheeks, she held out a little gray-gloved hand. When she spoke her
10   voice, full, sweet, and deliberate, proclaimed that its owner was accustomed to speak and be heard.

"Well, Mr. Easton, if you *will* make me speak first, I suppose I must. Don't you ever recognize old friends when you meet them in the West?"

The younger man roused himself sharply at the sound of her voice, seemed to struggle with a slight embarrassment which he threw off instantly, and then clasped her fingers with his left hand.

15   "It's Miss Fairchild," he said, with a smile. "I'll ask you to excuse the other hand; it's otherwise engaged just at present."

He slightly raised his right hand, bound at the wrist by the shining "bracelet" to the left one of his companion. The glad look in the girl's eyes slowly changed to a bewildered horror. The glow faded from her cheeks. Her lips parted in a vague, relaxing distress. Easton, with a little laugh, as if amused, was
20   about to speak again when the other forestalled him. The glum-faced man had been watching the girl's countenance with veiled glances from his keen, shrewd eyes.

"You'll excuse me for speaking, miss, but, I see you're acquainted with the marshal here. If you'll ask him to speak a word for me when we get to the pen he'll do it, and it'll make things easier for me there. He's taking me to Leavenworth prison. It's seven years for counterfeiting."

"Oh!" said the girl, with a deep breath and returning color. "So that is what you are doing out here? A marshal!"

"My dear Miss Fairchild," said Easton, calmly, "I had to do something. Money has a way of taking wings unto itself, and you know it takes money to keep step with our crowd in Washington. I saw this opening in the West, and—well, a marshalship isn't quite as high a position as that of ambassador, but—"

"The ambassador," said the girl, warmly, "doesn't call any more. He needn't ever have done so. You ought to know that. And so now you are one of these dashing Western heroes, and you ride and shoot and go into all kinds of dangers. That's different from the Washington life. You have been missed from the old crowd."

The girl's eyes, fascinated, went back, widening a little, to rest upon the glittering handcuffs.

"Don't you worry about them, miss," said the other man. "All marshals handcuff themselves to their prisoners to keep them from getting away. Mr. Easton knows his business."

"Will we see you again soon in Washington?" asked the girl.

"Not soon, I think," said Easton. "My butterfly days are over, I fear."

"I love the West," said the girl irrelevantly. Her eyes were shining softly. She looked away out the car window. She began to speak truly and simply without the gloss of style and manner: "Mamma and I spent the summer in Denver. She went home a week ago because father was slightly ill. I could live and be happy in the West. I think the air here agrees with me. Money isn't everything. But people always misunderstand things and remain stupid—"

"Say, Mr. Marshal," growled the glum-faced man. "This isn't quite fair. I'm needing a drink, and haven't had a smoke all day. Haven't you talked long enough? Take me in the smoker now, won't you? I'm half dead for a pipe."

The bound travelers rose to their feet, Easton with the same slow smile on his face.

"I can't deny a petition for tobacco," he said, lightly. "It's the one friend of the unfortunate. Good-bye, Miss Fairchild. Duty calls, you know." He held out his hand for a farewell.

"It's too bad you are not going East," she said, reclothing herself with manner and style. "But you must go on to Leavenworth, I suppose?"

"Yes," said Easton, "I must go on to Leavenworth."

The two men sidled down the aisle into the smoker.

The two passengers in a seat nearby had heard most of the conversation. Said one of them: "That
55   marshal's a good sort of chap. Some of these Western fellows are all right."

"Pretty young to hold an office like that, isn't he?" asked the other.

"Young!" exclaimed the first speaker, "why—Oh! didn't you catch on? Say—did you ever know an officer to handcuff a prisoner to his *right* hand?"

31. Which of the following phrases has the same meaning or most nearly has the same meaning as the word "influx" in line 1?
    A. arrival
    B. problem
    C. corporation
    D. travel

32. Which of the following phrases has the same meaning or most nearly has the same meaning as the word "forestalled" in line 20?
    A. investigated
    B. instigated
    C. intuited
    D. interrupted

33. Which of the following phrases has the same meaning or most nearly has the same meaning as the word "pen" in line 23?
    A. a writing utensil
    B. a hutch
    C. a ring
    D. a prison

Week 4

Week 4B: Infographics

On the SHSAT, there will several questions on interpreting infographics.

Tables

Tables present data on two variables using rows and columns. Rows run horizontally, and columns run vertically. Each individual box on a table is called a "cell."

Row 1, Column 1	Row 1, Column 2	Row 1, Column 3
Row 2, Column 1	Row 2, Column 2	Row 2, Column 3
Row 3, Column 1	Row 3, Column 2	Row 3, Column 3

Carefully read the title of the graph and the category that the rows and columns represent. Then, locate the relevant cell that you need to answer a question.

Suggested Price of Used Ford Explorers by Year Manufactured

Model	Suggested Retail Price
2008	$15,806.00
2009	$20,167.00
2010	$22,150.00
2011	$28,918.00

*Source: Kelley Blue Book

For example, according to the table above, the suggested retail price for a 2010 Ford Explorer is $22,150.

Graphs

Graphs are pictures of information based on data found in a data table. **Bar graphs** use bars to represent data that represents categories while **line graphs** use lines.

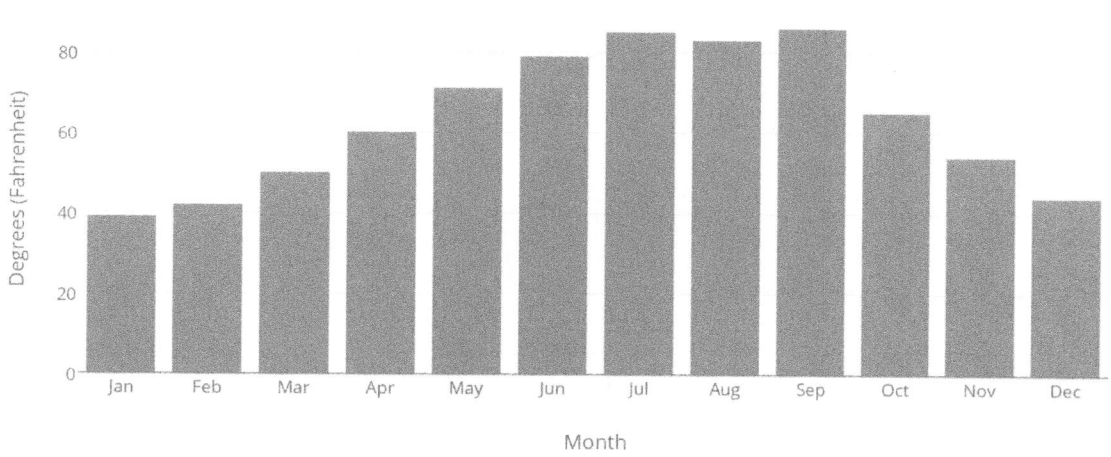

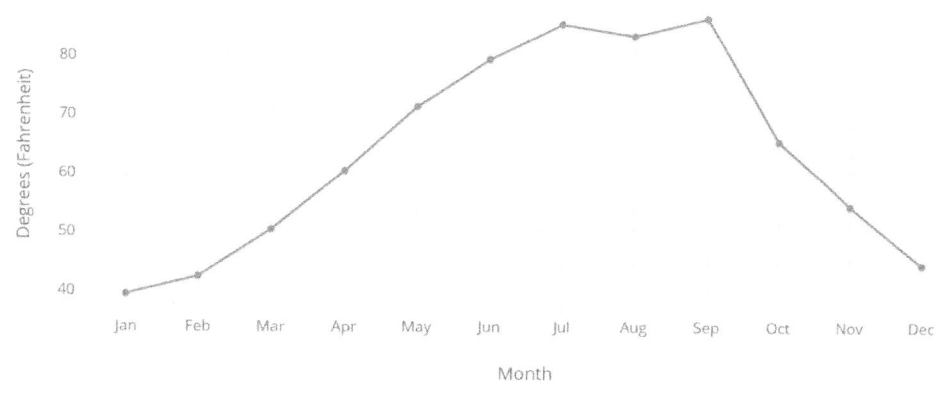

Source: U.S. Climate Data

According to the graphs above, the average high temperature in New York City in January is about 40 degrees while the average temperature in April is about 60 degrees.

Week 4

Pie charts are used to show percentages of a whole. They do NOT show percent change. According to the chart below, Lincoln won 59% of the electoral votes in the 1860 Presidential election while Breckenridge received 24%, Bell received 13%, and Douglas received 4%.

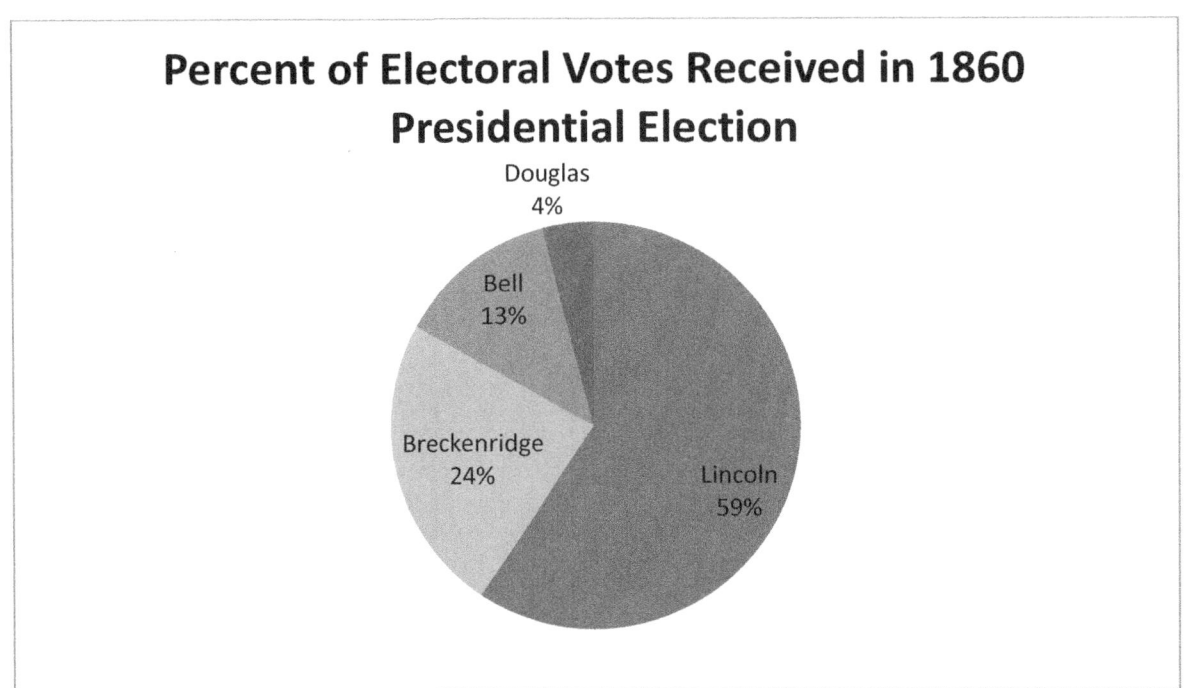

When interpreting graphs, make sure you read all labels and titles carefully. Go back to the graph or chart to determine accurate statements. For example, in the pie chart above, **wrong answer choices might say**

- "Lincoln won 24% of the electoral votes."

Breckenridge received 24% of the votes.

- "The number of votes Lincoln received increased by 59% from the previous election."

Pie charts provide no information about percent increase or decrease.

- "Lincoln received 59% more electoral votes than Breckenridge."

He received 59% of the total number of electoral votes, not 59% more than Breckenridge.

Week 4

Stacked bar graphs are also used to show distribution between categories. To find the value of each category, subtract the top value of each category from the bottom value of each category. Consider the graph below, which shows the preferred news sources of individuals in two classes.

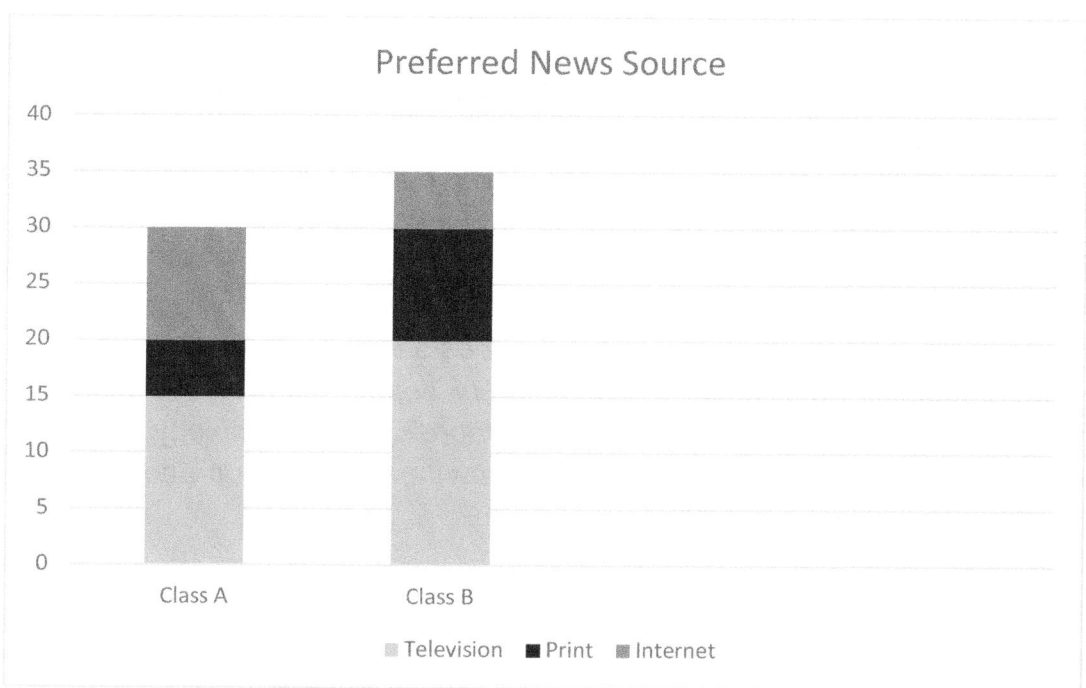

According to the figure

- There are 30 total individuals in Class A.
    - 10 prefer using the internet for news since the top bar extends from 20 to 30 and $30 - 20 = 10$ people.
    - 5 people prefer using print news sources since the middle bar extends from 15 to 20 and $20 - 15 = 5$
    - 15 people prefer television news sources since the bottom bar extends from 0 to 15 and $15 - 0 = 15$.
- In class B, there are 35 individuals. 20 prefer television news sources, 10 prefer print sources, and 5 prefer the internet.

For many questions, you will have to connect information from a passage to a graphic. Make sure that you carefully read the title and axes of all graphs so that you understand what is being measured. If necessary, find in the passage where the precise discussion of the topic being portrayed in the graph is located. Look for key words in the figure that appear in the passage.

Consider the sample below, which is adapted from the National Human Genome Research Institute's website (http://www.genome.gov/sequencingcosts/).

For many years, the National Human Genome Research Institute (NHGRI) *has tracked the costs associated with DNA sequencing performed at the sequencing centers funded by the Institute. This information has served as an important benchmark for assessing improvements in DNA sequencing technologies and for establishing the DNA sequencing capacity of the NHGRI Genome Sequencing Program (GSP). To illustrate the nature of the reductions in DNA sequencing costs, the graph shows hypothetical data reflecting Moore's Law, which describes a long-term trend in the computer hardware industry that involves the doubling of 'compute power' every two years. Technology improvements that 'keep up' with Moore's Law (technology whose costs are at or below the value predicted by Moore's Law) are widely regarded to be doing exceedingly well, making it useful for comparison.*

Figure 1

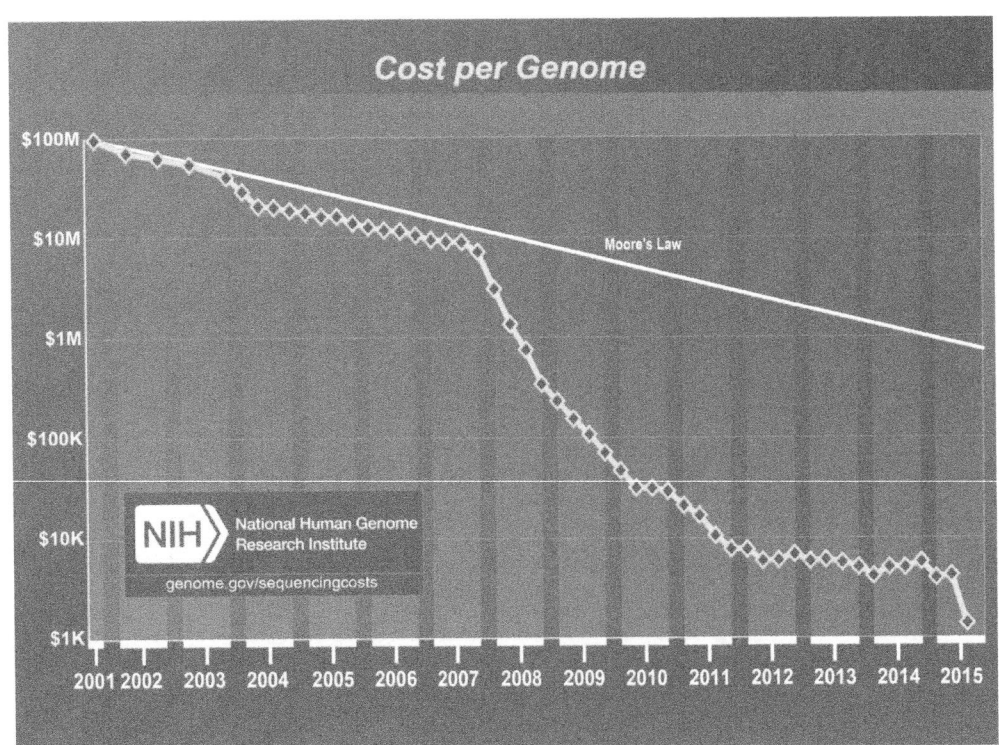

The line with the diamonds shows the actual cost per genome.

Sample 1: Based on the passage and the graphs, it can be inferred that improvements in DNA technology are regarded as doing

   A. poorly, because its costs have failed to keep up with Moore's Law.
   B. well, because its costs have kept up with Moore's Law.
   C. poorly, because its costs have exceeded Moore's Law.
   D. well, because its costs have failed to keep up with Moore's Law.

The costs have been lower than those predicted by Moore's Law. Thus, the technology is doing well. Choice B is correct.

Sample 2: During the year 2013, the cost per genome

   A. increased substantially from the previous year.
   B. decreased by more than 50% from the previous year.
   C. did not change appreciably throughout the year.
   D. was higher than the cost predicted by Moore's Law in 2012.

The cost per genome stayed almost the same. Choice C is correct.

Drill 1

The figures below are from the United States Census Bureau's report, "Home-Based Workers in the United States: 2010" by Peter J. Mateyka, Melanie A. Rapino, and Liana Christian Landivar (https://www.census.gov/prod/2012pubs/p70-132.pdf).

Figure 1

Type of Schedule (2010)	Onsite Workers (%)	Home Workers (%)
Regular daytime schedule	73.1	59.1
Regular evening shift	5.5	1.8
Regular night shift	2.8	.7
Rotating shift	3.5	1.4
Split shift	.8	1
Irregular schedule	12.1	30.5
Other	2.2	5.6

Figure 2

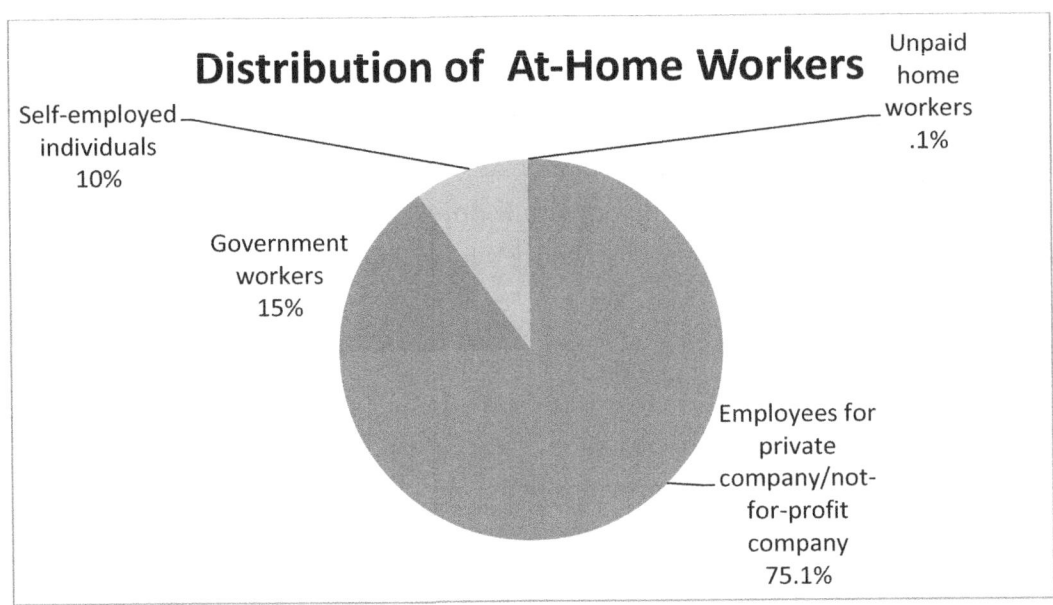

1. In 2010, what percentage of home workers worked a regular evening shift?
   A. .7
   B. 1.8
   C. 2.8
   D. 5.5

2. Which choice is best supported by the data in the Figure 1?
   A. Onsite workers are more likely than home workers to work a regular daytime schedule.
   B. The number of people who work at home is roughly equal to the number of people who work onsite.
   C. Onsite workers work more hours than home workers do.
   D. Homeworkers are more likely than onsite worker to work rotating shifts.

3. Which choice is best supported by the data in the Figure 2?
   A. Home workers are more likely to be self-employed than to work for the government.
   B. The number of home workers who are employees of private companies and nonprofits is greater than the number of home workers who are self-employed.
   C. Homeworkers spend more time doing unpaid tasks than onsite workers.
   D. The number of home workers who work for the government is roughly equal to the number of homeworkers who work for private companies and nonprofits.

Week 4

4. Taken together, the figures suggest that most people who work at home are
   A. government employees who work irregular schedules.
   B. employees of private companies or nonprofits who work irregular schedules.
   C. self-employed individuals who work regular daytime schedules.
   D. employees of private companies or nonprofits who work regular daytime schedules.

The excerpt below is adapted from the Environmental Protection Agency's website (http://www3.epa.gov/epawaste/nonhaz/municipal/).

Municipal Solid Waste (MSW)—more commonly known as trash or garbage—consists of everyday items we use and then throw away, such as product packaging, yard trimmings, furniture, clothing, bottles, food scraps, newspapers, appliances, paint, and batteries. This comes from our homes, schools, hospitals, and businesses. Each year EPA produces a report called Advancing Sustainable Materials Management: Facts and Figures 2013.

After 30 years of tracking MSW, the report has been expanded to include additional information on source reduction (waste prevention) of MSW, information on historical landfill tipping fees for MSW, and information on construction and demolition debris generation, which is outside of the scope of MSW. The new name also emphasizes the importance of sustainable materials management (SMM). SMM refers to the use and reuse of materials in the most productive and sustainable ways across their entire life cycle. SMM practices conserve resources, reduce wastes, slow climate change and minimize the environmental impacts of the materials we use. In 2013, Americans generated about 254 million tons of trash and recycled and composted about 87 million tons of this material, equivalent to a 34.3 percent recycling rate. On average, we recycled and composted 1.51 pounds of our individual waste generation of 4.40 pounds per person per day (Figure 1). Recycling and composting prevented 87.2 million tons of material away from being disposed in 2013, up from 15 million tons in 1980. This prevented the release of approximately 186 million metric tons of carbon dioxide equivalent into the air in 2013—equivalent to taking over 39 million cars off the road for a year.

Figure 1

Total MSW Generation (by Material), 2013
254 Million Tons (before recycling)

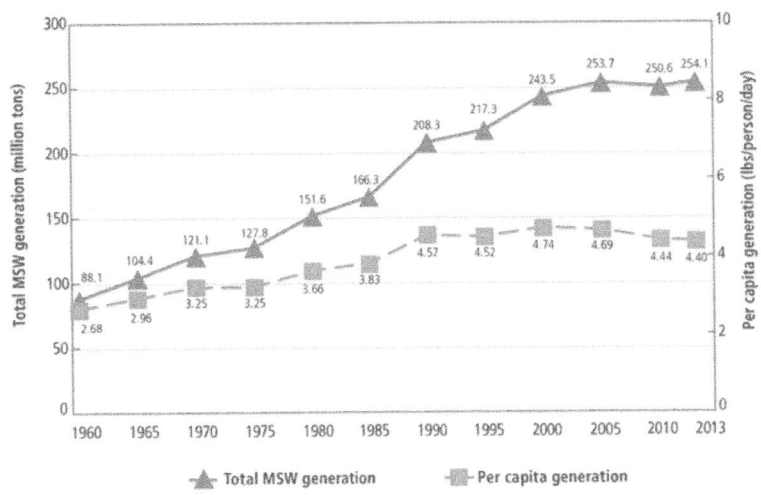

MSW Generation Rates, 1960-2013

Figure 2

Year	Total MSW recycling (million tons)	Percent recycling
1980	14.5	9.6
1990	33.2	16
2000	69.5	28.5
2013	87.2	34.3

Figure 3

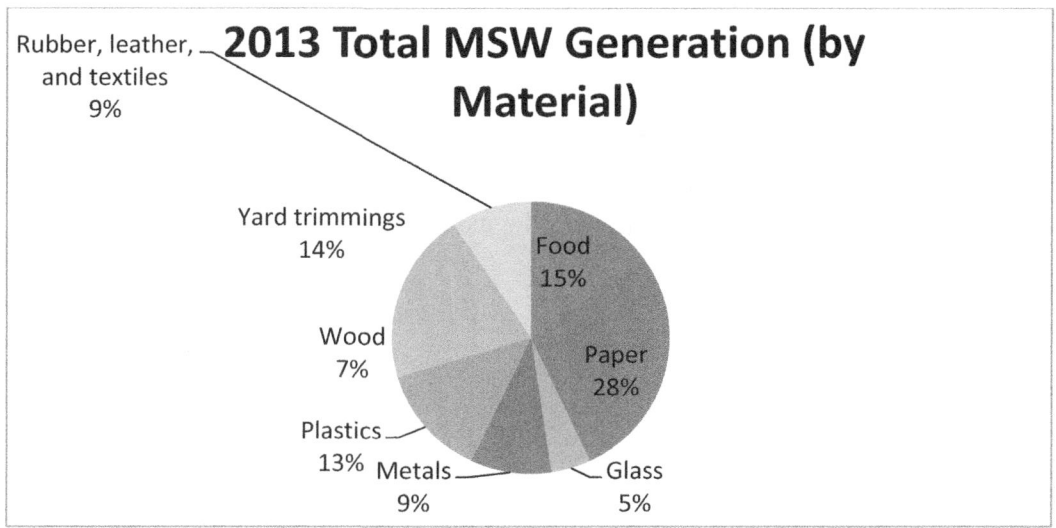

5. Between what years was there a decrease in per capita generation but an increase in MSW generation?
   A. 1960 and 1965.
   B. 1970 and 1975.
   C. 1980 and 1985.
   D. 1990 and 1995.

6. MSW generation increased by the greatest amount between
   A. 1970 and 1975.
   B. 1985 and 1990.
   C. 1990 and 1995.
   D. 2005 and 2010.

7. Based on the information provided, the change in per capita generation from 2010 to 2013 in Figure 1 can best be explained by
   A. an increase in recycling.
   B. a decrease in municipal waste generation.
   C. the removal of cars from the roads.
   D. a decrease in composting.

8. The data in Figure 2 support which idea?
   A. People in 2013 were less likely to dispose of waste unnecessarily than people in 1980.
   B. The failure to recycle is an indication of a lack of empathy.
   C. Cars in 2013 tended to pollute the environment less than those in 1980 did.
   D. Acting out of environmental consideration can be inconvenient.

9. The passage lists several examples of municipal solid waste in the first paragraph. Which of these examples is not shown in Figure 3?
   A. Yard trimmings
   B. Paint
   C. Herbicides
   D. Fertilizers

The following excerpt is adapted from the United States' Department of Agriculture report, *Factors Affecting Former Residents Returning to Rural Communities* by John Cromartie, Christiane von Reichert, and Ryan Arthun.
(http://www.ers.usda.gov/media/1844084/err185.pdf).

Persistent population loss is a challenge for many rural communities in the United States, especially those in more remote countries lacking scenic amenities. Young people often leave such communities to obtain an education, find a job, join the military, build personal relationships, or otherwise gain life experiences in a different locale. However, reducing rural
5   population loss and spurring economic development may depend less on retaining young adults after they graduate from high school and more on attracting them back later in life. Return migration plays a largely overlooked role in replenishing population numbers while raising education levels and labor supply, an increasing the social vitality of thousands of rural communications nationwide.

10 Many returned described positive aspects of small-town social life as bolstering their decisions to move home, including opportunities in the community to volunteer and take on leadership roles. Other factors that made a return move attractive were shorter drive times for work or shopping and proximity to outdoor recreation areas for camping, fishing, or hunting. The availability and quality of public community facilities, including schools, parks, bike paths, and
15 swimming pools, also cited as positive factors in their decisions to return.

Too much familiarity was often cited as a reason for not returning by people who preferred the greater sense of privacy available in big cities. Conversely, most returnees thrived in, or at least accepted, the tight-knit social networks of small towns. Lack of cultural event, shopping and dining options, and other urban amenities also were frequently mentioned by people with no
20 plans to return.

Figure 1

The figure shows population growth rates in metro areas, nonmetro areas, and the United States. 0 represents no net population change. A positive percent represents a percent increase from the previous year (1 represents a 1% population increase) and a negative percent represent a percent decrease from the previous year (-.4 represents a .4% population decrease).

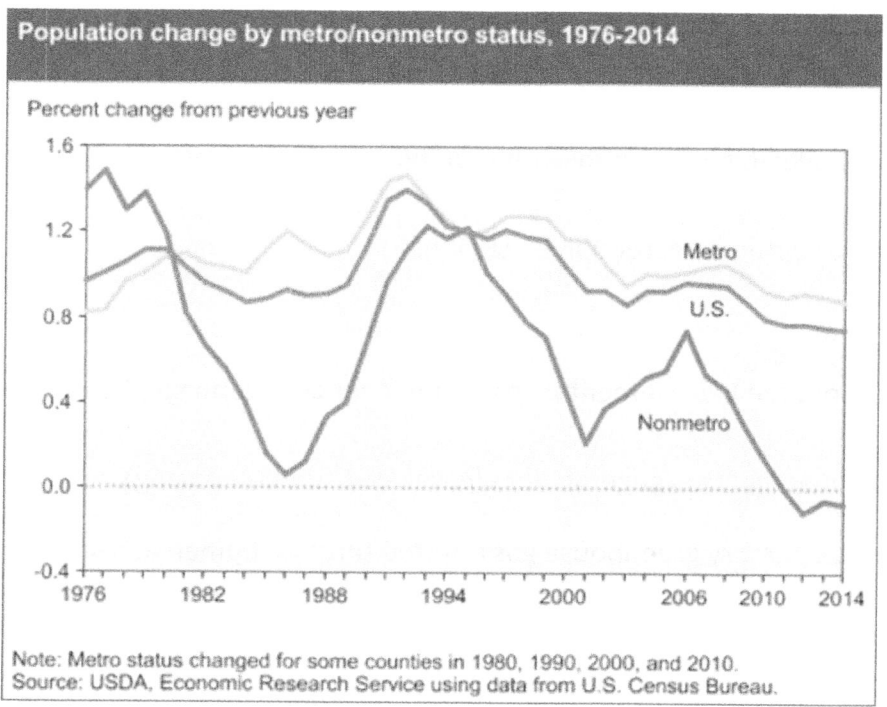

10. Of the following, the greatest difference between the growth rates in metro and nonmetro areas occurred in which year?
    A. 1976
    B. 1982
    C. 1988
    D. 1994

11. For the counties represented in the figure, 2010 to 2014 were characterized by
    A. smaller yearly percent increases in population growth in metropolitan areas than from 1988 to 1994.
    B. a decrease in the populations of metropolitan and nonmetropolitan areas.
    C. a smaller percent increase in the population of metropolitan areas than in the United States as a whole.
    D. roughly equal growth in metropolitan areas and nonmetropolitan areas.

Week 4

12. In the period of 1994 to 2006, the chart indicates that
    A. the population of the United States as a whole increased.
    B. the population of the United States decreased then increased.
    C. there was a mass migration of people from metro areas to nonmetro areas.
    D. growth rates in metro areas consistently rose.

13. According to the passage, the general change in the population of nonmetro areas from 2010 to 2014 can most strongly be explained by people's
    A. appreciation for tighter social networks.
    B. desire to take on leadership roles in the community.
    C. need for privacy.
    D. desire to be close to outdoor recreational activities.

The following excerpt if from the Environmental Protection Agency's webpage, "Overview of Greenhouse Gases" (http://www3.epa.gov/climatechange/ghgemissions/gases/co2.html#Reducing).

Carbon dioxide (CO_2) is the primary greenhouse gas emitted through human activities. In 2013, CO_2 accounted for about 82% of all U.S. greenhouse gas emissions from human activities. Carbon dioxide is naturally present in the atmosphere as part of the Earth's carbon cycle (the natural circulation of carbon among the atmosphere, oceans, soil, plants, and animals). Human activities are altering the carbon cycle—both by adding more CO_2 to the atmosphere and by influencing the ability of natural sinks, like forests, to remove CO_2 from the atmosphere. While CO_2 emissions come from a variety of natural sources, human-related emissions are responsible for the increase that has occurred in the atmosphere since the industrial revolution.

**Figure 1. U.S. Energy-Related CO_2 Emissions
1997 - 2007**

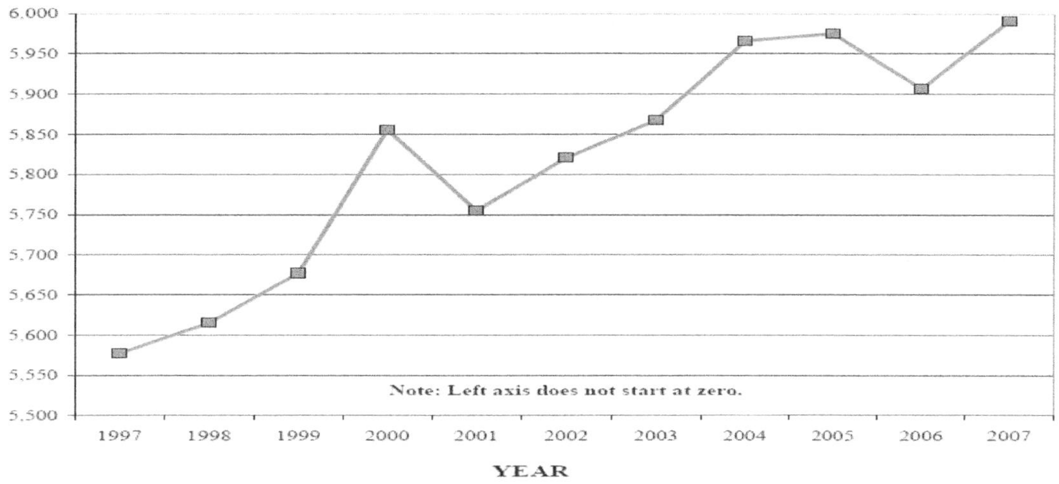

(Line chart showing U.S. energy-related CO_2 emissions from 1997 to 2007. Note: Left axis does not start at zero. Values range approximately from 5,580 in 1997, rising to about 5,855 in 2000, dropping to about 5,755 in 2001, then generally rising to about 5,990 in 2007.)

Source: U.S. Energy Information Administration, 2010(c).

14. According to the chart, between 2000 and 2001,
    A. carbon dioxide emissions in the United States reached its lowest point in the period of 1997 to 2007.
    B. carbon dioxide emissions in all industrialized countries decreased.
    C. carbon dioxide emissions in the United States decreased.
    D. there was no appreciable change in carbon dioxide emissions.

15. Does the data in the chart provide support for the author's claim that fossil fuels are the main cause of carbon dioxide emissions?
    A. Yes, carbon dioxide emissions have increased noticeably in the 10-year period shown.
    B. Yes, all sources of carbon dioxide come from fossil fuels.
    C. No, the chart provides no evidence of the effects of carbon dioxide emissions.
    D. No, the chart itself does not indicate what the specific sources of carbon dioxide are.

Week 4

The excerpt below is adapted from the United States' Census Bureau's "Research Trends in U.S. Entrepreneurship," by Ron S. Jarmin (http://researchmatters.blogs.census.gov/2014/08/14/recent-findings-on-trends-in-u-s-entrepreneurship/).

Two recent papers highlight findings based on the Census Bureau's Business Dynamics Statistics (BDS) that show declining rates of business dynamism over the last few decades. Census Bureau Business Dynamics Statistics provide data on number of establishments and year-to-year change in employment for births, deaths, expansions, and contractions by firm age and employment size.

A central finding in these papers is that rates of new firm start-ups have been declining since the early 1980s (see the figure from Decker et al. below). Seemingly, this trend is not of great concern. However, young entrepreneurial businesses are an important source of job creation in the U.S. economy. As these papers report, we do not have a satisfactory explanation for the declining pace of business dynamism. Nor do we fully understand the broader implications on productivity and economic growth. We need more research with data such as the BDS to resolve these gaps in our understanding of the economy.

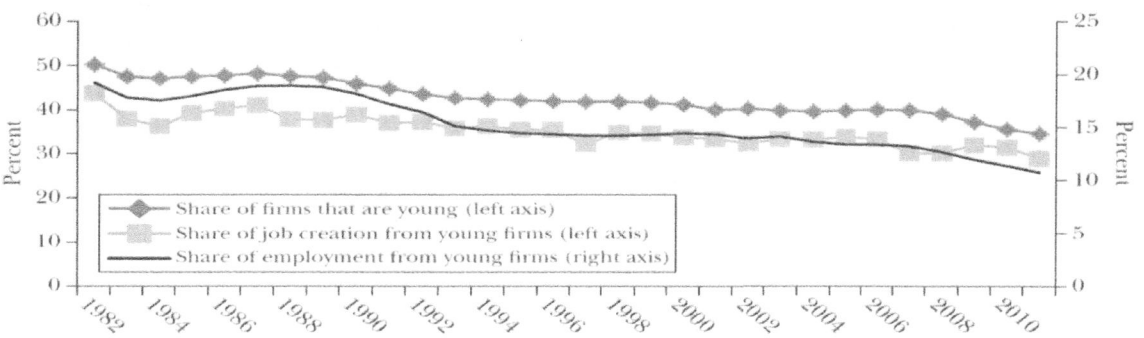

Declining Share of Activity from Young Firms (Firms Age 5 or Less)

Source: Author calculations from the US Census Bureau's Business Dynamics Statistics.
Note: Employment shares in each period based on the average of employment in period $t-1$ and t (the denominator of the Davis, Haltiwanger, and Schuh (1996) growth rate).

16. The period of 2004 to 2005 saw
    A. a decline in share of young firms by 45%.
    B. an unappreciable change in the share of firms that are young.
    C. proof that a large number of young firms than old firms went out of business in that period.
    D. a substantial increase in job creation at young firms.

17. The author would most likely state that the data are
    A. indicative of the growing vitality of entrepreneurship.
    B. evidence that the economy depends on young firms for its flourishment.
    C. too crude to draw definitive conclusions about the underlying causes of the decline of new firms.
    D. proof that productivity in the economy as a whole is set to decline in the next ten years.

Week 4

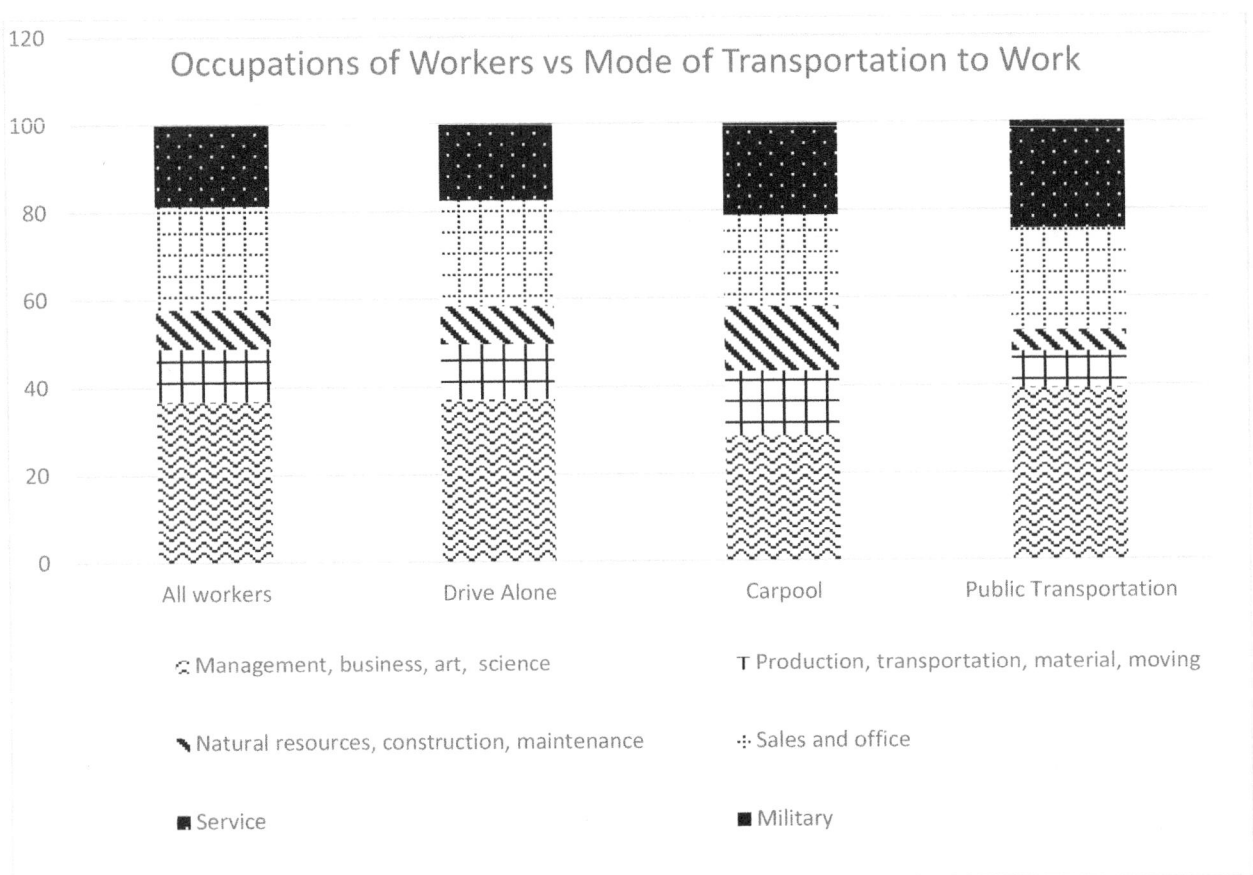

Source: https://www.titlemax.com/discovery-center/planes-trains-and-automobiles/how-americans-get-to-work/

18. The percent of people who drive alone and who work in sales or in an office is closest to which of the following?
   A. 14%
   B. 24%
   C. 60%
   D. 80%

19. Which of the following statements is best supported by the figure?
   A. The percent of people working in sales or an office is greater for those who carpool than those who take public transportation.
   B. For all workers, service work is more common than sales and office work.
   C. In comparison with people who carpool, people who drive to work alone have occupations in natural resources, maintenance, or construction at a rate that is closer to that of the working population as a whole.
   D. People who carpool to work are more likely to work in management, business, art, or science than those who take public transportation.

Week 4

The excerpt below is from the March 2025 blog "What is Generation Capacity" by the United States Department of Energy (source: https://www.energy.gov/ne/articles/what-generation-capacity).

[1] Capacity is the amount of electricity a generator can produce when it's running at full blast. The energy world can be a difficult place to navigate, especially if you're not speaking the same language. One term commonly thrown around is generation capacity. This is essentially one way experts in the field can measure the growth of energy resources ranging from wind to nuclear power.

[2] So what does it mean and how does it work? Let's break it down. When it comes to generation capacity, think maximum power output. Capacity is the amount of electricity a generator can produce when it's running at full blast. This maximum amount of power is typically measured in megawatts (MW) or kilowatts and helps utilities project just how big of an electricity load a generator can handle. U.S. nuclear generation capacity exceeded more than 99 gigawatts in 2023. That made up 8% of the country's total capacity and also let us know the total amount of electricity all 54 U.S. commercial nuclear power plants were capable of producing that year.

*It's important to note this is not the actual amount of electricity nuclear produced that year (18%), which we'll get to in a bit.

There are typically three types of capacity measures, according to the U.S. Energy Information Administration:

- **Nameplate generation capacity** – Determined by the manufacturer of the generator
- **Net summer generation capacity** – Determined by performance tests during peak demand between June 1 – September 30
- **Net winter generation capacity** – Determined by performance tests during peak demand between December 1 – February 28.

These numbers are all different, so it depends on which metric you want to measure. For instance, summer generation capacity is typically lower than winter generation capacity for thermal power plants because colder water is better at producing heat than warmer water.

Figure 1

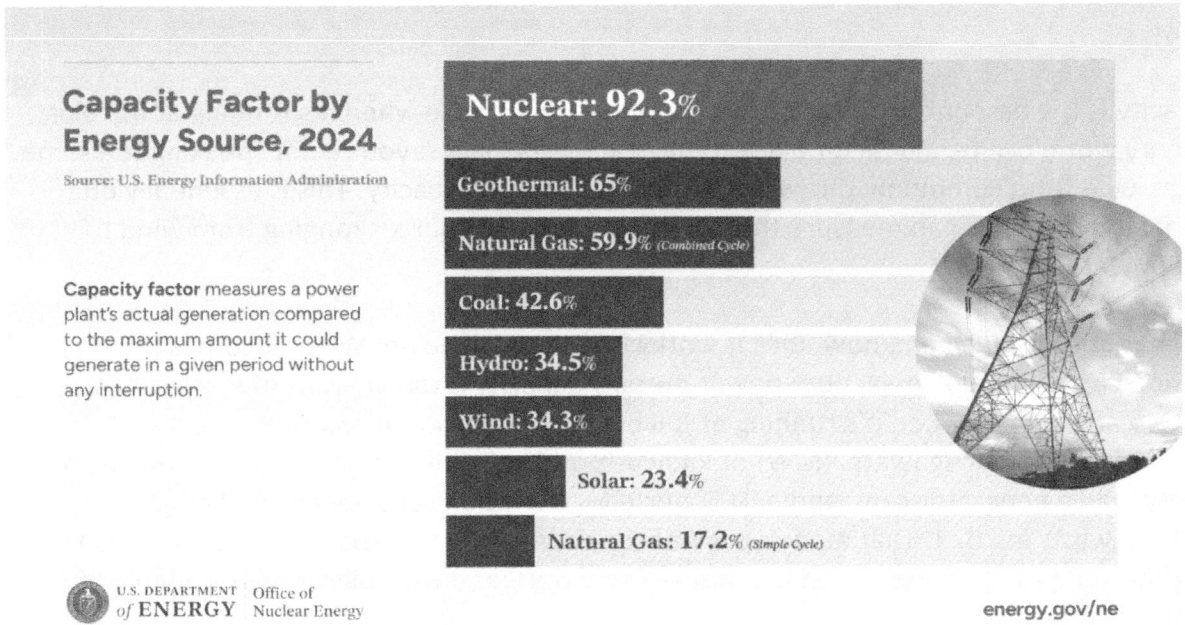

[3] Capacity factors allow energy buffs to examine the reliability of various power plants. It basically measures how often a plant is running at maximum power. A plant with a capacity factor of 100% means it's producing power all of the time. Nuclear has the highest capacity factor of any other energy source—producing reliable and secure power more than 92% of the time in 2024. That's nearly twice as much as a coal (42.36%) or natural gas (59.9%) plant that are used more flexibly to meet changing grid demands and almost 3 times more often than wind (34.3%) and solar (23.4%) plants.

Figure 2: Net Summer Generation Capacity and Generation

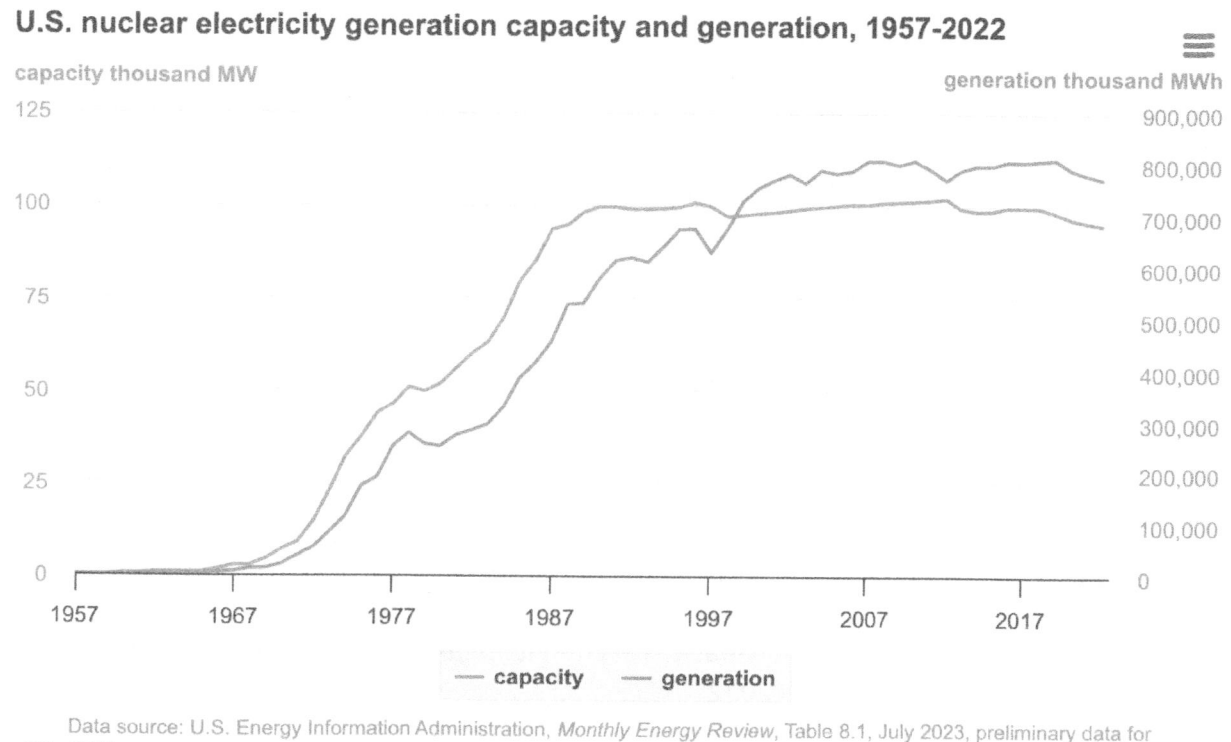

Capacity is not the same as electricity generation.

20. For the data shown in Figure 2, which of the following is closest to the value of the U.S. nuclear electricity generation capacity, in thousand MW, for 1978?
    A. 30
    B. 50
    C. 275,000
    D. 400,000

21. According to Figure 1, of the following, the difference between the power plant's actual generation and maximum possible generation is lowest for which of the following?
    A. Coal
    B. Solar
    C. Natural gas
    D. Hydro

22. Based on the text and Figure 1, which of the following best describes the relationship between wind energy and geothermal energy?
    A. Geothermal energy sources produce approximately twice as much electricity as do wind energy sources per unit of time.
    B. About twice as many secure and reliable sources of geothermal energy are available as are sources of wind energy.
    C. Wind energy plants are almost twice as efficient as are geothermal energy plants.
    D. Wind energy plants run at maximum power approximately half as often as geothermal energy plants.

23. Which of the following is best supported by Figure 2 for the United States?
    A. Nuclear electricity capacity in megawatts and nuclear electricity generation in megawatt hours had the same value in 1997.
    B. While both nuclear electricity generation and capacity generally increased sharply from 1967 to 1997, capacity and generation were more stable from 2007 to 2015
    C. Nuclear electricity generation reached its maximum value of close to 110 thousand MW in 2007 before alternately decreasing and increasing slightly through 2022.
    D. Nuclear electricity generation capacity reached its peak in 1997 and has steadily decreased each year through 2022.

24. Based on the passage and Figure 2, the net winter capacity for 1989 was most likely
    A. above 98 thousand MW
    B. between 75 thousand and 98 thousand MW
    C. between 50 and 75 thousand MW
    D. below 50 thousand MW

Week 4

The excerpt below is adapted from the National Institute of Health Blog, "Neuroscience: The Power of Curiosity to Inspire Learning" (http://directorsblog.nih.gov/2014/12/23/neuroscience-the-power-of-curiosity-to-inspire-learning/).

When our curiosity is piqued, learning can be a snap and recalling the new information comes effortlessly. But when it comes to things we don't care about—the recipe to that "delicious" holiday fruitcake or, if we're not *really* into football, the results of this year's San Diego County Credit Union Poinsettia Bowl—the new information rarely sticks. To probe why this might be so, neuroscientists Charan Ranganath and Matthias Gruber, and psychologist Bernard Gelman, all at the University of California at Davis, devised a multi-step experiment to explore which regions of the brain are activated when we are curious, and how curiosity enhances our ability to learn and remember.

The team recruited 19 students and asked them to rate more than 100 trivia questions. The students were encouraged to rate how confident they were that they knew the answer and their level of curiosity. The scientists next measured the brain activity of each student using an imaging technique called Functional Magnetic Resonance Imaging (fMRI). While lying in the scanner each participant was shown trivia questions that stumped them, some of which piqued their curiosity and others that didn't. As the students anticipated each answer, a photograph of a stranger flashed onto the screen. When the photo disappeared, a few seconds passed before the answer appeared. This sequence was repeated 112 times. Each student left the MRI scanner and took a quiz on the answers to the trivia questions and recall of the faces. When Ranganath's team scored the tests, they found the students recalled 71% of the answers that really piqued their curiosity compared to 54% of the answers that didn't. That, of course, wasn't surprising. When something interests us, we are more likely to remember it.

The intriguing result came when the researchers tested the students' ability to recall the faces. They found the students' ability to recognize faces was significantly higher during moments of great curiosity than during times of low curiosity. The team moved ahead to a second behavioral experiment and showed that the beneficial effect of extreme curiosity on trivia and face recollection persisted a day later. This indicates that the effects of curiosity, far from fleeting, help to build lasting memories. These results suggest a curious state of mind primes us to learn not just the things that interest us, but it helps us recall the peripheral information that we notice during our moments of wonder.

The figures below show the results of follow-up experiments on those described in the passage.

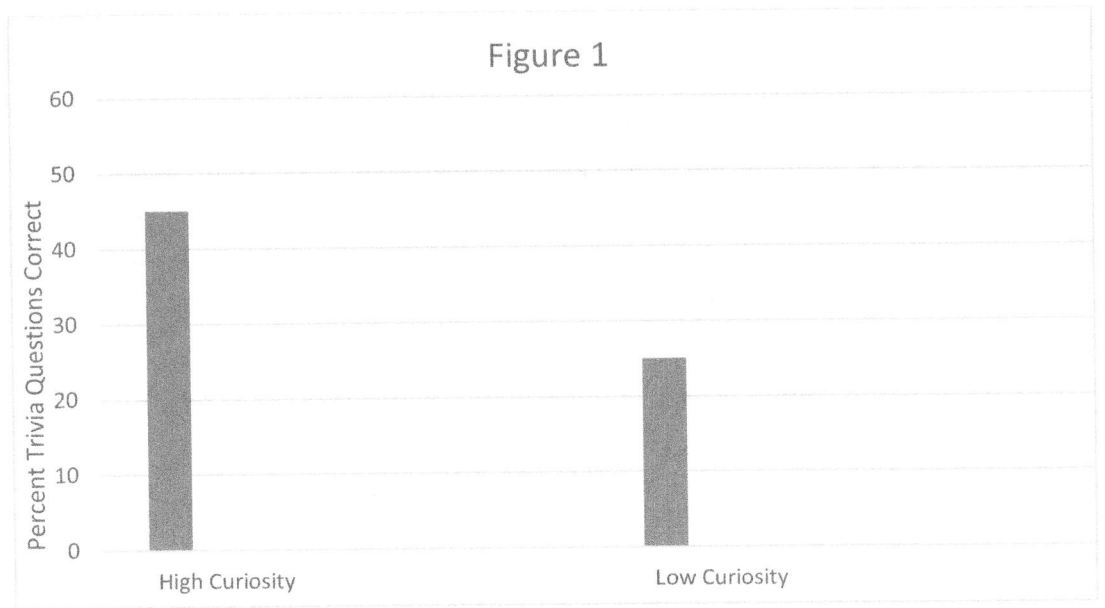

The data above is adapted from
https://www.sciencedirect.com/science/article/pii/S0896627314008046

25. The main purpose of the passage is to
    A. demonstrate how the findings of several of experiments have refined the understanding of the relationship between curiosity and memory.
    B. chronicle the history of competing theories about learning and cognition.
    C. present the results of contradictory yet revolutionary experiments on curiosity.
    D. assert that educators seeking to enhance their students' academic performance take measures to present their subjects in more interesting and compelling ways.

26. In the first paragraph (lines 1-8) there is a shift from
    A. an analysis of a study, to a personal anecdote, to the justification for a methodology.
    B. a presentation of an argument, to a consideration of a counterargument, to an explication of a rebuttal.
    C. a generalization, to a series of specific examples illustrating a phenomenon, to the identification of a study examining this phenomenon.
    D. a pronouncement of a claim, to an exploration of a case study, to a detailed description of a research project.

27. The main purpose of lines 9-17 ("The team...faces") is to
    A. assess an experiment's methodology.
    B. explain an experiment's conditions.
    C. document an experiment's discoveries.
    D. formulate an experiment's objective.

28. In the second and third paragraphs (lines 9-28) there is a shift from
    A. the analysis of a general principle to a discussion of topics for future research.
    B. the description of an experiment to a discussion of the experiment's findings.
    C. a critique of a scientific study to an analysis of the study's significance.
    D. a discussion of a scientific dilemma to a proposed solution to that dilemma.

29. As used in line 13, "piqued" most nearly means
    A. angered.
    B. roused.
    C. pointed.
    D. rejected.

Week 4

30. Which finding, if accurate, would undermine the interpretation of the results of the test scores on trivia questions that were included in Ranganath's study?
    A. Genetic differences between subjects also account for how well they memorize new information.
    B. The subjects already knew the answers to virtually all of the trivia questions they answered correctly prior to participating in the study.
    C. The researchers themselves had to look up the answers to most of the trivia questions included in the study.
    D. Older individuals answered less than 74% of the questions correctly even when they were highly curious.

31. The references to the fruitcake recipe and the football score (lines 2 to 4) primarily serve to
    A. illustrate the quality of typical products and events.
    B. outline the mechanism underlying a neural circuit.
    C. emphasize the connection between curiosity and knowledge retention with familiar situations.
    D. suggest that people rarely try to learn about matters with little practical value.

32. Phrases such as "learning can be a snap" (line 1) and "rarely sticks" (line 4) are likely included to
    A. render a potentially specialized biological discussion more approachable to a general audience.
    B. underscore how differences in genetics and experiences account for why some people learn more easily than others.
    C. stress the urgency of a new line of research into the mechanisms undergirding cognition and memory.
    D. offset the solemn nature of the work being discussed.

33. It can be inferred that the fMRI was used by the scientists to
    A. determine how often students answered questions accurately.
    B. help them gauge the students' interest level in different questions.
    C. ensure that students' brains were functioning normally.
    D. help the students better see the pictures used in the experiment.

Week 4

34. Which choice best supports the idea that the effect of curiosity on learning may be enduring?
    A. Line 16 ("This...112 times")
    B. Lines 21-23 ("The intriguing...curiosity")
    C. Lines 23-25 ("The team...later")
    D. Lines 26-27 ("These...interest us")

35. Which of the following situations best parallels the results of the behavioral experiments described in the last paragraph (lines 21-28)?
    A. A student uninterested in geography is better able to memorize geography facts while listening to music she likes.
    B. A person who likes baseball struggles to learn historical details about the sport.
    C. An art history enthusiast remembers the arrangement of plants on the table where she sat while reading art history trivia.
    D. A person with a strong interest in math becomes so absorbed in completing math problems that he forgets to attend an unrelated appointment.

36. The assertion in lines 19-20 ("When...it") can best be described as
    A. something surprising to most members of the scientific community.
    B. based primarily on anecdotal reports.
    C. persuasively founded on empirical evidence.
    D. likely to disprove earlier theories about cognition.

37. As used in the last paragraph, the word "intriguing" serves to
    A. suggest that researchers were somewhat surprised to find that subjects better remembered the faces of individuals when they were in a curious state.
    B. indicate that the idea that people have an easier time learning information they find interesting is fundamentally revolutionary.
    C. point out that the researchers had previously overlooked the connection between interest and building visual memories.
    D. reveal that researchers expected subjects to remember more faces than they actually did.

38. In Figure 2, the percent of photo recognition questions answered correctly by subjects with low curiosity was closest to
    A. 25%
    B. 30%
    C. 40%
    D. 45%

39. The figures suggest that curiosity level is most likely to make a difference in people's ability to remember
    A. the answers to trivia questions.
    B. peripheral information.
    C. the faces of people they were recently shown.
    D. faces of people they encounter in crowds.

40. Based on the passage and the figures, in which of the following situations would an individual stand the greatest chance of remembering something accurately?
    A. A person who dislikes animals is asked to remember the answer to a trivia question about ornithology, the study of birds.
    B. A stargazing enthusiast is asked to remember the face of a random person he is shown while studying astronomy trivia.
    C. A student is asked to remember the face of a professor she has not met during a moment of low curiosity.
    D. A jazz musician is asked to remember the answer to a trivia question about a jazz band.

41. Figure 1 can be used to answer which of the following questions addressed in the passage?
    A. To what extent do interested subjects remember the correct answer to trivia questions?
    B. How much more confident were subjects with high curiosity than were subjects with low curiosity in their answers to trivia questions?
    C. What trivia topics typically stumped subjects the most often?
    D. What differences did the MRI scan reveal about the brains of subjects with high curiosity and those with low curiosity?

42. Based on the passage, if there is enough information to answer this question, the difference between the two bars representing high curiosity in Figures 1 and 2 can best be explained by which of the following?
    A. People are generally more interested in learning new information than meeting new people.
    B. People make a more active attempt to memorize trivia in order to appear smarter.
    C. It is easier to become distracted by peripheral information when studying pictures than when learning trivia.
    D. There is not enough information in the passage to draw a definitive conclusion.

Week 4

Kweller Prep NEW SHSAT Grammar and Reading

Week 5

Week 5: Grammar Fundamentals

Basic Parts of Speech Overview

Nouns are words that name people, places, things, and abstract ideas (e.g., Bob, girl, dog, Paris, freedom, kindness).

1) **Common nouns** are general nouns that don't refer to specific people, places, things, and ideas.
2) **Proper nouns** refer to specific people, places, things, and ideas.

Common Noun Examples	Proper Noun Examples
author	Jules Verne
restaurant	Pete's Pizza
building	Eiffel Tower
person	Kenny
president	President of the United States

Pronouns are words that stand for nouns.

1) **Personal pronouns** refer to people, things, places, and ideas.
   - **He** wrote a research paper.

"He" refers to a specific male.

   - Shiloh saw **it** in the window.

"It" refers to something that is not a person, such as an item or an animal.

Personal Pronouns are classified by **person** and **number.**

	Singular (one)	Plural (two or more)
First Person (the speaker)	I/me	we/us
Second Person (the audience)	you	you
Third Person (all others)	he/him she/her it	they/them

2) **Reflexive pronouns** are followed by "self" or "selves" (*myself, yourself, himself, herself, us, themselves, itself*).

   - Reflexive: Ari bought **herself** a shirt.

Reflexive pronouns can also act as intensive pronouns. An intensive pronoun emphasizes the noun to which it refers.

   - Abby wrote the book **herself**.

"Herself" is not used as a substitute for a specific noun. It emphasizes that Abby was the person who wrote the book.

- That infraction **itself** won't disqualify him from playing.

"Itself" emphasizes the infraction, but it is not used as a substitute for any specific noun.

2) **Possessive pronouns** show ownership (*mine, yours, hers, his, ours, theirs*).
   - The money on the counter is **hers.**
   - The time is **yours** to use as you wish.

3) **Indefinite pronouns** don't stand for any specific person, thing, or amount.

Singular Indefinite Pronouns

another	little
anybody	much
anyone	neither
anything	nobody
each	no one
either	nothing
enough	one
everybody	other
everyone	somebody
everything	someone
less	something

- Can you give me **something** for my headache?
- **One** might disagree with that assessment.

Plural Indefinite Pronouns

both	others
few/fewer	several
many	they

- **Both** are good options.
- **Several** are located there.

Indefinite Pronouns That Take Plural and Singular Forms

all	any	more/most
none	some	such

- There is **some** for you to take home.
- **Some** are still waiting.

4) **Demonstrative pronouns** (*this, these, that, those*) stand for specific nouns.
   - I read about **that.**
   - Put **those** away!

Week 5

Adjectives are words that modify, or describe, nouns (e.g., big, wealthy, smart, generous).

Questions answered by adjectives include the following:

1) What kind?
    - An **old** house.
    - A **gym** membership.

2) How many?
    - **Five** horses.
    - I have a **few** books.

3) Which one? When demonstrative pronouns precede nouns, they act as demonstrative adjectives.
    - **This** calendar is from last year.
    - **These** people are friendly.

4) Whose? Possessive adjectives include *my, your, his, her, our, their,* and *its*.
    - **Darcy's** dress is over there.
    - **My** locker is on the top row.

Verbs are words that indicate action or states of being.

1) **Action verbs** indicate what nouns do.
    - I **gave** him a gift.
    - He **dove** off the diving board.

2) **Linking verbs** provide information about a noun. Specifically, they express states of being (*be, appear, seem, feel, remain, taste, smell, sound, look,* etc.)
    - The plate **is** on the table.
    - You **are** thirsty.
    - The task **seems** easy.
    - The pillow **feels** soft.
    - You **look** cold.

3) **Helping verbs** are verbs that are paired with action verbs in sentences.
    a. **Primary helping verbs** are generally variations of the words "be" (*am, is, are, was, were*), "do" (*do, does, did*), and "have" (*have, has, had*).
       - He **is** going to the movies.
       - She **did** know about the plan.
       - I **have** not revealed your secret.

b. **Modal helping verbs** modify the main verb's meaning to express possibility, permissibility, obligation, ability, probability, desire, or necessity (*can, could, may, might, will, would, shall, should, must, ought*).
- Possibility: He **might** call you.
- Permissibility: You **may** enter.
- Ability: She **can** read in three different languages.
- Obligation: We **must** follow the rules.
- Necessity: You **must** stay calm.
- Desire: I wish you **would** listen to your mother.
- Probability: The plan **should** go as expected.

Verbs are **conjugated** (change form) depending on the **subject** of the sentence and the **tense** of the verb. The subject is the noun performing the action of the verb (or whose state of being is described). The tense is the time period in which the verb is acting.

When a regular verb refers to something happening in the present, add an "-s" at the end of the verb when the subject is **singular** and in the **third person**. In most cases, if a verb ends in "-y," change the "-y" to "-ies" for third person singular subjects.

I walk.	I study.
You walk.	You study.
He/She **walks.**	He/She **studies.**
We walk.	We study.
They walk.	They study.

When a regular verb refers to an action happening in the past, add "-ed" to the end of the verb. For verbs ending in "-y," change the "-y" to "-ied."

- I/You/He/She/We/They **walked.**
- I/You/He/She/We/They **studied.**

The verb "to be" is irregular in both the present and past tense.

Present	Past
I am.	I was.
You are.	You were.
He/She is.	He/She was.
We are.	We were.
They are.	They were.

Irregular verbs do not conjugate normally. In some cases, they change form in the past tense.

- Irregular Present: I **buy** groceries.
- Irregular Past: I **bought** groceries.

Some irregular verbs change form in the perfect tenses (tenses where the verb is preceded by *have, has,* or *had*). The perfect tense also applies when "not" follows *have, has,* or *had.*

- Regular Verb: We **argued**/We **have argued.**
- Irregular Verb: The bell **rang**/The bell **has rung**.

Some Common Irregular Verbs

Verb	Past	Perfect (has, have, had + verb)
Begin	Began	Begun
Blow	Blew	Blown
Break	Broke	Broken
Choose	Chose	Chosen
Come	Came	Come
Draw	Drew	Drawn
Drink	Drank	Drunk
Drive	Drove	Driven
Eat	Ate	Eaten
Fall	Fell	Fallen
Forgive	Forgave	Forgiven
Freeze	Froze	Frozen
Give	Gave	Given
Go	Went	Gone
Grow	Grew	Grown
Know	Knew	Known
Ride	Rode	Ridden
Ring	Rang	Rung
Rise	Rose	Risen
Run	Ran	Run
See	Saw	Seen
Shake	Shook	Shaken
Sing	Sang	Sung
Sink	Sank	Sunk
Speak	Spoke	Spoken
Steal	Stole	Stolen
Swim	Swam	Swum
Take	Took	Taken
Write	Wrote	Written

Adverbs are words that modify verbs, adjectives, or other adverbs. Adverbs often end in "–ly" (e.g., strongly, kindly, newly, and beautifully).

- He thought **carefully** about his decision.

The adverb "carefully" modifies the verb "thought."

- He ran **very fast.**

The adverb "fast" modifies the verb "ran," and the adverb "very" modifies the adverb "fast."

- It is **terribly** cold outside.

The adverb "terribly" modifies the adjective "cold."

Prepositions are words that show relationships of time and place.

- I walk **to** the mall.
- The disk is **in** my hand.

Common Prepositions

about	before	for	onto	under
above	behind	from	opposite	underneath
across	below	in	outside	unlike
after	beneath	inside	over	until
against	beside	into	past	upon
along	between	like	since	via
among	beyond	of	through	with
as	by	off	toward	within
at	except	on	towards	without

A **phrase** is a group of words that functions as a single part of speech.

1) **Prepositional phrases** are strings of words beginning with a preposition. They often act as adjectives or adverbs.
    - He delivered the speech **with confidence**.

"With confidence" modifies the verb "delivered."

   - The increase **in prices** was concerning.

"In prices" modifies the noun "increase."

2) **Participial Phrases** are phrases that contain participles, verbs functioning as adjectives. The **present participle** ends in "-ing" (parking, writing, winning) and the **past participle** typically ends in "-ed," "-en," "-d," "-n," or "-t" (quoted, written, known, bent).

   - **Having succeeded in cracking the code,** the cryptologist was pleased with his accomplishment.

The participial phrase modifies the noun "cryptologist."

   - **Located between the café and the laundromat,** the supermarket attracts a lot of customers.

The participial phrase modifies the noun "supermarket."

Sometimes a participial phrase will appear at the end of a sentence.

- The company experienced a major setback after the scandal, **losing even its most loyal customers.**

The participial phrase modifies the noun "company."

3) **Appositives** are words or phrases that rename a noun or pronoun.
    - My uncle, **a man of few words,** shocked everyone with his friendly behavior at the party.

"A man of few words" functions as a noun that renames "my uncle."

- The experimental group, **or treatment group**, is exposed to a drug during clinical trials. On the other hand, the control group receives a placebo.

"Treatment group" is another term for the "experimental group."

Drill 1

For questions 1-20, select the part of speech of each underlined word or phrase.

1. The article included many <u>advanced</u> words.
    A. pronoun
    B. adjective
    C. adverb
    D. preposition
2. I was <u>thoroughly</u> impressed by your analysis.
    A. noun
    B. adjective
    C. verb
    D. adverb
3. The snow <u>is</u> falling quite rapidly.
    A. preposition
    B. noun
    C. verb
    D. adverb
4. The students had a discussion <u>about economic policy</u> that lasted for several hours.
    A. noun
    B. participial phrase
    C. prepositional phrase
    D. appositive
5. What did <u>they</u> tell you about the competition?
    A. noun
    B. pronoun
    C. preposition
    D. verb
6. Ellen has <u>six</u> rings in her jewelry box.
    A. noun
    B. pronoun
    C. adjective
    D. adverb

7. Howard examined the slide himself.
   A. preposition
   B. adverb
   C. adjective
   D. pronoun
8. Please introduce me to your friend.
   A. noun
   B. verb
   C. adverb
   D. pronoun
9. Smoke was coming out of the chimney.
   A. noun
   B. pronoun
   C. adjective
   D. adverb
10. There is a box underneath the couch.
    A. preposition
    B. noun
    C. pronoun
    D. verb
11. We have a special bond.
    A. noun
    B. preposition
    C. verb
    D. adjective
12. You solved the puzzle extremely quickly.
    A. adjective
    B. adverb
    C. preposition
    D. verb
13. I went to your house last night.
    A. adverb
    B. preposition
    C. pronoun
    D. verb
14. Working for days on end, Delia finally finished the paper.
    A. appositive
    B. participial phrase
    C. prepositional phrase
    D. adjective
15. My dog, an energetic creature, loves to play fetch.
    A. participial phrase
    B. prepositional phrase
    C. appositive
    D. adjective

16. The need <u>for improved working conditions</u> was the subject of the petition.
    A. prepositional phrase
    B. adverb
    C. participial phrase
    D. appositive
17. The heat of vaporization, <u>or heat of evaporation,</u> is the amount of heat required to change a quantity of a liquid into a gas without a change in temperature.
    A. preposition
    B. adverb
    C. verb
    D. appositive
18. I am <u>quite</u> concerned about your behavior.
    A. adjective
    B. adverb
    C. noun
    D. pronoun
19. He is so gullible; he will believe <u>anything</u> you tell him.
    A. noun
    B. adverb
    C. preposition
    D. pronoun
20. <u>Renowned for its unintended tilt to one side,</u> the Leaning Tower of Pisa is a freestanding bell tower in Italy.
    A. prepositional phrase
    B. participial phrase
    C. appositive
    D. noun

For questions 21-32, select the correct verb form.

21. They <u>complain</u> about everything.
    A. NO CHANGE
    B. have complain
    C. complains
    D. complaining
22. Miriam <u>talk</u> about that all the time.
    A. NO CHANGE
    B. have talk
    C. has talks
    D. talks
23. The application process has <u>begin.</u>
    A. NO CHANGE
    B. began
    C. begun
    D. beginning

Week 5

24. We have examine the artifact carefully.
    A. NO CHANGE
    B. examines
    C. examining
    D. examined
25. You is responsible for knowing that information.
    A. NO CHANGE
    B. are
    C. am
    D. was
26. Kelly had broke the glass.
    A. NO CHANGE
    B. break
    C. broken
    D. breaks
27. I have swum for one mile.
    A. NO CHANGE
    B. swim
    C. swam
    D. swimming
28. Craig were not telling the truth.
    A. NO CHANGE
    B. was
    C. be
    D. being
29. Have you did your homework?
    A. NO CHANGE
    B. do
    C. does
    D. done
30. I have go on an excursion through New Zealand.
    A. NO CHANGE
    B. went
    C. gone
    D. going
31. We have not drove here before.
    A. NO CHANGE
    B. drive
    C. drived
    D. driven
32. The batteries had ran out of power before the exam, so he had to borrow a calculator.
    A. NO CHANGE
    B. run
    C. runs
    D. running

Week 5

Clauses

A **main (independent) clause** has all the elements of a complete sentence.

A **complete sentence** contains a subject and a predicate verb, and it expresses a complete thought.

- A **subject** is the noun that performs an action or whose state of being is described.
- A **predicate verb** is a word that indicates what the subject is doing or reveals information about the subject's state of being.

- Independent Clause: Dan ran on the boardwalk.

The subject is "Dan" and the predicate verb is "ran." The sentence expresses a complete thought, so it is an independent clause.

- Independent Clause: He was at the concert.

The subject is "he" and the predicate verb is "was," which expresses the subject's state of being. The sentence expresses a complete thought.

A **dependent** clause contains a subject and a verb, but it does not express a complete thought.

- Dependent Clause: **Even though** I was tired.

The above clause is dependent because it cannot stand alone.

- Complete Sentence: I was tired.

Removing "even though" generates an independent clause.

- Complete Sentence: **Even though** I was tired, I still attended the party.

When the dependent clause is connected to an independent clause, the sentence becomes complete.

While you are not responsible for identifying the types of dependent clauses by name, it is useful to know some of the different forms dependent clauses take. The dependent clause in each sentence is in **bold**.

1) **Adverb (subordinate) clauses** are dependent clauses that function as adverbs. They answer questions such as "why?," "how?," "where?," "when?," "to what extent/degree?," "under what conditions?," and "with what goal/result?"
    - Cause: **Since it was raining,** she wore boots.
    - Purpose: I practiced **in order to improve my skills.**
    - Place: **Wherever there is trouble**, Carl is found.
    - Time: I listened to music **while I exercised.**
    - Condition: **In order to succeed**, you must work hard.
    - Concession: **Although I wanted to attend the event**, I had another obligation.
    - Degree: I studied **until I memorized the material.**

Common words found in subordinate clauses include *after, although, as, as soon as, because, before, even though, given that, if, in order to, once, provided that, since, though, unless, until, when, whenever, wherever, whether,* and *while.*

2) **Relative (adjective) clauses** are dependent clauses that function as adjectives. They answer questions such as "what kind?" and "which one?" They include relative pronouns *(who, which, whose, that, whom)* and relative adverbs *(when, where, why).*
   - The convention was attended by people **who like comic books.**
   - I liked the shirt **that had green stripes.**
   - I attended the university, **where I studied philosophy.**
   - Yesterday is **when I read the book.**

3) **Noun clauses** are clauses that stand for nouns. They function similarly to personal pronouns. Common pronouns included in noun clauses are *whichever, whatever, whoever,* and *whomever.*
   - **Whoever was at the game** had a good time.
   - I will eat **whatever you recommend.**
   - **That you called in advance** was important.

Note that the word "that" can sometimes mean "the fact that" when it begins a sentence. In this case, "the fact" was important.

Drill 2: Identify whether each clause is independent (I) or dependent (D).

Clause Write (I) or (D)

	Clause	Write (I) or (D)
1.	Because the explanation was so long.	
2.	The giraffe eats.	
3.	That is an interesting fact.	
4.	That you think the speech was good.	
5.	Whichever one you choose.	
6.	Whom the detective interviewed.	
7.	Which was on the table next to the napkins.	
8.	We dialed the number.	

9. In order that they improve their odds of being chosen.	
10. Once the decision was made.	
11. Where I discovered my talent.	
12. The tea is excellent.	
13. Unless you decide to change your mind.	
14. Whatever is going to make you happy.	
15. It is intriguing.	
16. Who attempted to contact me yesterday.	
17. While we went hiking in the rain.	
18. I enjoyed the show.	
19. We should celebrate.	
20. Until you scan the document.	

Kweller Prep NEW SHSAT Grammar and Reading

Week 6

Week 6: Sentence Formation

Coordinating conjunctions, the FANBOYS conjunctions **(for, and, nor, but, or, yet, so)**, connect two equal parts of a sentence (words, phrases, or clauses).

Conjunction	Relationship	Example
And	Continuation Addition	He is kind **and** smart. People will come **and** go into the building.
But, Yet	Contrast	The stew was visually appealing, **but** it had an unpleasant taste. The stew was visually appealing, **yet** it had an unpleasant taste.
Or	Alternative (when at least one alternative is true or happens)	I will order either the chicken **or** the fish.
Nor	Alternative (when each alternative is untrue or does not happen)	I will not eat the chicken, **nor** will I eat the fish.
So	Effect (result)	I was cold, **so** I put on a jacket.
For	Cause	I put on a jacket, **for** I was cold.

Correlative conjunctions appear in word pairs and connect equal grammatical items (words, phrases, clauses).

1) either…or
   - We will watch **either** a comedy **or** an action movie.
2) neither…nor
   - The explanation was **neither** accurate **nor** intelligible.
3) not only…but also
   - **Not only** do I think you made a great impression at the meeting, **but** I **also** think you will be given many exciting opportunities in the future.
4) both…and
   - Golden Retrievers are known for being **both** gentle **and** friendly.
5) whether…or
   - I wasn't sure **whether** you would attend the lecture **or** listen to the recording.
6) between…and
   - The competition was **between** the juniors **and** the seniors of the high school.

Conjunctive adverbs often connect two independent clauses. Within a sentence, conjunctive adverbs follow semicolons when introducing a new independent clause.

- The scientist was praised for conducting a comprehensive study; **nevertheless**, some people were skeptical of his conclusions.
- The chemicals in the laboratory are extremely toxic; **therefore**, employees are trained in basic safety procedures.

A single conjunctive adverb can be set off by commas in the middle of sentence to create a pause for effect. They may build off of the **previous sentence**, as in the second sentence below.

- I do not, **however,** recommend that one approach a wild deer.
- There are many ways to become involved in local government. You can, **for example,** create a petition or campaign for politicians who hold your views.

When the conjunctive adverbs are deleted, the sentences still make sense.

Conjunctive adverbs can also begin or end a sentence for emphasis.

- We still must attend the meeting, **however.**
- **Nevertheless**, I am concerned.

Common Conjunctive Adverbs

Addition	*furthermore, in addition, moreover, also, likewise*: show additional information. • I have a dog; in addition, I have a cat.
Contrast	*conversely, on the other hand, by contrast, on the contrary*: show opposites. • Sekou is tall; conversely, Clay is short. *however*: present a fact that is contrary to another. • Latasha was born in New York; however, she grew up in Illinois. *nevertheless, nonetheless, still*: present a fact that is contrary to another **and** that is surprising or unexpected. • Mike was cut from his high school's baseball team; nevertheless, he was the star player of his college's baseball team. • Lara campaigned hard for the position of class president; still, this was not enough to get her enough votes to win. *instead:* show an alternative. • Don't go on an extreme diet; instead, make healthier choices. *besides*: a benefit that contrasts with a negative situation. • The rain wasn't so bad; besides, it was nice after a snowy winter.
Cause-and-Effect	*as a result, accordingly, consequently, thus, therefore*: show result of a reason provided in the previous clause. • Pandas only digest a small portion of their food; therefore, they need to feed constantly in order to meet their nutritional needs.

Time	*first, next, now, then, subsequently, thereafter, finally, ultimately, at last*: show sequence.
	• I wrote the essay; subsequently, I edited it.
	in the meantime, meanwhile: show actions happening simultaneously.
	• He is cooking dinner; meanwhile, his brother is playing outside.
Emphasis	*indeed, certainly, of course, in fact*: emphasize a more surprising or important point related to a point previously mentioned.
	• Getting a PhD is no easy feat; in fact, many people spend years in school before completing the requirements of their degree programs.
Example	*for example, for instance*: show examples/evidence.
	• Cell membranes perform many important functions; for example, they protect cells from their surroundings.
Clarity/ Summary	*in other words, that is, all in all, in summary*: specify what is meant by an earlier clause.
	• The teacher is not infallible; in other words, she can make mistakes.
	Then: show the way something appears in order to sum up a point.
	• Her reasons for lying, then, are self-serving.

Subordinating conjunctions are conjunctions that make one clause dependent.

When a dependent clause precedes an independent clause, a comma is generally needed.

- **While** I like apples, I also like oranges.

A dependent clause that follows an independent clause does NOT necessarily require a comma.

- I did not speak to the professor **after** class ended.

Common Subordinating Conjunctions

Contrast	*whereas, while*: show opposites.
	• While Bob is tall, Clay is short.
	although, even though, though: presents a fact that is contrary to another.
	• Although Latasha was born in New York, she grew up in Illinois.
	• Even though I had a cold, I did not go to the doctor.
	rather than: show alternatives.
	• Rather than complain, I will make the best of the unpleasant situation.
	*despite, notwithstanding: without being affected by; in spite of.
	• Notwithstanding your efforts to cheer me up, I am still sad.
	• Despite my better judgment, I will heed your advice.
	*These words are prepositions, but they are sometimes tested with conjunctions.

Cause-and-Effect	*because, since, as*: show reason for a result. • Since I had to finish my homework, I did not go out with my friends. • She works at the camp, as her nametag indicates. *in order to, in order that, so, so that*: show goals • The scientist spent hours in the lab in order to make a fruitful discovery. • He worked a summer job so that he could make money. *whereby:* by means of which or through which. • The students use a system whereby they can communicate electronically. Note that the adverb *thereby* means "by means of that" or "for that reason" and is frequently used before a participle. • Enrico conducted a professional research study, thereby earning his professor's admiration.
Time/Place	*once, before, after, as soon as, by the time*: show sequence or timing. • As soon as I get the directions, I will read them. *when, whenever*: at any time or at any specific time. • Whenever I write an essay, I edit it. *wherever*: anywhere. • Wherever you go to school, you will learn a great deal. *until:* time up to when something happens or is possible. • I won't go until you talk to me. *while*: show actions happening simultaneously. • While he is cooking dinner, his brother is playing outside.
Condition	*provided that, as long as, so long as, if*: condition that must be satisfied for something else to happen. • As long as you answer the questions honestly, you will not get in trouble. *unless:* except if. • Unless you answer the questions honestly, you will get in trouble. *given that, granted that*: used when judging one thing based on something else being true. • Given that the law was unpopular, it was expected that there would be efforts to repeal it. *even if, even when, whether or not*: emphasizes a condition that will not change an outcome. • Even if you speak to him nicely, he will give you an attitude. *now that*: situation that is true and allows for other possibilities. • Now that I have arrived, the meeting can begin.

Drill 1

> (1) The "plum-and-pizza" model, a model of a thin crust pizza with a plum in the middle, is sometimes used by astronomers to describe the Milky Way Galaxy. (2) The plum represents the core of the galaxy, and the crust represents the galactic disk. (3) Because this model is fairly helpful, it has some problems. (4) The galactic disk is not rigid like a pizza crust; instead, it is a loose collection of matter.

1. Which sentence should be revised to correct a coordination or subordination error?
   A. Sentence 1
   B. Sentence 2
   C. Sentence 3
   D. Sentence 4

> Tammy got a job offer in a new town, for she had to move in order to have a shorter commute to her new job.

2. Which of the following edits should be made?
   A. Add "Although" before "Tammy."
   B. Add "Since" before "Tammy."
   C. Change "for" to "so."
   D. Change "for" to "or."

> The suggestions you gave us are neither practical or desirable.

3. Which of the following edits should be made?
   A. Change "or" to "nor."
   B. Change "neither" to "both."
   C. Change "or" to "and."
   D. Change "neither" to "so."

> Washington Irving wrote the short story "Rip Van Winkle," which not only is one of the first American short stories ever written while is still popular today.

4. Which of the following edits should be made?
   A. Change "not only" to "but only."
   B. Change "not only" to "neither."
   C. Change "while" to "and it."
   D. Change "while" to "but also."

> The results of the study will either be published in a journal and remain unreported.

5. Which of the following edits should be made?
   A. Change "and" to "yet."
   B. Change "and" to "or."
   C. Change "either" to "neither."
   D. Change "either" to "both."

> The commencement speakers encouraged the graduates to both follow their passions yet persist in the face of adversity.

6. Which of the following edits should be made?
   A. Change "yet" to "but."
   B. Change "yet" to "and."
   C. Change "both" to "either."
   D. Change "both" to "not only."

> The duck-billed platypus greatly resembles a duck; <u>therefore</u>, it is a mammal, not a bird.

7. Which of the following best replaces the underlined portion?
   A. subsequently
   B. also
   C. then
   D. however

> Many people believed that the rise of computer technology would decrease dependence on paper, and paper use has actually increased at offices in recent years.

8. Which of the following edits should be made?
   A. Change "and" to "but."
   B. Change "and" to "or."
   C. Change "Many people" to "Some people."
   D. Delete "actually."

> <u>Even though</u> there were so many items on the council's agenda, the meeting lasted two more hours than originally anticipated.

9. Which of the following best replaces underlined portion?
   A. Because
   B. Despite that
   C. Although
   D. While

> Jana did not discuss the details of her final project presentation with her classmates, <u>but</u> she wanted it to be a surprise.

10. Which of the following best replaces the underlined portion?
    A. so
    B. for
    C. yet
    D. nor

Week 6

> In Greek Mythology, Cassandra was a princess of Troy. Because she had the gift of being able to see the future, nobody ever believed her.

11. Which of the following edits should be made?
    A. Add "but" before "Cassandra."
    B. Add "and" before "nobody."
    C. Change "Because" to "Although."
    D. Change "Because" to "When."

> Leonardo da Vinci had a deep interest in engineering. In 1502, <u>in addition</u>, he made a design for a bridge that was ultimately built in 2001.

12. Which of the following best replaces the underlined portion?
    A. moreover
    B. however
    C. then
    D. for example

> The Bily Clocks Museum in Iowa hosts clocks that were made by hand <u>but also</u> is the site where Antonin Dvorak completed his ninth symphony.

13. Which of the following best replaces the underlined portion?
    A. and
    B. so it
    C. for it
    D. but

> Hilda's favorite bakery moved across town last year. When she walks past the site of its old location, <u>furthermore</u>, she can still smell the freshly baked bread in her mind.

14. Which of the following best replaces the underlined portion?
    A. for instance
    B. however
    C. in other words
    D. therefore

> The manager's proposal was highly controversial. She, <u>nevertheless</u>, struggled to get it approved by her colleagues.

15. Which of the following best replaces the underlined portion?
    A. however
    B. therefore
    C. for example
    D. likewise

> (1) I was originally opposed to the plan.
> (2) I changed my mind after doing more research.

16. Which of the following best combines the sentences?
    A. I was originally opposed to the plan, although I changed my mind after doing more research.
    B. Although I was originally opposed to the plan, I changed my mind after doing more research.
    C. I was originally opposed to the plan; therefore, I changed my mind after doing more research.
    D. Because I was originally opposed to the plan, I changed my mind after doing more research.

> (1) Installing solar panels can be costly.
> (2) This expense is ultimately offset by long-term savings in energy bills.

17. Which of the following best combines the sentences?
    A. Even though installing solar panels can be costly, this expense is ultimately offset by long-term savings in energy bills.
    B. Since installing solar panels can be costly, this expense is ultimately offset by long-term savings in energy bills.
    C. Installing solar panels can be costly, even though this expense is ultimately offset by long-term savings in energy bills.
    D. Installing solar panels can be costly; thus, this expense is ultimately offset by long-term savings in energy bills.

> (1) Avocado oils have healthy fatty acids.
> (2) Many people use them in recipes in place of less healthy alternatives, such as butter.

18. Which of the following best combines the sentences?
    A. Even though avocado oils have healthy fatty acids, many people use them in recipes in place of less healthy alternatives, such as butter.
    B. Avocado oils have healthy fatty acids; however, many people use them in recipes in place of less healthy alternatives, such as butter.
    C. Because avocado oils have healthy fatty acids, many people use them in recipes in place of less healthy alternatives, such as butter.
    D. Despite that avocado oils have healthy fatty acids, many people use them in recipes in place of less healthy alternatives, such as butter.

> (1) The newspaper industry has been hit hard in recent years by technological developments.
> (2) More Americans are turning to digital news sources.
> (3) The newspaper industry has seen a decline in profits.

19. Which of the following best combines sentences 2 and 3 to best clarify the relationship between the sentences?
    A. Although more Americans are turning to digital news sources, the newspaper industry has seen a decline in profits.
    B. More Americans are turning to digital news sources since the newspaper industry has seen a decline in profits.
    C. With more Americans turning to digital news sources, the newspaper industry has seen a decline in profits.
    D. In addition to more Americans turning to digital news sources, the newspaper has seen a decline in profits.

> (1) Many college students prefer traditional classrooms over virtual ones.
> (2) They believe they learn more when an instructor is present.

20. Which of the following best combines the sentences?
    A. Since many college students prefer traditional classrooms over virtual ones, they believe they learn more when an instructor is present.
    B. Many college students prefer traditional classrooms over virtual ones because they believe they learn more when an instructor is present.
    C. Although many college students prefer traditional classrooms over virtual ones, they believe they learn more when an instructor is present.
    D. Many college students prefer traditional classrooms over virtual ones, and they believe they learn more when an instructor is present.

Fragments

A complete sentence contains a subject and a predicate verb. It also expresses a complete thought. A sentence **fragment** is an incomplete sentence. There are several variations of fragments.

Subject and Verb-Related Fragments

1) **Error: Missing Subject**
If the subject is missing, the result is a fragment.

- Incorrect: Also recommends Claude talk to his guidance counselor.

There is no subject. Who also recommends that Claude talk to his guidance counselor?

- Correct: Claude's teacher also recommends that he talk to his guidance counselor.

2) **Error: Object in Improper Form**
The direct object of a sentence (what a verb acts on) must be a noun or pronoun.

- Incorrect: The company had significant **growing.**
- Incorrect: The company had significant **grows.**
- Correct: The company had significant **growth**.

The noun "growth" is the object of "had," not the gerund "growing" or the verb "grows."

3) **Error: Missing Verb**
If the main verb is missing, the result is a fragment.

- Incorrect: The hotel next to the doctor's office.

There is no verb to clarify the meaning of the sentence.

- Correct: The hotel **is** next to the doctor's office.
- Correct: The hotel next to the doctor's office **has** a pool.

4) **Error: Incomplete Verb**
If the main verb inappropriately ends in "-ing," replace the verb with one that can act as a main verb or add a helping verb such as "is," "are," "were," or "was."

- Incorrect: Saira **walking** to the store.
- Correct: Saira **is walking** to the store.
- Correct: Saira **walks** to the store.

Past participles (verbs ending in "-ed," "-en," "-d,""-t," or "-n") CANNOT act as main verbs unless they are attached to helping verbs.

- Incorrect: The book situated on the desk.
- Correct: The book **is** situated on the desk.

"Situated" describes the book's state of being, so a helping verb like "is" is needed.

- Correct: The man **situated** himself on the bench.

In this case, "situated" functions as the past tense of the action verb "situate," so no helping verb is needed.

Complete Thought Fragments

A sentence with a subject and a verb does not necessarily express a complete thought.

1) **Error: Dependent Clause Not Connected to an Independent Clause**

When a dependent clause stands alone, add more information to the sentence to complete the thought. Alternatively, remove the subordinating conjunction.

- Incorrect: **Once** Megan arrived home.

Possible Revisions

- Correct: Once Megan arrived home, she went to her room.

The addition of the independent clause completes the sentence.

- Correct: Megan arrived home.

The removal of the subordinating conjunction results in an independent clause.

2) **Error: Relative Clause Not Connected to an Independent Clause**

A relative clause contains a **relative pronoun** such as *that, who, whom,* or *which,* or a **relative adverb** such as *where, when,* or *why.*

Sample Relative Clauses
- **Where** he learned to fish.
- **Who** called me for help.
- **Which** is found in the Midwest.

A verb that is part of a relative clause cannot act as a main verb.

- Incorrect: The person **who biked on the street.**

The verb "biked" is part of the bolded relative clause and cannot function as the main verb.

- Correct: The person **who biked on the street is my neighbor**.

The addition of "is my neighbor" completes the sentence. When the relative clause is removed from the sentence, the result is a complete sentence ("The person is my neighbor").

3) **Error: Illogical Subordinating Conjunction or Adverb Used**
Be careful when using "where" or "when" to define subjects.

- Incorrect: A regular polygon is **when a polygon has equal sides and equal angles**.

A polygon is a what, not a when. No time relationship is indicated.

- Correct: A regular polygon is a polygon **that has equal sides and equal angles.**
- Correct: A regular polygon is a polygon **with equal sides and equal angles**

The first sentence connects the independent clause to a relative clause, and the second connects the independent clause to a prepositional phrase.

4) **Error: Sentence is Not Complete When Nonessential Terms Removed**

Nonessential terms are words, phrases, and clauses (relative clauses, participial phrases, appositives, etc.) that are NOT needed in a sentence. Nonessential terms in the middle of a sentence are typically set off by commas or dashes. The nonessential clauses in the two sentences below are in **bold**.

- The building**, which was recently renovated,** is now open for business.
- The child**, who was wearing a red shirt,** goes to school with my sister.

When nonessential terms are removed from a sentence, the result is a complete sentence.

- Incorrect: The Capitol Building, **which is located in Washington, D.C.,** where the legislature meets.

When the nonessential relative clause ("which is located in Washington D.C.") is removed, the resulting sentence is not complete. Instead, the sentence contains a subject connected to a relative clause beginning with "where."

- Correct: The Capitol Building, **which is located in Washington, D.C.,** is where the legislature meets.

The above sentence is correct. When the nonessential clause is removed, the result is a complete sentence ("The Capitol Building is where the legislature meets").

5) **Error: Coordinating Conjunction Follows a Dependent Clause**
A coordinating conjunction should not be used after a dependent clause.

- Incorrect: **While** the presentation was informative, **but** it was not interesting.

"While" and "but" are both contrast conjunctions. Only one is needed.

- Correct: **While** the presentation was informative, it was not interesting.
- Correct: The presentation was informative, **but** it was not interesting.

6) **Error: Relative Clause Follows a Dependent Clause**
A sentence containing a dependent clause followed by a relative clause is not complete.

- Incorrect: **When** I play board games with Stephen, **who** is always very competitive.

There is no independent clause. Either the subordinating conjunction or the relative pronoun should be removed. Alternatively, add an independent clause.

- Correct: **When** I play board games with Stephen, he is always very competitive.
- Correct: I play board games with Stephen, **who** is always very competitive.
- Correct: **When** I play board games with Stephen, **who** is always very competitive, I **have fun.**

Miscellaneous

1) When a modifying phrase (participial phrase, appositive, etc.) follows an independent clause, it is acceptable to use a comma.
    - The farmer spent hours working on the farm, an arduous undertaking indeed.

An "arduous undertaking indeed" describes the work that the farmer did.

- The unscrupulous judge was accused of running a **kangaroo court**, a court that ignores the principles of justice and operates dishonestly.

The definition of "kangaroo court" appropriately follows the comma.

Drill 2

(1) Null results, results in which the expected outcomes are absent, are of great value to researchers. (2) However, they are rarely published in popular journals. (3) This phenomenon is problematic. (4) Researchers often repeating these studies because they are unaware they have been done before.

1. Which sentence should be revised to correct a fragment?
    A. Sentence 1
    B. Sentence 2
    C. Sentence 3
    D. Sentence 4

The Niagara River, which flows north from Lake Erie to Lake Ontario, forming part of the border between the United States and Canada.

2. Which of the following edits should be made?
    A. Change "forming" to "being formed."
    B. Change "forming" to "forms."
    C. Delete "which flows north from Lake Erie to Lake Ontario."
    D. Change "part of the" to "the."

> The public health crisis in the small rural community having been alleviated because of improved access to vaccinations and medical care.

3. Which of the following edits should be made?
   A. Change "because of" to "as a result of."
   B. Change "having" to "was."
   C. Change "having" to "has."
   D. Change "and" to "in addition to."

> Talked to her brother on the phone in order to ask for advice.

4. Which of the following edits should be made?
   A. Change "ask" to "asking."
   B. Change "Talked" to "She talked."
   C. Change "Talked" to "She."
   D. Change "ask" to "ask him."

> (1) Author Gertrude Stein known for her unique usage of words and is of great interest to literary scholars. (2) She rejected literary norms by challenging conventions about grammar, style, and storytelling in general. (3) Though her works contained some famous quotes, most of her fiction was not commercially successful. (4) Her autobiography, however, was a bestseller.

5. Which of the following sentences should be revised to correct a fragment?
   A. Sentence 1
   B. Sentence 2
   C. Sentence 3
   D. Sentence 4

> If the majority of the committee likes the proposal, the chairwoman, who will approve it.

6. Which of the following edits should be made?
   A. Delete "the chairwoman."
   B. Change "the chairwoman, who" to "the chairwoman."
   C. Change "who" to "whom."
   D. Change "will" to "is going to."

> <u>Offering</u> words of inspiration, presented through the medium of poetry.

7. Which of the following edits to the underlined portion would correct the fragment?
   A. Because of
   B. Here are
   C. The reading of
   D. Here is

> In the paper, recommends doing something small each day if one feels unaccomplished.

8. Which of the following edits to the underlined portion would correct the fragment?
    A. the psychologist recommending
    B. being argued that
    C. the psychologist recommends
    D. states

> The Wren Library, located at Trinity College in Cambridge, which has a full-size statue of Lord Byron.

9. Which of the following edits should be made?
    A. Delete "located."
    B. Add "it is very famous," after the comma following "The Wren Library."
    C. Change "has" to "have."
    D. Delete "which."

> The labor union members demanded pay increasing from their employer.

10. Which of the following edits should be made?
    A. Change "increasing" to "increases."
    B. Change "demanded" to "demanding."
    C. Add "have" after "members."
    D. Delete "members."

> Usually devoted fans that purchase tickets as soon as they become available.

11. Which of the following edits should be made?
    A. Change "that" to "which."
    B. Delete "that."
    C. Change "purchase" to "purchasing."
    D. Change "become" to "are."

> A symphony being when an extended composition of Western classical music.

12. Which of the following best replaces the underlined potion?
    A. being
    B. when
    C. which is when
    D. is

> When the scientist boils the contents of the flask, adds a salt solution, and measures the alkene concentration.

13. Which of the following edits should be made?
    A. Change "boils" to "is boiling."
    B. Change "When the" to "The."
    C. Delete "and."
    D. Delete "the scientist."

Although Rachel and Leslie were supposed to contribute to the assignment equally, but Rachel did most of the work.

14. Which of the following edits should be made?
    A. Replace "Although" with "Despite."
    B. Delete "were."
    C. Delete "but."
    D. Replace "but" with "while."

Because water dissolves more substances than any other substance, therefore it is called the universal solvent.

15. Which of the following edits should be made?
    A. Delete "therefore."
    B. Change "Because" to "Since."
    C. Change "Because" to "Due to the fact that."
    D. Change "is called" to "has been called."

In the local newspaper, the culture section that presents information about art, dance, music, and photography.

16. Which of the following edits should be made?
    A. Add "being" after "section."
    B. Delete "that."
    C. Add "is" after "section."
    D. Delete "information."

Traders, who work several nightshifts during the week.

17. Which of the following best replaces the underlined portion?
    A. Traders, which
    B. Traders that
    C. Traders, they
    D. Traders

After the celebrity went on the talk show. He had to apologize for his insensitive remarks.

18. Which of the following best replaces the underlined portion?
    A. show; he
    B. show he
    C. show, he
    D. show, being that he

Walking in the rainforest, feeling as if I have entered another world.

19. Which of the following best replaces the underlined portion?
    A. feeling as if
    B. the feeling that
    C. I feel as if
    D. as though

Week 6

> From an open window, which light enters the bedroom.

20. Which of the following edits should be made?
    A. Change the comma to a semicolon.
    B. Change "enters" to "entering."
    C. Delete "which."
    D. Change "an open" to "a."

Run-On Sentences

Run-on sentences are sentences that contain two or more independent clauses that have been improperly combined. A **comma splice** is type of run-on that occurs when two independent clauses are separated by a comma.

- Incorrect: I had never given a speech before**, I** was nervous.

The sentence inappropriately contains two independent clauses that are only separated by a comma.

There are several ways to correct a comma splice.

1) Create two sentences.
   - I had never given a speech before**.** I was nervous.
2) Replace the comma with a **semicolon**. Note that when a semicolon is used, the clauses before and after the semicolon must be independent. That is, both clauses should be able to stand alone as complete sentences. In some cases, add a conjunctive adverb after the semicolon in order to clarify the relationship between the clauses.
   - I had never given a speech before**;** I was nervous.
   - I had never given a speech before**; therefore,** I was nervous.

Important: A conjunctive adverb introducing a second independent clause at the end of a sentence **MUST** follow a semicolon.

- Incorrect: Lucky's painting was a portrait**, conversely,** Judd's was an abstract.

The sentence contains a comma splice.

- Correct: Lucky's painting was a portrait**; conversely,** Judd's was an abstract.

The semicolon appropriately separates two independent clauses.

3) Add a subordinating conjunction to make one of the clauses dependent.
   - **Since** I had never given a speech before, I was nervous.

4) Add a coordinating conjunction (for, and, nor, but, or, yet, so) after a **comma.**
   - I had never given a speech before, **so** I was nervous.

5) Change one independent clause into a modifying phrase, a phrase that provides more details about a noun.
   - **Having never given a speech before,** I was nervous.

Important Points

1) A coordinating conjunction **should not** follow a semicolon.
    - Incorrect: Hieroglyphics were a system of writing that used pictures to represent words and sounds**; and** they were deciphered by Jean-François Champollion.
    - Correct: Hieroglyphics were a system of writing that used pictures to represent words and sounds**, and** they were deciphered by Jean-François Champollion.

2) An independent clause **should not** follow nonessential terms that are set off by commas in the middle of a sentence.
    - Incorrect: Herodotus, **who was a Greek historian**, he wrote about the Persian Empire.
    - Correct: Herodotus, **who was a Greek historian**, wrote about the Persian Empire.

The correct sentence is complete when the bolded relative clause is ignored.

3) Independent clauses usually cannot function as nonessential terms that are set off by commas. Phrases that contain a main verb with no subject should not be set off by commas.
    - Incorrect: Saturday Night Live, **it is a television show known for its comedic sketches**, has entertained audiences for decades.
    - Incorrect: Saturday Night Live, **is a television show known for its comedic sketches**, has entertained audiences for decades.

The first sentence uses an independent clause in the middle of a sentence, and the second uses a phrase with a main verb.

    - Correct: Saturday Night Live, **a television show known for its comedic sketches**, has entertained audiences for decades.
    - Correct: Saturday Night Live, **which is known for its comedic sketches**, has entertained audiences for decades.
    - Correct: Saturday Night Live, **known for its comedic sketches**, has entertained audiences for decades.

The first sentence has a nonessential appositive, the second has a relative clause, and the third has a participial phrase.

4) Creating a relative clause by changing a noun or pronoun to an appropriate relative pronoun *(who, whom, which)* can sometimes eliminate a comma splice.
    - Incorrect: I called my friend, **he** gave me advice.
    - Correct: I called my friend, **who** gave me advice.

5) Creating a prepositional phrase with "of which" or "of whom" can sometimes eliminate a comma splice. These phrases often follow indefinite pronouns (*all, both, each, many, most, some, etc.*)
    - Incorrect: The students gave presentations, **most** were excellent.
    - Correct: The students gave presentations, **most of which** were excellent.

Drill 3

> He was inspired by a family he knew, J.M. Barrie wrote *Peter Pan*, a wildly successful play.

1. Which edit should be made to correct the run-on?
   A. Change "he knew" to "he had known."
   B. Change "He was inspired" to "Inspired."
   C. Change "wrote" to "had written."
   D. Delete "wildly."

> Bella frequently networked at social events. This helped her land an opportunity at a startup, this is a newly established business.

2. Which edit should be made to correct the run-on?
   A. Delete "this is."
   B. Add a semicolon after "events."
   C. Change "this is" to "this being."
   D. Add "as such," after "startup."

> The author published several stories, each has a unique plot twist.

3. Which edit should be made to correct the run-on?
   A. Change "has" to "had."
   B. Change "each has" to "each of which has."
   C. Change "published" to "publishing."
   D. Change "each has" to "all have."

> The talk show host announced months in advance that she would not be renewing her contract, this gave time for the producers to find a replacement.

4. Which of the following edits should be made?
   A. Change "would not" to "will not"
   B. Change "this gave" to "it gave"
   C. Change "this gave" to "giving"
   D. Change "gave" to "gives"

> Many television cartoons operate on a floating timeline, this is a trope in which the characters do not age despite the years passing normally.

5. Which of the following best replaces the underlined portion?
   A. timeline; a
   B. timeline this is a
   C. timeline, is
   D. timeline, a

Week 6

The dogwood tree grew in the front yard in the late fall and winter, it is covered with berries.

6. Which of the following best replaces the underlined portion?
   A. yard, in
   B. yard; in
   C. yard; and in
   D. yard, in fact, in

After years of training, Hallie qualified for the National Championship, even then, she did not seem content.

7. Which of the following best replaces the underlined portion?
   A. Championship even then
   B. Championship, even, then
   C. Championship. Even then,
   D. Championship, even then

It was designed by Franklin Lloyd Wright, The Guggenheim Museum is visited by nearly 1.2 million people each year.

8. Which of the following edits should be made?
   A. Change "It was designed by" to "Designed by."
   B. Change "It was designed by" to "The museum was designed by."
   C. Delete "people."
   D. Add a comma after "Museum."

Katy never thought she would work on a political campaign, she was inspired by a candidate with a message that resonated with her.

9. Which of the following best replaces the underlined portion?
   A. campaign; but
   B. campaign; and
   C. campaign, but
   D. campaign, so

Henry Clay, he served as the Secretary of State under John Quincy Adams, founded the Whig Party, which was active in the mid-nineteenth century.

10. Which of the following edits should be made?
    A. Change "which was active" to "it was active."
    B. Change "he served" to "who served."
    C. Change "founded" to "he founded."
    D. Delete "which."

The intricate dance was performed by the duet partners, both of them had years of experience.

11. Which of the following edits should be made?
    A. Change "them" to "whom."
    B. Delete "of them."
    C. Change "had" to "have."
    D. Change "both of them" to "they."

The city hall would host a farmer's market every <u>Wednesday, on such days</u>, fruits and vegetables from local farms were sold.

12. Which of the following best replaces the underlined portion?
    A. Wednesday,
    B. Wednesday, which is when
    C. Wednesday; which is when
    D. Wednesday, here,

The students saw the Shakespeare play "Much Ado About Nothing" at the Sydney Opera <u>House, it is a</u> preeminent opera house with a modern expressionist design.

13. Which of the following edits best corrects the underlined portion?
    A. House, is considered a
    B. House, it serves as a
    C. House; a
    D. House, a

Jamal works in the <u>observatory, he provides</u> support for the workers who take shifts in the cold.

14. Which of the following best replaces the underlined portion?
    A. observatory; he provides
    B. observatory he provides
    C. observatory; providing
    D. observatory yet he provides

Many of the stories in the collection take place in different cities around the United States Cleveland, Los Angeles, and Detroit are some of these cities.

15. Which of the following edits should be made?
    A. Add a period after "the United States."
    B. Add a comma after "the United States."
    C. Add "some include" after "the United States."
    D. Change "take place" to "took place."

Painter Winslow Homer was fascinated by the sea, in *Cannon Rock*, rocks appeared flattened by the power of the ocean.

16. Which of the following best replaces the underlined portion?
    A. sea in
    B. sea, but in
    C. sea; in
    D. sea in,

At age eight, Mozart composed his first symphony, it was scored for two oboes, two horns, harpsichord, and strings.

17. Which of the following edits should be made?
    A. Replace "it" with "which."
    B. Add "yet" after the comma following "symphony."
    C. Delete "it."
    D. Add a semicolon after "age 8."

The owner of the multimedia conglomerate was convicted of embezzlement, this is considered a type of financial crime.

18. Which of the following best replaces the underlined portion?
    A. this is
    B. that is
    C. it is
    D. a

Dwight Eisenhower, who served as a general in World War II, before becoming President of the United States.

19. Which of the following is the correct version of the sentence?
    A. Dwight Eisenhower, serving as a general in World War II, before becoming President of the United States.
    B. Dwight Eisenhower, he served as a general in World War II, before becoming President of the United States.
    C. Dwight Eisenhower served as a general in World War II before becoming President of the United States.
    D. Dwight Eisenhower serving as a general in World War II before becoming President of the United States.

The company is embracing modern technology, it substituted in-person conferences with video conferences.

20. Which of the following best replaces the underlined portion?
    A. technology, substituting
    B. technology; substituting
    C. technology it substituted
    D. technology, it is substituting

Week 6

Week 6B: Bonus Reading Passage 1

The poem below is "Mother to Son" by Langston Hughes.

>   Well, son, I'll tell you:
>   Life for me ain't been no crystal stair.
>   It's had tacks in it,
>   And splinters,
> 5 And boards torn up,
>   And places with no carpet on the floor—
>   Bare.
>   But all the time
>   I'se been a-climbin' on,
> 10 And reachin' landin's,
>   And turnin' corners,
>   And sometimes goin' in the dark
>   Where there ain't been no light.
>   So boy, don't you turn back.
> 15 Don't you set down on the steps
>   'Cause you finds it's kinder hard.
>   Don't you fall now—
>   For I'se still goin', honey,
>   I'se still climbin',
> 20 And life for me ain't been no crystal stair.

1. The mother's character can best be described as
   A. resigned to her subordinate station in life.
   B. persistent in the face of adversity.
   C. wary of signs suggesting her troubles are subsiding.
   D. an intimidating and motivating force in her son's childhood.

Life for me ain't been no crystal stair.

It's had tacks in it,

2. Reread the excerpt above. The lines primarily serve to illustrate a contrast between the speaker's
   A. past comfort and present tribulations.
   B. lived experience and imagined possibilities.
   C. poor living conditions and desire for wealth.
   D. sadness over her own life and jealousy over the privilege of others.

3. In the context of the text, "crystal" most likely means
   A. sharp and precious.
   B. transparent and flawed.
   C. pointy and hurtful.
   D. clear and smooth.

**And boards torn up,
And places with no carpet on the floor—
Bare.**

4. Reread the excerpt above. These lines primarily serve to suggest that the speaker's life has been
   A. primarily defined by misfortune.
   B. too difficult for the speaker to bear.
   C. challenging and painful at times.
   D. smooth and clear-cut in its simplicity.

5. The dialect in the poem helps create a tone that is
   A. lighthearted.
   B. melancholy.
   C. conversational.
   D. condescending.

6. The "stair" referenced throughout can best be understood as
   A. a metaphor for the speaker's lived experiences.
   B. a feature of the speaker's childhood home.
   C. a figment of the speaker's imagination.
   D. a literal physical location fraught with challenges.

7. When the mother is on the stairs, she states that she
   A. climbs even when it is difficult to see.
   B. proceeds cautiously in the dark.
   C. avoids the tacks and splinters.
   D. frequently falls.

8. The "splinters" most likely refer most literally to
   A. literal pieces of woods.
   B. obstacles the speaker has faced.
   C. the pains experienced by the speaker's son.
   D. an injury for which the speaker could not afford medical care.

9. The mother's statements to her son in lines 17-19 primarily serve to
   A. warn him about dangers he will encounter.
   B. encourage him to persevere in the face of adversity.
   C. boast about her own unique capabilities.
   D. emphasize the length of the journey before him.

10. Which excerpt from the poem most clearly illustrates the speaker's resilience?
    A. "Don't you fall now—"
    B. "So boy, don't you turn back."
    C. "For I'se still goin', honey,"
    D. "And life for me ain't been no crystal stair."

Kweller Prep NEW SHSAT Grammar and Reading

Week 7

Week 7: Modifier Placement

Modifying phrases are phrases that describe nouns. In each example, the modifying phrase is in **bold** and the noun being modified is in *italics*.

Participial Phrases are phrases that contain participles, verbs functioning as adjectives. The **present participle** ends in "-ing" (e.g., parking, running) and the **past participle** typically ends in "-ed," "-en," "-n," "-d," or "-t" (e.g., quoted, written, known, bent).

- **Walking through the woods**, the *hiker* admired the beautiful scenery.
- **Delayed in its implementation**, the *new curriculum* was not taught in schools for another year.

Adjectival Phrases are phrases that begin with an adjective.

- **Uncomfortable with her boss's unethical request**, *Maura* decided to quit her job rather than comply.

Prepositional Phrases are phrases that begin with prepositions.

- **As a member of the band,** *I* helped compose the song.
- The *children* went to the amusement park, **with the most daring riding the fastest roller coaster.**

Appositive Phrases are phrases that rename a noun.

- *Pinball*, **an activity requiring great skill**, has lost popularity in recent years.
- **One of the best consultants in the electronics industry**, *Ana* was hired to help the fledgling business.
- **A document that indicates the rules of the organization**, *the charter* was signed by the company's founder last year.
- The 18th century saw the rise of the *French Salon*, **a gathering of men and women for intellectual and social exchange.**

A **misplaced modifier** results from a modifier being placed too far from the noun it modifies, thus making the meaning of the sentence unclear. Some common variations of misplaced modifiers include

1) **Misplaced Adjectives**

- Incorrect: The **plaid** kid's shirt is hanging up in the closet.

The sentence makes it seems as if the kid is plaid, instead of the shirt.

- Correct: The kid's **plaid** shirt is hanging up in the closet.

2) **Misplaced Adverbs**

- Incorrect: I **nearly** waited five hours for the mail to arrive.

This sentence inappropriately suggests that the speaker did not wait, but "nearly" (almost) waited.

- Correct: I waited **nearly** five hours for the mail to arrive.

In this sentence, "nearly" correctly modifies "five." The number of hours the speaker waited was almost five hours.

3) **Error: Misplaced Participles**

- Incorrect: I saw the tree **looking through the window.**

A tree cannot look through a window.

- Correct: I saw the tree **when I looked through the window**.

The modifying phrase can be changed to a main verb. In this sentence, a dependent clause beginning with "when" follows an independent clause, clarifying that the speaker looked.

4) **Error 4: Misplaced Relative Pronoun**

Pronouns such as "which," "who," and "where" should be close to the nouns they modify.

- Incorrect: The filmmaker showed his movie in the park, **which** was praised for its originality.

The sentence inappropriately suggests that the park was praised.

- Correct: In the park, the filmmaker showed his movie, which was praised for its originality.

The revised sentence makes it clearer that the movie was praised.

Dangling Modifiers

The noun that an introductory phrase describes must immediately follow the modifying phrase (with or without the articles "the", "a," or "an") in order to avoid a dangling modifier, a type of misplaced modifier.

- Incorrect: **Wanting to do well on his exam,** every night for a week *Kyle* studied.

The sentence inappropriately suggests that "every night" wanted to do well on his exam.

- Correct: **Wanting to do well on his exam,** *Kyle* studied every night for a week.

The noun "Kyle" correctly follows the participial phrase.

- Correct: Wanting to do well on his exam, *the ambitious Kyle* studied every night for a week.

In this case "ambitious" helps describe Kyle. It is still clear that Kyle is the noun being modified.

- Incorrect: **Selected for their keen sense of smell,** police investigations often use *dogs* to detect crime evidence.

The sentence inappropriately suggests that the police investigations have a keen sense of smell.

- Correct: **Selected for their keen sense of smell**, *dogs* are often used in police investigations to detect crime evidence.

The revision corrects the dangling modifier by clarifying that dogs are being described.

Incorrect answer choices will often include the possessive form (a noun followed by an apostrophe to show belonging) of the modified noun after the modifying phrase.

- Incorrect: **Respected for his kindness**, the *volunteer's time* was spent working with children.

The modifying phrase is supposed to describe the volunteer. As the sentence is written now, it appears that the *time* of the volunteer was respected for its kindness.

- Correct: **Respected for his kindness**, *the volunteer* spent his time working with children.

Occasionally, the modifying phrase itself must be changed to correctly modify a given noun. For example, a present participle is sometimes used when a past participle is needed. Such confusion usually occurs when one noun is acting on another.

- Incorrect: **Using it to promote relaxation**, *the product* has grown popular in recent years.

In this case, "using it" seems to describe people using the product. Since "the product" follows the comma, the result is a dangling modifier.

- Correct: **Used to promote relaxation**, *the product* has grown popular in recent years.

The modifying phrase describes the product.

- Incorrect: **After electing him as class president**, *Herb* was honored that his classmates supported him.

In context, "electing him" describes the classmates (they were the ones who elected Herb).

- Correct: **Having been elected as class president**, *Herb* was honored that his classmates supported him.

"Having been elected" clearly describes Herb, the person who was elected.

Week 7

Drill 1

(1) Lievens, who was a Dutch painter, was often compared to fellow painter Rembrandt during their lifetimes. (2) The works of Lievens are often mistook for those of Rembrandt, who likely borrowed techniques form Lievens. (3) Never settling on one specific painting style, the popularity of Lievens declined after his death. (4) In recent years, Lievens has begun to emerge from Rembrandt's shadow and is now recognized as a capable artist in his own right.

1. Which sentence should be revised to correct a misplaced modifier?
    A. Sentence 1
    B. Sentence 2
    C. Sentence 3
    D. Sentence 4

(1) Known for his murals in fresco, the paintings of artist David Siqueiros reflected social realism. (2) Not only was Siqueiros a skilled painter, but he was also a radical political activist. (3) While some people believed that art and politics should be treated as separate disciplines, Siqueiros saw them as deeply intertwined. (4) In fact, during his career, he painted several politically themed murals in order to educate the public through his art.

2. Which sentence should be revised to correct a misplaced modifier?
    A. Sentence 1
    B. Sentence 2
    C. Sentence 3
    D. Sentence 4

Pleased, a donation was made anonymously and discovered by the staff.

3. Which of the following is the best revision to the sentence above?
    A. Pleased, anonymously made was a donation discovered by the staff.
    B. A donation was made anonymously and discovered by pleased staff.
    C. Anonymously pleased, a donation was discovered by the staff.
    D. Left anonymously and discovered by staff, each donation was pleased.

Hiking along the trail, the beautiful scenery was admired by Dayna.

4. Which of the following is the best revision to the sentence above?
    A. She hiked along the trail, Dayna admired the beautiful scenery.
    B. The beautiful scenery, being admired by Dayna.
    C. Hiking along the trail, Dayna admired the beautiful scenery.
    D. Hiking along the trail, admiration was felt by Dayna about the beautiful scenery.

Located in the once booming business district, disrepair was the state of the old factory.

5. Which of the following is the best revision of the sentence above?
    A. Located in the once booming business district, the state of the old factory was one of disrepair.
    B. Located in the once booming business district, the old factory was in a state of disrepair.
    C. The once booming business district in the old factory was in a state of disrepair.
    D. The state of disrepair was the old factory in the once booming business district.

Week 7

The display is decorated with tiny crystals <u>trapped</u> formed by the hardening of liquid rocks below the Earth's surface.

6. Which of the following is the best placement for the underlined portion?
    A. After "display."
    B. After "formed."
    C. After "rocks."
    D. After "hardening."

Known for his contributions to genetics, Mendel's "Experiments on Plant Hybridization" described his studies of inheritance in pea plants.

7. Which of the following is the best revision of the sentence above?
    A. Knowing him for his contributions to genetics, Mendel's "Experiments on Plant Hybridization" described his studies of inheritance in pea plants.
    B. Known for his contributions to genetics, studies of inheritance in pea plants were described by Mendel in "Experiments on Plant Hybridization."
    C. Known for his contributions to genetics, Mendel described his studies of inheritance in pea plants in "Experiments on Plant Hybridization."
    D. Knowing him for his contributions to genetics, Mendel described his studies of inheritance in pea plants in "Experiments on Plant Hybridization."

<u>Choosing her for her shrewd marketing skills,</u> Emma was the campaign manager of the mayoral candidate.

8. Which of the following best replaces underlined portion?
    A. She was chosen for her shrewd marketing skills,
    B. Chosen for her shrewd marketing skills,
    C. They chose her for her shrewd marketing skills,
    D. Her marketing skills are shrewd,

Because it was too cold to walk home, Trevor took <u>wisely</u> the bus.

9. Which of the following is the best placement of the underlined portion?
    A. After "it."
    B. After "walk."
    C. After "Trevor."
    D. After "the."

The store ranging from luxury vehicles to cheap used cars sells automobiles.

10. Which of the following is the best revision for the sentence above?
    A. The store, ranging from luxury vehicles to cheap used cars, sells automobiles.
    B. The store sells automobiles ranging from luxury vehicles to cheap used cars.
    C. Ranging from luxury vehicles to cheap used cars, the store sells automobiles.
    D. Selling automobiles, ranging from luxury vehicles to cheap used cars, the store.

Week 7

> The horizontally labels were placed in the store on containers.

11. Which of the following is the best revision of the sentence above?
    A. The labels were placed on in the store containers horizontally.
    B. The labels were placed horizontally on the in the store containers
    C. The labels were placed horizontally on containers in the store.
    D. The labels horizontally were placed in the store on containers.

> Laura checked for factual and grammatical errors prior to submitting carefully her essay.

12. Which of the following is the best revision of the sentence above?
    A. Laura checked carefully for factual and grammatical errors prior to submitting her essay.
    B. Laura carefully prior to submitting her essay checked for factual and grammatical errors.
    C. Laura checked, prior to submitting her essay, factual and grammatical errors, carefully.
    D. Laura carefully, prior to submitting her essay, checked for errors, factual and grammatical included.

> At the park, fans of comedy in crowds waited for the artist to perform.

13. Which of the following is the best revision of the sentence above?
    A. At the park waited fans of comedy in crowds for the artist to perform.
    B. Fans of comedy in the park waited in crowds for the artist to perform.
    C. Waiting for the artist to perform, fans of comedy in crowds were at the park.
    D. At the park, crowds of comedy fans waited for the artist to perform.

> Driving down the street, an unusual billboard was noticed by me that made me laugh.

14. Which of the following is the best revision of the sentence above?
    A. An unusual billboard, driving down the street, made me laugh when I noticed it.
    B. I noticed an unusual billboard driving down the street that made me laugh.
    C. Driving down the street, I noticed an unusual billboard that made me laugh.
    D. It made me laugh, the unusual billboard driving down the street.

> An innovative style of music and improvisation, in the 1950s avant-garde jazz originated that challenged conventions of bebop.

15. Which of the following best corrects the dangling modifier in the sentence above?
    A. avant-garde jazz music that challenged conventions of bebop originated in the 1950s.
    B. the 1950s saw the origination of avant-garde jazz music that challenged conventions of bebop.
    C. the conventions of bebop were challenged in the 1950s by avant-garde jazz music.
    D. the origination of avant-garde jazz music challenged in the 1950s bebop conventions.

> To promote interest in their profession, master classes will be given by members of the speechwriting association on Saturday

16. Which of the following is the best revision of the sentence above?
    A. To promote interest in their profession, on Saturday master classes from members of the speechwriting association will be given.
    B. Members of the speechwriting association, on Saturday to promote interest in their profession, will give master classes.
    C. To promote interest in their profession, members of the speechwriting association will give master classes on Saturday.
    D. Members of the speechwriting association to promote interest on Saturday in their profession will give master classes.

> Norman moved to a village in Belgium attempting to lead a more idyllic life.

17. Which of the following edits should be made?
    A. Move "in Belgium" after "Norman."
    B. Change "attempting" to "in an attempt."
    C. Change "moved" to "moving."
    D. Change "attempting to" to "which attempted."

> (1) DNA microarrays represent an important development in the field of genetics.
> (2) Microarrays allow scientists to study an organism's entire genome.

18. Which of the following best combines the sentences?
    A. DNA microarrays, which allow scientists to study an organism's entire genome, represent an important development in the field of genetics.
    B. Because microarrays allow scientists to study an organism's entire genome, therefore they represent an important development in the field of genetics.
    C. Although DNA microarrays represent an important development in the field of genetics, they allow scientists to study an organism's entire genome.
    D. DNA microarrays represent an important development in the field of genetics, which allow scientists to study an organism's entire genome.

> (1) The human maze contained many twists, turns, and obstacles.
> (2) The twists, turns, and obstacles make it difficult for one to complete the maze quickly.

19. Which of the following best combines the sentences?
    A. Even though the human maze contains many twists, turns, and obstacles, it is difficult for one to complete it quickly.
    B. The quick completion of the maze for one person is difficult, which contained many twists, turns, and obstacles.
    C. The human maze contains many twists, turns, and obstacles, making it difficult for one to complete the maze quickly.
    D. Since it is difficult for one to complete the maze quickly, the human maze has many twists, turns, and obstacles.

> (1) Carnivorous plants are commonly found in bogs.
> (2) Carnivorous plants grow in acidic soil.
> (3) Carnivorous plants derive nutrients from trapping animals and bacteria.

20. Which of the following best combines the sentences?
    A. Carnivorous plants, which grow in acidic soil and are commonly found in bogs, derive their nutrients from trapping animals and bacteria.
    B. Carnivorous plants derive their nutrients from trapping animals and bacteria, which grow in acidic soil and commonly grow in bogs.
    C. Because they are commonly found in bogs, carnivorous plants grow in acidic soil and derive their nutrients from trapping animals and bacteria.
    D. Even though carnivorous plants derive nutrients from trapping animals and bacteria, they are commonly found in bogs, which grow in acidic soil.

Week 7B: Bonus Passage 2

The excerpt below is adapted from *A Daughter of the Samurai* by Etsu Inagaki Sugimoto.

[1] I was about eight years old when I had my first taste of meat. For twelve centuries, following the introduction of the Buddhist religion, which forbids the killing of animals, the Japanese people were vegetarians. In late years, however, both belief and custom have changed considerably, and now, though meat is not universally eaten, it can be found in all restaurants and hotels. But when I was a child, it was looked upon with horror and loathing.

[2] How well I remember one day when I came home from school and found the entire household wrapped in gloom. I felt a sense of depression as soon as I stepped into the "shoe-off" entrance, and heard my mother, in low, solemn tones, giving directions to a maid. A group of servants at the end of the hall seemed excited, but they also were talking in hushed voices. Of course, since I had not yet greeted the family, I did not ask any questions, but I had an uneasy feeling that something was wrong, and it was very hard for me to walk calmly and unhurriedly down the long hall to my grandmother's room.

[3] "Honourable Grandmother, I have returned," I murmured, as I sank to the floor with my usual salutation. She returned my bow with a gentle smile, but she was graver than usual. She and a maid were sitting before the black-and-gold cabinet of the family shrine. They had a large lacquer tray with rolls of white paper on it and the maid was pasting paper over the gilded doors of the shrine.

[4] Like almost every Japanese home, ours had two shrines. In time of sickness or death, the plain wooden Shinto shrine, which honours the Sun goddess, the Emperor, and the nation, was sealed with white paper to guard it from pollution. But the gilded Buddhist shrine was kept wide open at such a time; for Buddhist gods give comfort to the sorrowing and guide the dead on their heavenward journey. I had never known the gold shrine to be sealed; and besides, this was the very hour for it to be lighted in readiness for the evening meal. That was always the pleasantest part of the day; for after the first helping of our food had been placed on a tiny lacquer table before the shrine, we all seated ourselves at our separate tables, and ate, talked and laughed, feeling that the loving hearts of the ancestors were also with us. But the shrine was closed. What could it mean?

[5] "Pardon me, Honourable Grandmother," I persisted anxiously; "but is not the shrine being sealed with the pure paper of protection?"

[6] "Yes," she answered with a little sigh, and said nothing more.

[7] I did not speak again but sat watching her bent shoulders as she leaned over, unrolling the paper for the maid. My heart was greatly troubled.

[8] Presently she straightened up and turned toward me.

[9] "Your honourable father has ordered his household to eat flesh," she said very slowly. "The wise physician who follows the path of the Western barbarians has told him that the flesh of animals will bring strength to his weak body and also will make the children robust and clever like the people of the Western sea. The ox flesh is to be brought into the house in another hour and our duty is to protect the holy shrine from pollution."

[10] That evening we ate a solemn dinner with meat in our soup; but no friendly spirits were with us, for both shrines were sealed. Grandmother did not join us. She always occupied the seat of honour, and the vacant place looked strange and lonely. That night I asked her why she had not come.

[11] "I would rather not grow as strong as a Westerner—nor as clever," she answered sadly. "It is more becoming for me to follow the path of our ancestors."

[12] My sister and I confided to each other that we liked the taste of meat. But neither of us mentioned this to anyone else; for we both loved Grandmother, and we knew our disloyalty would sadden her heart.

[13] The introduction of foreign food helped greatly to break down the wall of tradition which shut our people away from the world of the West, but sometimes the change was made at a great cost. This could not be otherwise; for after the Restoration many samurai suddenly found themselves not only poor and at the same time separated entirely from the system that had given them support; but also, bound as firmly as ever by the code of ethics that for centuries had taught them utter contempt for money. The land was flooded, during those first years, with business failures; for many of these men were young, ambitious, and eager to experiment with new customs.

1. In the context of the passage as a whole, paragraph 1 primarily serves to
   A. explain why a widespread cultural practice lost favor.
   B. foreshadow how a breakdown of tradition has inflamed social tensions.
   C. convey the narrator's homeland's increasing acceptance of certain Western practices.
   D. express the narrator's nostalgia for a time in which meat was taboo in Japanese society.

2. Which excerpt from the text provides the best evidence that the narrator is perceptive to emotional cues?
   A. "I felt a sense of depression as soon as I stepped into the "shoe-off" entrance, and heard my mother, in low, solemn tones, giving directions to a maid" (paragraph 2).
   B. "'Honourable Grandmother, I have returned,'" I murmured, as I sank to the floor with my usual salutation." (paragraph 3)
   C. "But the gilded Buddhist shrine was kept wide open at such a time; for Buddhist gods give comfort to the sorrowing and guide the dead on their heavenward journey" (paragraph 4)
   D. "I did not speak again but sat watching her bent shoulders as she leaned over, unrolling the paper for the maid" (paragraph 7).

3. How do the details about the changes to the shrine in paragraph 4 contribute to the development of the plot?
   A. They provide context that clarifies why the narrator was able to deduce an impending change in her household's dynamics.
   B. They clarify the narrator's grandmother's plan for thwarting another character's agenda.
   C. They reveal the lack of respect the narrator's father has for his ancestral roots.
   D. They foreshadow how a traditional structure will be refashioned to accommodate a new set of customs.

4. In context, the statement "though meat is not universally eaten" (paragraph 1) functions to
   A. note the reversal of an aforementioned trend.
   B. highlight a growing divide between Japanese who embraced and those who rejected adopting new customs.
   C. suggest that the acceptance of meat in Japanese cuisine was highly controversial.
   D. introduce a minor qualification related to a previous assertion.

5. Which excerpt from the text best suggests that the narrator feels a deep connection to her native culture?
   A. "I had never known the gold shrine to be sealed; and besides, this was the very hour for it to be lighted in readiness for the evening meal" (paragraph 4)
   B. "we all seated ourselves at our separate tables, and ate, talked and laughed, feeling that the loving hearts of the ancestors were also with us" (paragraph 4).
   C. "The introduction of foreign food helped greatly to break down the wall of tradition which shut our people away from the world of the West, but sometimes the change was made at a great cost" (paragraph 13)
   D. "but also, bound as firmly as ever by the code of ethics that for centuries had taught them utter contempt for money" (paragraph 13)

My sister and I confided to each other that we liked the taste of meat. But neither of us mentioned this to anyone else; for we both loved Grandmother, and we knew our disloyalty would sadden her heart.

6. Reread the excerpt above from paragraph 12. In the context of the text, this excerpt serves to
   A. highlight a contrast between the narrator and her sister.
   B. dramatize the tension between a grandmother and her granddaughters.
   C. allude to a circumstance that presented the narrator with a moral conflict of sorts.
   D. suggest that an intergenerational rift is irrevocably unrepairable.

7. The decision to close the Buddhist shrine in the narrator's household can best be described as a
   A. rejection of traditional Japanese customs.
   B. reaction to a decision that violated sacred norms.
   C. celebration of the breakdown of cultural barriers.
   D. measure to prevent meat from entering the household.

"The wise physician who follows the path of the Western barbarians has told him that the flesh of animals will bring strength to his weak body and also will make the children robust and clever like the people of the Western sea."

"I would rather not grow as strong as a Westerner—nor as clever," she answered sadly. "It is more becoming for me to follow the path of our ancestors."

8. Reread the statements above from paragraphs 9 and 11. Taken together, these statements reveal that the narrator's grandmother
    A. believes that the health benefits of meat are marginal at best.
    B. considers cleverness an inherently barbaric trait.
    C. has a deep respect for ancestral Japanese traditions.
    D. thinks Westerners would do well to adopt vegetarian diets.

9. The "wall of tradition" (paragraph 13) can best be understood as
    A. a protective physical barrier between distrusting populations.
    B. a set of circumstances that functioned as an impediment to cultural diffusion.
    C. an obstacle that must be overcome to experience personal fulfillment.
    D. a code of ethics grounded in secular values.

10. A notable contradiction that the narrator sees in many of the samurai who went poor after the Restoration was that they
    A. pursued failed businesses despite knowing that their odds of succeeding were low because of their inexperience.
    B. were slow to warm up to interacting with foreigners despite having failed to make a living in their traditional roles.
    C. clung to the principles of a system that had failed to meet their basic needs.
    D. expected Western business to operate according to the same code of ethics as they did despite the failure of that code to launch many successful businesses.

Kweller Prep NEW SHSAT Grammar and Reading

Week 8

Week 8: Pronoun Agreement

Pronouns must agree with their antecedents, the nouns for which they stand. The pronouns and antecedents must agree in gender (male or female), number (singular or plural), and case (subjective or objective).

When the antecedent is a singular noun, the pronoun must be singular. When the antecedent is a plural noun, the pronoun must be plural.

Pronouns	Singular	Plural
Personal	I, me, he, him, she, her, you, it	they, them, we, us
Reflexive	myself, yourself, himself, herself, itself	ourselves, themselves
Possessive pronouns	mine, yours, his, hers	ours, yours, theirs
Possessive determiners	my, your, his, her, its	your, our, their

1) Use singular pronouns/determiners when referring to one noun and plural pronouns/determiners when referring to multiple nouns.
   - I read the story, and I really enjoyed **it.**

"It" refers to the story.

   - The campers appreciate when their counselors give **them** candy.

"Them" refers to campers.

   - **Samson** did **his** homework.
   - The **students** did **their** homework.

"His" refers to Samson and "their" refers to "students."

2) Use singular determiners when "each" is used.
   - **Each** of the snowflakes has **its** own unique pattern.

3) Use singular determiners when joining more than one singular noun by "or" or "nor."
   - Britney **or** Ava did **her** homework.
   - Neither Britney **nor** Ava did **her** homework.

4) Use plural determiners when joining more than one noun by "and."
   - Gene **and** Sonia did **their** homework.

In many sentences, the pronoun will not be located right next to the antecedent.

   - Incorrect: The **iguana**, known for **their** vegetarian **diets**, resides in the canopies of rainforests.

"Iguana" is a singular noun and "their" is a plural possessive determiner.

- Correct: The **iguana**, known for **its** vegetarian **diet**, resides in the canopies of rainforests.

The singular determiner "its" agrees with the singular noun "iguana."

- Correct: **Iguanas**, known for **their** vegetarian **diets**, reside in the canopies of rainforests.

The plural determiner "their" agrees with the plural noun "iguanas."

- Incorrect: The workers demanded improved benefits for **himself or herself**.
- Correct: The workers demanded improved benefits for **themselves.**

The plural "themselves" is needed to refer to workers.

Recall that **indefinite pronouns** are pronouns that do not stand for any specific noun. Possessive determiners must agree in number with indefinite pronouns (see fundamentals lesson).

- **Everyone** is in **her** seat.
- **Each person** gives **his or her** opinion.
- **One** must own up to **his or her** mistakes in order to learn from them.

Case Errors

Subjective	Objective
I, you, he, she, we, they, who	me, you, him, her, us, them, whom

Subjective pronouns are the subjects of sentences. Typically, they refer to nouns that perform actions.

- **He** called his sister on the phone.
- **They** saw the movie.
- **I am** standing below the ceiling.

Subjective pronouns often precede linking verbs.

- **She is** kind.
- **I was** chosen to give a speech.

Objective pronouns replace the objects of a verb or preposition in a sentence. They often function as recipients of actions.

- His sister called **him** on the phone.
- The movie was seen by **them.**
- The ceiling is above **me.**

When a pronoun is paired with a noun, **ignore the other noun** to determine whether the subjective case or the objective case is needed. Alternatively, substitute an objective or subjective plural form (*we, they, us, them*) in place of both the noun and the pronoun.

- Miles and **I** have to study for our history test.

"I have to study" is grammatically correct when "Miles" is ignored. "We have to study" is correct, so the subjective "I" is needed.

- Pass the homework to Marlon and **me**.

"Pass the homework to me" is grammatically correct when "Marlon" is ignored. "Pass the homework to us" is correct, so the objective "me" is needed.

Tips

1) Objective pronouns sometimes come between verbs and gerunds.
   - I heard **him talking** on the phone.
   - I saw **her arguing** with her classmate.

2) Only objective pronouns follow prepositions.
   - I went to the park **with him.**
   - The critique was directed **at her.**

<u>**Relative Pronoun Errors**</u>

1) **Who vs. Whom**

Who is a subjective relative pronoun that functions similarly to *he, she, we* and *they*. It typically comes after a subject (noun/pronoun) and before a verb. It also can come between two verbs.

- That is the person **who** sold those shoes to me.

The subjective "who" is needed between the subject and the verb. "He sold those shoes to me" is a correct variation of the relative clause.

Whom is an objective relative pronoun and functions similarly to *him, her, us,* and *them*. It often follows a preposition such as *to, with, of, for,* or *from*.

- The person **with whom** I spoke is my classmate.

The objective "whom" is needed. "I spoke with him" is a correct variation of this sentence.

2) **Who/Whom vs. That/Which**

"Who" and "whom" refer to people, and "that" and "which" refer to other nouns.

- The lawyer **who** defended the man on the news lives in California.
- The clothes **that** I bought are in shopping bags.

Sometimes a relative pronoun is needed instead of the personal pronoun in order to avoid creating a run-on sentence.

- Incorrect: After our company changed its computer system, I sought assistance from my manager, **she** was extremely helpful.
- Correct: After our company changed its computer system, I sought assistance from my manager, **who** was extremely helpful.

While "she" can refer to a manager, the sentence contains a comma splice. A relative clause properly follows the independent clause in the correct sentence. The appropriate relative pronoun between the subject and the verb is "who."

Pronoun Shifts

Personal pronouns are classified by both person and number.

Person	Definition	Examples
First Person	The writer (speaker).	I, me, we, us
Second Person	The audience; the person the writer is addressing.	you
Third Person	The people about whom the writer is writing.	he, she, him, her, one, they, them, it

Within a sentence, a writer cannot shift between the first, second, and third person when referring to the same person or people.

- **Incorrect**: When **one** reads, **you** can learn important lessons.

The original sentence inappropriately shifts from the third to the second person.

- **Correct:** When **you** read, **you** can learn important lessons.
- **Correct**: When **one** reads, **one** can learn important lessons.

Between sentences, writers must also be consistent.

- Incorrect: Blogging is a great way to express **yourself**. When **one** blogs, **you** can communicate **your** thoughts to the world and connect with likeminded people. **One** with a passionate interest should not hesitate to start a blog. **You** won't regret it!

The shift between the second and third person in the above excerpt is not stylistically appropriate.

Pronouns also should not shift in number inappropriately.

	Singular	Plural
First Person	I, me	we, us
Second Person	you	you
Third Person	he, she, him, her, one, it	they, them

A common error is one in which the pronoun does not agree in number with the noun it replaces.

- Incorrect: When **someone** gives you a compliment, you should thank **them.**
- Correct: When **someone** gives you a compliment, you should thank **him or her**.

"Someone" is singular, so "him or her" is appropriate.

Ambiguous Pronoun References

Sometimes, it is not clear to whom or what a particular pronoun refers. In such cases, it is preferable to use the precise noun to avoid confusion. In some cases, it may be acceptable to rewrite the sentence without any noun or pronoun

- Incorrect: The books are available for **them** to distribute.

It is not clear who "them" is.

- Correct: The books are available for **the store** to distribute

The unclear pronoun is replaced with a noun ("the store").

- Correct: The books are available for distribution.

The unclear pronoun is eliminated, and the sentence is reworded as needed to make it grammatical.

When more than one person of the same gender is present in a sentence, make sure there are no ambiguous pronouns.

- Incorrect: Jeanne and Maggie went to lunch, and **she** ate a cobb salad.

It is not clear which girl ate the cobb salad. The name should be given.

- Correct: Jeanne and Maggie went to lunch, and **Maggie** ate the cobb salad.

Drill 1

> The fire ravaged through the forest, burning down trees and destroying everything in whose path.

1. Which of the following best replaces the underlined portion?
    A. their
    B. its
    C. which
    D. his or her

> Many students rely on student loans to finance that education.

2. Which of the following best replaces the underlined portion?
    A. their
    B. its
    C. his or her
    D. one's

> Monitor speakers should be placed in the upright position; they are not meant to be placed on one's sides.

3. Which of the following best replaces the underlined portion?
    A. its
    B. that
    C. their
    D. whose

> Vail and myself attended the charity walk in New York City.

4. Which of the following edits should be made?
    A. Vail and me
    B. Us
    C. Vail and I
    D. Ourselves

The expert argued that if you study foreign languages, one's analytical skills will improve.

5. Which of the following edits should be made?
    A. Change "you" to "people."
    B. Change "you" to "they."
    C. Change "one's" to "your."
    D. Change "one's" to "his or her."

Every weekend during the summer, my friends and I would go surfing at the local beach. It was my special activity, one that united us.

6. Which of the following edits should be made?
    A. Change "my special activity" to "your special activity."
    B. Change "my special activity" to "our special activity."
    C. Change "us" to "we."
    D. Change "us" to "them."

The physics students discussed the work of Peter Higgs, he discovered the Higgs Boson particle.

7. Which of the following best replaces the underlined portion?
    A. that
    B. which
    C. who
    D. whom

Reservoirs created by dams do more than just prevent floods. Which also provide water for commercial and agricultural activities, including irrigation.

8. Which of the following best replaces the underlined portion?
    A. They also provide
    B. It also provides
    C. Them also provide
    D. Whom also provides

Boris and Christopher, who have been best friends since middle school, played a game of badminton. It was an intense game. Though they both played well, he won in the last round.

9. In the paragraph above, which pronoun should be replaced with a noun to correct an ambiguous pronoun error?
    A. who
    B. It
    C. they
    D. he

Week 8

> Vegetable oil at the top of a glass is less dense than the water under those.

10. Which of the following best replaces the underlined portion?
    A. one
    B. it
    C. them
    D. these

> The school district did not invest in additional buses because they had limited funding to do it.

11. Which of the following best replaces the underlined portion?
    A. it had limited funding to do it.
    B. funding for these buses was limited.
    C. they could not fund it.
    D. they could not fund them.

> The beluga whale, unlike the sperm whale, is known for whose elaborate songs.

12. Which of the following best replaces the underlined portion?
    A. one's
    B. its
    C. their
    D. our

> Each prospective student must submit your application before the deadline.

13. Which of the following best replaces the underlined portion?
    A. his or her
    B. their
    C. our
    D. one's

> It has long been unknown if Neanderthals, a species related to early modern humans, traveled by sea. The discovery of tools on Mediterranean islands suggest that we built boats.

14. Which of the following best replaces the underlined portion?
    A. it
    B. they
    C. he or she
    D. one

> Before the field trip to the national park, our teacher gave notes about its history to Tara and myself.

15. Which of the following edits should be made?
    A. Replace "our" with "their."
    B. Replace "myself" with "I."
    C. Replace "myself" with "me."
    D. Replace "its" with "their."

> As a speechwriter, Tenley always makes sure that her speeches capture the unique speaking styles of clients. Such attention to detail in one's work put her in high demand.

16. Which of the following best replaces the underlined portion?
    A. she
    B. her
    C. their
    D. our

> The executive of the consulting firm with which I had a meeting signed a contract with my company.

17. Which of the following best replaces the underlined portion?
    A. who
    B. whom
    C. him
    D. that

> The musicians performed the opening number herself.

18. Which of the following best replaces the underlined portion?
    A. himself
    B. ourselves
    C. themselves
    D. oneself

> In the movie about a small town, the actors skillfully portray the close-knit nature of we.

19. Which of the following best replaces the underlined portion?
    A. one.
    B. us.
    C. them.
    D. the townspeople.

> The amusement park attracted visitors them traveled thousands of miles.

20. Which of the following best replaces the underlined portion?
    A. whom
    B. who
    C. which
    D. they

> The identity of the prankster who left gnomes in people's gardens remains a mystery, though he did reveal in a note that he is a male. Whoever the trickster is, their motive is clear: to amuse the neighbors.

21. Which of the following edits should be made?
    A. Replace "who" with "whom."
    B. Replace "who" with "that."
    C. Replace "their" with "one's."
    D. Replace "their" with "his."

Week 8

The company whom invested in the venture earned a return on its investment.

22. Which of the following edits should be made?
    A. Change "whom" to "who."
    B. Change "whom" to "that."
    C. Change "its" to "one's."
    D. Change "its" to "their."

Nadia and Ashleigh played a game of basketball, and her won.

23. Which of the following best replaces the underlined portion?
    A. she
    B. the girl
    C. the player
    D. Ashleigh

(1) While on vacation, my friend Charlotte and I decided to go hunting for precious metals. (2) Charlotte told me that she had discovered precious metals while exploring mines, quarries, dumps, and sides of the road on her past vacations with her family. (3) At first, we did not find anything. (4) Given our previous successes, she urged me not to give up.

24. Which sentence has a pronoun agreement error?
    A. Sentence 1
    B. Sentence 2
    C. Sentence 3
    D. Sentence 4

The library, which bears the name of their founder, has recently been renovated.

25. Which of the following best replaces the underlined portion?
    A. who's
    B. his
    C. one's
    D. its

The organization was praised when they devoted resources to helping victims of the natural disaster.

26. Which of the following best replaces the underlined portion?
    A. it
    B. them
    C. themselves
    D. one

Week 8

> Colony Collapse Disorder occurs when the majority of worker bees in a hive die, leaving behind a queen bee, immatures bees, and nurse bees. There are many potential reasons for CCD, including pesticide poisoning and poor nutrition. Scientists are working hard to find ways to <u>stop that.</u>

27. Which of the following best replaces the underlined portion?
    A. stop it.
    B. end this.
    C. prevent this thing.
    D. alleviate this condition.

> Even in the middle of the summer, the air conditioning keeps me cool. My dog, like us, prefers to stay out of the hot sun.

28. Which of the following edits should be made?
    A. Change "me" to "I."
    B. Change "me" to "myself."
    C. Change "us" to "me."
    D. Change "us" to "it."

> While the idea of haggling over the prices of groceries may seem odd, maybe <u>them</u> shouldn't.

29. Which of the following best replaces the underlined portion?
    A. those
    B. they
    C. it
    D. one

> The researchers determined that <u>them have</u> found a new medical application of a microorganism in their studies.

30. Which of the following best replaces the underlined portion?
    A. they have
    B. one has
    C. he or she has
    D. it has

> After years of hardships, her and her family decided to move to a new town with a cheaper cost of living.

31. Which of the following edits should be made?
    A. Change "her and her family" to "she and her family."
    B. Change "her and her family" to "them."
    C. Change "her family" to "them."
    D. Change "her family" to "they."

Week 8

Week 8B: Bonus Reading Passage 3

The poem below is "Harvest Song" by Jean Toomer.

I am a reaper whose muscles set at sundown. All
    my oats are cradled.
But I am too chilled, and too fatigued to bind them.
    And I hunger.
5   I crack a grain between my teeth. I do not taste it.
I have been in the fields all day. My throat is dry.
    I hunger.
My eyes are caked with dust of oatfields at harvest-time.
I am a blind man who stares across the hills, seeking
10   stack'd fields of other harvesters.
It would be good to see them . . crook'd, split, and
    iron-ring'd handles of the scythes. It would be
    good to see them, dust-caked and blind. I hunger.
(Dusk is a strange fear'd sheath their blades are dull'd in.)
15   My throat is dry. And should I call, a cracked grain
    like the oats . . . eoho--
I fear to call. What should they hear me, and offer
    me their grain, oats, or wheat, or corn? I have
    been in the fields all day. I fear I could not taste
20   it. I fear knowledge of my hunger.
My ears are caked with dust of oatfields at harvest-time.
I am a deaf man who strains to hear the calls of other
    harvesters whose throats are also dry.
It would be good to hear their songs . . reapers of
25   the sweet-stalk'd cane, cutters of the corn . .
    even though their throats cracked and the
    strangeness of their voices deafened me.
I hunger. My throat is dry. Now that the sun has
    set and I am chilled, I fear to call. (Eoho, my
30   brothers!)
I am a reaper. (Eoho!) All my oats are cradled.
    But I am too fatigued to bind them. And I hunger.
    I crack a grain. It has no taste to it.
    My throat is dry . . .
35   O my brothers, I beat my palms, still soft, against the
    stubble of my harvesting. (You beat your soft
    palms, too.) My pain is sweet. Sweeter than

the oats or wheat or corn. It will not bring me
knowledge of my hunger.

1. What reason does the narrator give for not binding the notes?
    A. He hasn't cradled them yet.
    B. He is too tired.
    C. He doesn't know that he is hungry.
    D. He is too busy with other agricultural tasks.

2. The passage most directly suggests that the narrator's work
    A. is challenging but intellectually rewarding.
    B. requires long hours and is energy intensive.
    C. is more physically demanding than his previous job was.
    D. becomes more enjoyable with years of experience.

3. The passage indicates that the narrator suffers from all of the following EXCEPT
    A. exhaustion.
    B. pain.
    C. a dry throat.
    D. hallucinations.

4. The statement "you beat your soft palms, too" (line 36-37) exemplifies the narrator
    A. acknowledging a situation.
    B. being self-deprecating.
    C. expressing jealousy.
    D. downplaying his sense of camaraderie.

5. The "brothers" mentioned in the last stanza are most likely
    A. the narrator's biological siblings.
    B. all of the narrator's relatives.
    C. a general audience of men.
    D. the narrator's fellow reapers.

6. The narrator implies that his pain is "sweet" because it
    A. masks the bland taste of the oats.
    B. reminds him of the fruits of his labor.
    C. unites him with his coworkers.
    D. diminishes his feelings of starvation.

**I am a deaf man who strains to hear the calls of other
harvesters whose throats are also dry.**

7. Reread the excerpt above. These lines most directly emphasize the speaker's
    A. damaged hearing as a result of the work he performed.
    B. unbreakable emotional bonds with other workers in his profession.
    C. feelings of alienation during the course of his work.
    D. resignation about the long-term suffering his job will cause him.

8. Which excerpt from the poem best supports the idea that the speaker wishes to remain oblivious to his true feelings?
    A. "I am a blind man who stares across the hills, seeking/
        stack'd fields of other harvesters."
    B. "I fear knowledge of my hunger."
    C. "I crack a grain. It has no taste to it. /
        My throat is dry."
    D. "My pain is sweet. Sweeter than/
        the oats or wheat or corn."

Week 8

Kweller Prep NEW SHSAT Grammar and Reading

Week 9

Week 9: Verb Tense

Verb tense is the time in which a verb is acting. In the introductory lesson, we reviewed the basics of how verbs are conjugated. We will now examine the contexts in which different verb tenses are used.

Present Tense	Past Tense	Future Tense
<ul><li>To show a present action or state of being.<ul><li>The house is clean.</li><li>I see the sign.</li></ul></li><li>To show a habitual action.<ul><li>I play baseball.</li><li>He meets me every day after school.</li></ul></li><li>To indicate a future time.<ul><li>The restaurant closes at ten.</li></ul></li><li>To state a general truth.<ul><li>The Super Bowl is always on Sunday.</li></ul></li></ul>	<ul><li>To show a completed action or state of being.<ul><li>He swam one mile.</li><li>Yesterday she went to the zoo.</li></ul></li></ul>	<ul><li>To show an action that will or won't happen in the future.<ul><li>Tomorrow I will return her call.</li><li>Starting next month, the restaurant will offer discounts on select items.</li></ul></li></ul>

Pay attention for clues about the *time period* (today, yesterday, tomorrow, next week, etc.) in the context of a sentence to determine if an action is occurring presently, happened in the past, or will happen in the future.

Perfect tenses are tenses that require the helping verb *have*, *has*, or *had* followed by a **past participle.** Past participles are verbs ending in "-ed," "-d" "-t," "-n," or "-en" (e.g., spoken, asked, known, taught).

The **present perfect** tense describes actions that are currently happening and that started in the past. The present perfect takes the form of *have + past participle* and *has + past participle*.

- I **have been** studying Spanish since 6th grade.
- He **has written** an article for the newspaper every week since the beginning of the year.
- I **have been** here for three weeks.

The present perfect is also sometimes used to describe actions that will happen before another action in the future is completed.

- The bus will not leave until attendance **has been** taken.

The present perfect is often used in sentences with the simple present tense or simple past tense to highlight a change over time.

- You **have grown** so much since I last **saw** you.
- The amount of time people **spend** commuting **has increased** in recent years.

The **past perfect** tense indicates an action that was completed in the past before another past action or time period. The past perfect takes the form *had + past participle.*

- I **had gone** to the show before I received your message.
- We **had completed** the paper by the deadline.

The **future perfect** tense refers to actions that will be completed before another action or time period in the future. The future perfect takes the form *will have + past participle.*

- I **will have finished** my final exams by the end of June.
- He **will have** gone hiking before it rains.

The progressive tense is used to describe actions that were, are, or will be in progress. The progressive tense requires the use of a helping verb followed by a **present participle**.

- Past Progressive: I **was walking** down the street.
- Present Progressive: I **am walking** down the street.
- Future Progressive: I **will be walking** down the street.

A sentence cannot switch between verb tenses without reason.

- Incorrect: Because I **was** scared, I **scream.**

This sentence inappropriately shifts from the past to the present tense without reason. To correct this sentence, change "scream" to "screamed" so that the entire sentence is in the past tense.

Between sentences, verb tense must remain consistent unless there are clues in a sentence that indicate a time shift.

- Incorrect: During the conference, I **presented** a proposal to the committee. I then **listen** to the committee's feedback.

There is no reason for the sentence to switch to the present tense. "Listened" should follow "then." In order for the present tense to be correct, the writer needs to add more information that clarifies a change in time period.

- Correct: **Earlier today**, I presented a proposal to the committee members. **Now**, I am listening to their feedback.

The addition of "earlier today" and "now" clarify that there was a time shift.

"Would" and "could" are often used with the past tense to show conditions or possibilities.

- Correct: My grandfather **told** me stories so that I **would** be entertained.

"Can" and "will" are often used in sentences that include the present tense.

- Correct: My grandfather **tells** me stories so that I **will** be entertained.

Drill 1

Long before he became a successful physician, as a child, he <u>has seen himself</u> as a healer.

1. Which of the following best replaces the underlined portion?
   A. had saw himself
   B. had seen himself
   C. saw him
   D. sees himself

The number people who felt sleep-deprived at work has increased in recent years.

2. Which of the following edits should be made?
   A. Change "felt" to "had felt."
   B. Change "felt" to "feel."
   C. Change "has increased" to "had increased."
   D. Change "has increased" to "will increase."

When I approached the desk, I notice rows upon rows of papers stacked in an organized manner.

3. Which of the following edits should be made?
   A. Change "approached" to "have approached."
   B. Change "approached" to "will approach".
   C. Change "notice" to "noticed."
   D. Change "notice" to "have notice."

Ms. Newman's sales <u>will double</u> every year since she first opened up her company five years ago.

4. Which of the following best replaces the underlined portion?
   A. double
   B. doubled
   C. have doubled
   D. having doubled

> Next month, the government official <u>attending</u> a hearing with the congressional committee.

5. Which of the following best replaces the underlined portion?
    A. attends
    B. has attended
    C. will attend
    D. attended

> The scientist performed a chemical reaction that produced carbon dioxide, which <u>will exit</u> the flask as a gas.

6. Which of the following best replaces the underlined potion?
    A. exits
    B. has exited
    C. will have exited
    D. exited

> Last year, the school asked the researcher whether she will work as a visiting teaching professor for the following semester. Soon after, she accepted the job offer.

7. Which of the following edits should be made?
    A. Change "asked" to "has asked."
    B. Change "asked" to "asks."
    C. Change "will work" to "would work."
    D. Change "will work" to "worked."

> Since its beginning, the Slow Movement <u>opposed</u> actions that speed up the pace of life.

8. Which of the following best replaces the underlined portion?
    A. opposes
    B. will oppose
    C. had opposed
    D. has opposed

> We watched the game with anticipation and when a player gets a hit, we cheered.

9. Which of the following edits should made?
    A. Change "watched" to "watch."
    B. Change "gets" to "got."
    C. Change "gets" to "has gotten."
    D. Change "cheered" to "cheers."

> Although many people skip breakfast, studies show that a healthy breakfast helps people focus during the day and kept their weight under control.

10. Which of the following edits should be made?
    A. Change "skip" to "had skipped."
    B. Change "show" to "would show."
    C. Change "helps" to "helped."
    D. Change "kept" to "keep."

Week 9

While civics teachers generally refrain from sharing their personal political views with their students, they should understand that studying politics from an academic perspective required students to understand diverse political viewpoints and have the tools to formulate their own opinions.

11. Which of the following edits should be made?
    A. Change "refrain" to "had refrained."
    B. Change "should understand" to "would understand."
    C. Change "required" to "requires."
    D. Change "have the tools" to "having the tools."

"Welcome" shouts the museum tour guide. Some of the kids excitedly await to see the dinosaurs. Others attempted to break away and hide in a corner.

12. Which of the following edits should be made?
    A. Change "await" to "have awaited."
    B. Change "await" to "awaiting."
    C. Change "attempted" to "attempt."
    D. Change "hide" to "were hiding."

(1) First, the teacher illustrates how to apply the skill of the day with a model problem. (2) Then, he divides the class into small groups to work on practice problems. (3) He circulates the classroom, helping students as needed. (4) Finally, he gave the students a set of problems to complete independently.

13. Which sentence should be revised to correct an inappropriate shift in verb tense?
    A. Sentence 1
    B. Sentence 2
    C. Sentence 3
    D. Sentence 4

By the start of 1810, the United States Postal Service will deliver mail seven days a week.

14. Which of the following best replaces the underlined portion?
    A. delivers
    B. had delivered
    C. has delivered
    D. will have delivered

(1) Construction of the Eiffel Tower, an iron lattice tower in Paris, France, started in 1887. (2) Shortly after its construction was completed, it served as the entrance to the World's Fair in 1889, which honored the 100th anniversary of the storming of the Bastille. (3) Over time, it becomes a popular tourist destination, attracting people from all over the world. (4) Although it is now an architectural icon, it was initially criticized by artists, who believed it was a monstrous construction that violated conventional principles of aesthetics.

15. Which sentence should be revised to correct an inappropriate shift in verb tense?
    A. Sentence 1
    B. Sentence 2
    C. Sentence 3
    D. Sentence 4

Week 9B: Bonus Passage 4

The excerpt below is adapted from "Impressions of an Indian Childhood" by Zitkala-Sa.

[1] After my first three years of school, I roamed again in the Western country through four strange summers. During this time I seemed to hang in the heart of chaos, beyond the touch or voice of human aid. My brother, being almost ten years my senior, did not quite understand my feelings. My mother had never gone inside of a schoolhouse, and so she was not capable of comforting her daughter who could read and write. Even nature seemed to have no place for me. I was neither a wee girl nor a tall one; neither a wild Indian nor a tame one. This deplorable situation was the effect of my brief course in the East, and the unsatisfactory "teenth" in a girl's years.

[2] It was under these trying conditions that, one bright afternoon, as I sat restless and unhappy in my mother's cabin, I caught the sound of the spirited step of my brother's pony on the road which passed by our dwelling. Soon I heard the wheels of a light buckboard, and Dawée's familiar "Ho!" to his pony. He alighted upon the bare ground in front of our house. Tying his pony to one of the projecting corner logs of the low-roofed cottage, he stepped upon the wooden doorstep. I met him there with a hurried greeting, and, as I passed by, he looked a quiet "What?" into my eyes.

[3] When he began talking with my mother, I slipped the rope from the pony's bridle. Seizing the reins and bracing my feet against the dashboard, I wheeled around in an instant. The pony was ever ready to try his speed. Looking backward, I saw Dawée waving his hand to me. I turned with the curve in the road and disappeared. I followed the winding road which crawled upward between the bases of little hillocks. Deep water-worn ditches ran parallel on either side. A strong wind blew against my cheeks and fluttered my sleeves. The pony reached the top of the highest hill, and began an even race on the level lands. There was nothing moving within that great circular horizon of the Dakota prairies save the tall grasses, over which the wind blew and rolled off in long, shadowy waves. Within this vast wigwam of blue and green I rode reckless and insignificant. It satisfied my small consciousness to see the white foam fly from the pony's mouth.

[4] Suddenly, out of the earth a coyote came forth at a swinging trot that was taking the cunning thief toward the hills and the village beyond. Upon the moment's impulse, I gave him a long chase and a wholesome fright. As I turned away to go back to the village, the wolf sank down upon his haunches for rest, for it was a hot summer day; and as I drove slowly homeward, I saw his sharp nose still pointed at me, until I vanished below the margin of the hilltops.

[5] In a little while I came in sight of my mother's house. Dawée stood in the yard, laughing at an old warrior who was pointing his forefinger, and again waving his whole hand, toward the hills. With his

blanket drawn over one shoulder, he talked and motioned excitedly. As soon as he went away, I asked Dawée about something else.

[6] "No, my baby sister, I cannot take you with me to the party tonight," he replied. Though I was not far from fifteen, and I felt that before long I should enjoy all the privileges of my tall cousin, Dawée persisted in calling me his baby sister.

[7] That moonlight night, I cried in my mother's presence when I heard the jolly young people pass by our cottage. They were no more young braves in blankets and eagle plumes, nor Indian maids with prettily painted cheeks. The young men wore the white man's coat and trousers, with bright neckties. The girls wore tight muslin dresses, with ribbons at neck and waist. At these gatherings they talked English. I could speak English almost as well as my brother, but I was not properly dressed to be taken along. I had no hat, no ribbons, and no close-fitting gown. Since my return from school I had thrown away my shoes, and wore again the soft moccasins. While Dawée was busily preparing to go I controlled my tears. But when I heard him bounding away on his pony, I buried my face in my arms and cried hot tears.

[8] My mother was troubled by my unhappiness. Coming to my side, she offered me the only printed matter we had in our home. It was an Indian Bible, given her some years ago by a missionary. She tried to console me. After an uncertain solitude, I was suddenly aroused by a loud cry piercing the night. It was my mother's voice wailing among the barren hills which held the bones of buried warriors. She called aloud for her brothers' spirits to support her in her helpless misery. My fingers Grey icy cold, as I realized that my unrestrained tears had betrayed my suffering to her, and she was grieving for me.

During this time I seemed to hang in the heart of chaos, beyond the touch or voice of human aid.
1. Reread the sentence above from paragraph 1. Which excerpt from the text provides the best evidence to support this assertion?
    A. "The pony was ever ready to try his speed" (paragraph 3)
    B. "Suddenly, out of the earth a coyote came forth at a swinging trot that was taking the cunning thief toward the hills and the village beyond" (paragraph 4)
    C. "Upon the moment's impulse, I gave him a long chase and a wholesome fright" (paragraph 4)
    D. "My mother was troubled by my unhappiness" (paragraph 8)

2. The narrator implies her mother was incapable of comforting her primarily because
    A. the narrator responded better to encouragement presented in written rather than verbal form.
    B. her mother was unable to understand her due to significant differences in their lived experiences.
    C. the narrator looked down on her mother's character due to her lack of educational credentials.
    D. the mother's lack of formal education prevented her from perceiving subtle cues about the narrator's unhappiness.

Even nature seemed to have no place for me. I was neither a wee girl nor a tall one; neither a wild Indian nor a tame one. This deplorable situation was the effect of my brief course in the East, and the unsatisfactory "teenth" in a girl's years.

3. Reread the excerpt above from paragraph 1. The excerpt contributes to a central idea of the text by
    A. suggesting that the narrator's sense of alienation was compounded by a combination of biological and circumstantial factors.
    B. revealing that the narrator's teenage years were the most unhappy years of her life because her course in the East separated her from her family.
    C. underscoring the narrator's obsession with asserting her dominance within a social niche.
    D. describing physical characteristics of the narrator that prevent her from forging healthy relationships with others.

4. Dawée's response to the narrator's request to accompany him to the party can best be described as
    A. apprehensive and noncommittal.
    B. remorseful and apologetic.
    C. firm but affectionate.
    D. peevish and condescending.

5. The narrator's decision to untie the pony can best be described as
    A. a ploy to get her family members' attention.
    B. an elaborate plot to reestablish her connection with nature.
    C. a spontaneous means of alleviating her feelings of disquiet.
    D. a spirited decision to defy her mother's household rules.

6. How does paragraph 6 serve to advance the plot of the text as a whole?
   A. It contextualizes the interpersonal dynamics between narrator and Dawée.
   B. It presents an event that precipitated an emotional breakdown.
   C. It highlights the narrator's lingering disappointment in her cousin's choices.
   D. It underscores Dawée's inability to let go of an old habit.

7. As presented in paragraph 7, the teenagers at the party were described as
   A. being notably more proficient in English than the narrator.
   B. significantly older and more mature than the narrator.
   C. less traditional than the narrator in the garb they donned.
   D. rejecting the narrator for her failure to embrace social norms.

8. The narrator's mother most likely gave her the Indian Bible because
   A. the Bible had previously brought the narrator's mother solace during trying times, and she believed it could do the same for the narrator.
   B. she hoped it could bring the narrator comfort during her moment of despair.
   C. she wanted to acknowledge her appreciation for the narrator's educational achievements.
   D. the narrator needed a reminder of what was important in life after she became distressed by being excluded from a party.

My fingers Grey icy cold, as I realized that my unrestrained tears had _betrayed_ my suffering to her, and she was grieving for me.

9. Reread the sentence above. As used in the text, "betrayed" most nearly means
   A. revealed.
   B. deceived.
   C. transferred.
   D. hid.

Week 9

Kweller Prep NEW SHSAT Grammar and Reading

Week 10

Week 10: Subject Verb Agreement

Singular subjects require singular forms of verbs and plural subjects require plural forms of verbs.

Singular

- The **child talks.**
- The **committee has** voted.

Plural

- The **children play**.
- The **people have** voted.

When there are multiple subjects, the verb will be plural if the subjects are linked by the word "and."

- The **dog and the cat run.**

When "or" and "nor" join more than one subject, the verb must agree with the noun closest to the verb.

- Either the plate **or the forks are** on the table.
- Either the forks **or the plate is** on the table.

When phrases that suggest two nouns are being joined together or combined (*along with, joined to, combined with, in addition to, together with* and *as well as*) connect two nouns, the first noun determines whether a singular or plural verb is needed.

- **Palacio Real**, along with La Concha, **is** a popular tourist destination in Spain.

In this case, "Palacio Real" is the subject, so "is" is needed.

- **Palacio Real and La Concha are** popular tourist destinations in Spain.

In this case, both "Palacio Real" and "La Concha" are subjects, so "are" is needed.

When singular indefinite pronouns are used, singular verbs are needed. When plural indefinite pronouns are used, plural verbs are needed.

- **Each** of the cars **is** traveling over the speed limit.
- **Both** of you **have** improved a great deal.

When collective pronouns (pronouns standing for groups of people) act as subjects (audience, jury, committee, company, organization, government, family, etc.), singular verbs are generally used.

- The family *sits* at the table.
- The company **has** a forward-thinking mission.

The subject is not always next to the verb. In context, determine which noun is performing the action (in the case of action verbs) or is being described (in the case of linking verbs).

1) **Subject + Prepositional Phrase + Verb**

When a prepositional phrase is found between the subject and the verb, the subject before the prepositional phrase must agree with the verb.

- Incorrect: The **need** *for better education and job training programs* **are** responsible for the activist's demand for change.
- Correct: The **need** *for better education and job training programs* **is** responsible for the activist's demand for change.

The subject is "need," which requires the use of the singular verb "is." Although the plural word "programs" appears next to "is," it is part of the prepositional phrase "for better education and job training programs."

2) **Subject + Nonessential Elements + Verb**

Nonessential elements in the middle of a sentence (e.g., relative clauses and appositives) are typically set off by commas. A verb that appears after nonessential terms must agree with the subject that comes before the nonessential terms.

- Incorrect: The **diet program**, *which has been purchased by thousands of people,* **were** featured on the talk show.
- Correct: The **diet program**, *which has been purchased by thousands of people*, **was** featured on the talk show.

"Which has been purchased by thousands of people" is a nonessential relative clause. The "diet program" is the true subject. "The diet program was featured on the talk show" is the sentence without the prepositional phrase.

- Incorrect: **Tai Chi**, *a Chinese martial art associated with many health benefits*, **are** practiced by many people seeking to alleviate stress.
- Correct: **Tai Chi**, *a Chinese martial art associated with many health benefits*, **is** practiced by many people seeking to alleviate stress.

"Tai Chi" is the singular subject, and "is" is the verb. "Benefits" is part of the nonessential appositive set off by commas.

- Incorrect: **Proper nutrition**, *along with adequate rest*, **are** needed to promote optimal muscle growth.
- Correct: **Proper nutrition**, *along with adequate rest*, **is** needed to promote optimal muscle growth.

Only "proper nutrition" is the subject. "Adequate rest" is nonessential, as it is set off by commas.

- Correct: **Proper nutrition and adequate rest are needed** to promote optimal muscle growth.

In this case, there are two subjects joined by "and," so "are" is needed.

Drill 1

> The paper examines whether internship experience have value in helping students land jobs.

1. Which of the following edits should be made to correct a subject verb agreement error?
   A. Change "examines" to "examine."
   B. Change "examines" to "will examine."
   C. Change "have" to "has."
   D. Change "have" to "having."

> A group of software engineers having come together to work on an innovative educational product.

2. Which of the following edits should be made?
   A. Change "having come" to "comes."
   B. Change "having come" to "come."
   C. Change "having come" to "coming."
   D. Change "work" to "works."

> The countertop is composed of granite and containing baskets of fruit.

3. Which of the following edits should be made?
   A. Change "is" to "are."
   B. Change "is" to "have been."
   C. Change "containing" to "contain."
   D. Change "containing" to "contains."

> A collection of data points being graphed. Later, it will be analyzed.

4. Which of the following edits should be made?
   A. Change "being" to "has been."
   B. Change "being" to "have been."
   C. Change "will be" to "being."
   D. Change "will be" to "were."

> Today, the stars making up the constellation Taurus <u>has been</u> easy to spot in the Northern Hemisphere during the winter.

5. Which of the following best replaces the underlined portion?
   A. is
   B. was
   C. are
   D. were

> Bands of color next to each other on Jupiter having winds that move in opposite directions.

6. Which of the following edits should be made?
   A. Change "having" to "has."
   B. Change "having" to "have."
   C. Change "move" to "moving."
   D. Change "move" to "moves."

Only small portions of the original structure remaining at the archaeological site.

7. Which of the following best replaces the underlined portion?
   A. remains
   B. has remained
   C. remain
   D. having remained

Nueva Cancion, a genre of music that played a role in Latin American and Iberian social upheavals, have dealt with political themes.

8. Which of the following edits should be made?
   A. Change "originated" to "originating."
   B. Change "originated" to "originates."
   C. Change "have dealt" to "deal."
   D. Change "have dealt" to "deals."

Today, a governmental body of environmental regulators have helped monitor compliance with air pollution standards in the large industrial city.

9. Which of the following edits should be made?
   A. Change "have helped" to "helps."
   B. Change "have helped" to "help."
   C. Change "monitor" to "monitors."
   D. Change "monitor" to "monitoring."

Analysts at the lab study samples of bacteria and determines if toxins from them can be used to develop antibiotics that combat common infections.

10. Which of the following words in the sentence above must be revised to correct a subject verb agreement error?
    A. study
    B. determines
    C. develop
    D. combat

Morsels of fruit that grow on the Argania Tree attracting a horde of goats.

11. Which of the following edits should be made?
    A. Change "that grow" to "that grows."
    B. Change "that grow" to "having grown."
    C. Change "attracting" to "attract."
    D. Change "attracting" to "attracts."

Week 10

Ethologists, people who study animal behavior, was generally interested in behaviors animals inherit. Some of these scientists, by contrast, may study learned behaviors.

12. Which of the following best replaces the underlined potion?
    A. is
    B. are
    C. has been
    D. were

Corinne, along with some her colleagues, volunteering at the local animal shelter on the weekends.

13. Which of the following best replaces the underlined portion?
    A. volunteers
    B. volunteer
    C. having volunteered
    D. being volunteers

The decline in prices was bound to increase sales next month.

14. Which of the following best replaces the underlined portion?
    A. was
    B. are
    C. is
    D. were

The conversion of forestland into farms, ranches, or urban areas, though sometimes helpful to the economy, are devastating to delicate ecosystems.

15. Which of the following best replaces the underlined portion?
    A. devastate
    B. devastating
    C. have devastated
    D. devastates

The remarkable achievements of the prodigy being recognized on the television special.

16. Which of the following best replaces the underlined portion?
    A. has been
    B. have been
    C. having been
    D. was

Week 10

Week 10B: Bonus Passage 5

The excerpt below is adapted from a speech by Albert Lutuli in 1958 South Africa during the time of apartheid.

[1] If we are true to South Africa that must be our vision, a vision of South Africa as a fully democratic country. It cannot in honesty be claimed that she is yet really democratic, when only about a third of her people enjoy democratic rights, and the rest - notwithstanding the fact that they constitute the majority - are still subjected to apartheid rule. I emphasize the words are still, because I do believe firmly that it is not a state that can be perpetuated. Apartheid rule is the antithesis of democracy. Apartheid (a political system of minority rule by Whites) - in theory and in practice - is an effort, to make Africans march back to tribalism.

[2] Sometimes very nice and pretty phrases are used to justify this diversion from the democratic road. The one that comes to my mind is the suggestion that we Africans will "develop along our own lines". I do not know of any people who really have "developed along their own lines". My fellow white South Africans, enjoying what is called "Western civilization", should be the first to agree that this civilization is indebted to previous civilizations, from the East, from Greece, Rome and so on. For its heritage, Western civilization is really indebted to very many sources, both ancient and modern. There is really no possibility of anyone developing "along his own lines", as is often suggested. But in practice "developing along your own lines" turns out not to be development along your own lines at all, but development along the lines designed by the Government through the Native Affairs Department. Even in determining the laws that govern us and our development, there is no attempt to consult those who are affected. There is no contact between the governor and the governed at the present moment. " Developing along our own lines", has come to mean "developing along their lines - the Government`s lines". The essence of development along your own lines is that you must have the right to develop, and the right to determine how to develop. Its essence is freedom and - beyond freedom - self-determination. This is the vision we hold for our future and our development.

[3] One might ask, "Is this vision of a democratic society in South Africa a realizable vision? Or is it merely a mirage?" I say, it is a realizable vision. For it is in the nature of man, to yearn and struggle for freedom. The germ of freedom is in every individual, in anyone who is a human being. In fact, the history of mankind is the history of man struggling and striving for freedom. Indeed, the very apex of human achievement is FREEDOM and not slavery. Every human being struggles to reach that apex. It is sometimes suggested that people are "incited" to struggle for freedom. One wonders what that means. I admit that circumstances from time to time make it necessary to remind people of what lies at the apex. Naturally if I find a man in the mud, it is my duty to uplift him and remind him "You are not of the mud." If there be human beings who, for some reason or other, have forgotten their rights and wallow in the mud, it is the duty of all who see, to say to them "Don`t wallow in mud. Try to reach up to the apex." And the apex of human achievement and striving, as I have said, is freedom.

[4] The yearning for freedom is not peculiar to South Africa. The whole of Africa is emerging into freedom. We live in the midst of what has rightly been described as "Emergent Africa". Why should it be thought that Africans in this part of southern Africa are different from Africans in Ghana? Africans in Ghana have received full democracy. In Nigeria they are about to receive full democracy. How can it be suggested that the Africans in the Union of South Africa will not yearn, like their brothers in the North,

for freedom. The very fact that Africa is emerging to freedom should be a sign to all of us that our vision of democracy is coming and will be realized.

[5] Man must participate in all the aspects of life, political, social and religious. A man is not whole if he is deprived of participating in some aspects of life; he will grow to be a lopsided man. It is not our aim to produce among Africans lopsided citizens of South Africa. It is my firm belief that more and more South Africans, regardless of color, will come to see the justice of our cause, because it is not just our cause. It is a human cause and, I would say, a divine cause to try and build a climate in South Africa where human values will be respected.

1. According to Lutuli, South Africa will become fully democratic once
    A. citizens share the same political rights regardless of race.
    B. the number of representatives in government is equal between the races.
    C. cultural traditions of all racial groups are equally respected.
    D. certain provisions of apartheid are strengthened.

2. As used in paragraph 1, "antithesis" means
    A. friend.
    B. antidote.
    C. corollary.
    D. opposite.

3. Lutuli depicts apartheid as
    A. irreconcilable with democratic ideals.
    B. a necessary preliminary step on the road to democracy.
    C. flawed despite its lofty commitment to safeguarding individual freedoms.
    D. a byproduct of war between various cultural groups.

4. Lutuli implies that the end of apartheid rule is
    A. doubtful, given the reluctance of White South Africans to relinquish their high political standing
    B. noteworthy, since the system has been adopted by most nations.
    C. unknowable, since this political system is deeply entrenched in South African culture.
    D. inevitable, given the unsustainability of the system.

5. According to Lutuli, "nice and pretty phrases" (first sentence of paragraph 2)
    A. are employed to rationalize an unjustifiable system.
    B. reveal that politeness undergirds all sociopolitical interactions in daily life.
    C. weaken the arguments of government critics.
    D. protect democratic norms and institutions from ideological threats .

6. In the context of paragraph 2, Lutuli regards the argument that Black South Africans will develop along their own lines with
   A. mild skepticism.
   B. tempered agreement.
   C. outspoken incredulity.
   D. detached neutrality.

7. As used in the last sentence of paragraph 4, "realized" means
   A. remembered.
   B. achieved.
   C. understood.
   D. chased.

I admit that circumstances from time to time make it necessary to remind people of what lies at the apex

8. Reread the statement above from paragraph 3. This statement is an example of
   A. a concession that acknowledges a certain viewpoint is not completely unfounded.
   B. a pointed criticism of a popular myth.
   C. a description of a counterargument that rests on faulty assumptions.
   D. an explanation that demonstrates why liberty is an unnegotiable tenet of a just society.

9. Lutuli implies that meaningful social change
   A. is unlikely to happen in African countries outside of South Africa.
   B. will be engineered by the South African people themselves.
   C. will not happen anytime soon in South Africa.
   D. results primarily from meaningful economic change.

10. The statement "It is a human cause" (paragraph 5) most directly emphasizes
    A. the pervasiveness of a set of values associated with a political objective.
    B. the need of individuals to come to unanimous consent about certain principles in order to rectify a situation.
    C. that political leaders are directly responsible for assisting other humans outside their jurisdictions.
    D. the strategic transnational alliances that are required to make meaningful social progress.

11. Lutuli would most likely agree that the ability of Black South Africans to fully engage in social life
    A. is less important than their ability to engage in commercial life.
    B. functions as a prerequisite to attaining political liberties.
    C. is not possible so long as apartheid persists.
    D. would ensure that there is economic equality between the races.

12. A major theme of this speech is that
    A. economic freedom is the foundation of collective liberty.
    B. justice demands that individuals are free to develop in their own ways.
    C. people cannot have any significant political freedoms without economic equality.
    D. the laws of society should be created by legislative bodies that are demographically representative of the people they govern.

Kweller Prep NEW SHSAT Grammar and Reading

Week 11

Week 11: Punctuation

Common Functions of Commas

1) Use commas to separate items in a series or list.
- At the zoo, I saw lions, tigers, and bears.
- Before you take a big test, make sure to get plenty of rest, eat a nutritious meal, and relax your mind.

2) Use commas to set off nonessential phrases or clauses in the middle of a sentence. Nonessential information is information that can easily be removed from a sentence without changing the sentence's meaning.
    - My brother, **known for his stories of his travels across the globe,** invited me to go on vacation with him.
    - The cathedral, **which was built during medieval times,** exemplifies Gothic architecture.
    - My calculus class, **the hardest class offered in the math department,** ends next Tuesday.
    - The replica, **an accurate representation of the ship,** is made of wood.
    - The couch, **he discovered,** was damaged.

3) Use commas to set off parenthetical expressions, nonessential expressions that show commentary. Some common parenthetical expressions include *however, though, for example, in fact, needless to say,* and *as a matter of fact.*
    - Some tourists, **though**, did not take pictures.

4) Use commas to set off appositives, synonyms, or definitions.
    - Godfrey has an alpha, **or dominant,** personality type.
    - Organic compounds, **also known as carbon-based compounds**, exist in living organisms.

5) Use commas to separate an introductory phrase or dependent clause from an independent clause that follows.
    - Because many people refuse to believe that they are wrong, they tend to pay attention to information that confirms rather than contradicts their existing attitudes.
    - A staunch advocate of voting rights for women, Elizabeth Cady Stanton was one of the first women to launch organized women's suffrage movements in the United States.

6) Use commas to separate an independent clause from a nonessential (optional) phrase that follows.
    - Elliot studied daily, hoping to earn a good grade.

7) Use commas to separate coordinate adjectives. The order of coordinate adjectives can be switched.
    - It was an interesting, thought-provoking, and energetic presentation.

DON'T use commas

1) Before essential clauses or phrases (clauses or phrases that are needed for the sentence to retain its meaning). **Commas are rarely used before "that."**
    - The person **taking orders at the restaurant** is my friend.
    - The trophy **that I won** is on my desk.

2) To separate compounds subjects or objects.
    - Incorrect: **Meriwether Lewis, and William Clark** were the first Americans to explore the western portion of the United States.
    - Correct: **Meriwether Lewis and William Clark** were the first Americans to explore the western portion of the United States.

    - Incorrect: He is respected for his **kindness, and thoughtfulness.**
    - Correct: He is respected for his **kindness and thoughtfulness.**

3) To separate elements connected by coordinating conjunctions that are NOT independent clauses.
    - Incorrect: I read the **book, and** watched the movie.
    - Correct: I read the **book and** watched the movie.

4) Between a subject or subject clause and its verb.
    - Incorrect: **She, told** stories around the campfire.
    - Correct: **She told** stories around the campfire.

    - Incorrect: The **reason that I didn't believe him, was** the lack of evidence.
    - Correct: The **reason that I didn't believe him was** the lack of evidence.

5) Between a verb and its direct object (a noun or pronoun receiving the action of the verb).
    - Incorrect: He was **given, a** warning for his behavior, which was disruptive to the learning process.
    - Correct: He was **given a** warning for his behavior, which was disruptive to the learning process.

6) Before an intensive pronoun (pronoun ending in "self").
    - Incorrect: I'm not sure of the **answer, myself.**
    - Correct: I'm not sure of the **answer myself.**

7) Between an adjective and the noun it modifies.
    - Incorrect: The **blue, sweater** is in the drawer.
    - Correct: The **blue sweater** is in the drawer.

8) Between an adverb and the word (adjective, verb, or another adverb) it modifies.
   - Incorrect: I am **very, sorry.**
   - Correct: I am **very sorry.**

9) Between a preposition and its object.
   - Incorrect: Give the **note to, your** cousin.
   - Correct: Give the **note to your** cousin.

10) Before a preposition (unless the preposition is part of a nonessential phrase).
    - Incorrect: The **lack, of evidence** is alarming.
    - Correct: The **lack of evidence is** alarming.

11) Before a technical term, nickname, or unusually used term set off by quotes (unless a comma is needed regardless of the presence of quotation marks, such as when the quoted term begins a nonessential phrase in the middle of a sentence).
    - Incorrect: Henry Clay was known **as, "The Great Compromiser."**
    - Correct: Henry Clay was known **as "The Great Compromiser."**

12) Between cumulative adjectives (adjectives that build on one another and need to be placed in a certain order to modify a noun).
    - Incorrect: The **dark, blue, woolen** sweater was in the store.
    - Correct: The **dark blue woolen** sweater was in the store.

The phrase "a woolen, blue, dark sweater" would not make sense.

13) As part of a person's title when the name is needed for the sentence to be grammatically correct or logical.
    - Incorrect: Mayor**, Mary Smith,** gave a speech.
    - Correct: Mayor **Mary Smith** gave a speech.

The name "Mary Smith" is not optional: it is needed for the sentence to make sense.

14) Between a main verb and an infinitive phrase (a phrase that is in the form to+verb, such as *to walk*).
    - Incorrect: I **like, to** read historical fiction.
    - Correct: I **like to** read historical fiction.

Drill 1

> Common employers for law school graduates include <u>private firms universities and the government</u>.

1. Which of the following best revises the underlined portion?
   A. private, firms, universities, and, the government.
   B. private firms, universities and the government.
   C. private firms, universities, and the government.
   D. private, firms, universities and the government

> Parked in the long driveway was a new expensive blue sports car.

2. Which of the following edits should be made?
   A. Add a comma after "in."
   B. Add a comma after "long."
   C. Add a comma after "new."
   D. Add a comma after "expensive."

> At the gala, Helen wore a dress that she designed, herself.

3. Which of the following edits should be made?
   A. Delete the comma after "gala."
   B. Add a comma after "Helen."
   C. Add a comma after "dress."
   D. Delete the comma after "designed."

> The ouster of the CEO had a destabilizing effect on the organization prompting a power struggle from competing interests.

4. Which of the following edits should be made?
   A. Add a comma after "ouster."
   B. Add a comma after "destabilizing."
   C. Add a comma after "organization."
   D. Add a comma after "struggle."

> The practice of phone banking during political campaigns, though time-consuming is important for mobilizing voters.

5. Which of the following edits should be made?
   A. Add a comma after "banking."
   B. Delete the comma after "campaigns."
   C. Add a comma after "time-consuming."
   D. Add a comma after "is."

> Because she was on a budget, Sheree wanted to purchase cheap sturdy living room furniture.

6. Which of the following edits should be made?
   A. Add a comma after "purchase."
   B. Add a comma after "cheap."
   C. Add a comma after "sturdy."
   D. Add a comma after "room."

> The rain that falls on the grass and, flowers is a welcome relief from the drought.

7. Which of the following edits should be made?
   A. Add a comma after "rain."
   B. Delete the comma after "and."
   C. Add a comma after "flowers."
   D. Add a comma after "welcome."

> The new prime minister unlike her predecessor, did not mind giving regular press briefings.

8. Which of the following edits should be made?
    A. Add a comma after "new."
    B. Add a comma after "minister".
    C. Delete the comma after "predecessor."
    D. Add a comma after "regular."

> The chemist presented topics, such as acid base titration, in a clear logical manner.

9. Which of the following edits should be made?
    A. Delete the comma after "topics."
    B. Delete the comma after "titration."
    C. Add a comma after "clear."
    D. Add a comma after "logical."

> <u>American, marine biologist Rachel Carson</u> wrote about the detrimental effects of pesticides on the environment.

10. Which of the following best replaces the underlined portion?
    A. American marine biologist Rachel Carson,
    B. American marine biologist, Rachel Carson
    C. American marine biologist Rachel Carson
    D. American marine biologist, Rachel Carson,

> A <u>goal of, low-impact development is</u> to limit the impact of rainwater runoff when green infrastructure is designed.

11. Which of the following best corrects the underlined portion?
    A. goal of low-impact, development is
    B. goal, of low-impact development, is
    C. goal of low-impact development is,
    D. goal of low-impact development is

> The revival of the classic <u>play critics say</u> is true to the spirit of the original.

12. Which of the following best corrects the underlined portion?
    A. play, critics, say
    B. play, critics say,
    C. play, critics say
    D. play critics say,

> In 1935, <u>the newly formed, Works Projects Administration</u> was headed by Harry Hopkins.

13. Which of the following best corrects the underlined portion?
    A. the newly formed Works Projects Administration
    B. the newly, formed Works Projects Administration,
    C. the newly, formed, Works Projects Administration
    D. the newly formed Works Projects Administration,

Week 11

Though a few of the participants in the study were able to complete the puzzle in under five minutes the majority of them took at least ten minutes to finish the task.

14. Which of the following edits should be made?
    A. Add a comma after "Though"
    B. Add a comma after "few."
    C. Add a comma after "five minutes."
    D. Add a comma after "took."

Modern architecture is characterized by simple plain geometric forms.

15. Which of the following edits should be made?
    A. Add a comma after "architecture."
    B. Add a comma after "simple."
    C. Add a comma after "plain."
    D. Add a comma after "geometric."

Albert Einstein became famous for his contributions, including the theory of relativity. For years however, he struggled and failed to create a single unified theory that combined gravity with electromagnetism.

16. Which of the following edits should be made?
    A. Add a comma after "famous."
    B. Add a comma after "years."
    C. Add a comma after "that."
    D. Add a comma after "gravity."

Corn husks, which are around, 40% cellulose by weight can be used to encase foods.

17. Which of the following best revises the underlined portion?
    A. around 40% cellulose, by weight
    B. around 40% cellulose by weight,
    C. around, 40% cellulose by weight,
    D. around 40% cellulose by weight

By the time the warm, summer, weather, arrived dozens of people had rented apartments in the small beach community.

18. Which of the following best revises the underlined portion?
    A. warm summer weather arrived,
    B. warm, summer weather arrived,
    C. warm summer, weather arrived,
    D. warm, summer weather, arrived

The professor used many of the same <u>materials strategies and methodologies</u> that she learned from her statistics course.

19. Which of the following best revises the underlined portion?
    A. materials, strategies, and, methodologies
    B. materials, strategies, and methodologies
    C. materials, strategies, and methodologies,
    D. materials strategies, and methodologies

<u>Actress Hattie McDaniel was,</u> the first African American to win an Academy Award in the category of acting.

20. Which of the following best revises the underlined portion?
    A. Actress, Hattie McDaniel, was
    B. Actress, Hattie McDaniel was
    C. Actress Hattie McDaniel was
    D. Actress Hattie McDaniel, was

According to the article three-dimensional models of yeast genomes cannot account for the radial placement of loci in the nucleus.

21. Which of the following edits should be made?
    A. Add a comma after "article."
    B. Add a comma after "three-dimensional."
    C. Add a comma after "models."
    D. Add a comma after "radial."

A recipe <u>taken from the pages of,</u> a manuscript recipe book was popular with students at the college.

22. Which of the following best revises the underlined portion?
    A. taken, from the pages, of
    B. taken, from the pages of
    C. taken from the pages of
    D. taken from, the pages of

The <u>large corporation, as the founder points out</u> started as a small pet project.

23. Which of the following best revises the underlined portion?
    A. large corporation, as the founder points out,
    B. large corporation as the founder points out,
    C. large, corporation as the founder points out
    D. large corporation as the founder points out

The charity received <u>donations, from a small nonprofit company</u> based in England.

24. Which of the following best revises the underlined portion?
    A. donations from a small nonprofit company
    B. donations from a small, nonprofit company
    C. donations from a small nonprofit, company
    D. donations, from a small nonprofit company,

A sedimentary rock is formed when <u>sediment, is weathered from a source area and</u> deposited to an area of deposition.

25. Which of the following best revises the underlined portion?
    A. sediment is weathered from a source area, and
    B. sediment is weathered from a source area, and,
    C. sediment, is weathered from a source area, and
    D. sediment is weathered from a source area and

There are often telltale sign that a piece of art is not genuine. An article explained, though that even some experts can't tell the difference between authentic works and forgeries.

26. Which of the following edits should be made?
    A. Add a comma after "though."
    B. Add a comma after "experts."
    C. Add a comma after "authentic."
    D. Add a comma after "works."

John Quincy Adams' public speaking <u>skills earned, him the nickname</u> "Old Man Eloquent."

27. Which of the following best corrects the underlined portion?
    A. skills, earned him the nickname
    B. skills earned him the nickname,
    C. skills earned him the nickname
    D. skills, earned him the nickname,

<u>In collaboration, with Missouri-born author Langston Hughes, Alabama-born author</u> Zora Hurston wrote *Mule Bone.*

28. Which of the following best corrects the underlined portion?
    A. In collaboration with Missouri-born, author Langston Hughes, Alabama-born, author
    B. In collaboration with Missouri-born author, Langston Hughes, Alabama-born author,
    C. In collaboration with Missouri-born author Langston Hughes, Alabama-born, author
    D. In collaboration with Missouri-born author Langston Hughes, Alabama-born author

<u>Two 8-feet-wide blue weather balloons,</u> were floating in the sky.

29. Which of the following best corrects the underlined portion?
    A. Two, 8-feet-wide blue weather balloons
    B. Two, 8-feet-wide, blue weather balloons
    C. Two 8-feet-wide blue weather balloons
    D. Two, 8-feet-wide, blue, weather, balloons

> The Parthenon in Athens, Greece which is one of the most prominent ancient Greek buildings, exemplifies Doric architecture.

30. Which of the following edits should be made?
    A. Delete the comma after "Athens."
    B. Add a comma after "Greece."
    C. Add a comma after "prominent."
    D. Delete the comma after "buildings."

> The responsibilities of the actuary include compiling statistical data, analyzing the economic cost associated with certain events preparing reports, and presenting findings to executives.

31. Which of the following edits should be made?
    A. Add a comma after "responsibilities."
    B. Add a comma after "economic."
    C. Add a comma after "events."
    D. Delete the comma after "reports."

> My advisor who collaborated with me to decide on a topic for my thesis, pointed me to useful resources and gave me feedback on my writing.

32. Which of the following edits should be made?
    A. Add a comma after "advisor."
    B. Add a comma after "with me."
    C. Add a comma after "useful."
    D. Add a comma after "resources."

Week 11B: Bonus Passage 6

The passage below is "To One Coming North" by Claude Mckay.

At first you'll joy to see the playful snow,
Like white moths trembling on the tropic air,
Or waters of the hills that softly flow
Gracefully falling down a shining stair.

5   And when the fields and streets are covered white
And the wind-worried void is chilly, raw,
Or underneath a spell of heat and light
The cheerless frozen spots begin to thaw,

Like me you'll long for home, where birds' glad song
10 Means flowering lanes and leas and spaces dry,
And tender thoughts and feelings fine and strong,
Beneath a vivid silver-flecked blue sky.

But oh! more than the changeless southern isles,
When Spring has shed upon the earth her charm,
15 You'll love the Northland wreathed in golden smiles
By the miraculous sun turned glad and warm.

1. The speaker believes that at first the listener will
   A. grow impatient waiting for the first snowfall.
   B. enjoy watching the snow.
   C. play joyfully in the snow.
   D. prefer the snow to warm weather.

2. As the winter progresses, the speaker
   A. plans to move back home.
   B. misses their home.
   C. grows to appreciate the cold.
   D. regrets moving North.

3. The speaker appreciates spring for
   A. reminding them of home.
   B. thawing the roads.
   C. its changelessness.
   D. transforming the North.

4. It can be inferred that the speaker ultimately
   A. hates the North because of the weather.
   B. will return to the South.
   C. appreciates living in the North.
   D. moved to the North primarily to experience different seasons.

5. An important theme developed in this work is the
   A. importance of honoring one's roots.
   B. beauty of change.
   C. ephemerality of joy.
   D. need to let go of the past.

6. Which line in the poem contributes to the nostalgic tone?
   A. Line 1 ("At first...snow")
   B. Line 8 ("The cheerless...thaw")
   C. Line 9 ("Like me...song")
   D. Line 13 (But oh...isles")

Kweller Prep NEW SHSAT Grammar and Reading

Week 12

Week 12: Transitions

A sentence can be grammatically correct without being logical. A logical sentence is one that makes sense. Recall from lesson 2 that conjunctions within sentences must show the correct relationship (contrast, comparison, cause-and- effect, sequence, etc.) in context.

- Illogical: Missy studied hard for the test, **but** she got a perfect score.

If Missy studied hard, one would expect her to do well on the test. The coordinating conjunction "but" illogically suggests a contrasting relationship. In this case, "and" or "so" would be more logical.

Recap of Some Common Transitions (see Lesson 6 for more comprehensive lists)

Compare	as, like, likewise, similarly
Contrast	alternatively, although, by contrast, but, conversely, even though, in contrast to, nevertheless, nonetheless, on the other hand
Addition	also, and, aside from, in addition, furthermore, moreover, what's more
Time	as, at last, finally, first, next, previously, subsequently, ultimately
Cause	as, because, due to the fact, for, since
Effect	as a result, accordingly, consequently, hence, therefore, thus, to these ends
Example	for example, for instance
Emphasis	indeed, in fact
Clarity	in other words
Concession	admittedly, granted
Conclusion	in conclusion, in summary , in short
Definition	as such, in broad terms
Detail	particularly, specifically

> Typically, scientific papers are organized in chronological order. Effective papers often break this general pattern.

Sample: Which word should be added at the beginning of the second sentence (with adjusting capitalization as needed)?

- A. Consequently,
- B. However,
- C. For instance,
- D. As such,

"Typically" indicates what scientific papers usually do. The second sentence indicates that while these papers are usually chronological, the best papers do NOT always follow this format. Therefore, a contrast transition is needed. Choice B is correct.

Drill 1

> Some people who frequently interrupt others when they speak are intentionally disrespectful. Others are just eager and want to show the people they are interrupting that they are engaged with what they are saying—even to the point of completing their sentences.

1. Which transition should be added the beginning of the second sentence(with adjusting capitalization as needed)?
    - A. Also,
    - B. For example,
    - C. However,
    - D. Subsequently,

> (1) Actuaries apply math and financial theory to analyze and manage risks. (2) Working as an actuary is both financially rewarding and intellectually stimulating. (3) Many people agree that the actuarial field is satisfying.

2. Which of the following transitions should be added at the beginning of the third sentence(with adjusting capitalization as needed)?
    - A. Indeed,
    - B. Furthermore,
    - C. Nevertheless,
    - D. For instance,

> Genetic counselors inform people about their risks of developing certain diseases based on genetic test results. Genetic counselors must have strong communication skills to be effective.

3. Which of the following transitions should be added at the beginning of the second sentence(with adjusting capitalization as needed)?
    - A. However,
    - B. Likewise,
    - C. Furthermore,
    - D. Consequently,

> The young entrepreneur started many failed businesses. She became successful when she launched an educational software company.

4. Which of the following transitions should be added to the beginning of the second sentence(with adjusting capitalization as needed)?
   A. Eventually,
   B. Similarly,
   C. Thus,
   D. For instance,

> In late December through January, there are relatively few hours of daylight in Iceland. By July, there is midnight sun.

5. Which of the following transitions should be added to the beginning of the second sentence(with adjusting capitalization as needed)?
   A. Later, though,
   B. Soon, of course,
   C. By the same token,
   D. Therefore,

> 3-D printing has many advantages in medicine. It can be used for tissue and organ fabrication.

6. Which of the following transitions should be added to the beginning of the second sentence? (with adjusting capitalization as needed)?
   A. On the contrary,
   B. Nevertheless,
   C. At the same time,
   D. For instance,

> Aristotle's *Art of Rhetoric* is generally considered essential reading for students of rhetoric. Professor Miller chose not to include this work in her rhetoric class's curriculum.

7. Which of the following transitions should be added to the beginning of the second sentence(with adjusting capitalization as needed)?
   A. In effect,
   B. However,
   C. Thus,
   D. For example,

> Upton Sinclair's *The Jungle* exposed unsanitary conditions in the meatpacking industry and led to a public outcry for federal reforms. The Federal Meat Inspection Act and Pure Food and Drug Act were passed to protect consumers from harmful food products.

8. Which of the following transitions should be added to the beginning of the second sentence(with adjusting capitalization as needed)?
   A. In addition,
   B. Likewise,
   C. Nonetheless,
   D. Subsequently,

(1) In business, a mastermind group is a group of peers who offer each other support and accountability with their professional goals. (2) Though there are many advantages of such groups, there are also reasons you should be cautious about joining one. (3) If people in your group are not responsible, they may not hold you accountable. (4) If group members are less accomplished than you, you may find that you are more of a mentor than a beneficiary of your peers' advice.

9. Which of the following transitions should be added to the beginning of the fourth sentence (with adjusting capitalization as needed)?
    A. Conversely,
    B. In addition,
    C. Therefore,
    D. For example,

(1) There are many health benefits associated with ginger. (2) Ginger helps reduce exercise-induced pain. (3) Ginger helps relieve nausea and digestive issues.

10. Which of the following transitions should be added to the beginning of the third sentence (with adjusting capitalization as needed)?
    A. Furthermore,
    B. However,
    C. Therefore,
    D. For instance,

It is very costly to treat certain largely preventable health conditions. It is important that we invest in preventive medicine, which helps patients avoid developing these conditions in the first place.

11. Which of the following transitions should be added to the beginning of the second sentence (with adjusting capitalization as needed)?
    A. However,
    B. Instead,
    C. Therefore,
    D. For instance,

Telecommuting policies benefit both employees and employers by increasing productivity and boosting morale. Employers should consider allowing their employees to telecommute when possible.

12. Which of the following transitions should be added to the beginning of the second sentence (with adjusting capitalization as needed)?
    A. Likewise,
    B. Accordingly,
    C. Nevertheless,
    D. However,

> The goal of the organization is to foster a spirit of entrepreneurship. The organization provides loans and training to women to start their own businesses.

13. Which of the following transitions should be added to the beginning of the second sentence(with adjusting capitalization as needed)?
    A. In summary,
    B. To these ends,
    C. By the same token,
    D. However,

> There are many ways to improve your vocabulary. You can study root words, make flashcards, or play vocabulary games.

14. Which of the following transitions should be added to the beginning of the second sentence(with adjusting capitalization as needed)?
    A. Also,
    B. Similarly,
    C. For example,
    D. However,

> The drought has hurt ranchers, who must spend more money on water to feed livestock and water plants. It hurts the timber industry who may lose trees to forest fires.

15. Which of the following transitions should be added to the beginning of the second sentence (with adjusting capitalization as needed)?
    A. For instance,
    B. Similarly,
    C. Therefore,
    D. Nevertheless,

Week 12B: Bonus Passage 7

The excerpt below is adapted from *Don Quixote* by Miguel Cervantes.

[1] Once upon a time, in a village in La Mancha, there lived a lean, thin-faced old gentleman whose favorite pastime was to read books about knights in armor. He loved to read about their daring exploits, strange adventures, bold rescues of damsels in distress, and intense devotion to their ladies. In fact, he became so caught up in the subject of chivalry that he neglected every other interest and even sold many acres of good farmland so that he might buy all the books he could get on the subject. He would lie awake at night, absorbed in every detail of these fantastic adventures. He would often engage in arguments with the village priest or the barber over who was the greatest knight of all time. Was it Amadis of Gaul or Palmerin of England? Or was it perhaps the Knight of the Sun?

[2] As time went on, the old gentleman crammed his head so full of these stories and lost so much sleep from reading through the night that he lost his wits completely. He began to believe that all the fantastic and romantic tales he read about enchantments, challenges, battles, wounds, and wooings were true histories. At last he fell into the strangest fancy that any madman has ever had: he resolved to become himself a knight errant, to travel through the world with horse and armor in search of adventures. First he got out some rust-eaten armor that had belonged to his ancestors, then cleaned and repaired it as best he could. Although the head-piece of the helmet was intact, unfortunately, the visor that would have protected the face was gone. Not to be discouraged by this deficiency, however, he fashioned another out of some pieces of stiff paper and strips of iron. In his eyes it was without a doubt the most splendid helmet ever fashioned.

[3] Don Quixote set about with all his powers of persuasion to persuade a laborer of the village, whose name was Sancho Panza (/sahn*cho/ pahn*za/), to accompany him as his squire. At last, with the promise that Don Quixote would someday make him governor of his very own island, the country bumpkin agreed to leave his wife and children and follow the knight. The tall, lean knight sat upon bony Rocinante*, while the plump Sancho Panza climbed astride his ass named Dapple, a leather wine bottle and well-stocked saddlebags at his side. And so this unlikely pair set off in search of adventures.

[4] As they crossed the plain of Montiel, they spied dozens of windmills. "Fortune has smiled on us," said Don Quixote to his squire. "Yonder stand more than thirty terrible giants. I will fight them and kill them all, and we shall make ourselves rich with the spoils."

[5] "What giants?" asked Sancho Panza.

[6] "Those giants there, with the long arms," said the knight.

[7] "Be careful, sir," said the squire. "Those are not giants, but windmills, and what seem to be their arms are the sails which turn the millstone."

[8] "If you are afraid of them, then go say your prayers," said Don Quixote. "But I shall engage them in battle." Immediately, he spurred his horse forward, and, paying no 5 attention to Sancho Panza's shouted warnings, he cried, "Do not run, you cowards, for a lone knight assails you!" Just then a slight wind caused the windmills to begin turning. "I fear you not, though you have more arms than the giant Briareus," cried the knight. "I ride forth in the name of fair Dulcinea!" Covering himself with his shield and thrusting forth his lance, he spurred Rocinante toward the nearest windmill. His lance pierced one of the whirling sails, which immediately wrenched it with such force that the horse was dragged along and the knight sent rolling across the ground. He lay without moving as Sancho Panza trotted to his side.

[9] "Oh dear," said Sancho, "didn't I warn your worship to watch what you were doing when attacking those windmills?"

[10] "I believe," replied the knight, "that some evil enchanter turned those giants into windmills to rob me of a glorious victory. But I shall prevail over him in the end."

[11] "As God wills," said Sancho, helping the knight to his feet. They climbed upon Rocinante and Dapple once more and continued on their way.

[12] Just as Don Quixote desired, he and Sancho Panza encountered many dangerous and unusual adventures in the days that followed; for so often did the knight mistake shepherds, holy men, and peasant girls for miscreant knights, evil enchanters, and ladies in distress, that he was continually involved in ridiculous quarrels and brawls. No matter how frantically Sancho urged him to see things as they really were, Don Quixote paid no attention to him. But although these absurd encounters were matters of great seriousness to the knight, many who witnessed them were delighted and amused. Gradually, his exploits became known all over the countryside, and there were few who had not heard of that flower of chivalry, Don Quixote de la Mancha.

*Rocinante: the name of Quixote's horse

1. The first paragraph contributes to the development of the plot primarily by
    A. explaining an influential incident that led Quixote to have a break from reality.
    B. establish a character's obsession with a certain type of literature.
    C. illustrating the extent to which Quixote's interpretations of stories of knighthood differ from those of his peers.
    D. reveal Quixote's fixation with combatting forces of injustice.

2. Which of the following excerpts from the passage best illustrates Quixote's resourcefulness and creativity?
    A. "In fact, he became so caught up in the subject of chivalry that he neglected every other interest and even sold many acres of good farmland so that he might buy all the books he could get on the subject" (paragraph 1)
    B. "He would lie awake at night, absorbed in every detail of these fantastic adventures" (paragraph 1)
    C. "At last he fell into the strangest fancy that any madman has ever had: he resolved to become himself a knight errant, to travel through the world with horse and armor in search of adventures" (paragraph 2)
    D. "Not to be discouraged by this deficiency, however, he fashioned another out of some pieces of stiff paper and strips of iron" (paragraph 2)

3. Paragraph 3 most strongly suggests that Sancho Panza joined Don Quixote out of
    A. a need to prove himself to his family.
    B. a self-interested desire to enhance his station in life.
    C. flattery that someone as esteemed as Don Quixote gave him attention.
    D. sympathy for Don Quixote's mission.

4. To create his costume, Quixote
    A. used a helmet that belonged to his ancestors and painted over the parts that were unsightly.
    B. sold some acres of his land to afford a traditional helmet on which he performed simple repairs.
    C. did minor fixes to an existing helmet and created the visor with loose materials.
    D. constructed an entire helmet from scratch, using pieces of paper and iron.

5. Don Quixote's response to Sancho Panza in paragraph 10 can best be described as
    A. an admission of poor judgment.
    B. a celebration of vindication.
    C. a rationalization for an occurrence.
    D. a prediction of an obstacle.

6. Which of the following excerpts from the text most directly suggests that Quixote's interpretations of his adventures are not accurate?
    A. "As time went on, the old gentleman crammed his head so full of these stories and lost so much sleep from reading through the night that he lost his wits completely" (paragraph 2)
    B. "Don Quixote set about with all his powers of persuasion to persuade a laborer of the village, whose name was Sancho Panza (/sahn*cho/ pahn*za/), to accompany him as his squire" (paragraph 3)
    C. " 'I ride forth in the name of fair Dulcinea!' Covering himself with his shield and thrusting forth his lance, he spurred Rocinante toward the nearest windmill" (paragraph 8)
    D. "Just as Don Quixote desired, he and Sancho Panza encountered many dangerous and unusual adventures in the days that followed; for so often did the knight mistake shepherds, holy men, and peasant girls for miscreant knights, evil enchanters, and ladies in distress, that he was continually involved in ridiculous quarrels and brawls" (paragraph 12)

"Yonder stand more than thirty terrible giants. I will fight them and kill them all, and we shall make ourselves rich with the spoils."

7. Read the excerpt above from paragraph 4. This excerpt most directly reveals that Don Quixote
    A. is primarily motivated by a desire to amass wealth.
    B. believes the windmills are forces he is meant to battle.
    C. sees the windmills as a sign that he must search for and destroy monstrous giants.
    D. feels compelled to engage in warfare despite his terror.

8. Which of the following is the best evidence that Sancho Panza respects Don Quixote in the story?
    A. He addresses Quixote as "your worship."
    B. He helps Quixote up after he is hurt.
    C. He abandons his family to travel with Quixote.
    D. He admires Quixote's active imagination.

9. One purpose of paragraph 12 is to
    A. convey the extent to which Don Quixote's resolve is shaken during his various misadventures.
    B. highlight how the absurdity of Quixote's mission has caused Sancho Panza to consider abandoning him.
    C. characterize how other people react to the adventures of Don Quixote.
    D. contrast the various types of encounters that Don Quixote and Sancho Panza faced on their mission.

10. How do Don Quixote's actions affect Sancho Panza?
    A. They cause him to ridicule Quixote for their absurdity.
    B. They lead Panza to worry about Quixote and attempt to ground him in reality.
    C. They cause Panza to feed into Quixote's delusions for his own amusement.
    D. They lead Panza to ask townspeople for advice on how to help Quixote see things clearly.

Kweller Prep NEW SHSAT Grammar and Reading

Week 13

Week 13: Concise and Precise Language

Concision

It is important to avoid using redundant (repetitive) language in writing. Writers should not repeat words or use words with the same meaning unless absolutely necessary.

Every year, the company has annual growth in its sales.

Sample: Which of the following best replaces the underlined portion?
   A. has
   B. has yearly
   C. annually has
   D. each year has

By definition, something that happens "every year" must be "annual." Choice A is correct. It lacks repetitive information, unlike the other choices.

Precision

Precise language is language that is **highly specific.**

- Vague Sentence: The city spent **a lot of money** to repair damages to the bridge.
- Precise Sentence: The city spent **3 million dollars** to repair damages to the bridge.

"A lot of money" is too vague. The revised sentence makes it clear exactly how much was spent.

- Vague Sentence: Economists who are **more aware** of human psychology **may know better** why **certain people** make **financial choices the way they do**.
- Precise Sentence: Economists who are **knowledgeable** about human psychology are **better equipped** to understand the **purchasing decisions of customers.**

Overall, the first sentence uses very weak language (shown in bold). Who are the "certain people?" What are the "financial choices?" The second sentence is much more precise than the first. Not only do economists need to have a "basic awareness" about psychology, but they also need to be knowledgeable. They are equipped (have the tools) to understand customer's purchasing decisions.

Sample: Which of the following sentences uses the most precise language?
   A. People wanting to change careers can take measures to explore new options.
   B. People seeking to change careers can take courses in subjects that interest them or consult with a career counselor.
   C. People wanting a new career can learn about new careers at locations where other people go to find new careers.
   D. A person interested in changing careers might want to learn information about new careers or engage in activities related to the pursuit of these careers.

Choice A is too vague. What measures should people take?
Choice C is too vague. At what locations can people learn about new careers?
Choice D is too vague. How would people learn information? What kinds of activities would they do?
Choice B is correct. It contains two specific recommendations (taking courses and consulting with a career counselor)

Style

Academic writing will typically use a **formal** style rather than an **informal** one. Formal writing is more likely to be grammatically correct, well-structured, and polite. Informal writing, on the other hand, may be looser with grammatical structures and contain more conversational vocabulary.
- Formal: The students ignored the rules.
- Informal: The kids in the class blew off doing what they were supposed to do.

The formal sentence uses vocabulary that is appropriate for writing. While the informal sentence is fine for casual conversations and informal forms of writing (like blogs or emails), it is not appropriate for formal writing. "Blew off" is a colloquial expression. "Kids in the class" can be more concisely and formally expressed as "students." "Doing what they were supposed to do" is also very casual.

Drill 1

> The official <u>frequently many times</u> cited a quote from an article that has since been debunked.

1. Which of the following best corrects the underlined portion?
   A. oftentimes
   B. often repeatedly
   C. constantly regularly
   D. frequently

> New technologies have largely transformed life in small towns. In addition, shifts in cultural attitudes <u>have in addition</u> caused changes.

2. Which of the following best corrects the underlined portion?
   A. also
   B. have as well
   C. have
   D. in addition to new technologies

> An article in a scientific journal examines the problems and flaws associated with the wisdom of the crowds.

3. Which of the following edits should be made?
   A. Delete "in a scientific journal."
   B. Delete "and flaws."
   C. Change "problems" to "shortcomings."
   D. Change "examines" to "looks at."

> A famous and renowned political cartoon by Benjamin Franklin, *Join or Die* includes a snake cut into portions representing different American colonies or regions.

4. Which of the following edits should be made?
   A. Change "renowned" to "well-known."
   B. Delete "and renowned".
   C. Delete "into portions."
   D. Change "regions" to "areas."

> In English class, we studied written works, novels, poems, and short stories.

5. Which of the following edits should be made?
   A. Delete "English"
   B. Delete "written works,"
   C. Delete "novels,"
   D. Delete "class"

> The tree may <u>reach, get up to, and attain</u> a height of 100 feet.

6. Which of the following is the best revision to the underlined portion?
   A. reach
   B. reach to and achieve
   C. get up to and progress towards
   D. attainably achieve

> After failing to qualify for nationals, the swimmer <u>adjusted and modified</u> his training routine.

7. Which of the following is the best revision to the underlined portion?
   A. altered and modified
   B. variably adjusted
   C. modified
   D. changed and revised

> The law needs to <u>move up and on with</u> advancements in technology.

8. Which revision to the underlined portion best employs a formal style?
   A. keep pace with
   B. follow the beat of
   C. stay on the level of
   D. get in line with

Week 13

> The lack of a clean water supply in the town is pretty important.

9. Which revision to the underlined portion best employs a formal style?
   A. kind of a big deal.
   B. a serious issue.
   C. something that can't be put on the back burner.
   D. a really tricky thing to fix.

10. Which choice best maintains a formal style?
    A. One of the big things behind acid rain was the letting go of sulfur dioxide and nitrogen oxide.
    B. One of the primary causes of acid rain was the emission of sulfur dioxide and nitrogen oxide.
    C. One of the major reasons leading up to acid rain was the giving off of sulfur dioxide and nitrogen oxide.
    D. A huge deal behind acid rain was the release of sulfur dioxide and nitrogen oxide.

11. Which choice best maintains a formal style?
    A. Professional development classes can help teachers improve their teaching skills.
    B. Everything you learn at professional development classes can help teachers learn things that will make them better at teaching.
    C. Professional development classes can make teachers better at a lot of different things related to teaching.
    D. Professional development classes can help teachers learn whatever they need to learn to have better teaching skills.

12. Which choice best maintains a formal style?
    A. The people at the party hooted and hollered about the disgusting edibles.
    B. The partygoers went on and on about how bad the food tasted.
    C. The partygoers complained about the unappetizing food.
    D. The partygoers said a lot of bad things about the awful food at the party.

> The farmer dedicates time to work.

13. Which of the following revises the underlined portion with the most precise language?
    A. certain agricultural tasks.
    B. matters related to farming.
    C. weeding and mulching.
    D. protecting his crops.

14. Which of the following sentences uses the most precise language?
    A. Many entities put together fake flavors at their organizations that are similar to real ones.
    B. Many scientists produce artificial flavors in workplaces that are like real.
    C. Many flavorists manufacture artificial flavors in laboratories that rival natural flavors.
    D. Many workers make products that resemble natural flavors.

> The researchers <u>tested how various things</u> affected the brains of growing children.

15. Which of the following revises the underlined portion with the most precise language?
    A. conducted studies on how some actions
    B. looked at how certain activities
    C. examined how reading over the summer
    D. analyzed how intellectually engaging practices

> The journalist <u>disapproved of certain stuff for</u> its effect on the community.

16. Which of the following revises the underlined portion with the most precise language?
    A. scolded certain policies due to
    B. criticized the property tax increase for
    C. wrote about the property tax increase with regards to
    D. analyzed a new policy and

17. Which of the following sentences uses the most precise language?
    A. The four highest paid actors on the movie set will be guests on a talk show.
    B. Some of the actors who were paid well for their roles in the movie will attend the talk show.
    C. Four actors on the movie set who were paid highly for their roles will be guests on a talk show.
    D. Some of highest paid actors on the movie set will attend the talk show.

18. Which of the following sentences uses the most precise language?
    A. The senator received over 2,000 calls from his constituents in one day, a 900% increase from the day before.
    B. The senator received a lot of calls from his constituents in small duration of time, a huge increase from a short time ago.
    C. The senator received over 2,000 calls from his constituents in one day, a substantial increase from the day before.
    D. The senator received a huge number of calls from his constituents one day, a 900% increase from the day before.

19. Which of the following sentences uses the most precise language?
    A. Workers who are aware of how to write well may appear better to people they deal with at work.
    B. Workers with crisp writing skills may be perceived as more intelligent to coworkers and clients.
    C. Workers who write well may come off as smart to diverse workplace acquaintances.
    D. Workers who are aware of skills related to the act of writing in a good manner may have a positive reputation among many kinds of people.

20. Which of the following sentences uses the most precise language?
    A. Picasso's *Guernica* was a mural-sized oil painting that symbolically criticized the Spanish Civil War through violent imagery.
    B. Picasso's *Guernica* was kind of artwork that brought attention to the Spanish Civil War through its visual features.
    C. Picasso's *Guernica* was a large painting that portrayed the Spanish Civil War through drawn pictures.
    D. Picasso's *Guernica* was a mural-sized oil painting that features strong artistic choices to illustrate Picasso's opinion about the Spanish Civil War.

21. Which of the following sentences uses the most precise language?
    A. A team of archaeologists discovered artifacts from an ancient shipwreck during a dig in an African desert.
    B. A group of people found remainders left over from an old ship in a desert in Africa.
    C. A team of experts found ancient things while digging in an African ecosystem.
    D. A team of archaeologists discovered ship parts during a dig in an African locale.

Week 13B: Mixed Review

> The classification of a person as a duke, baron, marquess, or another title of nobility have a long history in the four home nations of the United Kingdom.

1. Which edit should be made to correct this sentence?
   A. Change *classification* to *designation*.
   B. Change *another title* to *other titles*.
   C. Change *nobility* to *nobilities*.
   D. Change *have* to *has*.

> Jillian has a major exam tomorrow, nevertheless, she has decided to go to a concert instead of study.

2. Which edit should be made to correct this sentence?
   A. Add a comma after *major*.
   B. Change the comma after *tomorrow* to a semicolon.
   C. Delete the comma after *nevertheless*.
   D. Add a comma after *concert*.

> How you can make an impact on elections outside of your home state is through campaign donations, for example, the money may be used to pay for the travel expenses of campaign workers or create advertisements that mobilize voters.

3. Which edit should be made to correct this sentence?
   A. Change *your* to *one's*.
   B. Add a comma after *home state*.
   C. Change comma after *donations* to a semicolon.
   D. Delete the comma after *example*.

> (1) The hotel restaurant had a strict formal dress code.
> (2) Brandon was not allowed to be seated because he was wearing sweatpants and a t-shirt.

4. What is the best way to combine the sentences to clarify the relationship between the ideas?
   A. Although the hotel restaurant had a strict formal dress code, Brandon was not allowed to be seated because he was wearing sweatpants and a t-shirt.
   B. The hotel restaurant had a strict formal dress code, but Brandon was not allowed to be seated because he was wearing sweatpants and a t-shirt.
   C. Since the hotel restaurant had a strict formal dress code, Brandon was not allowed to be seated because he was wearing sweatpants and a t-shirt.
   D. The hotel restaurant had a strict formal dress code; the result being that Brandon was not allowed to be seated because he was wearing sweatpants and a t-shirt.

> (1) Zoos are often critiqued by animal rights activists.
> (2) They contend that zoo animals are treated as objects on display rather than as living creatures with dignity.

5. What is the best way to combine the sentences to clarify the relationship between the ideas?
   A. Zoos are often critiqued by animal rights activists, who contend that zoo animals are treated as objects on display rather than as living creatures with dignity.
   B. Zoos are often critiqued by animal rights activists, they contend that zoo animals are treated as objects on display rather than as living creatures with dignity.
   C. Zoos are often critiqued by animal rights activists, but they contend that zoo animals are treated as objects on display rather than as living creatures with dignity.
   D. Although zoos are often critiqued by animal rights activists, they contend that zoo animals are treated as objects on display rather than as living creatures with dignity.

> The singer who adapted a classic song said that her desire to stay true to the spirit of the original meaning that she had to make certain artistic sacrifices.

6. What is the best revision of *meaning?*
   A. will have meant
   B. means
   C. meant
   D. will mean

> Ryan did some stuff to compare the intensity of different physical exercises.

7. What is the most precise revision for *Ryan did some stuff*?
   A. Ryan did some things
   B. Ryan took concrete action steps
   C. Ryan engaged in an activity
   D. Ryan conducted an experiment

> George Santayana, an acclaimed writer and philosopher is known for his insightful, popular aphorisms.

8. Which edit should be made to correct this sentence?
   A. Delete the comma after *Santayana.*
   B. Add a comma after *writer.*
   C. Add a comma after *philosopher.*
   D. Delete the comma after *insightful.*

Botticelli's *The Birth of Venus* was painted in Florence Italy, and while it is the subject of extensive study by art historians, it portrays a relatively straightforward scene in Greek mythology.

9. Which edit should be made to correct this sentence?
    A. Add a comma after **Florence.**
    B. Delete the comma after **Italy.**
    C. Delete the comma after **historians.**
    D. Add a comma after **relatively.**

In an effort to restore the damaged wetland, a bill last year was signed by the governor that established procedures to clean the water.

10. How should this sentence be revised?
    A. Trying to restore the damaged wetland, procedures for cleaning the water were established in a bill signed by the governor last year.
    B. Last year, in an effort to restore the damaged wetland, the governor signed a bill that established procedures to clean the water.
    C. The governor signed a bill, in an effort to restore the damaged wetland, that established procedures to clean the water last year.
    D. The governor, last year to restore the damaged wetland, signed a bill that established procedures to clean the water.

Last fall, Sadie's boss asked her if she gave a speech at the charity event the following December.

11. Which edit should be made to correct the sentence?
    A. Delete the comma after **fall.**
    B. Change **asked** to **asks.**
    C. Change **gave** to **would give.**
    D. Add a comma after **following.**

Week 13

(1) The university invested in a program to provide stipends for students who take on unpaid internships that may help them land jobs after graduation.
(2) This spiked applications for such internships among students.

12. What is the best way to combine the sentences to clarify the relationship between the ideas?
    A. The university invested in a program to provide stipends for students who take on unpaid internships that may help them land jobs after graduation; this effort, however, spiked applications for such internships among students.
    B. The university invested in a program to provide stipends for students who take on unpaid internships that may help them land jobs after graduation, resulting in a spike in applications for such internships among students.
    C. The university invested in a program to provide stipends for students who take on unpaid internships that may help them land jobs after graduation, and it was so that there was a spike in applications for such internships among students.
    D. While the university invested in a program to provide stipends for students who take on unpaid internships that may help them land jobs after graduation, there was a spike in applications for such internships among students.

Desha enrolled in an intensive online chemistry course. This chemistry experiment enthusiast decided to order it so that she could perform experiments at home.

13. What is the most precise revision of **order it?**
    A. order some of her own
    B. order materials related to chemical sciences
    C. order a chemistry kit
    D. order a scientific product as part of this course

There is some disagreement over the fairness of the United Nations, which, according to some critics is distant from the people and gives disproportionate influence to the five permanent members of the United Nations Security Council.

14. Which edit should be made to correct this sentence?
    A. Add a comma after **disagreement.**
    B. Delete the comma after **which.**
    C. Add a comma after **critics.**
    D. Add a comma after **people.**

> The healthiest way to deal with problems with a colleague or boss are generally not to avoid the person entirely but rather to address the concerns openly but respectfully.

15. Which edit should be made to correct this sentence?
    A. Change *healthiest* to *healthy.*
    B. Change *are generally* to *is generally.*
    C. Change *but rather* to *although.*
    D. Add a comma after *openly.*

> Students of psychology may benefit in a variety of ways related to their interactions with others because they learn things about how people behave.

16. What is the most precise revision of this sentence?
    A. Students of psychology may be clued into human behavior which improves their relationships with diverse peoples.
    B. Students of psychology learn insights into human behavior that may help them form better relationships with friends, family members, and colleagues.
    C. Students of psychology learn about people, which in turn helps them interact with people with different backgrounds and interests.
    D. Students of psychology learn factoids about human behavior that aid them in certain facets of their lives.

> The ability to analyze common themes and motifs across various literary works have been especially important to Beth during her time as an English major.

17. Which edit should be made to correct this sentence?
    A. Change *to analyze* to *of analyzing.*
    B. Add a comma after *literary works.*
    C. Change *have been* to *has been.*
    D. Add a comma after *English.*

> Because games in the youth soccer league are very competitive, many coaches had their athletes train while they are on summer vacation rather than wait until school starts in the fall.

18. Which edit should be made to correct this sentence?
    A. Change *are very competitive* to *were very competitive.*
    B. Change *had their* to *have their.*
    C. Change *are on summer vacation* to *will be on summer vacation.*
    D. Change *starts* to *will start.*

> (1) Cassowaries are flightless birds.
> (2) Cassowaries are native to the tropical forests of New Guinea.
> (3) Cassowaries are generally shy creatures but may inflict injuries on humans or other animals when provoked.

19. What is the best way to combine these sentences?
    A. Although cassowaries are flightless birds and are native to the tropical forests of New Guinea, they are generally shy creatures but may inflict injuries on humans or other animals when provoked.
    B. Because cassowaries are flightless birds, native to the tropical forests of New Guinea, they are generally shy creatures, but they may inflict injuries on humans or other animals when provoked.
    C. By being generally shy creatures except when provoked, as they may inflict injuries on humans or other animals, cassowaries are flightless birds and native to the tropical forests of New Guinea.
    D. Cassowaries, flightless birds that are native to the tropical forests of New Guinea, are generally shy creatures but may inflict injuries on humans or other animals when provoked.

> Known for its climbing routes and giant sequoia trees, millions of people visit Yosemite Park during the spring and summer months each year.

20. What is the best revision of this sentence?
    A. Each year during the spring and summer months, millions of people visit Yosemite Park, which is known for its climbing routes and giant sequoia trees.
    B. Millions of people visit Yosemite Park during the spring and summer months each year known for its climbing routes and giant sequoia trees.
    C. During the spring and summer months, known for its climbing routes and giant sequoia trees, millions of people visit Yosemite Park.
    D. Millions of people Yosemite Park, which is known for its climbing routes and sequoia trees during the spring and summer months.

> Glenda is a capable resourceful leader who does whatever it takes to meet her clients' deadlines and educates herself on the latest trends in her industry.

21. Which edit should be made to correct this sentence?
    A. Add a comma after **Glenda is.**
    B. Add a comma after **capable.**
    C. Add a comma after **deadlines.**
    D. Change **herself** to **Glenda.**

> In 1860, a lithographer Milton Bradley, created *The Checkered Game of Life,* which became America's first popular parlor game.

22. Which edit should be made to correct this sentence?
    A. Delete the comma after **1860.**
    B. Add a comma after **lithographer.**
    C. Delete the comma after **Life.**
    D. Add a comma after **first.**

> (1) Agatha Christie was inspired by the many archaeological visits she did with her husband Max.
> (2) The writings of Agatha Christie include intricate details of different locations and characters based on real archaeologists.

23. What is the best way to combine the sentences to clarify the relationship between the ideas?
    A. She was inspired by the many archaeological visits she did with her husband Max, Agatha Christie included intricate details of different locations in her writings and characters based on real archaeologists.
    B. Inspired by the many archaeological visits she did with her husband Max, real archaeologists were the basis for many characters and many intricate details of different locations that were included in Agatha Christie's writings.
    C. Inspired by the many archaeological visits she did with her husband Max, Agatha Christie included in her writings both intricate details of different locations and characters based on real archaeologists.
    D. Inspiring many archaeological visits she did with her husband Max, the writings of Agatha Christie include intricate details of different locations and characters based on real archaeologists.

> (1) Political action committees date back to 1943.
> (2) Political action committees raise money from members to help fund campaigns.

24. What is the best way to combine the sentences to clarify the relationship between the ideas?
    A. Although political action committees date back to 1943, they raise money from members to help fund campaigns.
    B. Political action committees raise money from members to help fund campaigns, which date back to 1943.
    C. Political action committees date back to 1943, although they raise money from members to help fund campaigns.
    D. Political action committees, which date back to 1943, raise money from their members to help fund campaigns.

> The novel contained elements that were a depiction and representation of events in the life of the author.

25. What is the best revision of **depiction and representation?**
    A. representative depiction
    B. depictive portrayal
    C. depiction that was a portrayal
    D. depiction

> With its distinctive shape, the 60-feet high Delicate Arch have become a famous tourist attraction in Utah.

26. Which edit should be made to correct this sentence?
    A. Change *its* to *their.*
    B. Add a comma after *high.*
    C. Change *have* to *has.*
    D. Add a comma after *famous.*

Week 13

> After reviewing the arguments from both parties, five thousand dollars in punitive damages was awarded to the plaintiff by the judge.

27. How should this sentence be revised?
    A. After reviewing the arguments from both parties, the plaintiff was rewarded five thousand dollars by the judge in punitive damages.
    B. Punitive damages, five thousand dollars, was awarded by the judge to the plaintiff, after reviewing the arguments from both parties.
    C. After reviewing the arguments from both parties, the judge awarded five thousand dollars in punitive damages to the plaintiff.
    D. The plaintiff, after reviewing the arguments from both parties, was awarded five thousand dollars in punitive damages by the judge.

> Scientists think maybe there are a whole lot of Earth-sized planets orbiting in the habitable zone of sun-like stars in the Milky Way.

28. What is the most precise revision for *Scientists think maybe there are a whole lot of*?
    A. Scientists believe there are many
    B. Scientists approximate that there are billions of
    C. Scientists hypothesize that there are more than 1 million but fewer than 1 trillion
    D. Scientists estimate that there are about 11 billion

> The investigation into the financial dealings of the governor and his associates have uncovered years' worth of crimes, such as money laundering and fraud.

29. Which edit should be made to correct this sentence?
    A. Change *into* to *onto*
    B. Change *have uncovered* to *has uncovered*
    C. Change *years'* to *years*
    D. Delete the comma after *crimes*

> On a cold Wednesday, the Senator, who was holding a town hall for her constituents, offered free hot chocolates, and coffee for all who attended.

30. Which edit should be made to correct this sentence?
    A. Delete the comma after **Wednesday.**
    B. Delete the comma after **Senator.**
    C. Delete the comma after **constituents.**
    D. Delete the comma after **chocolates.**

> The newspaper, featured a series of well-researched, provoking editorials on the gubernatorial candidates that are sure to sway some voters.

31. Which edit should be made to correct the sentence?
    A. Delete the comma after **newspaper.**
    B. Delete the comma after **well-researched.**
    C. Add a comma after **provoking.**
    D. Add a comma after **candidates.**

> The washing machine in Kiara's house was not functioning properly. Many of the parts were worn out because they used it before Kiara moved in.

32. What is the most precise revision of **they used it before Kiara moved in**?
    A. it had been used by certain people
    B. they used it previously to wash their clothes
    C. the previous owners of the house used it before Kiara moved in
    D. it had been used by them previously before Kiara moved in

> The interior of the building is decorated very modestly, while the exterior contained many ornate and elaborate designs.

33. Which edit should be made to correct the sentence?
    A. Change **decorated** to **decorating.**
    B. Change the comma after to **modestly** to a semicolon.
    C. Add a comma after **exterior.**
    D. Change **contained** to **contains.**

> The physical therapy center, which is located just a few blocks from the train station, is hiring many high school students interested in the medical field to perform various tasks, such as cleaning the office answering phones, bringing patients ice and heating pads, and assisting patients in their workouts.

34. Which edit should be made to correct this sentence?
    A. Add a comma after **students.**
    B. Add a comma after **office.**
    C. Add a comma after **ice.**
    D. Delete the comma after **pads.**

Week 13

> (1) Plantains and bananas have similar appearances.
> (2) Bananas are generally eaten raw while plantains are generally eaten cooked.

35. What is the best way to combine the sentences to clarify the relationship between the ideas?
    A. Although plantains and bananas have similar appearances, bananas are generally eaten raw while plantains are generally eaten cooked.
    B. Plantains and bananas have similar appearances, although bananas are generally eaten raw while plantains are generally eaten cooked.
    C. Since plantains and bananas have similar appearances, bananas are generally eaten raw while plantains are generally eaten cooked.
    D. Although plantains and bananas have similar appearances, whereas bananas are generally eaten raw while plantains are generally cooked.

> Joanna, one of the most dedicated talented swimmers on her team, won the 100-meter freestyle, earning her a spot in the national championships.

36. Which edit should be made to correct this sentence?
    A. Add a comma after *most.*
    B. Add a comma after *dedicated.*
    C. Add a comma after *talented.*
    D. Change *earning* to *this earned.*

> Some employers do not want to spend the money on professional development for their employees, but others contend that the investment is worthwhile because they enable companies to keep workers' skills sharp.

37. Which edit should be made to correct this sentence?
    A. Change *their* to *his or her.*
    B. Change the comma after *employees* to a semicolon.
    C. Change *but* to *so.*
    D. Change *they enable* to *it enables.*

> The zoologist, who regularly lectures at universities, explains that although it is true that bats and birds both have wings, while this fact does not mean that they are more closely related to each other than bats and humans, which are both mammals.

38. Which edit should be made to correct this sentence?
    A. Change *explains* to *explain.*
    B. Change the comma after *wings* to a semicolon.
    C. Delete *while.*
    D. Delete the comma after *humans.*

Week 13

The Metropolitan Museum of Art contains various, eighteenth-century paintings, many of which reflect the influence the of the Enlightenment and Neoclassicism.

39. Which edit should be made to correct this sentence?
    A. Delete the comma after **various.**
    B. Delete the comma after **paintings.**
    C. Add a comma after **which.**
    D. Change **reflect** to **have reflected.**

This year, the company made a lot of revenue, a tremendous increase from last year.

40. Which of the following is the most precise revision of this sentence?
    A. This year, the company made millions of dollars in revenue, which amounts to a 40% increase from last year.
    B. This year, the company took in $20 million, a big jump from last year.
    C. This year, the company made $20 million in revenue, a 40% increase from last year.
    D. This year, the company made several million dollars, a notable rise from the previous year.

There is a lack of funding for the reparation of crumbling and falling apart roads and bridges in the small town.

41. Which of the following is the most concise and precise revision to this sentence?
    A. There is too little funding to repair crumbling roads and bridges in the small town.
    B. There is not enough money to fix broken areas in the community.
    C. There aren't sufficient resources to address transportation issues in the small town.
    D. There is a lack and shortage of monies to fix the broken roads and bridges in the town.

Kombucha, a fermented tea believed to have been originated in Manchuria, is touted for its many health benefits; in addition, kombucha is purported to aid in digestion and lower hypertension.

42. Which edit should be made to correct the sentence above?
    A. Change **have been** to **be.**
    B. Delete the comma after **Manchuria.**
    C. Change **in addition** to **for example.**
    D. Change **purported** to **reported.**

> Pamperos are strong cold southwesterly winds that sweep down over the pampas of Argentina from the Andes towards the Atlantic Ocean.

43. Which edit should be made to correct this sentence?
    A. Add a comma after **Pamperos.**
    B. Add a comma after **strong.**
    C. Add a comma after **winds.**
    D. Add a comma after **Andes.**

Kweller Prep NEW SHSAT Grammar and Reading

Week 14

Week 14: Effective Writing in Paragraphs

Crafting arguments

A **claim** is an assertion that an author makes that conveys his or her view about a topic or issue. A **thesis statement** articulates a claim that the writer will **support** with evidence and reasoning. The thesis statement is generally found in the first paragraph of the passage, often as the concluding sentence.

- Sample Claim: *Employers should adopt measures to make their employees engaged.*

This sentence provides an argument that the author is setting out to prove.

- Sample Reasoning: *Engaged employees are more likely to take their work seriously and be more productive.*

This sentence provides a clear rationale for why the author believes employers should adopt measures to engage their employees.

- Sample Evidence: *A study showed that companies with highly engaged employees have higher levels of revenue growth than their competitors.*

This sentence provides clear evidence (a study based on data) that provides credence for the author's assertion.

All details mentioned in a paragraph must be directly **relevant**, or related, to the main point of the paragraph. The following statement would provide little to no support for the sample claim above.

1) *Many employees who are not engaged at work seek out hobbies that give them pleasure.*

While this sentence is loosely tied into the topic of employee engagement, it does not necessarily provide convincing evidence for why employers should seek to engage their employees in the workplace.

---

(1) A common category of recycled waste is compost, which consists of organic debris such as food scraps, egg shells, wood, and leaves. (2) People who compost generally collect compost in a bin, wait for it to decompose, and then finally use it in their yards, gardens, and lawns. (3) Many websites provide resources for people unfamiliar with composting.
(4) There are many reasons one should consider composting. (5) It enriches the soil with nutrients and reduces the need for chemical fertilizers. (6) Glass recycling is another type of recycling that protects the environment. (7) Composting helps soil retain moisture, thus reducing storm water runoff and energy costs. (8) In large quantities, compost can be converted to natural gas.
(9) When organic matter that is not composted is sent to landfills, it is unable to break down properly, leading to the release of methane, a harmful greenhouse gas that warms the environment. (10) This problem is gaining attention, prompting many people to dispose of their compost responsibly. (11) Some large cities, like San Francisco, now require people and businesses to put compost in separate bins. (12) If you are not able to use compost yourself, disposing of compost in separate bins is an environmentally friendly— and far less time-consuming— alternative. (13) People who ignore compost laws are often shamed.

Sample: Which sentence best replaces sentence 3 to introduce the topic of the passage?
   A. People should consider recycling compost in order to benefit the environment.
   B. Composting is an enjoyable pastime that strengthens people's ties to nature.
   C. People should compost because it reduces their energy costs.
   D. People should think carefully before deciding to compost.

The topic highlights the main point and hints at supporting details, as choice A does. The author stresses the environmental benefits of composting and encourages people who can't compost to at least dispose of compost in compost bins. Choice B is incorrect because the passage never states that composting is enjoyable. Choice C mentions one minor detail that is only briefly mentioned. Choice D is too negative. The passage focuses mostly on the pros of composting.

Sample: Which sentence best follows and supports sentence 5?
   A. Chemical fertilizers have helped farmers increase crop production for decades.
   B. Chemical fertilizers may contribute to problems such as waterway pollution and mineral depletion of the soil.
   C. If you compost instead of use fertilizers, be careful to avoid attracting rodents.
   D. There is a lively debate among farmers about the relative pros and cons of chemical and organic fertilizers.

Sentence 5 states that compost helps the environment by reducing the need for chemical fertilizers. Choice B highlights potential environmental problems associated with these fertilizers, thus emphasizing why an alternative to fertilizers is positive for the environment.

Sample: Which sentence is irrelevant to the argument presented in the passage and should be deleted?
   A. Sentence 1
   B. Sentence 3
   C. Sentence 6
   D. Sentence 7

The paragraph focuses on composting, not glass recycling. Sentence 6 awkwardly inserts a sentence about glass recycling that goes unexplained. The sentence should be deleted. Choice C is correct.

Sample: Which concluding sentence should replace sentence 13 to better support the information in the passage?
   A. Clearly, it is in the best interest of the environment for people and communities to be mindful of how they handle their compost.
   B. Smaller and medium-sized cities may also revise their composting laws.
   C. Ultimately, composting is the most effective way of combatting air pollution.
   D. Cities must work together to find the best way to combat methane pollution.

Choice A is correct. The passage focuses on the environmental benefits of composting. Choice B is incorrect because the passage does not mention composting laws in smaller cities. Choice C is incorrect because the passage never compares composting to other means of fighting pollution. Choice D is incorrect because the passage never suggests cities must work together to combat methane pollution.

Information in paragraphs must be presented in a coherent order. Each sentence should provide a logical transition from the sentence preceding it to the one following it.

(1) Bioprospecting is the search for scientific information from genetic or biochemical resources, such as national parks. (2) In the 1960s, researchers discovered the microorganism *Thermus aquaticus* in a Yellowstone hot spring and learned how to grow it in a laboratory. (3) By 1985, scientists were able to utilize an enzyme found in this organism, Taq polymerase, in polymerase chain reactions (PCR). (4) PCR is useful in various applications, such as DNA fingerprinting for criminal investigations, medical diagnoses, and genetic engineering. (5) Since then, bioprospecting has led to other important discoveries, such as materials used in the creation of life-saving drugs. (6) Not only has bioprospecting helped improve people's health, but it has also strengthened local economies.

(7) For all its benefits, there are some reasons to be concerned about bioprospecting. (8) Bioprospecting can have negative environmental impacts. (9) Thus, the balance of ecosystems is often disrupted. (10) The economic benefits of bioprospecting may also be exaggerated. (11) While pharmaceutical companies certainly reap rewards, there is growing concern that some of them cheat local communities out of profits. (12) The process of extracting microorganisms may be disruptive to the habitats in which they are found. (13) Currently, there are no clear guidelines for how indigenous populations should be rewarded for the work they do to develop and nurture biological resources.

(14) There is also debate over whether or not private bioprospectors should profit from the organisms they discover on public lands. (15) Though private bioprospectors given permission to conduct research should be allowed to profit off their findings, it only seems fair that the national parks are in some way compensated for this as well. (16) These negotiations should be made transparent to the public, as the parks are a public resource owned by no private individual. (17) While no one could have anticipated that studying organisms in the hot springs of Yellowstone Park would have led to an extremely lucrative discovery, it is now known that the microorganisms found in these springs have potential to be valuable. (18) Without permission of the parks to study their lands, researchers might never have had the opportunity to make certain discoveries. (19) It is important that national parks and research companies engage in negotiations prior to research, preferably with the aid of a third party with expertise in the law.

PCR is a process that allows scientists to replicate DNA quickly and cheaply.

Sample: Where should the sentence be added to best maintain the organization of the first paragraph? (sentences 1-6)

    A. *Between sentences 1 and 2.*
    B. *Between sentences 2 and 3.*
    C. *Between sentences 3 and 4.*
    D. *Between sentences 4 and 5.*

The new sentence explains what PCR is. It should follow sentence 3 (which announces its discovery) and precede sentence 4 (which identifies contexts in which PCR is used). Choice C is correct.

> Many pharmaceutical companies partner with communities that provide the raw materials needed to make medicines, thus providing a stream of revenue for these communities.

Sample: Where should sentence be added to best support the ideas in the first paragraph? sentences 1-6)
- A. Between sentences 3 and 4.
- B. Between sentences 4 and 5.
- C. Between sentences 5 and 6.
- D. At the end of the paragraph (after sentence 6.)

Sentence 6 states that bioprospecting benefits local economies. The new sentence elaborates on this idea by explaining how local communities are helped. Choice D is correct.

Sample: Where should sentence 12 be moved to improve the organization of the second paragraph? sentences 7-13)
- A. At the beginning of the paragraph (before sentence 7).
- B. Between sentences 8 and 9.
- C. Between sentences 10 and 11.
- D. At the end of the paragraph (after sentence 13).

Sentence 8 states that bioprospecting has negative environmental impacts. Sentence 12 expands on this idea by clarifying how the environment might be harmed. Sentence 9 draws the conclusion that the balance of ecosystems is disrupted. Choice B is correct.

Sample: Where should sentence 19 be moved to improve the organization of the third paragraph? (sentences 14-19)
- A. Between sentences 14 and 15.
- B. Between sentences 15 and 16.
- C. Between sentences 16 and 17.
- D. Between sentences 17 and 18.

Sentence 16 builds off of sentence 19 with the phrase "these negotiations." As the paragraph is written now, it is not clear after reading sentence 15 to which negotiations sentence 16 is referencing. Sentence 19 mentions that negotiations are needed, and sentence 16 elaborates on this idea by stating that they should be transparent. Choice B is correct.

Drill 1

(1) There is considerable scientific debate over the effects of screen-based technology on the brain. (2) In addition, there are political disagreements over how much regulation should be applied to such media.

(3) In general, computer usage seems to be most positively associated with improvements related to quick and basic information processing. (4) For example, people who play certain computer games are often better at performing tasks that require processing visual information quickly. (5) These games also help people develop improved reaction times and a better ability to shift focus between tasks.

(6) Computer use can also improve our ability to learn. (7) For example, playing certain educational video games can increase students' interest in certain subjects. (8) Students also learn better when they are actively engaged in a task. (9) When they play math games online as part of their studying, they are more likely to master the skills they learn in school.

(10) However, people should not conclude that playing computer games makes people smarter. (11) In addition, improved skills in one area are not transferable to improvements in other areas. (12) For example, improved visual-spatial skills will not make someone better at math. (13) Not only does computer use not make you "smarter" in the most fundamental sense, but excessive computer use can also reduce cortical thickness of the brain and impair cognitive functioning. (14) Computer addiction is often caused by anxiety, depression, or boredom.

(15) The precise effects of computers on the brain are complex and still not completely understood. (16) While computers can be invaluable tools for learning, there are limits to how much they can aid in cognitive development.

1. Which sentence should be added at the end of the first paragraph to best support the claim presented in the passage?
    A. Overall, screen-based technology likely helps people develop certain cognitive skills at the expense of others.
    B. People should carefully consider which computer games they choose to play.
    C. Although there is hesitation to embrace screen-based technology, they are essential for success in today's world.
    D. It is important for people to engage in activities that strengthen cognitive skills in multiple areas.

2. Which of the following would best follow and support sentence 4?
   A. Computer games may also give people the skills to solve certain types of problems.
   B. Of course, these benefits must be weighed against the harm that violent video games can have on children's psychological development.
   C. In one study, people who played video games for 10 days were better able to shift their focus between visual images.
   D. Some parents still forbid their children from playing video games because these games distract them from their schoolwork.

> Playing the game "Civilization," a game in which students build empires, ignited student learning in history and was linked with higher history grades.

3. Where should the above sentence be added to best supports the ideas in the third paragraph? (sentences 6-9)
   A. Between sentences 6 and 7.
   B. Between sentences 7 and 8.
   C. Between sentences 8 and 9.
   D. At the end of the paragraph (after sentence 9).

4. Which of the following would best follow and support sentence 10?
   A. The violent nature of some of these games may make people desensitized to violence.
   B. In fact, playing these games does not help, and may even hinder, our ability to think deeply and creatively.
   C. Speed reading classes do not necessarily enhance actual comprehension.
   D. Intelligence is typically defined as the ability to acquire knowledge and skills.

5. Which sentence is irrelevant to the argument presented in the passage and should be deleted?
   A. Sentence 1
   B. Sentence 2
   C. Sentence 3
   D. Sentence 4

6. Which sentence is irrelevant to the argument presented in the fourth paragraph and should be deleted? (sentences 10-14)
   A. Sentence 11
   B. Sentence 12
   C. Sentence 13
   D. Sentence 14

(1) In the 21st century, the role of the librarian is changing. (2) With copies of virtually all books present online, some public libraries are shutting down for financial reasons. (3) Those who love libraries should not despair, however.

(4) Contrary to what some people might argue, librarianship will remain an important profession in the foreseeable future. (5) Librarians play an important but different role in the digital age. (6) For example, they act as curators of vast sources of electronic information. (7) Many classroom teachers also are beginning to see the value of curating digital content themselves in their classrooms.

(8) Librarians working at schools are now more than ever intertwined with the lives of faculty, researchers, and students. (9) Librarians must keep up with the latest trends so that they can better support student and faculty researchers. (10) They often help researchers understand the resources that are available to them to meet their needs. (11) They may also help researchers showcase their projects. (12) Some trends include scholarly communication, laws regarding data and management and open access, and e-books.

(13) In fact, some librarians are specially trained in child development, thus allowing them to perform these services more effectively. (14) Librarians perform important community services. (15) Some librarians are trained to provide adults with computer and research skills needed for success in the workforce. (16) They also can act as a resource to help people fill out electronic forms, such as tax forms. (17) Libraries are also champions for young people. (18) Libraries often provide services for families, such as child parent-child workshops and free or low-cost tutoring.

(19) The physical libraries themselves serve important social functions. (20) Libraries serve as incubators for peer learning, and many university students find the library to be an excellent place for group project meetings and study sessions with friends. (21) Libraries can also provide opportunities for social networking. (22) For example, some libraries provide workshops for entrepreneurs to connect with each other and receive advice from mentors and volunteers. (23) Lastly, libraries can help foster a sense of community beyond academia and work-related matters. (24) Many newer libraries have lounge spaces or coffee shops where people can socialize and relax. (25) The librarian can assist these groups by pointing them to appropriate resources for their schoolwork.

7. Which sentence would best follow and support sentence 2?
   A. Many people form human chains in front of libraries to protect them from destruction.
   B. Some communities would rather use public tax dollars towards more urgent matters, such as funding for hospitals and schools.
   C. Book stores are facing similar challenges in today's economic climate.
   D. Governments should avoid investing in resources that the majority of the public do not regularly use.

8. Which sentence would best follow and support sentence 3 to introduce the topic of the passage?
   A. Libraries and the librarians who work there are well-positioned to meet people's needs in the 21st century.
   B. Libraries are popular because they are useful to both teachers and students.
   C. Asking a librarian for help with research is more convenient than attempting to find sources on one's own.
   D. Libraries have provided opportunities for working professionals to network.

9. Which sentence includes an example that would best follow and support sentence 15?
   A. The resources that libraries provide are free for all.
   B. Students often prefer to study in the library despite the fact that they can access the internet at home.
   C. Librarians may help people develop their resumes and search for jobs during tough economic times.
   D. Research skills are rarely taught by teachers, who assume students will develop these skills in libraries.

10. Which sentence is irrelevant to the argument presented in the passage and should be deleted?
    A. Sentence 3
    B. Sentence 5
    C. Sentence 6
    D. Sentence 7

11. Where should sentence 12 be moved to improve the organization of the third paragraph? (sentences 8-12)
    A. At the beginning of the paragraph (before sentence 8).
    B. Between sentences 8 and 9.
    C. Between sentences 9 and 10.
    D. Between sentences 10 and 11.

> For example, they may create institutional repositories that store researchers' work.

12. Which sentence should the above sentence follow to support the ideas in the third paragraph? (sentences 8-12)
    A. Sentence 8
    B. Sentence 9
    C. Sentence 10
    D. Sentence 11

13. Where should sentence 13 be moved to improve the organization of the fourth paragraph? (sentences 13-18)
    A. Between sentences 14 and 15.
    B. Between sentences 15 and 16.
    C. Between sentences 16 and 17.
    D. At the end of the paragraph (after sentence 18).

14. Where should sentence 25 be moved to improve the organization of the fifth paragraph? (sentences 19-25)
    A. Between sentences 19 and 20.
    B. Between sentences 20 and 21.
    C. Between sentences 21 and 22.
    D. Between sentences 22 and 23.

15. Which concluding sentence should be added at the end of the passage to support the argument presented in the passage?
    A. Clearly, budget cuts will render librarians obsolete in the 21st century.
    B. Though most libraries will disappear, the ones that will remain will be paragons of digital content curation.
    C. The broadening of librarians' skills and services in response to the growing relevance of electronic information means that librarians will continue to play an important role in society.
    D. The Internet will be a valuable tool to individuals without access to libraries.

---

(1) Some critics of free markets lament that consumer choices are often associated with "immoral" consequences. (2) For example, many people purchase products from certain chain stores because of their minimal expense, even though the workers who produce these products often are underpaid or subject to abusive working conditions. (3) What's more, some products are produced in ways that are harmful to the environment since complying with environmental standards is often costly. (4) Adam Smith was a famous political philosopher who analyzed the importance of acting in one's own economic self-interest. (5) In recent years, the "fair trade" movement has been touted as one solution to some of the market's "ethical problems."

(6) Fair trade products are sold with a certification that they are produced by workers who are paid fairly. (7) Sales of these products can also more broadly improve the lives of people in the communities where these products are produced. (8) Chocolate is an especially popular fair trade product. (9) Fair trade products are also better for the environment. (10) Many are produced by farmers who use agricultural methods that enrich the soil, promote biodiversity, and protect ecosystems. (11) One technique that fair trade producers often use is crop rotation. (12) As a result, the soil that is not used at any given time has a chance to recover. (13) The money gained from sales is often invested in housing, infrastructure, healthcare, and education.

(14) Fair trade products don't always have their intended benefits. (15) For one, fair trade products are generally of better quality since they are produced by farmers and artisans who take pride in their work and use the best production methods available to them. (16) Fair trade food products usually taste better. (17) For example, fair trade coffee is often said to be less bitter and more flavorful than other coffee. (18) More importantly, fair trade food products may be safer to ingest since they are likely to be produced in smaller quantities and without the use of harmful chemicals.

(19) Of course, fair trade products come at a price. (20) They are more expensive than comparable products without the fair trade certification, thus turning off some price-conscious shoppers. (21) However, the expense does not deter many customers. (22) A possible explanation is that human concerns with matters of justice may override simple "rational" cost-benefit analyses.

16. Which sentence would best follow and support sentence 21?
    A. In fact, fair trade product certified sales increased by 63% in 2011.
    B. Fair Trade International is an organization that assesses the effectiveness of fair trade Programs.
    C. The number of fair trade banana producers declined between 2013 and 2014.
    D. Common examples of fair-trade products are coffee, cocoa, flowers, and even gold.

17. Which sentence is irrelevant to the argument presented in the passage and should be deleted?
    A. Sentence 1
    B. Sentence 2
    C. Sentence 3
    D. Sentence 4

> In addition, the workers work under safe and fair conditions and generally have a say in how the business in the run.

18. Where should the above sentence be added to best supports the ideas in the second paragraph? (sentences 6-13)
    A. Between sentences 6 and 7.
    B. Between sentences 7 and 8.
    C. Between sentences 8 and 9.
    D. Between sentences 9 and 10.

19. Which sentence is irrelevant to the argument presented in the passage and should be deleted?
    A. Sentence 8
    B. Sentence 9
    C. Sentence 15
    D. Sentence 17

20. Where should sentence 13 be moved to improve the organization of the second paragraph? (sentences 6-13)
    A. Between sentences 6 and 7.
    B. Between sentences 7 and 8.
    C. Between sentences 9 and 10.
    D. Between sentences 10 and 11.

21. Which of the following best replaces sentence 14 to improve the organization of the third paragraph?
    A. For the less empathetically minded, there are plenty of "selfish" reasons to support fair trade products.
    B. Many experts want to talk about how fair trade products benefit communities.
    C. If fair trade products are to remain profitable, we must analyze all the benefits of the fair trade movement.
    D. Buying fair trade is the only way to ensure your food is healthful and tasteful.

22. Which sentence would best follow and support sentence 11?
    A. Some researchers are looking for alternative techniques to circumvent traditional crop rotation.
    B. Different agricultural techniques are used depending on the climate of the region.
    C. This process involves planting crops in different parts of the soil at different times.
    D. Many farmers previously weren't able to rotate crops because the land available to them was small.

23. Which concluding sentence should be added after sentence 22 to support the argument presented in the passage?
    A. Purchasing fair trade products is the best way to be an ethical participant in the market.
    B. Most economists are confident that the fair trade movement is sustainable despite the high costs associated with it.
    C. The popularity of fair trade shopping is an extraordinary example of how human morality can prevail, even when there are market incentives to make choices that have less ethical consequences.
    D. It is undeniable that fair trade sales always benefit surrounding local economies.

---

(1) The desire of humans to expand their horizons, from Columbus's sails across Atlantic to the American colonists' expansion to the West coast, is undeniable. (2) In the past several decades, this desire has prompted humans to accomplish space travel. (3) For many scientists and nonscientists alike, the next logical frontier is a manned mission to Mars. (4) In fact, NASA (The National Aeronautics and Space Administration) is hoping to have humans orbit Mars by 2033 and land there on a later mission.

(5) It is impossible to deny how groundbreaking and exciting a successful mission to Mars would be for its own sake. (6) More importantly, such a mission can also have some practical benefits, as supporters of such missions like to point out. (7) For one, the research conducted during the mission can teach us knowledge that can help us push our limits as a species. (8) After all, if we can use technology to make Mars inhabitable, then we can certainly take steps to protect earthly habitats that are threatened by climate change and other ecological threats. (9) For the United States, there are also political reasons to desire a mission to Mars.

(10) Despite the allure of Mars, traveling there in the near future may not be such a wise investment. (11) Theoretically, oxygen for breathing can be extracted from water from Martian soil, but it is not certain that a water source on Mars even exists. (12) On the journey to Mars, astronauts would be packed in close quarters for eight months. (13) It is not clear how a long period in space in such conditions will affect astronauts psychologically. (14) Even with the best technology available, the crew will have little room for error: space debris, technical malfunctions, and equipment failures, to name a few, are all dangers that the astronauts will face. (15) If the trip to Mars itself is a success, the next challenge becomes living on Mars. (16) Mars is a wasteland with conditions incompatible for human survival without serious intervention. (17) Astronauts would have to find a reliable source for creating breathable oxygen. (18) At high levels, oxygen can be toxic to humans. (19) Lastly, the cost of such an expedition would be exorbitant: likely hundreds of billions of dollars. (20) We would need a good reason to justify using taxpayer money that can be used for addressing problems on Earth, like crumbling infrastructure and environmental threats.

(21) While the idea of traveling to Mars is exhilarating, we should not let it cloud our better judgment.

24. Which sentence should follow sentence 4 to state the main claim of the passage?
    A. There are many dangers associated with traveling to Mars.
    B. While the idea of traveling to Mars is appealing, it is important to pause for consideration before pursuing such an ambitious undertaking.
    C. Life on Earth may be improved by technology associated with a mission to Mars.
    D. It is unlikely astronauts will be able to survive on Mars.

In addition, the technological advancements needed to make a mission to Mars possible themselves may also be applied to various fields on Earth, such as to studies related to addressing environmental challenges.

25. Where should sentence be added to best support the ideas in the second paragraph? (sentences 5-9)
    A. At the beginning of the paragraph (before sentence 5)
    B. Between sentences 5 and 6.
    C. Between sentences 6 and 7.
    D. Between sentences 7 and 8.

Week 14

26. Which sentence would best follow and support sentence 9?
    A. International cooperation is a hallmark of advancements in space travel.
    B. A successful trip to Mars would highlight America's leadership in the world.
    C. Congressional elections in the United States are held every two years.
    D. The Space Race was a 20th century competition between the United States and the Soviet Union in spaceflight capability.

27. After which sentence should sentence 11 be moved to improve the organization of the third paragraph? (sentences 10-20)
    A. Sentence 12
    B. Sentence 14
    C. Sentence 16
    D. Sentence 17

28. Which sentence is irrelevant to the argument presented in the passage and should be deleted?
    A. Sentence 12
    B. Sentence 16
    C. Sentence 18
    D. Sentence 20

Week 14

Week 14 Bonus Drill: TEI (Technology Enhanced Items)

Part 1: Reading

The excerpt below is from the EPA article "Using Cool Roofs to Reduce Heat Islands" Source: https://www.epa.gov/heatislands/using-cool-roofs-reduce-heat-islands

What is a Cool Roof?

[1] A cool roof absorbs and transfers less heat from the sun to the building compared with a more conventional roof. A high solar reflectance, or albedo, is the most important characteristic to understand in terms of how well a cool roof reflects heat from the sun away from a building. A high thermal emittance—how well a cool roof sheds the heat it does absorb—also plays a role, particularly in climates that are warm and sunny. Together, these properties reduce temperatures on the roof, inside the building, and in the surrounding ambient air.

[2] Buildings with cool roofs use less air conditioning, save energy, and have more comfortable indoor temperatures. For example, in non-air-conditioned residential buildings, cool roofs can lower maximum indoor temperatures by 1.2–3.3°C (2.2 to 5.9°F).

[3] Cool roofs also impact surrounding areas by lowering temperatures outside of buildings and thus mitigating the heat island effect.

Figure 1

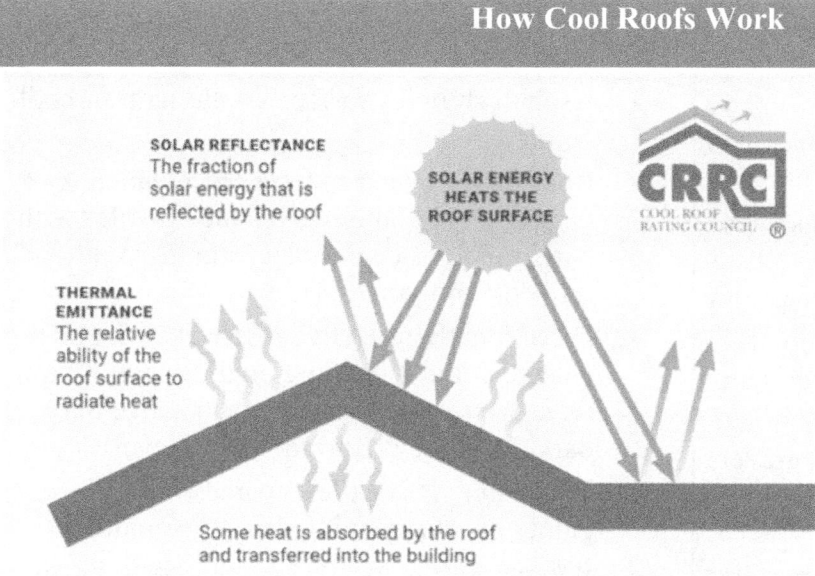

[4] This illustration depicts the flow of radiant energy as heat between the sun, roof surface, building interior, and surroundings. The higher solar reflectance, the more solar energy is reflected away from the cool roof surface. Some of the solar energy is absorbed by the roof as heat. The higher the thermal emittance, the more of this absorbed heat is radiated away from the roof surface. (Image courtesy of Cool Roof Rating Council.)

Products for Different Roofing Types

[5] Building owners and roofing contractors have used cool roofing products for many years on commercial, industrial, and residential buildings. They may be installed on low-slope roofs (such as the flat or gently sloping roofs typically found on commercial, industrial, and office buildings) or the steep-sloped roofs used on houses and residential buildings.

[6] The product technologies used for cool roofs vary by the roof's type, as shown below.[2]

Figure 2

Low-slope Cool Roof Products	Steep-slope Cool Roof Products
- Asphaltic membranes surfaced with reflective granules - Liquid-applied roof coatings with light or cool colors - Fluid-applied membranes (used for waterproofing and protection of bitumen or metal roofs) with light or cool colors - Roofing aggregate, such as gravel, that is light- or cool-colored - Single-ply membranes (prefabricated sheets that are rolled onto the roof) with light- or cool-colored pigments	- Asphalt shingles surfaced with light- or cool-colored granules - Roofing tiles such as terra cotta, which is naturally cool; alternatives include tiles with a light or cool-color glaze, and tiles with reflective polymer coatings - Directionally reflective materials, which change color depending on the angle of view (e.g., white when viewed from above but dark when viewed from ground level) - Metal shingles or tiles, coated with reflective paint or surfaced with reflective granules - Polymer or composite shingles coated with light or cool-colored pigments - Wood shingles or shakes, which are naturally cool

[7] The cost difference between a cool roof and conventional roofing materials varies by product type. Products that use certain reflective pigments (e.g., infrared reflective pigments) tend to cost more than products with conventional pigments. Ongoing costs of cool roofs may include periodic maintenance to keep the roof clean and maximize its reflectance, particularly for low-sloped cool roofs.

[8] Cool walls—exterior walls that are made more reflective through white or light-colored paints or cladding or products that use special pigments—perform services similar to those of cool roofs. Their potential for heat reduction and energy savings is comparable to that of cool roofs across all of California and U.S. climate zones 1–4, especially on older structures where walls are typically less well-insulated than roofs.

Co-Benefits of Cool Roofs

[8] Cool roofs provide a number of benefits beyond urban heat island mitigation, including:

- *Reduced energy use:* A cool roof lowers the amount of heat transferred to the building, which allows it to stay cooler and use less energy for air conditioning. In air-conditioned residential buildings, solar reflectance from a cool roof can reduce peak cooling demand by 11–27%.
- *Reduced air pollution and greenhouse gas emissions:* By lowering energy use, cool roofs decrease the associated air pollution and greenhouse gas emissions. When applied at a scale large enough to affect ambient temperatures, cool roofs could reduce the formation of ground-level ozone (which is heat-dependent) and reduce cooling energy use across a city.
- *Improved human health and comfort:* Cool roofs can help reduce the adverse health impacts of heat islands, such as heat exhaustion, respiratory difficulties, dizziness and cramps, and heat-induced death. One United Kingdom study showed that cool roofs, when implemented across a city, could offset 18% of heat-related mortality associated with the heat island effect.

[9] Because cool roofs reflect sunlight and reduce solar heat gain into a building, they may increase energy use in buildings during winter months in cold climates. However, this so-called "heating penalty" is typically offset by summer cooling energy savings. Several factors can limit or reduce the heating penalty of cool roofs in winter. The sun's angle in winter is lower and days are shorter than in summer, reducing the effect of cool roofs on wintertime energy use. Effective insulation and energy-efficient design can also reduce impacts. Buildings in areas with heavy and long-lasting snow cover would have the lowest heating penalty from cool roofs, since the roofs will be covered with reflective snow for most of the winter. To maximize the energy savings and heat island benefits of cool roofs, building owners should consider implementing energy efficiency improvements such as insulation and air sealing.

1. Which of the following choices represent actions performed by cool roofs that directly serve to keep buildings cool AND that are directly illustrated by the drawing of the cool roof in Figure 1?
   Select all answers that apply.
   ☐ Some light that strikes the roofs enters the building as solar and heat energy.
   ☐ Some heat trapped in the interior building exits through the cool roof.
   ☐ Some heat absorbed by the roof surface is radiated into the atmosphere.
   ☐ Some solar energy that strikes the roof is returned to the atmosphere.
   ☐ The cool roof permanently traps excessive heat in the roofing material itself.

2. Based on the text, which attributes are relevant to each type of roof product? You may select more than one answer for each row.

Attribute	Low-slope Cool Roof Products	Steep-slope Cool Roof Products
Generally not used for personal homes.	☐	☐
Include asphalt-based products.	☐	☐
Include light- and cool-colored pigments.	☐	☐
May offer heat reduction savings comparable to cool walls.	☐	☐
Often include shingles.	☐	☐
Especially prone to regular maintenance costs.	☐	☐

3. Reread the section below. Underline the two sentences that give quantitative evidence for the benefits of cool roofs.

Cool roofs provide a number of benefits beyond urban heat island mitigation, including:

- *Reduced energy use:* A cool roof lowers the amount of heat transferred to the building, which allows it to stay cooler and use less energy for air conditioning. In air-conditioned residential buildings, solar reflectance from a cool roof can reduce peak cooling demand by 11–27%.
- *Reduced air pollution and greenhouse gas emissions:* By lowering energy use, cool roofs decrease the associated air pollution and greenhouse gas emissions. When applied at a scale large enough to affect ambient temperatures, cool roofs could reduce the formation of ground-level ozone (which is heat-dependent) and reduce cooling energy use across a city.
- *Improved human health and comfort:* Cool roofs can help reduce the adverse health impacts of heat islands, such as heat exhaustion, respiratory difficulties, dizziness and cramps, and heat-induced death. One United Kingdom study showed that cool roofs, when implemented across a city, could offset 18% of heat-related mortality associated with the heat island effect.

For questions 4 and 5, reread the paragraph below.

Because cool roofs reflect sunlight and reduce solar heat gain into a building, they may increase energy use in buildings during winter months in cold climates. However, this so-called "heating penalty" is typically offset by summer cooling energy savings. Several factors can limit or reduce the heating penalty of cool roofs in winter. The sun's angle in winter is lower and days are shorter than in summer, reducing the effect of cool roofs on wintertime energy use. Effective insulation and energy-efficient design can also reduce impacts. Buildings in areas with heavy and long-lasting snow cover would have the lowest heating penalty from cool roofs, since the roofs will be covered with reflective snow for most of the winter. To maximize the energy savings and heat island benefits of cool roofs, building owners should consider implementing energy efficiency improvements such as insulation and air sealing.

4. For the paragraph above, underline the sentence where the author most directly introduces the idea that a concern about cool roofs is overstated.

Week 14

5. What does the author state or imply about cool roofs in this paragraph? Select all answers that apply.
   ☐ Geographic factors can worsen the heating penalty of cool roofs.
   ☐ Cool roofs may increase demand for heating during the winter months.
   ☐ Energy-efficient design choices typically fully eliminate the heating penalty.
   ☐ Conventional roofs may be less subject to a heating penalty because more sunlight striking the roofs warms the building.
   ☐ Areas with shorter days during the winter see less of a heating penalty with cool roofs because the lower angle of the sun's rays prevents them from being reflected by the roofs.
   ☐ Areas with more snowfall have a lower heating penalty for cool roofs because conventional roofs behave more similarly to cool roofs under such conditions.

The passage below is adapted from "May's Night Sky Notes: How Do We Find Exoplanets?" by Kate Troche.

Source: https://science.nasa.gov/solar-system/skywatching/night-sky-network/may2025-night-sky-notes/

[1] Astronomers have been trying to discover evidence that worlds exist around stars other than our Sun since the 19th century. By the mid-1990s, technology finally caught up with the desire for discovery and led to the first discovery of a planet orbiting another sun-like star, Pegasi 51b. Why did it take so long to discover these distant worlds, and what techniques do astronomers use to find them?

[2] One of the most famous exoplanet detection methods is the **transit method**, used by Kepler and other observatories. When a planet crosses in front of its host star, the light from the star dips slightly in brightness. Scientists can confirm a planet orbits its host star by repeatedly detecting these incredibly tiny dips in brightness using sensitive instruments. If you can imagine trying to detect the dip in light from a massive searchlight when an ant crosses in front of it, at a distance of tens of miles away, you can begin to see how difficult it can be to spot a planet from light-years away! Another drawback to the transit method is that the distant solar system must be at a favorable angle to our point of view here on Earth – if the distant system's angle is just slightly askew, there will be no transits. Even in our solar system, a transit is very rare. For example, there were two transits of Venus visible across our Sun from Earth in this century. But the next time Venus transits the Sun as seen from Earth will be in the year 2117 – more than a century from the 2012 transit, even though Venus will have completed nearly 150 orbits around the Sun by then!

[3] Spotting the Doppler shift of a star's spectra was used to find Pegasi 51b, the first planet detected around a Sun-like star. This technique is called the **radial velocity or "wobble" method.** Astronomers split up the visible light emitted by a star into a rainbow. These spectra, and gaps between the normally smooth bands of light, help determine the elements that make up the star. However, if there is a planet orbiting the star, it causes the star to wobble ever so slightly back and forth. This will, in turn, cause the lines within the spectra to shift ever so slightly towards the blue and red ends of the spectrum as the star wobbles slightly away and towards us. This is caused by the blue and red shifts of the star's light. By carefully measuring the amount of shift in the star's spectra, astronomers can determine the size of the object pulling on the host star and if the companion is indeed a planet. By tracking the variation in this periodic shift of the spectra, they can also determine the time it takes the planet to orbit its parent star.

[4] Finally, exoplanets can be revealed by **directly imaging** them, such as this image of four planets found orbiting the star HR 8799! Space telescopes use instruments called **coronagraphs** to block the bright light from the host star and capture the dim light from planets. The Hubble Space Telescope has captured images of giant planets orbiting a few nearby systems, and the James Webb Space Telescope has only improved on these observations by uncovering more details, such as the colors and spectra of exoplanet atmospheres, temperatures, detecting potential exomoons, and even scanning atmospheres for potential biosignatures!

Figure 1

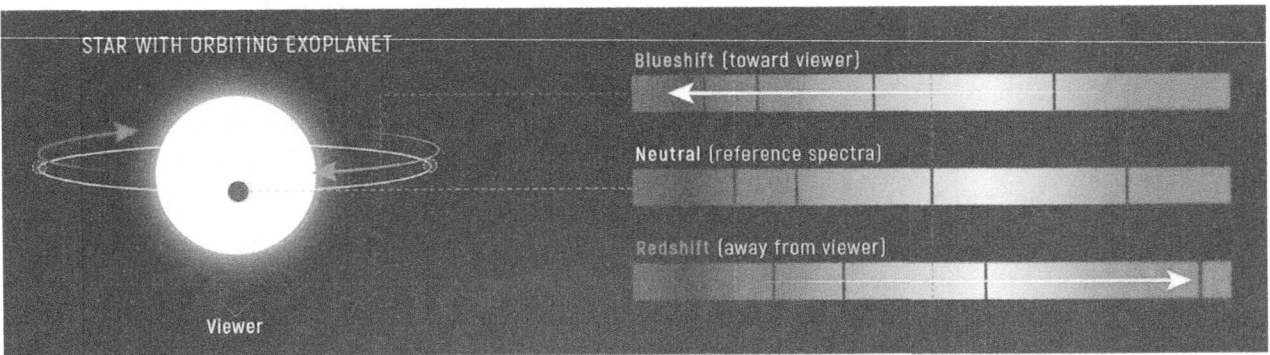

Figure 2

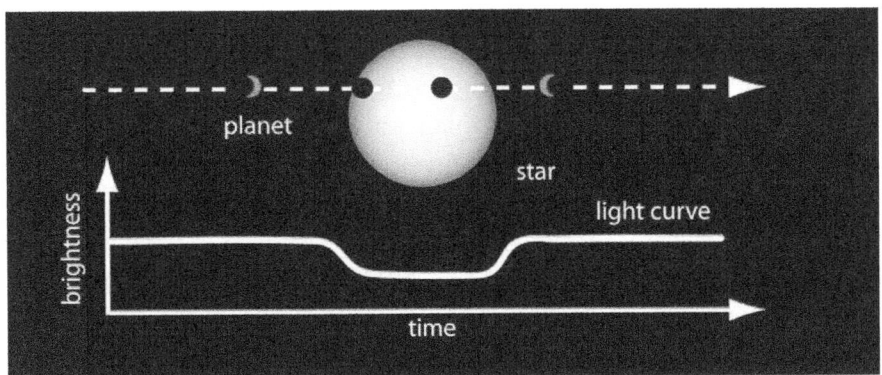

Credit: NASA's Ames Research Center

Figure 3

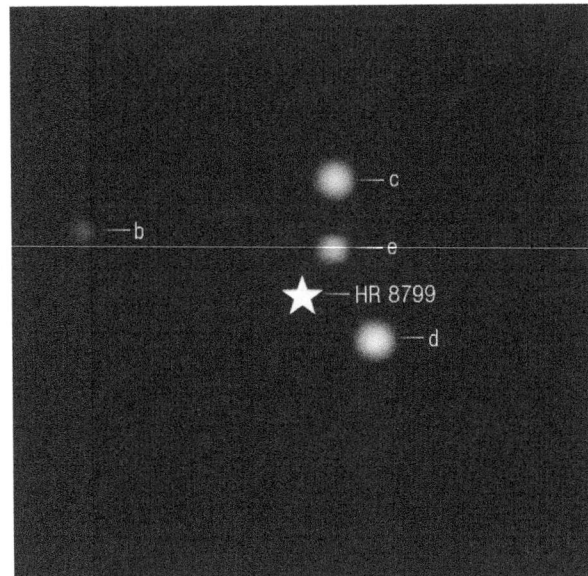

Week 14

6. Based on the descriptions in the text, identify the numbers of the figures (1,2, or 3) that correspond to each method in the table.

Method	Figure Number
Transit Method	
Wobble Method	
Direct Imaging	

For questions 7 and 8, reread paragraph 2 below.

One of the most famous exoplanet detection methods is the **transit method**, used by Kepler and other observatories. When a planet crosses in front of its host star, the light from the star dips slightly in brightness. Scientists can confirm a planet orbits its host star by repeatedly detecting these incredibly tiny dips in brightness using sensitive instruments. If you can imagine trying to detect the dip in light from a massive searchlight when an ant crosses in front of it, at a distance of tens of miles away, you can begin to see how difficult it can be to spot a planet from light-years away! Another drawback to the transit method is that the distant solar system must be at a favorable angle to our point of view here on Earth – if the distant system's angle is just slightly askew, there will be no transits. Even in our solar system, a transit is very rare. For example, there were two transits of Venus visible across our Sun from Earth in this century. But the next time Venus transits the Sun as seen from Earth will be in the year 2117 – more than a century from the 2012 transit, even though Venus will have completed nearly 150 orbits around the Sun by then!

7. Underline the sentence that uses an analogy to shed insight into a scientific process.

8. Based on the text, which of the following is true about transits and/or the transit method? Select all answers that apply.
   ☐ It takes advantage of the fact that a planet's brightness increases and dips as it orbits its host star.
   ☐ Its utility is as a method of planet identification is limited in part by its position relative to Earth.
   ☐ Transits are rarely detected by this method in our own solar system because of limitations in the sensitivity of instruments.
   ☐ Not every orbit of a planet around its star produces a transit visible from Earth.

9. Based on the text, which of the following is true about the wobble method? Select all answers that apply.
   - ☐ It exploits the fact that planets wobble at regular intervals as they orbit a star.
   - ☐ The extent of the shift in a star's spectra allows scientists to use this method determine if a companion to a star is a planet or another celestial body.
   - ☐ Scientists use this method to determine a planet's rotation rate as it orbits a star at regular intervals.
   - ☐ It was employed successfully to identify an exoplanet orbiting a star before the transit method or direct imaging were.

10. Based on the text, which statements are true for each method? You may select more than one answer for each row.

Attribute	Transit Method	Wobble Method
An indirect way of detecting exoplanets.	☐	☐
Takes advantage of properties of planets occurring at predictable intervals.	☐	☐
Detection method directly attributable to the motion of stars.	☐	☐
Detection method directly attributable to shifts in light's brightness.	☐	☐
Provides information about orbital periods.	☐	☐

The excerpt below is adapted from the 2023 U.S. Department of Interior's blog "Celebrating 50 Years of Success in Wildlife Conservation."

Source: https://www.doi.gov/blog/endangered-species-act-celebrating-50-years-success-wildlife-conservation

[1] This year marks the 50th anniversary of the Endangered Species Act, providing the opportunity to reflect on the progress made and the work ahead for protecting our nation's endangered species and their habitats. The Act has saved hundreds of species from extinction and continues to protect and preserve some of our most beloved animals and plants. It has also helped to create a better understanding of how human activities can impact the environment and how we can work together to protect it. Perhaps most importantly, this anniversary is a reminder that conservation efforts are essential for stemming the worsening impacts of climate change, protecting biodiversity and preserving our planet for ourselves and future generations.

[2] The ESA was enacted in 1973 as a response to the declining populations of many species of animals and plants. The Act was designed to protect and recover species at risk of extinction and to promote the conservation of ecosystems and habitats necessary for the survival of those species. Each of these species is a part of the web of life, each with a unique cultural and biological community, performing services that are essential to our combined well-being. By conserving them, guided by the best-available science, we help protect healthy air, land, and water for everyone.

[3] The innovative and determined actions taken by the Interior Department's U.S. Fish and Wildlife Service team members and partners over these past decades have helped prevent some species from needing the protection of the Act and provided the critical information for decision-making that contributes to the success of the Act.

The ESA was enacted to protect and recover species at risk of disappearing forever. It has become one of the most significant wildlife conservation laws in the United States and has proven instrumental in protecting numerous species.

Iconic Species Make a Remarkable Comeback

[4] In its first 50 years, the ESA has been credited with saving 99% of listed species from extinction thanks to the collaborative actions of federal agencies, state, local and Tribal governments, conservation organizations and private citizens. Here are some of the notable successes.

The Bald Eagle: We Nearly Lost Our National Symbol

[5] In the mid-1900s, our national symbol was in danger of extinction throughout most of its range. The species was listed as endangered in 1967 (under the Endangered Species Preservation Act of 1966, a predecessor to the ESA). Bald eagle populations were negatively impacted by habitat destruction and degradation, as well as illegal shooting and the contamination of their food source—largely from the insecticide Dichlorodiphenyltrichloroethane, known as DDT.

Habitat protection afforded by the ESA, the federal government's banning of DDT, and conservation actions taken by the American public helped bald eagles make a remarkable recovery. They were removed from the list of endangered species in 2007. Bald eagle sightings are now common during both the nesting season and throughout the winter. The recovery of the bald eagle is a testament to the effectiveness of the ESA in conserving and recovering imperiled species.

Kirtland's Warbler Exceeds Recovery Expectations

[6] The Kirtland's warbler is a small, yellow-bellied songbird found in the jack pine forests of Michigan, Wisconsin and Ontario. Threatened by habitat loss and parasitism, the species was listed under the ESA in 1973. Multiple partners worked to restore the warbler's habitat and control parasitic threats. Thanks to their efforts, the species rebounded from 170 breeding pairs in the 1970s and '80s to 2,300 breeding pairs in 2019, exceeding recovery plan goals. The warbler was removed from the endangered species list in 2019.

American Alligators Are Living Fossils That Continue to Survive

[7] The American alligator is a member of the crocodile family – living fossils from the Age of Reptiles – who have survived on earth for over 200 million years. The American alligator populations reached an all-time low in the 1950s, primarily due to market hunting and loss of habitat. The species was listed as endangered in 1967 but made a significant recovery due to ESA protections and was removed from the list of endangered species in 1987. The recovery of the American alligator highlights the importance of habitat protection and conservation efforts in promoting species recovery.

Whooping Crane's Steady Recovery Is a Tall Order

[8] The whooping crane occurs only in North America, specifically within Canada and the United States, and is North America's tallest bird. Though it once ranged throughout the Great Plains and Gulf Coast regions, the Whooping Crane population was decimated by hunting and habitat loss. The whooping crane was listed as endangered in 1970, has made a steady recovery, and its population has increased from just 21 individuals in 1941 to over 500 individuals today. The whooping crane's progress toward recovery demonstrates the power of species management and reintroduction programs in promoting species recovery under the ESA.

Peregrine Falcons Demonstrate That Conservation Can Save a Species

[9] It is estimated that prior to the 1940s, there were approximately 3,875 nesting pairs of peregrines in North America. From the 1940s through the 1960s the total population dropped dramatically, due in large part to the introduction of synthetic pesticides to the environment. By 1975, there were only 324 known nesting pairs of American peregrine falcons in the United States. This incredibly fast hunter was listed as endangered in 1970 but has made a remarkable recovery due to the banning of the pesticide DDT and conservation efforts. It was removed from the list of endangered species in 1999. The recovery of the peregrine falcon demonstrates the importance of reducing threats and promoting conservation efforts to promote species recovery.

The Next 50 Years of the ESA

[10] These ESA success stories demonstrate the effectiveness of the ESA in conserving and recovering imperiled species and highlight the importance of continued efforts to protect and conserve species threatened with extinction. Animals, plants, insects, and all living things are part of the balance of nature that our world relies on, but today there are still species at risk of being lost forever. Plants and wildlife make our lives better. And they need our active protection. We have an obligation to protect our planet's biodiversity now and for future generations.

11. Review the five events listed below. Place the following events in chronological order by filling in the table. For example, the event that happened first should be placed into the row labeled "Event 1," and the event that happened last should be placed into the row labeled "Event 5."

DDT is banned in the United States.	The bald eagle is officially considered to no longer be in danger of extinction.	2,300 breeding pairs of Kirtland's warblers are estimated to exist in the wild.	The estimated number of peregrine falcons in the wild was 3,875.	The American alligator is listed as an endangered species under the Endangered Species Preservation Act.

Event 1	
Event 2	
Event 3	

Week 14

Event 4	
Event 5	

Week 14

12. Based on the text, which statements are true for each species? You may select more than one answer for each row.

Attribute	Peregrine Falcon	Bald Eagle	Kirtland's Warbler
Faced threats to its natural habitat.	☐	☐	☐
Chemicals used by humans were largely responsible for declines in its populations.	☐	☐	☐
Was removed from the endangered species list within 30 years of first being listed.	☐	☐	☐
Hunting from humans was a major reason it was listed as endangered.	☐	☐	☐
Parasitic threats were a key danger for this species.	☐	☐	☐
Initially listed as endangered under a predecessor to the ESA.	☐	☐	☐

13. Which of the following species is no longer listed as endangered? Select all answers that apply.
    ☐ Bald eagle
    ☐ Kirtland's warbler
    ☐ Peregrine falcon
    ☐ Whooping crane
    ☐ American alligator

14. Reread the paragraph below. Underline the sentence that most directly identifies the aim of the ESA.

The ESA was enacted in 1973 as a response to the declining populations of many species of animals and plants. The Act was designed to protect and recover species at risk of extinction and to promote the conservation of ecosystems and habitats necessary for the survival of those species. Each of these species is a part of the web of life, each with a unique cultural and biological community, performing services that are essential to our combined well-being. By conserving them, guided by the best-available science, we help protect healthy air, land, and water for everyone.

15. Based on the text, which of the following is true about the ESA? Select all answers that apply.
    - ☐ Its impact is limited to species that have been officially listed as endangered.
    - ☐ The act is credited with saving the majority of species listed under it.
    - ☐ The act has been employed to save both plants and animals.
    - ☐ Humans themselves benefit from the impact of the ESA.
    - ☐ Its success in saving certain species may hinge on cooperation from multiple entities.

The passage below is from the 2024 article "Making Mars' Moons: Supercomputer Offer 'Disruptive' Explanation."

[1] A NASA study using a series of supercomputer simulations reveals a potential new solution to a longstanding Martian mystery: How did Mars get its moons? The first step, the findings say, may have involved the destruction of an asteroid.

[2] The research team, led by Jacob Kegerreis, a postdoctoral research scientist at NASA's Ames Research Center in California's Silicon Valley, found that an asteroid passing near Mars could have been disrupted – a nice way of saying "ripped apart" – by the Red Planet's strong gravitational pull.

[3] The team's simulations show the resulting rocky fragments being strewn into a variety of orbits around Mars. More than half the fragments would have escaped the Mars system, but others would've stayed in orbit. Tugged by the gravity of both Mars and the Sun, in the simulations some of the remaining asteroid pieces are set on paths to collide with one another, every encounter further grinding them down and spreading more debris.

[4] Many collisions later, smaller chunks and debris from the former asteroid could have settled into a disk encircling the planet. Over time, some of this material is likely to have clumped together, possibly forming Mars' two small moons, Phobos and Deimos.

[5] To assess whether this was a realistic chain of events, the research team explored hundreds of different close encounter simulations, varying the asteroid's size, spin, speed, and distance at its closest approach to the planet. The team used their high-performance, open-source computing code, called SWIFT, and the advanced computing systems at Durham University in the United Kingdom to study in detail both the initial disruption and, using another code, the subsequent orbits of the debris.

[6] In a paper published Nov. 20 in the journal Icarus, the researchers report that, in many of the scenarios, enough asteroid fragments survive and collide in orbit to serve as raw material to form the moons.

[7] "It's exciting to explore a new option for the making of Phobos and Deimos – the only moons in our solar system that orbit a rocky planet besides Earth's," said Kegerreis. "Furthermore, this new model makes different predictions about the moons' properties that can be tested against the standard ideas for this key event in Mars' history."

[8] Two hypotheses for the formation of the Martian moons have led the pack. One proposes that passing asteroids were captured whole by Mars' gravity, which could explain the moons' somewhat asteroid-like appearance. The other says that a giant impact on the planet blasted out enough material – a mix of Mars and impactor debris – to form a disk and, ultimately, the moons. Scientists believe a similar process formed Earth's Moon.

[9] The latter explanation better accounts for the paths the moons travel today – in near-circular orbits that closely align with Mars' equator. However, a giant impact ejects material into a disk that, mostly, stays close to the planet. And Mars' moons, especially Deimos, sit quite far away from the planet and probably formed out there, too.

[10] "Our idea allows for a more efficient distribution of moon-making material to the outer regions of the disk," said Jack Lissauer, a research scientist at Ames and co-author on the paper. "That means a much smaller 'parent' asteroid could still deliver enough material to send the moons' building blocks to the right place."

[11] Testing different ideas for the formation of Mars' moons is the primary goal of the upcoming Martian Moons eXploration (MMX) sample return mission led by JAXA (Japan Aerospace Exploration Agency). The spacecraft will survey both moons to determine their origin and collect samples of Phobos to bring to Earth for study. A NASA instrument on board, called MEGANE – short for Mars-moon Exploration with GAmma rays and Neutrons – will identify the chemical elements Phobos is made of and help select sites for the sample collection. Some of the samples will be collected by a pneumatic sampler also provided by NASA as a technology demonstration contribution to the mission. Understanding what the moons are made of is one clue that could help distinguish between the moons having an asteroid origin or a planet-plus-impactor source.

[12] Before scientists can get their hands on a piece of Phobos to analyze, Kegerreis and his team will pick up where they left off demonstrating the formation of a disk that has enough material to make Phobos and Deimos.

[13] "Next, we hope to build on this proof-of-concept project to simulate and study in greater detail the full timeline of formation," said Vincent Eke, associate professor at the Institute for Computational Cosmology at Durham University and a co-author on the paper. "This will allow us to examine the structure of the disk itself and make more detailed predictions for what the MMX mission could find."

[14] For Kegerreis, this work is exciting because it also expands our understanding of how moons might be born – even if it turns out that Mars' own formed by a different route. The simulations offer a fascinating exploration, he says, of the possible outcomes of encounters between objects like asteroids and planets. These events were common in the early solar system, and simulations could help researchers reconstruct the story of how our cosmic backyard evolved.

16. The table below gives several steps in a sequence of events Kegerreis's team proposed. Put the events in chronological order by labeling them a whole number from "1" to "5" such that "1" is the first event and "5" is the last.

Event	Step in Hypothesized Sequence
A disk formed around Mars as a result of the products of multiple collisions.	
The gravitational pull of Mars disrupted an asteroid passing by it.	
Material from the disk clumped together to form moons.	
Asteroid pieces that remained in Mars' orbit collided, grinding each other down over a long period of time.	
Some rocky fragments from the disrupted asteroid were strewn outside of Mars' orbit, and others stayed in its orbit.	

17. Which of the following identifies an aspect of Kegerreis's team's hypothesis that is SIMILAR to an attribute of one of the two leading hypotheses discussed in paragraphs 8 and 9? Select all answers that apply.
    ☐ Debris formed a disk that formed the moons.
    ☐ The debris that formed the moons included material originating from the Martian surface.
    ☐ Mars' moons contain at least some material deriving from asteroids.
    ☐ Tidal forces disrupted an asteroid passing by Mars.
    ☐ Celestial bodies captured by Mars' gravity remained intact.

For question 18, read the excerpt below.

[8] Two hypotheses for the formation of the Martian moons have led the pack. One proposes that passing asteroids were captured whole by Mars' gravity, which could explain the moons' somewhat asteroid-like appearance. The other says that a giant impact on the planet blasted out enough material – a mix of Mars and impactor debris – to form a disk and, ultimately, the moons. Scientists believe a similar process formed Earth's Moon.

[9] The latter explanation better accounts for the paths the moons travel today – in near-circular orbits that closely align with Mars' equator. However, a giant impact ejects material into a disk that, mostly, stays close to the planet. And Mars' moons, especially Deimos, sit quite far away from the planet and probably formed out there, too.

[10] "Our idea allows for a more efficient distribution of moon-making material to the outer regions of the disk," said Jack Lissauer, a research scientist at Ames and co-author on the paper. "That means a much smaller 'parent' asteroid could still deliver enough material to send the moons' building blocks to the right place."

18. Underline the sentence that identifies an expectation that would need to be met to make the giant impact hypothesis more convincing.

For question 19, return to the same excerpt.

[8] Two hypotheses for the formation of the Martian moons have led the pack. One proposes that passing asteroids were captured whole by Mars' gravity, which could explain the moons' somewhat asteroid-like appearance. The other says that a giant impact on the planet blasted out enough material – a mix of Mars and impactor debris – to form a disk and, ultimately, the moons. Scientists believe a similar process formed Earth's Moon.

[9] The latter explanation better accounts for the paths the moons travel today – in near-circular orbits that closely align with Mars' equator. However, a giant impact ejects material into a disk that, mostly, stays close to the planet. And Mars' moons, especially Deimos, sit quite far away from the planet and probably formed out there, too.

Week 14

[10] "Our idea allows for a more efficient distribution of moon-making material to the outer regions of the disk," said Jack Lissauer, a research scientist at Ames and co-author on the paper. "That means a much smaller 'parent' asteroid could still deliver enough material to send the moons' building blocks to the right place."

19. Underline the sentence that identifies an advantage that one of the leading hypotheses has over the other.

[8] Two hypotheses for the formation of the Martian moons have led the pack. One proposes that passing asteroids were captured whole by Mars' gravity, which could explain the moons' somewhat asteroid-like appearance. The other says that a giant impact on the planet blasted out enough material – a mix of Mars and impactor debris – to form a disk and, ultimately, the moons. Scientists believe a similar process formed Earth's Moon.

[9] The latter explanation better accounts for the paths the moons travel today – in near-circular orbits that closely align with Mars' equator. However, a giant impact ejects material into a disk that, mostly, stays close to the planet. And Mars' moons, especially Deimos, sit quite far away from the planet and probably formed out there, too.

[10] "Our idea allows for a more efficient distribution of moon-making material to the outer regions of the disk," said Jack Lissauer, a research scientist at Ames and co-author on the paper. "That means a much smaller 'parent' asteroid could still deliver enough material to send the moons' building blocks to the right place."

20. According to the text, which of the following is true about the MMX mission? Select all answers that apply.
    ☐ Its main objective is to examine hypotheses for how Mars' moons formed.
    ☐ The mission itself will use a supercomputer to determine if it is possible for Martian material to have formed the moons.
    ☐ Samples from Phobos and Deimos will be collected for chemical analysis.
    ☐ The mission will be developed and spearheaded by NASA.
    ☐ Kegerreis's team will attempt to make predictions about what the mission can find through further studies.

The passage below is adapted from "The Yellow Wallpaper" by Charlotte Perkins Gilman.

[1] John laughs at me, of course, but one expects that in marriage. John is practical in the extreme. He has no patience with faith, an intense horror of superstition, and he scoffs openly at any talk of things not to be felt and seen and put down in figures. John is a physician. You see he does not believe I am sick! And what can one do? If a physician of high standing, and one's own husband, assures friends and relatives that there is really nothing the matter with one but temporary nervous depression—a slight hysterical tendency—what is one to do? My brother is also a physician, and also of high standing, and he says the same thing. So I take phosphates or phosphites—whichever it is, and tonics, and journeys, and air, and exercise, and am absolutely forbidden to "work" until I am well again. Personally, I disagree with their ideas. Personally, I believe that congenial work, with excitement and change, would do me good. But what is one to do? I did write for a while in spite of them; but it DOES exhaust me a good deal—having to be so sly about it, or else meet with heavy opposition. I sometimes fancy that in my condition if I had less opposition and more society and stimulus—but John says the very worst thing I can do is to think about my condition, and I confess it always makes me feel bad.

[2] So I will let it alone and talk about the house. The most beautiful place! It is quite alone, standing well back from the road, quite three miles from the village. I don't like our room a bit. I wanted one downstairs that opened on the piazza and had roses all over the window, and such pretty old-fashioned chintz hangings! but John would not hear of it. He is very careful and loving and hardly lets me stir without special direction. I have a schedule prescription for each hour in the day; he takes all care from me, and so I feel basely ungrateful not to value it more.

[3] The paint and paper look as if a boys' school had used it. I never saw a worse paper in my life. One of those sprawling flamboyant patterns committing every artistic sin. It is dull enough to confuse the eye in following and pronounced enough to constantly irritate and provoke study. The color is repellent, almost revolting; a smoldering unclean yellow, strangely faded by the slow-turning sunlight. John does not know how much I really suffer. Out of one window I can see the garden, those mysterious deep-shaded arbors, the riotous old-fashioned flowers, and bushes and gnarly trees. I always fancy I see people walking in these numerous paths and arbors, but John has cautioned me not to give way to fancy in the least. He says that with my imaginative power and habit of story-making, a nervous weakness like mine is sure to lead to all manner of excited fancies, and that I ought to use my will and good sense to check the tendency.

[4] But I must not think about that. This paper looks to me as if it KNEW what a vicious influence it had! There is a recurrent spot where the pattern lolls like a broken neck and two bulbous eyes stare at you upside down. I get positively angry with the impertinence of it and the everlastingness. Up and down and sideways they crawl, and those absurd, unblinking eyes are everywhere. There is one place where two breadths didn't match, and the eyes go all up and down the line, one a little higher than the other.

[5] There comes John's sister. Such a dear girl as she is, and so careful of me! I must not let her find me writing. She is a perfect and enthusiastic housekeeper and hopes for no better profession. I verily believe she thinks it is the writing which made me sick! But I can write when she is out and see her a long way off from these windows. John says if I don't pick up faster, he shall send me to Weir Mitchell in the fall. But I don't want to go there at all. I had a friend who was in his hands once, and she says he is just like John and my brother, only more so!

[6] There is a very funny mark on this wall, low down, near the mopboard. A streak that runs round the room. It goes behind every piece of furniture, except the bed, a long, straight, even *smooch*, as if it had been rubbed over and over. I wonder how it was done and who did it, and what they did it for. Round and round and round—round and round and round—it makes me dizzy! I really have discovered something at last. Through watching so much at night, when it changes so, I have finally found out.

[7] The front pattern *does* move—and no wonder! The woman behind shakes it! Sometimes I think there are a great many women behind, and sometimes only one, and she crawls around fast, and her crawling shakes it all over. Then in the very bright spots she keeps still, and in the very shady spots she just takes hold of the bars and shakes them hard. And she is all the time trying to climb through. I think that woman gets out in the daytime! And I'll tell you why—privately—I've seen her! I can see her out of every one of my windows!

21. In the first paragraph, the narrator employs which of the following techniques? Select all answers that apply.
    - ☐ Extended metaphors.
    - ☐ Repetitive constructions.
    - ☐ Personal confession.
    - ☐ Personification of inanimate objects.
    - ☐ Detailed imagery.

22. Read the paragraph below. Underline the sentence that most directly reveals that the narrator has deceived her loved ones.

John laughs at me, of course, but one expects that in marriage. John is practical in the extreme. He has no patience with faith, an intense horror of superstition, and he scoffs openly at any talk of things not to be felt and seen and put down in figures. John is a physician. You see he does not believe I am sick! And what can one do? If a physician of high standing, and one's own husband, assures friends and relatives that there is really nothing the matter with one but temporary nervous depression—a slight hysterical tendency—what is one to do? My brother is also a physician, and also of high standing, and he says the same thing. So I take phosphates or phosphites—whichever it is, and tonics, and journeys, and air, and exercise, and am absolutely forbidden to "work" until I am well again. Personally, I disagree with their ideas. Personally, I believe that congenial work, with excitement and change, would do me good. But what is one to do? <u>I did write for a while in spite of them; but it DOES exhaust me a good deal—having to be so sly about it, or else meet with heavy opposition.</u> I sometimes fancy that in my condition if I had less opposition and more society and stimulus—but John says the very worst thing I can do is to think about my condition, and I confess it always makes me feel bad.

23. Consider the themes below.

The restorative power of intellectual outlets.
Gender discrimination in professional settings.
The subordination of women in marriage.
The destructive effects of isolation on personal happiness.
The power of an unrestrained imagination.

In the table below, identify which theme is most directly related to the corresponding quote. One theme will not be used.

Quote	
"And what can one do? If a physician of high standing, and one's own husband, assures friends and relatives that there is really nothing the matter with one but temporary nervous depression—a slight hysterical tendency—what is one to do?"	
"The front pattern *does* move—and no wonder! The woman behind shakes it! Sometimes I think there are a great many women behind, and sometimes only one, and she crawls around fast, and her crawling shakes it all over."	
"Personally, I believe that congenial work, with excitement and change, would do me good."	
"The color is repellent, almost revolting; a smoldering unclean yellow, strangely faded by the slow-turning sunlight. John does not know how much I really suffer."	

Week 14

24. Select which attributes the narrator states or implies about each character. Select all answers that apply.

Attribute	John	John's sister	The narrator's brother
Has a high social status	☐	☐	☐
Complicit in the narrator's treatment plan.	☐	☐	☐
Believes the narrator should avoid writing.	☐	☐	☐
Works as a physician.	☐	☐	☐
Oversees the narrator's prescriptions.	☐	☐	☐

25. Select the best answers for both blanks.

"He is very careful and loving and hardly lets me stir without special direction."

In the context of the passage as a whole, the statement above can primarily be characterized as (i)_____ and suggests John's attentiveness (ii)_____

Blank i	Blank ii
ironic	is a reflection of his deep expertise in mental health conditions.
mendacious	removes the narrator's doubts about the efficacy of her treatment plan.
adulatory	is a mere façade to keep up appearances as a doting husband.
recriminatory	may reflect his controlling nature.

Week 14

Part 2: Grammar

For questions 26 to 30, read the passage below.

(1) Hummingbird migration is not completely understood, as much of what we do know about hummingbirds is determined from "banding studies." (2) In banding studies, individual hummingbirds are trapped, and given identification numbers, which are written on aluminum foil and wrapped around their legs. (3) Scientists conduct these studies in order to learn about the natural history and habits of different species of hummingbirds. (4) The age of hummingbirds can be estimated by examining their bills with a hand lens upon capture. (5) Evidence from various studies suggest that many birds follow a set route each year, demonstrating loyalty to particular sites. (6) For example, the ruby-throated hummingbird shows a high degree of fidelity approximately one fifth of birds return to the same site year after year.

(7) In the United States, hummingbirds typically migrate to the North during the spring and to the South during the winter however, the precise reasons why they migrate are not completely understood. (8) Some scientists believe that hummingbirds primarily migrate in order to follow flower populations. (9) Hummingbirds eat the nectar from flowers, so it makes sense that they would travel to locations where the flowers they feed on are in full bloom. (10) Other scientists believe that hummingbirds primarily migrate to follow insects. (11) Although it is thought that hummingbirds migrate on the backs of geese, this belief is a myth. (12) Overall, scientists still have a lot to learn about why hummingbirds migrate. (13) Hummingbirds usually migrate alone to avoid detection by predators.

26. The passage above has 13 sentences labeled from 1 to 13. In the blanks below, write in the numbers corresponding to the three sentences that should be deleted from the passage for the sake of logic and cohesion.

Sentence ___
Sentence ___
Sentence ___

27. Without adjusting the capitalization, insert a comma or colon to fix the sentence.
   For example, the ruby-throated hummingbird shows a high degree of fidelity approximately one fifth of birds return to the same site year after year.

28. Without adjusting the capitalization, insert a comma, semicolon, or colon to fix the sentence.
   In the United States, hummingbirds typically migrate to the North during the spring and to the South during the winter however, the precise reasons why they migrate are not completely understood.

29. Underline the word in this sentence that either has an unnecessary comma after it OR is missing a comma that should be present after it.
   In banding studies, individual hummingbirds are trapped, and given identification numbers, which are written on aluminum foil and wrapped around their legs.

30. Underline the word that produces a grammatical error in the sentence below.
   Evidence from various studies suggest that many birds follow a set route each year, demonstrating loyalty to particular sites.

31. Underline ONE word that should be deleted from this sentence to eliminate the redundancy error.
   In the beginning, the camper was initially concerned about hiking along the trail, but his worries quickly subsided once he saw the beautiful scenery.

32. Underline TWO words in the sentence below that result in a redundancy error.
As a result of assimilation programs, many Native American groups have lost aspects of their cultures, such as widespread use of their native languages. Yet efforts by Indian and Alaskan native elders to teach their native languages to younger generations <u>raised</u> and <u>lifted</u> these languages from obscurity.

33. Underline the word in the sentence below that is grammatically incorrect.
The mantis shrimp is one of the strongest animals in the world on a pound for pound basis. This crustacean, using clubs at the ends of <u>their</u> forelegs, produces quick and powerful strikes to its prey.

34. Add missing punctuation that is needed to make this sentence grammatically correct.
Male tanagers can consume carotenoids to make their feathers darker, an honest signal of fitness to potential mates. The ability of some tanagers to manipulate light to give their feathers a darker appearance without actually having to consume the carotenoids, though, can serve as a dishonest signal of fitness.

35. Add missing punctuation that is needed to make this sentence grammatically correct.
Consistent with the vision of its founders, the nonprofit serves to promote a nurturing, inclusive environment for students to develop their artistic skills.

36. Underline the word in the sentence below that is grammatically incorrect.
Throughout her career, Jane Addams, founder of the Hull House, sought to improve education for children, documenting social illnesses, and <u>promote</u> feminist values.

37. Select the best answers for each of the three blanks.

Managed care networks seek to promote disease management and preventative care. The ability of managed care networks to meet these goals (i)_____ integral to lowering costs. Many companies hire representatives to regularly contact clients to make sure that (ii) _____are engaging in healthful behaviors. They will often encourage at-risk patients to seek medical care during times when they are experiencing minor health issues. (iii)_____ precludes more catastrophic health disasters that would be costlier for companies to cover.

Blank i	Blank ii	Blank iii
is	he or she	That
are	them	This practice
being	they	Doing it
to be	whom	It

38. Select the best answers for each of the three blanks.
Some social psychologists question if there is such thing as a genuinely altruistic good deed and instead argue that seemingly generous actions have (i)_____. For example, students may engage in community service to be more "competitive" for admission to selective colleges. A rider on the bus may give (ii)_____ seat to an elderly person to avoid negative social judgement by observers. By definition, altruistic acts are done to help others without expectation of any benefit in return. The empathy-altruism hypothesis argues that evidence from both psychological experiments and neuroimaging suggests that people high in empathy may help others out of genuine concern for their welfare, (iii)_____those lower in empathy may engage in helping behaviors for more selfish reasons.

Blank i	Blank ii	Blank iii
selfish motivations?	their	which
selfish motivations.	our	while
selfish, motivations?	his or her	instead,
selfish, motivations.	whose	however,

Week 14

39. Select the best answers for each of the three blanks.

Mohammad Yunus, the Founder of the Grameen Bank in Bangladesh, is a pioneer in the concept of microcredit. Since Yunus perceived traditional banks as profit-seeking entities primarily serving the wealthy, he established the Grameen Bank to serve disadvantaged populations. Under the microcredit model, the bank gives small loans to individuals (i) _____ are too poor to qualify for (ii) _____. Each time a borrower repays the loan, he or she is entitled to an even larger loan. Due to the success of the Grameen Bank, microfinance institutions (iii) _____ now a global phenomenon.

Blank i	Blank ii	Blank iii
whom	traditional bank loans	will be
which	traditional bank loans owing to a lack of funds	has become
who	traditional bank loans due to a dearth of income	are
they	traditional bank loans in an impoverished state	is

40. Select the best answers for each of the three blanks.

Both the *Harry Potter* series and the *Hunger Games* trilogy portray young protagonists who experience what is often (i)_____ a "hero's journey." In *Harry Potter*, the titular character is a valiant wizard who takes on supernatural forces of evil. (ii)_____ in *The Hunger Games*, Katniss Everdeen becomes a somewhat reluctant hero against an oppressive regime. In both cases, the characters rely on the help of their friends and (iii)_____ all while navigating ordinary challenges associated with being teenagers. Both characters came from humble beginnings before assuming heroic roles with humility and courage.

Blank i	Blank ii	Blank iii
dubbed	Nevertheless,	allies;
dubbed,	Specifically,	allies
dubbed:	Similarly,	allies,
dubbed—	For instance,	allies and

41. Select the best answers for each of the three blanks.

The Mycenaean civilization flourished in Greece from 1650 to 1200 B.C. The Mycenaeans were the first people to speak the Greek language and were influenced by the culture of the Minoans, who resided in Crete. While later Greeks often told stories about this (i)_____ Homer in *Iliad* and *Odyssey*, there was no evidence that the Myceneans actually existed until (ii) _____ Heinrich Schliemann made a discovery in 1876. He found artifacts from this lost civilization high in the mountains of (iii)_____ golden masks, bronze weapons, and palaces that illustrated the wealth of Mycenaean rulers.

Blank i	Blank ii	Blank iii
group they included	Archaeologist	Mycenae, such as:
group, they included	archaeologist:	Mycenae:
group, including	archaeologist	Mycenae,
group such as,	archaeologist;	Mycenae

42. Select the best answers for each of the three blanks.

Many marine mammals rely heavily on (i)_____ a process whereby they use sound waves to locate objects and gain information about their surroundings. By emitting sound waves and interpreting their reverberations off of objects, marine mammals can get a sense of these (ii) _____ shapes and positions. (iii) _____ echolocation essentially functions as a means by which these animals "see the world." This is especially important in areas where water is dark or murky.

Blank i	Blank ii	Blank iii
echolocation	objects	Therefore,
echolocation,	object's	On the other hand,
echolocation;	objects'	For example,
echolocation, this is	objects':	Nonetheless,

Colorado-based artist Gregg _____ to use his work to share his perspective as both an Indigenous person and human being, believes in using his craft to produce accurate portrayals of Indigenous experiences and shatter stereotypes.

43. Which of the following best completes the text so that it conforms to the conventions of Standard English? Select all answers that apply.
    ☐ Deal, seeking
    ☐ Deal, whom seeks
    ☐ Deal, that seeks
    ☐ Deal, who seeks
    ☐ Deal, he seeks
    ☐ Deal seeks

A California sea lion who achieved fame in 2013 for her ability to bob her head to a rhythm reentered the <u>limelight she appeared</u> in a new study that showed her synchronization matched or surpassed that of humans.

44. Which of the following corrects the underlined portion? Select all answers that apply.
    ☐ limelight; she appeared
    ☐ limelight, appearing
    ☐ limelight. She appeared
    ☐ limelight appeared
    ☐ limelight; appearing
    ☐ limelight when she appeared

One of the most popular items traded along the Silk Road, a network of ancient trade routes connecting the East and the West, was jade, _____ for its appearance, rarity, durability, and spiritual significance.

45. Which of the following best completes the text so that it conforms to the conventions of Standard English? Select all answers that apply.
    ☐ it was highly prized
    ☐ it is highly prized
    ☐ highly prized
    ☐ which was highly prized
    ☐ prizing

Key

Week 1

Drill 1

1. **B.** "Insourcing" is hiring people in-house, as the last paragraph explains.
2. **A.** The band preferred not to outsource, but insource, as explained in the last paragraph. They did "shake up conventional norms" (lines 3-4), tour year-round (lines 4-5), and reward loyal fans (lines 7-9).
3. **D.** Many companies adopted a customer-first model that focused on meeting the needs of their clients (lines 9-11).
4. **C.** The band made money from merchandise sales (lines 14-15).
5. **A.** The last paragraph explains how one business strategy (insourcing) helped the band. Choice B describes the second paragraph.
6. **B.** The sentence marks a shift from a commentary on the band's musical style to a different characteristic of the band that has gained scholarly attention, namely its business model. The rest of the passage elaborates on the band's business model and its role in its success.
7. **C.** The long maturation periods suggest that mastodons required care for a long time (lines 22-23).
8. **D.** The ridged molars were characteristics of the mammoths, not the mastodons (lines 15-16). The mastodons did have cone-like cusps (line 16), low-domed heads (line 7), and large, long tusks (line 7).
9. **C.** The arrowhead was evidence that humans hunted mastodons (lines 11-12).
10. **C.** The debate hasn't been completely resolved since there is "still some debate" (line 26).
11. **B.** The judgment that mastodons were social creatures is based on their similarities to elephants, but scientists still can't be completely sure (lines 19-21). Thus, it is a reasonable judgment based on scientific analysis of the similarities between mastodons and elephants.
12. **B.** Carbon from the teeth provided a treasure trove of information (lines 17-18).
13. **C.** While the results from carbon studies may be accurate and may reflect differences between individual mastodons, that is not why they are mentioned. Rather, they provide evidence for the dietary preferences of animals. In this case, they confirm the different preferences of mastodons and mammoths.

14. **A**. The fourth paragraph speculates about mastodon behavior, including their social and migratory behavior. The paragraph notes similarities with elephants, not differences, as Choice B indicates.
15. **B**. The previous sentence mentions that the preservation of the mastodon's death was connected to a practical purpose. The last sentence expands on this by stating that the skeletons were likely stored as meat under a pond.
16. **B**. It was believed that the window between the living and the dead opened on October 31st (lines 6-7). In other words, the boundary loosened.
17. **D**. The jack-o-lanterns were made to ward off evil spirits (lines 8-10).
18. **A**. Masks, costumes, and jack-o-lanterns were all mentioned in the second paragraph as being associated with Samhain. Apple bobbing was described as being associated with the modern-day version of Halloween (line 17).
19. **A**. Tricking is outlawed in some countries for the disruption and damage it causes (lines 22-23).
20. **C**. Lines 13-18 provide background information about how Halloween began in the United States with a wave of Scottish and Irish immigration. The previous paragraph discusses the religious traditions.
21. **D**. People left out food and drink for deceased loved ones seeking hospitality (lines 10-12).
22. **A**. People may perceive bright red apple-flavored drinks as sweeter (lines 14-15).
23. **B**. People were asked to guess flavors when the color of drinks was shown or manipulated.
24. **A**. The paragraph concludes that color, which is a visual cue, impacts how we perceive taste (lines 18-19).
25. **B**. Colorimeters are used to ensure the food is perfectly hued (line 27).
26. **A**. Blue lemonade and green ketchup are examples of products that are colored in a way that counters our expectations but have nonetheless been marketed successfully (lines 32-33).
27. **A**. The color of the food is manipulated to drive sales since people associate green meat with meat that has gone bad.
28. **C**. The last paragraph concedes that visual cues do not completely control our food preferences, as other factors can override visual cues, such as a desire to be adventurous. Thus, there are limits to the power of visual cues.
29. **C**. That companies dye meat a different color to appear more appealing to customers suggests they are aware of the power of visual cues to shape dietary choices.
30. **C**. Sea stars hide from predators in the coral reef (lines 16-19).
31. **B**. The paragraph focuses on the anatomy of sea stars, such as their digestive and nervous systems.

Key

32. **C.** Suction is used for feeding, which is ingestion (lines 9-10).
33. **C.** Regeneration allows sea stars to regrow missing lines (lines 20).
34. **B.** Sea stars eat sea urchins. Sea stars are threatened by the virus Sea Star Wasting Syndrome (lines 31), warming waters (line 32), and harvesting by humans (lines 30-31).
35. **D.** Keystone organisms maintain the balance, or stability, of an ecosystem (lines 21-222).
36. **A.** Nightingale believed mental and physical health were linked, or intertwined (lines 28-29).
37. **B.** The school was for nurses (lines 39-40), though it was connected to a medical program.
38. **D.** Nightingale did not identify unusual military capabilities as a reason for high death rates. More soldiers died from disease than combat. She did identify factors of the high death rate as including bad drainage (line 23), poor hygiene (lines 15-16), and unsanitary living quarters (lines 15-16).
39. **B.** Nightingale defied her family's expectations much to her mother's "protest" by becoming a nurse instead of marrying someone in the upper class (lines 5-7, 11-13).
40. **B.** Clarke taught Nightingale that men and women can be equal (lines 10-11).
41. **A.** The speaker is charmed, or captivated, by autumn.
42. **D.** The poets sing a dirge and seem to lament on the death associated with autumn, such as of the flowers. Thus, their attitude is somber.
43. **A.** The woods provide the speaker with a sense of peacefulness, or tranquility.
44. **C.** Hope is described as a thing with feathers that perches in the soul. A bird has feathers and perches. Thus, hope is like a bird.
45. **B.** The song is a tune without words, or lyrics.
46. **D.** The song never stops. Thus, it is a steady force.
47. **A.** Hope asks nothing of the speaker. Thus, it is undemanding.
48. **B.** The speaker cannot explain why he is sick and tired, which his subjective, or personal, experience during the lecture.
49. **A.** The speaker was bored with the facts and figures. He felt sick and tired, so he walked out. While sitting outside under the stars, he experienced perfect silence, or peacefulness.
50. **B.** There is a contrast between the knowledge taught by the astronomer and the actual experience of sitting under the stars. There is also a contrast between the settings of the lecture room indoors and the outdoors.
51. **D.** The mask "grins and lies." In other words, it smiles dishonestly. "With torn and bleeding hearts we smile" further suggests that the people smiling are actually sad, or torn up inside.
52. **B.** The mask hides people's true feelings. Thus, it represents deception, or dishonesty.
53. **A.** The souls of the people cry and are tortured. Thus, they feel tormented. They also have "torn and bleeding hearts."

Key

54. **A.** The second stanza suggests that the world is not "wise" or aware of how the "we" really feel. They only see the "we" in their masks that hide their unhappiness. "Let the world dream otherwise" in the last stanza indicates that the world is not aware that the souls are tortured.
55. **A.** The man "labored hard" (worked hard) toward his dream.
56. **B.** The man is resilient because despite experiencing difficulties, he maintains a hopeful attitude and maintains his dream.
57. **D.** The man saw a gleam (light) through the darkness of the clouds. In context, the storm and clouds seem to represent the obstacles he faced. The fact that he still had his dream and saw a gleam shows that he felt hopeful.
58. **C.** Helen felt anger and bitterness in the weeks leading up to Anne Sullivan's arrival (lines 9-10). In other words, she was irritated.
59. **B.** Helen compared herself to a ship without a compass or sounding line with no idea how close to the harbor she was (lines 11-16). In other words, she was like a directionless ship (a ship wandering without direction).
60. **B.** Helen says that more than all things else, Anne loved Helen (lines 17-19).
61. **B.** Helen took childlike pleasure in imitating Anne in spelling monkey, but she had no idea what language was or that she was even spelling a word or that words existed (lines 22-26).
62. **D.** Lines 15-17 indicate that problems included the cold (inclement weather), starvation (food scarcity), and hunting from animals and each other (predation).
63. **C.** Prometheus felt bad for the humans, and he wanted to give them fire so that they could cook food, stay warm, and have shelter. He believed they lived no better than beasts (line 18-20). Thus, he wanted humans to live under more dignified, or honorable, circumstances.
64. **A.** Jupiter did not want humans to become strong and wise like the Mighty Folk and possibly overthrow him (lines 23-26). Thus, he was concerned about his own standing, or status, being jeopardized.
65. **A.** Prometheus taught them how to cook, tame animals, and build houses (lines 37-50). Though he taught them how to build weapons, he didn't teach them how to fight.
66. **C.** The Mighty Folk are more powerful than the humans and Jupiter (the king of the gods) is one of them, as he makes clear in his conversation with Prometheus. Thus, the Mighty Folk are divine beings, or gods.
67. **C.** Lines 13-21 indicate that the older man is glum-faced, or gloomy-looking.
68. **B.** Lines 17-18 indicate that Miss Fairchild's face became one of bewildered horror when she saw the handcuffs.
69. **B.** The older man says that Mr. Easton is a marshal taking him to prison (lines 22-24). Thus, he claims Mr. Easton is performing his occupational duties.

Key

70. **D.** Mr. Easton is headed to Leavenworth. However, he is going as the prisoner. The passenger at the end realizes that a marshal would not cuff a prisoner to his right hand; thus, the older man is actually the marshal.
71. **A.** The speaker walks purposefully. She was walking up a mountain "With many things to do/Important business of my own/And other people's too." She had important business to attend to."
72. **A.** Prejudice will not let the speaker past, which frustrates her. The fact that she notes her strength and time were limited hints at growing impatience, which culminates in her screaming at Prejudice.
73. **B.** The speaker says that Prejudice was a mass of "obdurate ill will." "Obdurate" means "stubborn." Thus, Prejudice resembled a massive monument for its stubborn refusal to move.
74. **D.** The speaker ultimately walked around Prejudice by acting as if it wasn't there, or by pretending it didn't exist.
75. **A.** While Prejudice was as mad (enraged) as the speaker, it refused to move. Thus, it was steadfast, or determined, it is resolved.
76. **C.** The speaker adapted to the inconvenient truth that there was no reasoning or pleading with Prejudice. The only way to get around it was to pretend it did not exist.
77. **B.** The mountain setting parallels the speaker's uphill battle against Prejudice, which doesn't let her pass through.
78. **D.** While some of the women are happy and others overworked, what they share is their preoccupation with their own loved ones and lack of concern for others they do not know personally.
79. **B.** In the second stanza, the speaker asks questions that have implicit (implied) positive answers. The speaker does believe the women feel entitled to ignore the sorrow in the world and that such sorrow doesn't affect them.
80. **A.** The speaker expresses outrage at the complacency (contentment) of a class of individuals (mothers) who limit their love to a small group of people.
81. **A.** The rebels were those who the speaker passed with a "nod" or "polite meaningless words." Thus, they were ordinary people in his community who were insignificant to him personally. They merely exchanged pleasantries.
82. **B.** The speaker exchanged pleasantries at the "close of the day" from "counter or desk" (a likely reference to their work). Thus, he mostly saw them after work, in the late afternoon or early evening.
83. **A.** The speaker comes off as snobbish and seems to think he is "above" the rebels. He describes their houses common and seems to find his interactions with them repetitive, or annoying. He is merely being polite, but he has no interest in developing genuine friendships with them. We later learn that he even makes fun of them to his companions.
84. **B.** Before the rebellion, the speaker would often tell a "mocking tale or a gibe" to his companions about the rebels.

85. **C.** The speaker is very conflicted about his feelings. When reflecting on one leader, he describes his as "daring" and "sweet in his thought." Yet he describes another as a "drunken, vainglorious lout," but he still "numbers" (acknowledges) him for his role in the fight and therefore pays his respects to him for his sacrifice. He also repeats the idea that "a terrible beauty is born," showing his mixed feelings about the rebellion. While some beautiful results might come from it, there has also been great tragedy. Overall, while the speaker is sympathetic to the rebels and ponders that might be forever remembered, he also critiques some of them and believes they have paid a terrible price.
86. **B.** The speaker calls the woman "ignorant," suggesting that she is uninformed. She spends her night arguing, presumably about politics, showing that she is passionate.
87. **C.** The purpose and resolve of the rebels was unmovable (they had "hearts with one purpose alone"). They were like stones in that stones are unaffected even as everything around them changes (e.g. the riders and animals that splash through a stream and the even the clouds change minute by minute, but the stone remains constant "in the midst of it all").
88. **D**. The speaker asserts that we know their (the rebels') dreams and we know that they are dead. Thus, we know the ideals they were willing to die for, so he is still uncertain if their deaths were pointless or if they were bewildered by excess love. It is also not clear how exactly historians will remember them.
89. **A.** The rebellion was terrible because many people lost their lives. But it was also beautiful because the rebels will be remembered for their sacrifice. Wearing green will now have a changed meaning, implying the sacrifices will be honored. Thus, the idealism and change associated with rebellion can be beautiful.
90. **A.** The narrator asserts that the story is not a fancy sketch but was told by a clergyman who vouched for its truth (promised it was truthful). Thus, the narrator attempts to dispel any doubts that the story is fictional before telling it, sensing that it might seem unrealistic.
91. **B.** The first paragraph highlights the narrator's awe and admiration of Scoresby. We learn that he was a celebrated figure whom the narrator saw as a demigod. The assertion that he is a fool marks a transition to a discussion of how Scoresby is inept and has benefited greatly from luck despite his poor qualifications.
92. **C.** According to the clergyman, "He went through on that purely superficial "cram," and got compliments too, while others, who knew a thousand times more than he, got plucked. By some strangely lucky accident—an accident not likely to happen twice in a century—he was asked no question outside of the narrow limits of his drill." Thus, Scoresby was fortunate that he was only tested on the narrow range of topics that he happened to study by chance.

93. **A.** The clergyman complains that people misinterpreted Scoresby's performance and "took his idiotic blunders for inspirations of genius; they did, honestly! His mildest blunders were enough to make a man in his right mind cry; and they did make me cry—and rage and rave too, privately." The clergyman was in "a sweat of apprehension" because each of his blunders "increased the luster of his reputation!" Thus, most people did not share the negative opinion of Scoresby that the clergyman had, so the word choice of the clergyman dramatizes this point by highlighting his frustrations that nobody else could perceive the military man's flaws.
94. **D.** The clergyman states, "He is just as good and sweet and lovable and unpretending as a man can be, but he doesn't know enough to come in when it rains. Now that is absolutely true. He is the supremest donkey in the universe." He suggests that Scoresby is a good person (he is friendly) but he is dim, or dumb.
95. **C.** The fact that the clergyman inserted himself in Scoresby's exams suggests he was not actually a man of repose (rest) and inaction. Rather, he was very proactive.
96. **A.** The background information about the author's urban existence clarifies why she was so taken aback by seeing a deer at work, as she was not accustomed to such human-animal interactions.
97. **B.** The practical conclusions the author makes about how companion animals support health and well-being is grounded in empirical evidence from several research studies suggesting that health and behavioral outcomes in children can be improved through human-animal interventions.
98. **B.** The description of three studies (related to children with diabetes, autism, and ADHD) serves as three separate pieces of supporting evidence to support the larger claim about the well-being benefits of interactions with companion animals.
99. **A.** The end of paragraph 1 into the beginning of paragraph 2 makes a broader point about the health/well-being benefits of human-animal interactions. By the end of the paragraph, it transitions to how research on such interactions in a particular group of people (children) supports this argument, setting the stage for the discussion of several research studies in the ensuring paragraphs.
100. **C.** The author presents scientific studies that illustrate the health/well-being benefits of human-animal interactions on children with diabetes, autism, and ADHD, respectively. These studies are used to support the author's broader point of view about the value of human-animal interactions.
101. **D.** The fact that the anxiety levels of children dropped after playing with the guinea pigs best supports the idea that interacting with animals can improve health and well-being. Reducing anxiety is a positive health outcome.
102. **D.** D provides an example of children interacting with real animals and then engaging in a more healthful behavior (monitoring glucose) as a result of such behavior.
103. **C.** The hypothesis that interactions with dogs help children focus their attention is a potential causal mechanism (means, or way) by which such interactions result in improved executive functioning skills.

Key

104. **C.** Tillie frequently boasts about Thea's accomplishments, to the point where she turns other people off. Thea's father is proud of Thea, but he always feels the need to compliment his other children when someone comments on how remarkable Thea is. Thus, he seems more modest and less publicly boastful about Thea's traits and abilities.
105. **B.** The second paragraph describes patterns of behavior in Thea and her siblings that serve to differentiate her from them. Specifically, she is described as more independent than they are. She is not demanding of others (unlike her siblings) and generally keeps to herself.
106. **B.** The paragraph highlights the strength of the bond between Tillie and Thea, illustrating how Thea feels beholden to Tillie's whims, which in turn shapes her behavior (by causing her to help Tillie more than she otherwise would prefer).
107. **C.** The excerpt shows that Thea is committing to helping Tillie rehearse. It also hints at her frustration through her critiques ("I don't see the point in it"), which is consistent with the passage's assertion that Thea was ashamed of Tillie's acting skills. That Thea only chimed in occasionally rather than often and enthusiastically might suggest she resented having to help Tillie, as she only helped her out of obligation.
108. **A.** The men attending rehearsals just to oblige Tillie parallels Thea and her family catering to Tillie's whims to oblige her, such as by helping her rehearse.
109. **B.** Tillie's refusal to agree to the club members' request for Thea to play the lead annoyed them, leading to Tillie getting a cold reception and Thea having a new crop of enemies. Thus, the remark precipitated tension between Tillie and other characters.
110. **A.** This sentence introduces that certain neurons (MCH neurons) may play a role in promoting forgetting, and the passage will later support this with results from studies showing that activation of these neurons during REM sleep is associated with forgetting.
111. **B.** The sentence provides descriptive information on some of the technical features of REM sleep, providing context for understanding the study (the effects of activating/inhibiting MCH neurons seemed to matter most during this very specific stage of sleep, not wakefulness or sleep in general).
112. **C.** While the study described in this passage might be the first to show how REM sleep might promote forgetting, the idea that sleep might play a role in useful forgetting has been around for a long time. Crick is mentioned to provide an illustrative example of one scientist in the past who speculated this might be the case.
113. **C.** Paragraphs 5 and 6 help justify the importance of the research on the relationship between sleep and forgetting, since understanding this relationship can shed insight into understanding certain disorders.
114. **C.** Paragraph 11 described the unexpected finding of the researchers' study, namely that activating MCH neurons seemed to enhance forgetting while inhibiting them promoted remembering. Paragraph 12 is important in part because it corroborates (supports) these findings by mentioning further studies that suggest the findings in paragraph 11 are correct.
115. **A.** The sentence lists a variety of factors associated with disrupting the ways of life of American Indian tribes who lives by the Santa Fe Trail, leading to tensions the passage goes on to describe.

116. **C.** That Hancock's campaign just led to more raids by American Indian tribes and inflamed hostilities shows that it was not successful in its goal to establish peace.
117. **B.** The main problem discussed early on in the passage was the tension between American Indian tribes and those using the trail, which led to violent raids. Because the Santa Fe Trail had essential commercial functions, Fort Larned served as an outpost to protect travelers, commerce, and mail. Militarily, it functioned as an outpost from which successful military campaigns were done by the United States government to stop attacks. Diplomatically, it also served to establish peaceful relations with tribes through treaties.
118. **D.** The beginning of the paragraph briefly summarizes a failed military campaign by Hancock, noting it was unsuccessful in ending hostilities with American Indian tribes. The end of the paragraph highlights a more successful later campaign by Custer, which did end raids by certain tribes.
119. **C.** Only C provides an example of a physical change made to Fort Larned (changing the material used) as a result of safety concerns (the new material was more durable).
120. **B.** Paragraph 7 provides a general discussion of the efforts of the United States government to establish peaceful relations with American Indian tribes. The sentence in paragraph 8 transitions into a more specific discussion of the features of certain treaties, such as what the tribes were offered.
121. **A.** Information about how the trail failed to keep pace with the convenience of more modern inventions (the railroad) in the final paragraph helped clarify why Fort Larned was shut down.
122. **A.** The fact that the wolves usually travel alone or in pairs made their presence in a large pack that threatened the narrator and his companion (the central conflict of the passage) somewhat unexpected. The narrator likely highlights this fact about wolves to partially account for why he was off guard and had no warning.
123. **B.** The paragraph reinforces the idea that the narrator is in fact facing a dangerous situation, and assumptions he holds about wolves (e.g., that they are cowardly) do not align with his current conflict.
124. **C.** Although the narrator was surprised by the pack of wolves since they usually only hunt singly or alone, he knew that they sometimes travel in larger groups at the end of winter.
125. **B.** The narrator states, " a thin coating of ice in the inequalities of the hard, frost-bound trail, making a treacherous footing for the horses' hoofs." Thus, the icy trail most directly posed a threat to the horses.
126. **C.** Once the horses were clear of the steep grade and thick underbrush along it, they were able to move with a freer trot on the level trail. Thus, the steeper trail before made it more difficult for their legs to move freely.
127. **A.** That the horses moved suddenly and violently suggests they were scared, which could be because they sensed the presence of the wolves. This sudden change in behavior likely alarmed the narrator. Soon after that, he noticed the dark forms that were the wolves.

128. **B.** Paragraph 1 hints at the narrator's interaction with wolves starting in paragraph 5. Paragraphs 2 and 3 provide some background information on why the narrator was in the area in the first place and describes his actions leading up to the encounter.

129. **C.** The narrator presents a common, comforting idea about wolves that he notes can only be broken by direct experience with the animals, proving that they are in fact dangerous. The false sense of security can be shaken upon a dangerous encounter.

Week 2

Drill 1

1. **C.** Customers who recorded for free were more likely to pay for other products and services, such as merchandise and concert tickets. Thus, it is likely that the band tolerated this practice in exchange for increased business (lines 13-16).
2. **D.** "Ahead of its time" means innovative, or doing something characteristic of a later age. The band was innovative in the way it did business (lines 2-4). The band used innovative practices such as the customer-first orientation before it became popular with other businesses (lines 7-11).
3. **A.** The Grateful Dead gained paying customers when they allowed their concerts to be recorded for free. It is implied that businesses gave "free stuff" with hopes they would get paying customers.
4. **C.** The last paragraph explains that one advantage of insourcing over outsourcing is greater control of the product. If the band had relied on outsourcing, it can be inferred they would have less control.
5. **B.** The last paragraph states that the position of the bones shows natural causes were likely not the cause of death. Rather, the mastodon seemed to serve a practical purpose, a source of meat for hunters. Thus, "human pressures," seemed to play a role in the extinction.
6. **A.** Since mastodons are often confused with mammoths, with whom they are closely related, it can be inferred they had some similarities in appearance (lines 13-15).
7. **B.** The mastodon discovered had one of the most complete skeletons found in a long time (line 29).
8. **B.** The author states that studies show the mammoth and mastodon are only distantly related. Thus, looks can be deceiving (the fact that the mastodon looks like the mammoth is misleading).
9. **A.** Because mastodons often had what they needed to live comfortably, this likely limited their need to migrate (lines 23-25).
10. **C.** Dressing up in costumes in exchange for food has occurred for centuries, as shown by the example of guising (lines 23-26).
11. **A.** The holiday was originally celebrated by immigrant communities in the United States (line 15). Thus, European traditions were preserved.
12. **B.** The last paragraph explains how Halloween provides adults with an escape from dwelling on the stresses of their normal lives. Thus, the holiday helps them feel less stressed.

13. **B.** In both the wine study and the milk study, experts had a harder time making accurate descriptions when they could not see the correct color of what they were tasting. Thus, even experts' perception of taste is linked to color.
14. **D.** The last paragraph states that people may eat foods that eat disgusting if the other senses (such as smell) take precedence, they have positive memories of the food, or want to be adventurous. D may be true, but the passage never mentions this. The passage does say that parents might be encouraged that their children may still want to eat healthy foods that look unappealing (e.g. for any of the reasons discussed before). It does not mention people eating foods that they think have an unpleasant appearance for the sole reason that their health will be danger if they do not.
15. **A.** The author says that people sometimes eat foods that look unappealing becomes other senses override, or supersede, the appearance (lines 34-35).
16. **A.** The passage states that people typically associate green meat with meat that has gone bad. It can be inferred this is why companies must dye them brown (line 30-31).
17. **B.** If sea stars are removed, the population of mussels rises uncontrollably. This is similar to the relationship between grizzlies and elk.
18. **D.** Sea stars eat mussels and keep their population in check. If the population of sea stars is increased in an ecosystem, a likely result is the decrease in the mussel population.
19. **C.** Lines 30-34 describe human and ecological threats to sea stars. Due to these factors, many people want to protect them and treat them as endangered species.
20. **A.** Lines 24-29 describe how kelp populations may be threatened if sea stars don't keep populations of organisms that feed on kelp, such as sea urchins. Kelp is important for the environment and provide a habitat for many organisms.
21. **C.** Kelp absorbs carbon dioxide, a substance that contributes to global warming. Thus, kelp may protect against global warming (lines 27-29).
22. **B.** The term may be misleading, since star fish are not fish, but echinoderms (lines 5-6).
23. **B.** Nightingale used statistical findings to convince the Royal Commission to adopt certain practices (lines 32-35), so she used data analysis. The third paragraph makes clear that Nightingale observed the living conditions of the soldiers directly.
24. **B.** Nightingale's family expected her to marry someone in her class and disapproved of her desire to become a nurse. Thus, her mom likely would approve if she did not start a career and instead raised a family.
25. **A.** The nursing profession reflects the influence of Nightingale (lines 3-4). Thus, the tasks of nurses are likely mentioned in order to give examples of ways Nightingale influenced the profession.
26. **B.** The nickname was likely one of respect, as the soldiers who called her this were reassured by her presence (lines 20-22).

Key

27. **A.** In context, the author argues that although the field of nursing has changed over the years, Nightingale's influence is still felt today. Thus, while the field of nursing has not remained static (unchanged), Nightingale still made an important impact on the field. That changes have been made to nursing does not diminish her accomplishments.
28. **B.** The narrator describes features of nature she has observed in great detail. She seems to be attuned to her natural surroundings.
29. **B.** The poem is about autumn, which occurs at the end of the calendar year.
30. **C.** While the mourners lament the autumn, the narrator believes it also signals cheerful times, such as Christmas. Thus, the narrator thinks the views are alarmist, or exaggerated (while it is a time of death in certain respects, it is also a time of peacefulness and cheerfulness).
31. **B.** While the mourners lament the autumn, the narrator believes it also signals cheerful times, such as Christmas. Thus, the mournful songs do not reflect the narrator's more positive feelings about autumn.
32. **A.** If the loss of beauty is not a loss, then the absence of beauty is not necessarily bad. For example, the narrator finds peacefulness in the autumn woods.
33. **A.** Hope sounds sweetest in the Gale, which is a strong wind. The difficult weather conditions likely refer to difficult times.
34. **B.** Only a really sore storm (bad storm) can abash hope. Thus, it hope's power can only be dampened under truly difficult circumstances.
35. **C.** Hope is found in all kinds of environments. Thus, it is a pervasive, or widespread, force.
36. **B.** The narrator seems bored with the facts and figures presented by the astronomer, to the point that he walks out of the lecture early. This reaction contrasts with those of the other attendees, who applaud.
37. **C.** The narrator seems disappointed in the lecture. Rather than talking about the stars, he is fixated on the calculations he is expected to form. He ends up feeling sick and tired and walking out of the room. Thus, he seemed bored.
38. **A.** The speaker wandered out by himself after quickly feeling sick and tired. It can be inferred that the lecture was not actually over.
39. **A.** The speaker was bored by the lecture about astronomy (stars), but he was captivated by stars he saw in the sky. Thus, knowledge of a topic does not always convey the deeper meaning or value of observed phenomena (e.g. observation of stars).
40. **C.** The "them" refers to the rest of the world who only see the speaker in the mask, which hides his authentic feelings. Thus, these people do not accept the speaker as he or she really is.
41. **B.** "The torn and bleeding hearts" suggests that the people are suffering inside, but they smile anyway. Thus, the people who smile publicly keep their suffering private.
42. **C.** The mask most likely refers to outward superficial expressions of behavior, such as smiles, which "lie" and hide the wearers' true feelings.
43. **A.** The phrase suggests that for all of his life (forever before his eyes), his dream colored, or affected, the way he saw, or perceived, the world.

44. **B**. "Raging tempests" are violent storms. This is likely meant figuratively to indicate the challenges the man faced in laboring hard towards his dream, which was filled with great toil and strife (trouble and conflict).
45. **A**. We are told that the man "failed at last" after working hard. Despite the storms (challenges he faces), he still has his dream. Thus, it is implied that he has not yet actually achieved his dream, but he is holding on to hope.
46. **C**. The man says that the tempest will be short. The man's bark will come to port, meaning he will eventually arrive where he needs to despite the challenges he faced. Thus, the problem of the storm is temporary and manageable.
47. **A**. Helen compared herself to a ship without a compass or a sounding line to help the reader understand how lost she felt before her education.
48. **B**. Helen did not know any words before her education. It can be inferred that the cries of her soul were wordless because she was lost and unhappy, but she had no concept of language to articulate what exactly it was she needed.
49. **A**. Before her education, Helen felt lost. After she began learning words, the world took on a new meaning for her, and she began to feel joy. Thus, light likely represented knowledge (specifically knowledge of words).
50. **C**. Helen struggled to learn the difference between mug and water. She grew irritated with Anne's repeated attempts to teach her and broke the doll (lines 29-34). It is likely that she broke it because she was frustrated by the lesson.
51. **A**. All objects now had a name and were part of a "new sight" she had. They quivered with life because they now had names, which, in turn, gave rise to thoughts (lines 49-51). Thus, the objects had a new meaning for her, one with language.
52. **B**. The mystery of language was revealed to her (lines 45-46) during that day. She then was eager to learn new words and was hopeful for the future.
53. **C**. The last paragraph indicates that Helen's eyes filled with tears because she felt repentance (regret) and sorrow for what she had done (namely, breaking the doll). Thus, it can be inferred that she tried to fix it out of guilt.
54. **D**. Hephaestus was always thinking about the past (lines 6-8). Thus, he is likely to reflect on painful past experiences.
55. **C**. Jupiter made clear that he was fine with humans continuing to live like beasts. He feared if they became wise, they could overthrow the Mighty Ones (lines 23-26). Humans were suffering while the Mighty Ones were living idly. Thus, it can be inferred that the Mighty Ones were crassly indifferent (insensitively uncaring) to humans.
56. **B**. Prometheus wanted to make the world wiser and better. In the last paragraph, he taught humans to be more self-sufficient and looked forward to a new Golden Age. It can be inferred that this is a time of human advancement.
57. **A**. When the first passenger is surprised at how young Mr. Easton is to be a marshal, the second passenger notes that he didn't "catch on" (realize the truth). Marshals don't cuff people to their right hand, suggesting that the older man actually was the marshal.
58. **D**. Mr. Easton made a joke about his other hand being "engaged "at the moment. Miss Fairchild was initially horrified when she saw the handcuffs. Since he and Miss Fairchild knew each other, it can be inferred Mr. Easton was embarrassed by the fact he was handcuffed to the older man.

Key

59. **B**. The older man had shrewd eyes and was watching Miss Fairchild's countenance carefully (lines 20-21). This suggests that he is perceptive, as he noticed that she was distressed by seeing Mr. Easton in the cuffs. He then lied that Easton was the marshal, showing his sensitive side, saving Mr. Easton embarrassment.
60. **B**. Mr. Easton tells the lie after noticing Miss Fairchild's reaction. By doing so, Miss Fairchild is no longer horrified and is actually impressed by Mr. Easton being a marshal. Thus, the older man was probably trying to protect Mr. Easton from embarrassment.
61. **B**. Miss Fairchild clearly thinks fondly of Mr. Easton. For example, she greets him enthusiastically, calls him a dashing Western hero, and assures him that she is not romantically involved with the ambassador. Thus, her feelings can best be described as those of admiration.
62. **C**. Lines 27-29 suggest that Mr. Easton values money. He notes that he needed money to keep step with the crowd in Washington. In his lie for why he became a marshal, he implies that the job opening was lucrative. We also learn that the crime committed was counterfeit, or a money crime (we can infer that even though the old man lied that he himself committed this crime, this was likely the actual crime committed by Easton). Thus, Easton's love for money likely got him into trouble.
63. **D**. Miss Fairchild is described as having elegant taste and appearing like someone who travels often (lines 1-3). It can be inferred that she values classiness, or sophistication.
64. **C**. Mr. Easton says that money is needed to keep step with the crowd in Washington, D.C. It can be inferred that he felt the need to spend extravagantly.
65. **B**. Miss Fairchild is clearly fond of Mr. Easton. When Mr. Easton notes that being a marshal is not at the same level of being an ambassador (lines 28-29), Miss Fairchild retorts that the ambassador "doesn't call anymore" and that he never should have (line 30). She then goes on to compliment Mr. Easton for being a dashing Western hero. It can be inferred that the ambassador is someone from Miss Fairchild's past who once had a romantic interest in her.
66. **C**. The title of the poem suggests that the child is a chimney sweeper. Thus, he is described as a "little black thing" because he is likely covered in soot.
67. **B**. The child cries in notes of woe, or melancholy.
68. **B**. The speaker asked the child where his parents are after seeing him crying, implying that the speaker is concerned.
69. **A**. The last stanza reveals that the child's parents think he is happy because he dances and sings, but he implies that he is in misery. The fact that he cries notes of woe also suggests he is unhappy. Thus, outward appearances can be deceiving.
70. **A**. The child dances and sings, which make some people (like his parents) think he is happy. He says that his parents think they have done him no injury, implying that they actually have injured him. He also makes a reference to "our misery." Thus, his happy behavior belies, or is contrary to, his real emotions.

71. **D.** The child's parents think he is happy because he dances and sings. Thus, they dressed him in clothes of death. The child says that his parents think they have done him no injury, implying that they actually have injured him. Thus, they are oblivious to impact of their actions (likely their decision to have him work as a chimney sweeper).
72. **B.** The speaker addresses the other factory workers as "sisters" and refers to herself as having to perform the same tasks they do. She is like a fellow factory worker.
73. **B.** The meals seem hurried, or rush. They have to take their rations "quickly" (line 9). The bell rings to start working again when they are "not half-done eating" (line 19).
74. **A.** The bell, not other indications of time (e.g. the sun rising), dictate the girls' schedules. Thus, it overrules other standards of time.
75. **C.** The factory girls seem grateful for meal hours. For example, at noon, the bell rings merrily when they dine (lines 13-16).
76. **D.** "Sisters" literally refers to the coworkers who share a common experience of toiling hard during the workday. The term is likely intended to create solidarity over this shared experience.
77. **A.** The bell is a demanding taskmaster at times, signaling that the workers must go to their stations and work. It is also a welcome respite, or break, when signaling meals and the end of the work day.
78. **A.** "Ding dong ding, - our toil is ended/Joyous bell, good night, good night" suggests that it is nighttime and the end of the work day. Since the work is very laborious, the narrator would likely feel joyful to go home and rest.
79. **B.** "Toil" refers to hard, or grinding, work. Thus, it can be inferred that the work is physically demanding.
80. **A.** Words like "bleak," "weary," "dreary," and "fearing" create a tense or suspenseful atmosphere. The speaker hears noises that scare him, which turn out to be a raven.
81. **B.** On a quiet, dreary night, the speaker is "pondering" (contemplating) while feeling "weak and weary."
82. **D.** The speaker eagerly awaits the morning and wants to cease feeling sorrow for the lost Lenore, who the passage makes clear is lost to him forever.
83. **C.** The author is nervous when he hears the noises. He comforts himself by assuring himself it is no more than a strange visitor or the wind.
84. **B.** The speaker is initially intrigued by the raven and can't help but smile. He talks to the raven as if he is some noble person.
85. **C.** Other friends in the past have come and gone (they leave him by the morning), much like a passing emotion. The speaker hopes the sadness he is feeling now for losing Lenore will go away.
86. **C.** The speaker realizes that she (Lenore) will never sit on the cushions again. He realizes she is gone forever.
87. **A.** The bird answers "nevermore" when the speaker says that the bird will leave him and when he states that he will forget Lenore, suggesting his grief is permanent. Despite his attempts to not think about her, the raven functions as a symbol reminding him that his grief is permanent.
88. **C.** The speaker grows increasingly angry with the bird's responses, as first rationalizing it by imagining that "nevermore" is the only word it can utter. He calls him a thing of evil when it implies he will never forget Lenore. He continues to curse the bird after it says he will never be reunited with Lenore. Thus, the speaker does not like what the raven is telling him.

89. **A.** Since the clergyman is the only person who doubts the worthiness of Scoresby's accolades, this might suggest that he is not giving Scoresby enough credit for his accomplishments and is undervaluing his worth. The reader has reason to at least somewhat doubt the clergyman's assessment.
90. **C.** The clergyman believed people were misinterpreting Scoresby's blunders and stated that people "misinterpreted his performance every time—consequently they took his idiotic blunders for inspirations of genius; they did, honestly!" Scoresby's apparent superiority was illusory as he was a blunderer, from the clergyman's perspective.
91. **B.** The clergyman seemed to have compassion and pity for Scoresby and saw him as a crippled child. At the same time, he clearly looked down on his abilities, implying that he saw himself as superior.
92. **A.** The clergyman believes Scoresby benefitted by chance, not because he had any discernible strategy or plan.
93. **A.** The quote implies that in almost all cases where someone employed the same strategy as Scoresby (99 out of 100), the outcome would have been disastrous. Only by chance did the outcome work out well despite Scoresby's bad judgment. Thus, his reputation for greatness by be unwarranted, as he benefitted from luck.
94. **B.** The clergyman would agree that one's reputation (in this case Scoresby's reputation for military greatness) can overshadow one's true character (in reality, the clergyman believed Scoresby was a fool).
95. **D.** The clergyman repeatedly insults Scoresby for being a fool who blunders, but he inadvertently reveals that he may be a hard worker. The fact that Scoresby was willing to drill with the clergyman may hint at his level of dedication.
96. **B.** Self-monitoring of glucose levels is an example of taking personal responsibility. Kids were more likely to do this after the animal intervention.
97. **C.** The author was shocked in the moment, as she was used to living in urban environments where such animal-human interactions are not typical. However, once she introspected on the research about the relationship between such interactions and human well-being, it made more sense to her in hindsight why there would be deer near her work.
98. **C.** "Speculated" means that the researchers were taking an educated guess in making this assertion. Specifically, the causal mechanism they suggested (that unconditional acceptance by the animals is what caused the children to be calm) should be regarded as tentative. It is possible another factor about the interaction caused the children to calm down instead.
99. **B.** "Accustomed" means "used to." The incident in the first paragraph with the deer that the narrator found shocking is now one that she is used to, as she sees animals at her work all the time.
100. **B.** The narrator compliments the NIH for its research on human-animal interactions and its promising findings on how they might improve health outcomes in children. It can be reasonably inferred she would support continued research on this topic to further advance knowledge in the field.
101. **B.** When Thea's mother advises her to make sure Tillie's performance isn't any worse than it needs to be, she implies that Tillie is not a skilled actress.
102. **B.** That all the Kronborgs are worthy suggests they all have positive attributes. That Thea is different suggests that she stands out (from Tillie's perspectives) even among other worthy people, magnifying how impressive Thea is to Tillie.
103. **D.** Thea generally didn't bother anyone, but her occasional sudden bursts of temper were alarming to her mother. Thus, certain uncharacteristic (unusual) behavior was jarring, or upsetting to her mother.

Key

104. **A.** That Thea's father makes it a point to compliment his other children whenever others comment on how remarkable Thea is shows he does not want to appear partial to Thea.
105. **B.** The scientists drew conclusions about mice's memory for familiar objects based on the amount of time they spent sniffing them relative to how long they spent sniffing new objects. Thus, the time they spend seems to allow to scientists to gauge how subjectively familiar these objects seem to the mice. Specifically, it seems they spend more time sniffing objects that seem new.
106. **D.** If the hippocampus is a memory center of the brain, we can infer damage to it would interfere with memories. Forgetting details of the episodic details of one's life seems like a likely symptom.
107. **B.** The passage indicates that sleep plays a role in storing memories (paragraph 4), but the study featured in the passage suggests it also may help us forget useless information. Thus, sleep seems to play a role in the interplay between which information is stored and which is discarded.
108. **B.** The sentence indicates that the study provides direct evidence that REM sleep (a phase of sleep) plays a role in deciding which memories to store. Thus, a goal was to determine if there is a relationship between REM sleep and memory for learned information, namely which information is retained and which is forgotten.
109. **C.** While quotes A and B indicate effects of activating or inhibiting MCH neurons during REM sleep, they do not make clear if the effects were limited to REM sleep. C indicates that unlike in REM sleep, there is no effect of turning on/off these neurons outside of REM sleep (when awake or when in other stages of sleep). Thus, it makes clear MCH's role is limited by the time in which it is activated or suppressed.
110. **A.** Scientists drew conclusions about the role of MCH neurons in memory by examining mice's performance on memory exams when these neurons were manipulated during REM sleep. Since such neurons are found in humans as well, scientists can infer that they might function similarly in humans.
111. **B.** Though basic research is concerned with increasing understanding of biological topics rather than applying knowledge to interventions, the passage notes that clinical advances are not possible without basic research and that research often builds on previous research in unexpected ways. Thus, basic research does have the potential to spur advances that benefit human health.
112. **C.** The government simultaneously engaged in military and peaceful efforts to end hostilities with native American tribes, suggesting that a multipronged approach was needed to achieve this goal. The contrast transitions emphasize that military tactics were not the only ones used.
113. **A.** Since visitors can get a glimpse of life was like during that time by visiting many of the buildings, it is implied that the buildings must at least somewhat retain the character of how they were when people lived there.
114. **C.** The author notes that Fort Larned preserves the buildings, stories, and historical themes associated with it and that the Santa Fe Trail was one of the most important transportation routes of its time. The author also notes that Fort Larned was one of the most important defense posts along this trail before the fort was no longer needed after the railroad became popular. The author discusses how visitors can still see the fort to get a glimpse of what life was like there. Given its historical importance, the author would probably agree its preservation is important for preserving stories and historical themes of a notable time in history.
115. **B.** Given that the wolves are surrounding him and his companion and that he asked his companion if he had his gun, it can be inferred the narrator knew decisive action must be taken quickly to neutralize the threat the wolves posed.

Key

116. **C.** The descriptions of the ghostlike figures of the wolves and the terrified horses create an eerie mood emphasizing the danger they pose, along with the allusion to the scary stories of mountaineers who have confronted wolves' danger.
117. **A**. As the wolves quietly surround the narrator while keeping pace with the horses, he begins to feel uneasy.
118. **A**. The wolves have not yet attacked the narrator and his companion, but their stealthy surrounding of them builds tension and establishes them as a looming threat, thus creating a tense and menacing (threatening) mood.
119. **C.** The narrator finds the quiet perseverance of the wolves unsettling, making him uneasy. He goes on to say a sound such as a howl or growl would have been a relief.
120. **C.** "Black mass" suggests that the wolves were in large numbers and difficult to see. That they filled the "whole width of the trail" suggests they kept pace with the narrator and his companion and had them surrounded.

Key

Week 3

Drill 1

1. **B.** Darla was able to adapt to her new town when she bonded with peers over a shared interest (art).
2. **A.** The mother is initially uncomfortable with Amy's career choice, but she comes to accept it when her daughter achieves success. Note that Choice D is incorrect because there is no evidence Amy's mother thought she had no talent.
3. **B**. The author believes that the alarm, or fears, about the decline of reading is exaggerated. While people are reading less fiction, they are still reading quality nonfiction.
4. **C**. An innovative development (wheat-resistant starch) has many health benefits, such as improving gastrointestinal health.
5. **B**. Dolley Madison served an indirect but important role in politics. Her parties allowed people with different political views to come together, laying the foundation for political cooperation. A is too broad. The passage does not provide a biography about Dolley Madison's life as a whole: it only focuses on her White House renovation project and weekly drawing room parties. D is too specific because the beauty of the White House is only a minor detail. The main focus of the passage is on the social and political impact of the parties. C is incorrect because there is no mention of other First Ladies.
6. **D**. The passage primarily focuses on the economic (financial) and environmental advantages associated with geothermal energy, such as reduced energy costs and less pollution than other energy sources. A is too specific. Volcanoes are only briefly mentioned as one possible source of geothermal energy. C is too specific. The passage only briefly mentions limitations of solar energy in the context of illustrating the benefits of geothermal energy. B is too broad. The passage focuses on the benefits of geothermal energy, not multiple energy sources.
7. **B**. The passage focuses on how art changed during the Renaissance. Specifically, art became more realistic. Choice C is contradicted by the passage. Art before the Renaissance did not accurately portray emotions. There is no support for A and D. Perspective is mentioned as one of several techniques used during the Renaissance and *The Last Summer* is mentioned as one (likely of many) famous paintings.

8. **C.** The paragraph focuses on how Roosevelt combatted abusive big business practices. Choice A is contradicted by the passage. The passage focused on how Roosevelt limited the power of business in order to strengthen competition, not strengthen the hold of big businesses over industries. Choice B is only loosely supported by the passage, which briefly mentions that businesses helped increase the standard of living. For the most part, the passage focuses on efforts by Roosevelt to weaken big business to protect the common people. Choice D is too specific. The Northern Security Company is mentioned as one company that limited competition. The paragraph as a whole does not focus on this one company.

9. **B**. The paragraph focuses on how different playwrights' political beliefs influence their writings. For example, Aeschylus supported democracy and wrote plays criticizing nondemocratic forms of government. Euripides distrusted democracy, which was reflected in his writings. A and C are not directly supported by the passage. At best, only Aeschylus would agree with these claims. Choice D is not directly supported by the passage. At best, only Euripides would agree with this claim.

10. **D.** Anthropologists no longer see cultures as isolated units. Rather, they recognize cultures as interactive units in a global context. Culture isn't shared equally, but power struggles affect how different people experience culture. Overall, anthropologists' approaches to studying culture has become more diverse and complex. Choice A is a minor detail from the passage. Choices B and C are contradicted by the passage. Anthropologists still engage in academic analysis, and power is not shared equally in most cultures.

11. **A.** The passage focuses on the innovative business practices of the Grateful Dead. Choices C and D are too specific. They are minor details used to support the broader point that the band had innovative business practices. Choice B is incorrect because the passage does not focus on the band's musical abilities, nor does it suggest that their music is significantly better than all their contemporaries.

12. **A.** The passage focuses on the traits, or characteristics, of mastodons, a long-extinct animal. Choice B is incorrect because the passage does not discuss future research projects on environmental pressures. Choice C is incorrect because the passage briefly mentions the discovery of a skeleton. Choice D is incorrect because the passage only briefly discusses how bones are analyzed (their carbon content is examined).

Key

13. **B.** The passage examines historical practices that influenced modern-day Halloween. Choice A is incorrect because the passage does not discuss the influence of European religions on American religions (the passage makes clear that Halloween does not have a religious dimension in America). Choice C is incorrect because the passage does not mention Halloween in modern Ireland, but in historical Ireland. Choice D is incorrect because the passage does not discuss modern-day Halloween outside the United States. Rather, it examines how historical European traditions and holidays (like Samhain) influenced Halloween.

14. **C.** The passage primarily focuses on the role of vision in how we perceive test, including how the appearance of food shapes our expectations about food and ability to correctly identify its flavor. Choice A is too specific. The wine experiment is just one example used to support the broader point about the role of vision in taste perception. Choice B is too broad. The passage does not focus on the scientific workings of the brain and the eye in general. Rather, it is only concerned with vision in relation to foods. Choice D is too specific and is only briefly mentioned in the passage.

15. **A.** The passage describes the features of sea stars and their importance to the environment. The other choices are too specific: they deal with points that provide support for sea stars' environmental importance.

16. **A.** The passage focuses on Florence Nightingale's influence on the nursing profession. Choice B is a minor detail briefly discussed in the passage supporting Nightingale's influence on nursing. Choice C is only briefly alluded to in the passage. We learn that labor was seen as inappropriate for upper class women and the passage indirectly suggests Nightingale's accomplishments may have helped changed attitudes. However, the passage mostly focuses on the nursing profession, not upper-class women. Choice D is too broad. The passage only mentions history of the nursing profession, not medicine in general.

17. **A.** Helen Keller reflects on a transformative episode in her life early in her education, a time that she learned the concept of language. This would later open doors for her and connect her to the world.

18. **B.** The story explains how humans came to acquire fire, an element of the human condition.

19. **A.** Easton encounters a friend from his past while he is handcuffed and being sent off to prison, but the marshal prevents the encounter from getting more awkward by lying that he himself is the criminal and Easton is the marshal.

20. **A.** The first paragraph highlights the author's admiration for Scoresby and the fact he is a decorated war hero. All this information may account for why the clergyman's subsequent critique of Scoresby might seem inappropriate, or incongruous.

21. **B.** We learn of Scoresby's failure through the perspective of the clergyman, who recounts various episodes of Scoresby's incompetence with language that is melodramatic, or overdramatic (e.g. calling him a donkey and a fool).

Key

22. **A.** The sentence shows the clergyman's resignation that Scoresby will be celebrated for the results of his actions, even if he stumbled into a positive outcome by "luck." Thus, impact may override intention in matters of public opinion.
23. **C.** The clergyman's perspective of Scoresby's success, if it is accurate, exemplifies how one can benefit from luck rather than skill. A confluence of positive circumstances seemed to help Scoresby succeed over more potentially more qualified individuals. For example, people who knew more than him did worse than him on his preliminary exam because he was lucky enough to be tested on the one topic he studied.
24. **A.** The passage is a satirical (humorous) commentary on the shallowness of hero worship. Many people idolize Scoresby when it is likely that this is at least partially unjustified if the clergyman's perceptions are even partially correct. Even if Scoresby is more qualified than the clergyman cares to admit, others' admiration for him (including the author's) is over the top and superficial, as shown when the author admitted to thinking of him as a demigod.
25. **A.** The struggles of those who suffer "broken" lives will eventually "beat" (harm) the homes of those who selfishly limit their love. This suggests that the domestic happiness of those who are selfish will be compromised
26. **A.** The speaker believes that people, especially mothers, should be aware of problems that exist in the world and work to promote human progress: "The one first duty of all human life/Is to promote the progress of the world/In righteousness, in wisdom, truth and love." She criticizes many women for not knowing or not caring about the suffering of people they do not know personally. Those who are fortunate should help those who are not and show them love. Thus, women should see their role in promoting progress as just and important.
27. **C.** The lines convey the idea that motherhood is not inconsistent with, but complementary to, humanitarian principles. A mother's care is the first step to a broader and friendly peace within all nations, as it raises the standard for how we should act with one another. The speaker goes on to argue that women should extend their love beyond their homes to those who are suffering.
28. **B.** The speaker is critical of women and people in general who don't care about the suffering of others or fulfil their duty to promote the progress of the world. She even calls such people "selfish" and says they cannot keep their small domestic peace while others starve and are neglected.
29. **B.** B is the most complete summary, encompassing key ideas from all three paragraphs about the health and well-being benefits of service animals to children with a variety of conditions, such as diabetes, autism, and ADHD. It lists highlights from key ways children benefit.
30. **A.** A clarifies the author's central view that, clinically (medically), animals can improve health and well-being in humans.
31. **A.** The excerpt reveals the respect Tillie has for Thea, as she thinks she is unique even among her other worthy family members and romanticizes about possibilities for her future, suggesting Tillie has faith in her niece.

32. **B.** In context, the excerpt emphasizes how odd and fallible (capable of follies, or errors) Tillie is. Despite her flaws, she had intuitions (perceptions) that belie (contradict) her deficits. This supports the larger theme that people who lack knowledge in one domain might make up for it with other skills. Specifically, Tillie seems to exemplify "people who are foolish about the more obvious things of life are apt to have peculiar insight into what lies beyond the obvious." While Tillie's mind is far from perfect, she does seem to have some degree of insight, specifically when it comes to Thea's special nature.

33. **C.** On the subject of Tillie bragging about Thea, Tillie made them tired. This suggests they found her boastfulness off-putting.

34. **B.** The passage suggests that Tillie is not a good actress. For example, Thea's mom advises her to help Tillie "tone her down a shade" so that she does not perform any worse than need be. Still, the drama club was important to Tillie, and her devotion helped keep it together. This suggests one need not be particularly talented in an endeavor in order to have a meaningful impact on it.

35. **C.** The phrases make clear there is a deliberate, controlled process by which certain information is forgotten. Thus, it is implied that sleep helps organisms discard (forget) information that is not needed for their well-being.

36. **C.** C provides the most complete summary. The paragraph notes that sleep's role in helping people retain memories has long been known and studied. It also points out that it has long been suspected sleep also helps us forget memories, and more recent studies have shown that sleep helps prune (reduce) synaptic connections, suggesting sleep does help us forget. The last major point of the paragraph was that it was not until a recent study (the one in Dr. Kilduff's lab) that provided insight into how this might happen.

37. **B.** The key finding through experiments with mice was that activating MCH neurons (during REM sleep only, not during wakefulness or other stages of sleep) seemed to enhance forgetting. This may be done to forget unimportant information.

38. **B.** B suggests that Fort Larned was historically important and notes that it had many significant functions.

39. **C.** The emphasis on the raids by American Indian tribes along the trail that threatened the safety of travelers and traders most clearly conveys the tensions that were inflamed between these groups.

40. **B.** B provides the most complete summary. The Indian Bureau was created to establish peaceful solutions to the tensions between American Indians and those who used the trail. They created treaties in which they agreed to pay annuities to various tribes in exchange for keeping the peace. Once tribes moved to reservations and the threat of violence was not as pressing, Fort Larned was no longer an agent for the Indian Bureau (1868).

41. **D.** That the government sought to engage in more peaceful solutions, such as treaties, shows that they knew military campaigns would be inadequate to establishing peace.

42. **A.** The wolves' stealth, or sneakiness, made an already tense situation even eerier. The narrator would have preferred they made some sound. The silence made him more scared.

43. **C.** C provides the most complete summary. The first 40 miles of the trek were on a zigzagging hill with thick underbrush and the conditions were treacherous for the horses. Once they reached the level grade, the horses could trot more freely, a welcome relief indeed.

44. **D.** The wolves moved silently like ghosts, crossing back and forth but keeping pace with the narrator and his companion, forming a large mass along the trail.

Week 4

Drill 1

1. **A.** The problems are serious, or severe.
2. **B.** Surprise is a factor, or circumstance, that contributed to the advantage of the army.
3. **B.** Seats must be reserved, or ordered, in advance.
4. **A.** The protest approached, or came close to, the level of a riot.
5. **C.** The sense of timing is keen, or sharp.
6. **C.** The pattern of abuse was obvious, or easy to notice.
7. **B.** The evidence enables, or permits, the detectives to draw conclusions.
8. **D.** It is not in Finley's character, or personality, to argue.
9. **A.** The rash behavior was not fitting, or appropriate, of someone expected to act rationally.
10. **B.** The disaster was avoided by pure, or absolute, luck.
11. **A.** The band had a loyal group of followers, its fanbase.
12. **D.** The strategies were implemented, or put into practice.
13. **B.** Clients who receive free stuff are more prone, or likely, to purchase paid services.
14. **C.** The animals grabbed hold of, or taken hold of, people's imagination.
15. **B.** There is debate over the main, or most important, cause of mastodons' extinction.
16. **C.** Halloween invokes associations with, or brings to mind, images of trick treating, costumes, and haunted houses.
17. **A.** There was an upsurge, or increase, in immigration.
18. **C.** Halloween now has a less religious aspect, or component.
19. **D.** Taste includes, or involves, multiple senses.
20. **B.** People connect, or relate, different colors to different tastes.
21. **A.** Companies make foods that go against, or oppose, our expectations.
22. **C.** People are charmed, or dazzled, by the appearance of starfish.
23. **B.** The ability to change color gives starfish a means, or way, of protection.
24. **B.** The discovery of starfish in some areas shows that their numbers have increased.
25. **B.** The job was once disdained, or looked down upon.
26. **A.** "Station" refers to social class, in this case the upper class.
27. **B.** The school allowed Nightingale to share her ideas on a larger level.
28. **C.** Helen kept confusing the difference between "mug" and "water."
29. **B.** Her wordless thought can best be described as a consciousness, or perception, that she was going out into the sunshine.
30. **A.** Helen unsuccessfully, or ineffectively, tried to fix the doll.
31. **A.** There was an inflow, or arrival, of passengers onto the train.
32. **D.** The older man interrupted Easton before he could tell Miss Fairchild the truth.

Key

33. **D.** Mr. Easton is headed to prison (the penitentiary).

Week 4B
Drill 1

1. **B.** According to the table, the percentage of home workers working regular evening shifts is 1.8%.
2. **A.** 73.1% of onsite workers work a regular daytime schedule while only 59.1% of home workers do.
3. **B.** According to the second figure, a greater percentage of home workers work for private companies/non-profits (75.1%) than are self-employed (10%).
4. **D.** According to the first figure, most home workers work regular daytime schedules. According to the second figure, most home workers work for private companies/non-profits.
5. **D.** Per capita generation decreased from 4.57 to 4.52 but MSW generation increased from 208.3 to 217.3.
6. **B.** The line increases by the greatest amount from 1985 to 1990, approximately 42 million tons.
7. **A.** According to the passage, recycling helps decrease the impact of MSW generation. During the years when per capita generation decreased, the recycling rate increased.
8. **A.** The recycling rate increased from 9.6% to 34.3%.
9. **B.** Paint is not indicated explicitly on the figure, but it is listed in the passage. Herbicides and fertilizers are not listed in either the figure or the passage.
10. **C.** The distance between the lines representing metro and nonmetro is greatest in 1988, about a .8% difference.
11. **A.** The growth rate from 1988 to 1994 in metro areas was higher than from 2010 to 2014.
12. **A.** The growth rate of the United States was positive in the period. The population increased.
13. **C.** The population in nonmetro areas decreased. One reason the author gives for people leaving nonmetro areas is a desire for privacy in cities. The other choices list reasons why people would want to move to nonmetro areas.
14. **C.** According to the figure, emissions decreased from about 5,850 to 5,750.
15. **D.** The chart only shows total emissions, not the sources of emissions.
16. **B.** The number of young firms stayed about the same.
17. **C.** The author says that entrepreneurship is declining, but the reasons are not completely understood.
18. **B.** Subtract the percent at the top of the bar from the percent at the bottom. $83\% - 59\% = 24\%$.
19. **C.** The percent of people who work in natural resources, construction, and transportation is more comparable to that of the general population for those who drive alone than for those who carpool since the bars are approximately the same thickness (about 9% each). The percent of those who carpool working in these fields is about 15%.
20. **B.** The top line for 1978 represents U.S. nuclear energy capacity, which according to the y-axis on the left is close to 50 thousand MW.
21. **C.** The closer the percentage the capacity factor is to 100%, the closer the actual generation is to the maximum generation, meaning the difference is smallest. Of the choices, natural gas has the highest percentage.
22. **D.** The text clarifies that the capacity factor shows what percent of the time the plant is producing power. Since wind energy has a capacity factor of 34.3%, which is around half that of geothermal

Key

(65%), wind energy plants run at maximum power about half as often as do geothermal energy ones.
23. **B.** The lines for both capacity and generation increased significantly from 1967 to 1997, as shown by the sharp positive slopes. We see these values become more stable as relatively flat horizontal lines with only slight changes year to year from 2007 to 2015.
24. **A.** Figure 2 shows the net capacity for summer was around 98 thousand MW in 1989. The passage states that net capacity is generally higher for winter, so the value was likely above this number for winter.
25. **A.** The passage describes various experiments on the correlation between interest level (curiosity) and memory. These experiments have shed insight into how these concepts are connected.
26. **C.** The generalization is that learning is easy when it relates to matters one finds interesting but not to matters that are not interesting. Then examples are given of information that "rarely sticks." Finally, a study examining the connection between curiosity and learning is discussed.
27. **B.** The lines describe the experimental conditions. They illustrate the procedures used in testing the relationship between curiosity and memory.
28. **B.** The experiment's procedures are described. Then, the significance of the findings is noted. Specifically, a curious state of mind makes it easier for people to learn.
29. **B.** Some questions roused, or provoked, the curiosity of the students.
30. **B.** If the subjects already knew the correct answers, it could undermine the results because they did not actually learn the answers during the study.
31. **C.** The author argues that people effortlessly learn matters that interest them and do not learn information that doesn't interest them as easily. The recipe and the football game results exemplify information people might find uninteresting and therefore struggle to learn. Thus, there is a connection between curiosity and learning.
32. **A.** The informal tone of these phrases helps engage a general audience by making an otherwise technical and specialized topic seem more approachable.
33. **B.** The fMRI shows brain activity. Since the study examined the relationship between curiosity and learning, it can be inferred that the level of activity shown might correlate with curiosity.
34. **C.** The effects of curiosity on memory continued the next day, suggesting that curiosity may have a long-term impact on memory. The following lines even clarify that these results suggest that curiosity helps us build lasting memories.
35. **C.** The last paragraph discusses how people remember peripheral information when studying topics that interest them. Just as someone learning trivia in an interesting subject remembers faces that they are shown during that time, someone studying an interesting topic may remember background details (in this case the arrangement of plants).
36. **C.** The assertion is backed by empirical evidence, namely the experiments described in the passage showing that curiosity is associated with memory.
37. **A.** In context, the word "intriguing" emphasizes the fascinating nature of the finding that subjects also better remembered the faces they were shown while learning trivia in subjects that interested them.
38. **B.** According to Figure 2, the subjects with low curiosity recognized the faces a little over 30% of the time.
39. **A.** There was a greater difference in subjects' ability to remember for trivia questions.
40. **D.** People best remember trivia questions during periods of high curiosity, as exemplified by situation D.

Key

41. **A.** The graph shows the correlation between curiosity and correct answers to trivia questions.
42. **D.** The passage does not specify why people are better at remembering trivia than faces during moments of high curiosity.

Key

Week 5

Drill 1

1. **B.** The adjective "advanced" modifies the noun "words."
2. **D.** The adverb "thoroughly" modifies the adjective "impressed."
3. **C.** "Is" acts as a helping verb in the verb phrase "is falling."
4. **C.** "About economic policy" is a prepositional phrase that modifies "the discussion."
5. **B.** "They" is a personal pronoun.
6. **C.** "Six" modifies the noun "rings."
7. **D.** "Himself" is an intensive pronoun.
8. **B.** "Introduce" is an action verb.
9. **A.** "Smoke" is a substance.
10. **A.** "Underneath" is a preposition of location.
11. **A.** "Bond" is an abstract idea.
12. **B.** "Extremely" is an adverb that modifies the other adverb "quickly."
13. **B.** "To" is a preposition of location.
14. **B.** The participial phrase with the participle "working" describes "Delia."
15. **C.** The appositive phrase renames "dog."
16. **A.** The phrase begins with the preposition "for" and modifies "need."
17. **D.** "Heat of evaporation" renames "heat of vaporization."
18. **B.** "Quite" describes the adjective "concerned."
19. **D.** "Anything" is an indefinite pronoun.
20. **B.** The participial phrase with the participle "renowned" describes the Leaning Tower of Pisa.
21. **A.** "Complain" is the present tense of the regular verb "complain" when the subject is "they."
22. **D.** "Talks" is the present tense of the regular verb "talk" when the subject is singular and in the third person.
23. **C.** "Has begun" is the present perfect tense of the irregular verb "begin."
24. **D.** "Have examined" is the present perfect tense of "examine."
25. **B.** The irregular verb "be" becomes "are" when "you" is the subject in the present tense.
26. **C.** "Had broken" is the past perfect tense of the irregular verb "break."
27. **A.** "Have swum" is the present perfect tense of the irregular verb "swim."
28. **B.** "Was" is the past tense of "be" when the subject is singular and in the third person.
29. **D.** "Have done" is the present perfect tense of the irregular verb "do."
30. **C.** "Have gone" is the present perfect tense of the irregular verb "go."
31. **D.** "Have driven" is the present perfect tense of the irregular verb "drive." "Have not" is used in the present perfect tense.
32. **B.** "Had run" is the past perfect tense of the irregular verb "run."

Drill 2

1. **Dependent.** The sentence is an adverb clause expressing causation.
2. **Independent.** The sentence has a subject and a verb, and it expresses a complete thought.

Key

3. **Independent.** The sentence has a subject and a verb, and it expresses a complete thought.
4. **Dependent.** "That" functions as "the fact that."
5. **Dependent.** The sentence is a noun clause.
6. **Dependent.** The sentence is a relative clause with a relative pronoun.
7. **Dependent.** The sentence is a relative clause with a relative pronoun.
8. **Independent.** The sentence has a subject and a verb, and it expresses a complete thought.
9. **Dependent.** The sentence is an adverb clause expressing a purpose.
10. **Dependent.** The sentence is an adverb clause expressing a time relationship.
11. **Dependent.** The sentence is a relative clause with an adverb.
12. **Independent.** The sentence has a subject and a verb, and it expresses a complete thought.
13. **Dependent.** The sentence is an adverb clause expressing a condition.
14. **Dependent.** The sentence is a noun clause.
15. **Independent.** The sentence has a subject and a verb, and it expresses a complete thought.
16. **Dependent.** The sentence is a relative clause with a relative pronoun.
17. **Dependent.** The sentence is an adverb clause expressing a time relationship.
18. **Independent.** The sentence has a subject and a verb, and it expresses a complete thought.
19. **Independent.** The sentence has a subject and a verb, and it expresses a complete thought.
20. **Dependent.** The sentence is an adverb clause expressing a condition.

Key

Week 6

Drill 1

1. **C.** A contrast transition, such as "although," should begin the sentence to highlight the contrast relationship between the idea that model is helpful and also has problems. "Because" inappropriately suggests a cause-and-effect relationship.
2. **C.** "So" shows the proper cause-and-effect relationship. Tammy moved as a result of getting a job offer in a new town. "For" suggests that Tammy got a new job because she moved.
3. **A.** "Neither...nor" is a word pair.
4. **D.** "Not only...but also" is a word pair.
5. **B.** "Either...or" is a word pair.
6. **B.** "Both...and" is a word pair.
7. **D.** "However" shows the contrast relationship between the platypus's appearance and classification.
8. **A.** "But" shows the correct contrast relationship between the expectation about the decline of paper use and the reality (its use did not actually decrease). "And" incorrectly suggests an addition relationship.
9. **A.** "Because" shows the correct cause-and-effect relationship. The detailed agenda caused the meeting to last longer. "Even though" inappropriately suggests a contrast relationship.
10. **B.** "For" shows the correct cause-and-effect relationship. Because Jan wanted her presentation to be a surprise, she did not share the details.
11. **C.** "Although" shows the correct contrast relationship. Cassandra could see the future, but nobody believed her. "Because" inappropriately suggests a cause-and-effect relationship.
12. **D.** The design for the bridge is an illustrative example of da Vinci's interest in engineering.
13. **A.** "And" shows the proper addition relationship between the two facts about the museum.
14. **B.** "However" shows the contrast relationship between the bakery having moved and Hilda still being able to smell the bread in her mind.
15. **B.** "Therefore" shows the correct cause-and-effect relationship. Because the proposal was controversial, many people did not agree with it.
16. **B.** "Although" shows the correct contrast relationship between originally opposing the plan and later agreeing to it. Choice A puts "although" with the wrong clause. The speaker agrees to the plan despite originally opposing it.
17. **A.** "Even though" shows the correct contrast relationship between the high expense of installing the solar panels and the long-term cost savings. Choice C puts "even though" with the wrong clause.
18. **C.** "Because" shows the correct cause-and-effect relationship. People use avocado as a substitute because of its healthy properties.

Key

19. **C.** Choice C makes it clearest that the decline in profits was an effect of more people turning to digital media. Choice B suggests that more people turning to digital media is the effect (rather than the cause) of declining newspaper profits.
20. **B.** "Because" shows the correct cause-and-effect relationship. Students prefer classrooms because they believe they learn more when an instructor is present.

Drill 2

1. **D.** "Repeating" is not a main verb. "Repeat" should be used instead.
2. **B.** "Forming" is not a main verb. "Forms" should be used instead.
3. **C.** "Having been" is not a main verb. "Has been" should be used instead.
4. **B.** The original sentence lacks a subject. "She" acts a subject for the verb "talked."
5. **A.** "Known" is incorrectly used as a main verb. "Is known" or "was known" would have been correct.
6. **B.** The sentence lacks a main verb. "Will approve it" is part of the relative clause "who will approve it." When "who" is deleted, "will approve it" acts as a main verb.
7. **B.** The sentence lacks a subject and main verb. "Here are" is a proper subject and plural predicate.
8. **C.** The original sentence lacks a subject. Choice C corrects this error by making the subject "the psychologist."
9. **D.** The sentence lacks a main verb. "Which has a" is part of a relative clause. When "which" is deleted, "has" acts as a main verb.
10. **A.** "Increases" is a proper object (a noun) to the verb "demanded."
11. **B.** "Purchase" acts as a main verb when "that" is deleted. Otherwise, it is part of a relative clause, and the sentence lacks a main verb.
12. **D.** "Being" is not a main verb. "Is" is an appropriate main verb.
13. **B.** The sentence is a dependent clause. Deleting "when" makes it independent.
14. **C.** A coordinating conjunction cannot connect a dependent clause to an independent clause. "But" should be deleted.
15. **A.** A conjunctive adverb like "therefore" should introduce an independent clause following a dependent clause. "Therefore" should be deleted.
16. **B.** "Presents" acts as a main verb when "that" is deleted. Otherwise, it is part of a relative clause.
17. **D.** "Works" acts as a main verb when "who" is deleted. Otherwise, it is part of a relative clause.
18. **C.** The first sentence is a dependent clause and cannot stand alone. It should be connected to the independent clause that follows by a comma.
19. **C.** The sentence lacks a subject. "I" is the subject and "feel" is the main verb.

20. **C.** The original sentence connects an introductory prepositional phrase to a relative clause. Deleting "which" allows "light" to act as a main subject and "enters" to act as a main verb.

Drill 3

1. **B.** The original sentence contains a comma splice. Eliminating "he was" results in an introductory participial phrase followed by an independent clause.
2. **A.** The second sentence contains a comma splice. Deleting "this is" creates an appositive phrase after the independent clause.
3. **B.** The original sentence contains a comma splice. Adding "of which" before "has" makes the independent clause a phrase.
4. **C.** The original sentence contains a comma splice. Changing "this gave" to "giving" creates a nonessential participial clause following the independent clause.
5. **D.** The original sentence contains a comma splice. Deleting "this is" creates an appositive phrase after the independent clause.
6. **B.** The original sentence contains two complete sentences improperly combined. Adding a semicolon after the first independent clause corrects the error.
7. **C.** The original sentence separates two complete sentences by a comma. A period should be used to separate the sentence into two separate sentences.
8. **A.** The original sentence contains a comma splice. Deleting "it was" changes the first independent clause into a participial phrase.
9. **C.** The original sentence contains a comma splice. Adding the coordinating conjunction "but" after the comma corrects the error and shows the contrast relationship between the clauses. Katy ended up working on a campaign despite thinking she never would.
10. **B.** The original sentence contains an independent clause between commas. Changing "he" to "who" creates a nonessential relative clause.
11. **A.** The original sentence contains a comma splice. Changing "of them" to "of whom" makes the second independent clause a phrase.
12. **B.** The original sentence contains a comma splice. Changing "on such days" to "which is when" makes the second independent clause a relative clause.
13. **D.** The original sentence contains a comma splice. Deleting "it is" creates an appositive phrase after the relative clause.
14. **A.** The sentence contains a comma splice. Changing the comma to a semicolon appropriately separates the independent clauses.
15. **A.** The sentence inappropriately combines two independent clauses into one sentence. Adding a period after "United States" appropriately creates new complete sentences.
16. **C.** The sentence contains a comma splice. Changing the comma to a semicolon appropriately separates the independent clauses.

Key

17. **A.** The original sentence contains a comma splice. Changing "it" to "which" changes the second independent clause to a relative clause.
18. **D.** The original sentence contains a comma splice. Deleting "this is considered" creates an appositive phrase after the relative clause.
19. **C.** Choice C has a main subject and a main verb, and it expresses a complete thought. Choices A lacks a main verb when the participial phrase between commas is ignored. Choice B inappropriately uses an independent clause between commas. Choice D inappropriately uses "serving" as a main verb.
20. **A.** The second sentence is a participial phrase and can't stand alone as a full sentence. It should be connected to the independent clause before it by a comma.

Key

Week 6B: Bonus Reading Passage 1

1. **B.** The mother is persistent (determined) because she keeps climbing the stairs even though it is difficult. She never gives up in the face of obstacles.
2. **B.** The line shows a contrast between the speaker's lived experience (which has been like a stair filled with tacks) and hypothetical state of being (a life like a "crystal stair" without troubles).
3. **D.** The stair is not clear and smooth (like a crystal stair). Rather, the stair has been filled with splinters and tacks.
4. **C.** The stair is comparable to the speaker's life. It is filled with challenges (tacks, splinters, darkness, no carpets), but the speaker still deals with them and perseveres.
5. **C.** The dialect is very conversational, or informal. It is not written entirely in standard English. For example, she uses words like "a'int" and spellings like "turnin'" and "reachin'" that mirror her spoken English.
6. **A.** The speaker compares her life to a stair. Thus, it is a metaphor (comparison) for her lived experiences. Her life, like the stair, has been rough and filled with challenges.
7. **A.** "I'se been a-climbin' on… And sometimes goin' in the dark/Where there ain't been no light." Even when there is no light and it is hard to see, the speaker keeps walking.
8. **B.** Stairs are a metaphor for the speaker's life. It has not been a crystal stair (an easy life), as it is filled with splinters (painful challenges).
9. **B.** The tone at the end of the poem is meant to be encouraging. The mom calls the son "honey" and reassures him that she herself has kept going, so he can too.
10. **C.** That the speaker keeps going is evidence of her resilience (mental strength and toughness in the face of challenges).

Key

Week 7

Drill 1

1. **C.** The introductory participial phrase described Lievens, not Lievens' popularity. "Lievens" should be the first word after the comma ("Never settling on one specific painting style, Lievens became less popular after his death").
2. **A.** The introductory participial phrase describes Siqueiros, not his paintings. "Siqueiros" should be the first word after the comma ("Known for his murals in fresco, David Siqueiros created paintings that reflected social realism").
3. **B.** The original sentence inappropriately suggests that the donation was pleased. Choice B makes it clear that "pleased" modifies the "staff" and "anonymously" modifies "donated."
4. **C.** The original sentence inappropriately suggests that scenery went hiking. Choice C corrects the dangling modifier by clarifying that Dayna hiked.
5. **B.** The original sentence inappropriately suggests that disrepair was located in the district. Choice B corrects the dangling modifier by clarifying that the factory was located there.
6. **C.** "Trapped" should be moved after "rocks" to clarify that the rocks are trapped below the Earth's surface.
7. **C.** The original sentence inappropriately suggests that Mendel's paper, rather than Mendel himself, was the person known for his contributions to genetics. Choice C corrects the dangling modifier.
8. **B.** The modifying phrase needs to describe Emma (the first word after the comma), but it seems to describe the people who chose Emma. Choice B appropriately uses a modifying phrase that describes Emma (Emma was chosen).
9. **C.** "Wisely" modifies "took." It should appear between "Trevor" and "took."
10. **B.** The original sentence inappropriately suggests that the store, rather than the cars, ranged from cheap used cars to luxury vehicles. Choice B corrects this error.
11. **C.** The original sentence inappropriately suggests that "horizontally" modifies "labels" rather than the way the labels were placed. It also does not make it clear that the labels were placed on containers that happened to be in the store. Choice C appropriately shows that "horizontally" modifies "placed," that "on the containers" modifies "horizontally," and that "in the store" modifies "containers."
12. **A.** The original sentence does not make it clear that "carefully" modifies "checked." Choice A corrects this error.
13. **D.** The original sentence does not make it clear that the fans themselves were standing in crowds. It suggests that the comedy was in crowds. Choice D corrects this error.
14. **C.** The original sentence suggests that the billboard was driving. Choice C corrects the dangling modifier by clarifying that the speaker ("I") was driving.

15. **A.** The original sentence suggests that the 1950s was a style of music. Choice A corrects the dangling modifier by clarifying that avant-garde jazz was the style.
16. **C.** The original sentence has a dangling modifier. C makes it clear that "to promote interest in their profession" modifies "members."
17. **B.** The original sentence suggests Belgium was attempting to live a more idyllic lifestyle. Choice B clarifies that Norman was the one who moved.
18. **A.** Choice A appropriately creates a nonessential relative clause beginning with "which" between commas ("which" refers to the microarrays). Note that Choice D has a misplaced modifier ("which" does not describe "genetics." Choice B is not properly constructed ("because" and "therefore" should not both be used). Choice C inappropriately shows a contrast relationship.
19. **C.** Choice C appropriately uses a participial phrase that makes it clear that the difficulty of completing the maze was a result of the twists, turns, and obstacles. Choice B has a misplaced modifier ("which" should refer to the maze, not "difficult"). Choice A inappropriately shows a contrast relationship. Choice D inappropriately suggests that the twists, turns, and obstacles are the result of, rather than the cause of, the maze being difficult to complete.
20. **A.** Choice A appropriately uses a nonessential relative clause in the middle of the sentence ("which" refers to carnivorous plants). Choice B has a misplaced modifier ("which" should not refer to the animals and bacteria). Choice C inappropriately suggests a cause-and-effect relationship. Choice D inappropriately suggests a contrast relationship and contains a misplaced modifier ("which" should not refer to the bogs).

Week 7B: Bonus Reading Passage 2

1. **C.** The fact that meat is now served in restaurants after centuries of being forbidden in Japanese culture and the fact that even in the narrator's childhood meat was frowned upon provide evidence that Japanese culture has begun to embrace Western practices (in this case, meat eating).
2. **A.** That the narrator sensed the sense of gloom in the household as soon as she walked in shows that she is perceptive of emotional situations.
3. **A.** The narrator is able to piece together that something in her household has changed based on the fact that the Buddhist shrine is closed, leading her to wonder what this development means.
4. **D.** The clause introduces a qualification to an earlier point that custom and belief had changed a great deal. Though meat was becoming more popular, not all Japanese people ate it (so there were limits to its popularity).
5. **B.** B shows that the narrator feels the presence of her ancestors during meals, suggesting her connection to her roots.
6. **C.** The narrator felt conflicted about enjoying the meat, knowing her grandmother would not approve since meat consumption violates tradition.
7. **B.** The shrine was closed to protect it from the "pollution" that the meat would bring to the household. This decision was a reaction to the narrator's father's decision to allow meat into the household.
8. **C.** The quote shows the grandmother's respect for ancestral traditions: she clings to them despite conceding benefits of meat to the body and mind.
9. **B.** The "wall of tradition" separated the Japanese people from other cultures. Thus, it was an impediment to cultural diffusion (spread of cultural ideas and artifacts between cultures). The introduction of foreign food helped to break down this barrier.
10. **C.** The narrator states, "not only poor and at the same time separated entirely from the system that had given them support; but also, bound as firmly as ever by the code of ethics that for centuries had taught them utter contempt for money." Thus, the system the samurai were born into did not meet their basic needs, yet they still clung to the code of ethics (set of principles) it provided.

Key

Week 8

Drill 1

1. **B.** The singular possessive "its" agrees with "the fire" (the path belongs to the fire).
2. **A.** The plural possessive "their" agrees with "the students" (the education belongs to the students).
3. **C.** The plural possessive "their" agrees with "monitor speakers" (the sides belong to the speakers).
4. **C.** The subjective "Vail and I" (the equivalent of "we") is needed since "Vail and I" act as subjects.
5. **C.** "Your" is consistent with "you."
6. **B.** "Our" agrees with "my friends and I."
7. **C.** "Who" is used between a subject and a verb. "Who" refers to "Peter Higgs."
8. **A.** "They" refers to "reservoirs."
9. **D.** "He" can refer to either Boris or Christopher, so it is a vague pronoun.
10. **B.** "It" refers to the oil.
11. **B.** The original sentence uses the vague "they" and "do it." Choice B makes it clear that funding for buses was limited. Choice A uses the vague "do it." Choices C and D use the plural "they" to refer to the singular "school district."
12. **B.** The singular possessive "its" agrees with "the beluga whale" (the songs belong to the whale).
13. **A.** "Each" requires the singular possessive determine "his or her."
14. **B.** "They" refers to "Neanderthals."
15. **C.** The objective pronoun "me" is needed ("me" is the object of "gave").
16. **B.** The possessive determiner "her" agrees with "Tenley" (the "work" belongs to "Tenley").
17. **B.** "Which" cannot refer to a person. "Whom" should follow the preposition "with."
18. **C.** "Themselves" agrees with "musicians."
19. **D.** The noun "townspeople" clarifies which people the actors portrayed.
20. **B.** "Who" refers to people ("the visitors") and is between a subject and a verb.
21. **D.** The singular possessive "his" is needed. "His" agrees with the "prankster," who is male.
22. **B.** "Whom" cannot refer to a company. "That" is needed instead.
23. **D.** "Ashleigh" is needed to clarify which of the two girls won.
24. **D.** The passage makes clear that Charlotte had success on her previous trips. "Our" should be "her" (the speaker did not find precious metals with Charlotte on previous occasions).
25. **D.** The singular possessive "its" agrees with "library" (the founder belongs to the library).
26. **A.** "It" refers to "the organization."

27. **D.** "Stop that" is too vague. Choice D uses the most precise language (scientists are trying to alleviate the condition Colony Collapse Disorder).
28. **C.** The second sentence has a pronoun shift. "Me" in the second sentence is consistent with "me" in the first sentence.
29. **C.** "It" refers to "the idea."
30. **A.** "They" refers to "the researchers."
31. **A.** "She and her family" (the equivalent of "they") is needed because "she and her family" act as plural subjects performing the action.

Key

Week 8B: Bonus Passage 3
1. **B.** The speaker did not bind the notes because he is too "fatigued," or tired.
2. **B.** The speaker says he has been in the fields "all day." Thus, it can be inferred that he works long hours. He also says that he is fatigued, suggesting the work is tiring.
3. **D.** The speaker mentions being hungry, fatigued, in pain, and having a dry throat.
4. **A.** The speaker acknowledges the fact that other harvesters beat their palms too.
5. **D.** The speaker is most likely referring to the "harvesters whose throats are also dry"/ "the reapers of the sweet stalk'd cane" who live similar experiences to him in the field. "Brothers" is used to show solidarity, or unity.
6. **D.** The pain is sweet because it will not bring him knowledge of his hunger (make him aware he is hungry). Thus, his feelings of starvation are diminished.
7. **C.** That the speaker strains to hear the other reapers suggests his feelings of alienation, or isolation from them.
8. **B.** The speaker does not want to know about his hunger. He is trying to remain oblivious to his suffering.

Drill 1

1. **B.** The past perfect is needed because the physician saw himself as a healer before he became an adult. "Had seen" is the correct past perfect form of "see."
2. **B.** The present tense "feel" is needed since the sentence describes the number of people who feel sleep-deprived today.
3. **C.** The sentence has a verb tense shift. The past tense "approached" requires the past tense "noticed."
4. **C.** The present perfect is needed to show that sales continue to increase today.
5. **C.** The future "will attend" is needed to describe a future action ("next month").
6. **D.** The sentence contains a verb tense shift. The past tense "performed" requires the past tense "exited."
7. **C.** "Would work" is needed since the question was asked in the past.
8. **D.** The present perfect "has opposed" is needed because the movement began in the past and exists today.
9. **B.** The original sentence has a verb tense shift. The past tense "watched" and "cheered" require the past tense "got."
10. **D.** The original sentence has a verb tense shift. The present tense "skips" and "helps" require the present tense "keeps."
11. **C.** The sentence takes place in the present tense (it describes what teachers should understand about studying politics today). "Required" should be "requires."
12. **C.** The original sentence has a verb tense shift. The present tense verbs "shouts" and "await" require the present tense "attempt."
13. **D.** The original passage has a verb tense shift. The entire paragraph takes place in the present tense. The present tense "gives" is needed.
14. **B.** The past perfect "had delivered" is needed since the action was completed before a time in the past (1810).
15. **C.** The paragraph takes place in the past, describing the history of the Eiffel Tower. The present tense "becomes" should be in the past tense as "became."

Week 9B: Bonus Passage 4

1. **C.** The narrator's chasing of the coyote shows her impulsiveness, or proneness to chaos.
2. **B.** The narrator says, "my mother had never gone inside of a schoolhouse, and so she was not capable of comforting her daughter who could read and write." The implication is that her mother lacked similar experiences to her daughter, which left her ill-equipped to comfort her since she could not relate to her or understand her fully.
3. **A.** The narrator believes that the combination of her time in the East and her being a teenager led to her deplorable situation in which she felt alienated, or isolated. She did not feel like she belonged ("even nature" had no place for her).
4. **C.** Dawée's is firm about the fact that the narrator cannot attend, yet he is affectionate by calling her "baby sister."
5. **C.** The narrator untied the pony after feeling restless and unhappy. Overall, it was an impulsive decision to alleviate her feelings of disquiet (uneasiness).
6. **B.** The excerpt shows Dawée's refusal to let the narrator attend the party, leading to her breakdown in the next paragraph.
7. **C.** The teenagers did not wear traditional Indian clothes (garb), and the narrator lacked the proper attire to attend the party.
8. **B.** The narrator's mother knew the narrator was sad and tried to comfort (console her). She brought the narrator the Indian Bible because it was the only written material she could find, hoping that the narrator would find comfort in it.
9. **A.** The narrator's crying revealed (made clear) her suffering to the mother.

Week 10

Drill 1

1. **C.** The singular subject "internship experience" requires the singular verb "has."
2. **A.** The singular subject "group" requires the singular verb "comes."
3. **D.** The singular subject "countertop" requires the singular verb "contains."
4. **A.** The singular subject "collection" requires the singular verb "has been."
5. **C.** The plural subject "stars" requires the plural verb "are." The present tense is needed since it describes "today."
6. **B.** The plural subject "bands" requires the plural verb "have."
7. **C.** The plural subject "portions" requires the plural verb "remain."
8. **D.** The singular subject *Nueva Cancion* requires the singular verb "deals."
9. **A.** The singular subject "governmental body" requires the singular verb "helps."
10. **B.** The singular verb "determines" should become "determine," in agreement with the plural subject "analysts."
11. **C.** The plural subject "morsels" requires the plural verb "attract."
12. **B.** The plural subject "ethologists" requires the plural verb "are." The present tense is needed in context, so "were" is incorrect.
13. **A.** The singular subject "Corinne" requires the single verb "volunteers."
14. **C.** The singular subject "decline" requires the singular verb "is." The past tense should not be used since the decline is expected to go into effect in the future.
15. **D.** The singular subject "conversion" requires the singular verb "devastates."
16. **B.** The plural subject "efforts" requires the plural verb "have been."

Key

Week 10B: Bonus Passage 5

1. **A**. Lutuli argues that South Africa cannot be fully democratic when only one third of the people have democratic rights. The implication is that all people must have equal political rights for a society to be truly democratic.
2. **D**. Under apartheid rule, Black South Africans lack democratic rights. Thus, apartheid is the opposite of democracy (it is contrary to democracy).
3. **A**. Apartheid is the "antithesis" (opposite) of democracy. Thus, it is irreconcilable (incompatible) with democratic ideals. Society cannot be truly democratic so long as apartheid exists.
4. **D**. Lutuli implies that the end of apartheid is inevitable (unavoidable) since the system cannot be sustained (continued, or perpetuated, indefinitely): "I emphasize the words are still, because I do believe firmly that it is not a state that can be perpetuated."
5. **A**. According to Lutuli, nice and pretty phrases "justify this diversion from the democratic road." In other words, polite language is used to rationalize an indefensible governing system that is antithetical to democracy.
6. **C**. Lutuli's attitude towards the argument that people should "develop along their own lines" is one of outspoken incredulity (vocal disbelief). In practice, people really develop along the lines the government wants them to. People cannot develop along their own lines without genuine freedom.
7. **B**. Lutuli is hopeful that his vision for democracy (his goal to bring democracy to South Africa) will be attained, or achieved.
8. **A**. Lutuli makes the concession that the viewpoint that people need to be incited to struggle for freedom is true to an extent. When people are discouraged, they may need some outside encouragement to persevere and pursue their goals.
9. **B**. Lutuli discusses the history of mankind as being a struggle for freedom. He wants human beings to try and reach the apex (high point) of freedom. The implication is that the South African people themselves will fight for their rights and work to bring about meaningful change.
10. **A**. Lutuli emphasizes that the demand for a free and just society is a "human cause" that applies not just to South Africa, but to other countries as well. Thus, ideals of liberty associated with the movement to eliminate apartheid in South Africa are pervasive (widespread).
11. **C**. Lutuli argues that apartheid prevents Black South Africans from being truly free and independent. Thus, their ability to engage fully in social life is not possible so long as their political rights are undermined under the apartheid system.
12. **B**. Throughout the passage, Lutuli emphasizes the importance of freedom in a democratic society. He argues that people cannot "develop along their own lines" unless they have the right to develop and determine how they will develop. Once people are free, they can fully participate in all aspects of life.

Key

Week 11

Drill 1

1. **C.** Commas should separate the three items in the series. No comma should be between the adjective "private" and the noun "firms." No comma should follow "and."
2. **C.** A comma should separate the coordinate adjectives "new" and "expensive" (their order can be switched).
3. **D.** No comma should precede the intensive pronoun "herself."
4. **C.** A comma should follow the independent clause and introduce the participial phrase beginning with "prompting" that follows.
5. **C.** The nonessential phrase "though time-consuming" should be set off by commas.
6. **B.** A comma should separate the coordinate adjectives "cheap" and "sturdy" (their order can be switched).
7. **B.** No comma is needed between the compound objects "grass" and "flowers."
8. **B.** The nonessential phrase "unlike her predecessor" should be set off by commas.
9. **C.** A comma should separate the coordinate adjectives "clear" and "logical" (their order can be switched).
10. **C.** No comma should appear between the adjective "American" and the noun phrase "marine biologist." No comma should appear between the title "marine biologist" and the noun "Rachel Carson" (the name is needed for the sentence to make sense). No comma is needed between the subject "Carson" and the verb "wrote."
11. **D.** No comma should appear between the subject "goal" and the essential prepositional phrase beginning with "of." There should be no comma between the adjective "low-impact" and the noun "development." No comma should separate the verb "is" and the infinitive phrase "to limit."
12. **B.** The nonessential expression "critics say" should be set off by commas.
13. **A.** No comma should separate the adverb "newly" and the adjective "formed." No comma should separate the adjective "formed" and the noun "Works Project Administration." No comma should separate the subject "Works Projects Administration" and the verb "was."
14. **C.** A comma should separate the dependent clause ending in "five minutes" from the independent clause that follows.
15. **B.** A comma should separate the coordinate adjectives "simple" and "plain" (their order can be switched).
16. **B.** The parenthetical "however" should be set off by commas.

17. **B**. The relative clause "which are around 40% cellulose by weight" should be set off by commas. No comma should appear between the preposition "around" and its object "40% cellulose." No comma should separate "40% cellulose" from the prepositional phrase that modifies it ("by weight").
18. **A**. A comma should separate the introductory prepositional phrase ending in "arrived" from the independent clause that follows. No comma should appear between the cumulative adjectives "warm" and "summer." No comma should appear between the adjective "summer" and the noun "weather."
19. **B**. Commas should separate the items in the list. No comma is needed before the essential relative clause beginning with "that."
20. **C**. No comma should set off the name "Hattie McDaniel" because it is needed for the sentence to be correct. No comma is needed between the verb "was" and the predicate.
21. **A**. A comma should follow the introductory phrase ending in "article."
22. **C**. No comma should appear between the verb "taken" and the prepositional phrase "from the pages." No comma should appear between "pages" and the prepositional phrase "of a manuscript recipe book."
23. **A**. The parenthetical expressions "as the founder points out" should be set off by commas.
24. **A**. No comma should separate the noun "donations" from the prepositional phrase "from a small nonprofit company." No comma should separate the cumulative adjectives "small" and "nonprofit." No comma should separate the adjective "nonprofit" from the noun "company."
25. **D**. No comma should separate the noun "sediment" from the verb "is." No comma should separate the verb phrases connected by "and." No comma should follow "and."
26. **A**. The parenthetical "though" should be set off by commas.
27. **C**. No comma is needed between the noun "skills" and the verb "earned." No comma is needed between the verb "earned" and the object "him." No comma is needed to introduce the nickname.
28. **D**. A comma is needed after the introductory phrase ending in "Hughes." No commas should be between the cumulative adjectives "Missouri-born" and "author" or between "Alabama-born" and "author." No comma should follow "author" since the names of the authors are essential.
29. **C**. No commas should appear between the adjectives (they are cumulative). No comma should appear between the adjective "weather" and the noun "balloons." No comma should appear between the noun "balloons" and the verb "were."
30. **B**. A comma is needed after "Greece" to set off the relative clause starting with "which."
31. **C**. A comma after "reports" is needed to separate the items (the different responsibilities of actuaries) in the series.
32. **A**. Add a comma after "advisor" to set off the nonessential relative clause.

Week 11B: Bonus Passage 6

1. **B.** The speaker says at first "you'll joy to see the playful snow." In other words, you will enjoy watching the snow.
2. **B.** The third stanza makes clear that the listener will long for home (miss home). At home in the South are flowering lanes and dry weather.
3. **D.** The speaker appreciates the way spring changes the North, making it "wreathed in golden smiles" and "glad and warm."
4. **C.** The poem ends on a positive note. The speaker says that the listener will love the North when spring comes, as it is "wreathed in golden smiles." It can be inferred that the speaker appreciates living in the North despite missing home at certain points in the winter.
5. **B.** The poem examines the beauty of change. It both discusses the beauty of changing seasons and the beauty of moving to a new home.
6. **C.** The speaker expresses nostalgia in line 9 (a longing for the past). In this case, the speaker longs for home during winters in the North.

Week 12

Drill 1

1. **C.** A contrast transition is needed to show the different motivations of people who interrupt others.
2. **A.** A transition of emphasis confirms that the actuarial field is satisfying, as the previous sentence indicates.
3. **D.** A cause-and-effect transition is needed. Genetic counselors need good communication skills in order to work with their clients.
4. **A.** A time transition is needed. Though the entrepreneur failed at first, she eventually (later) found success.
5. **A.** "Later" is the correct transition to show the time relationship. "Though" shows the appropriate contrast in terms of the number of daylight hours.
6. **D.** An example transition is needed because the second sentence gives an example of a medical application.
7. **B.** A contrast transition is needed to show the difference between what is generally considered essential reading and Professor Miller's decision to not include the book in the syllabus.
8. **D.** A transition of time is needed. First, the book exposed abuses in the meatpacking industry. Then (subsequently), reforms were passed.
9. **B.** An addition transition is needed to show a second problem associated with mastermind groups.
10. **A.** An addition transition is needed to show a second health benefit of ginger.
11. **C.** A cause-and-effect transition is needed to show that investment in preventive medicine is needed due to the high costs of treating health problems that could have been prevented (if people get preventive care, they are less likely to become sick).
12. **B.** A cause-and-effect transition is needed to show that employers should consider telecommuting policies since these policies benefit employers and employees.
13. **B.** "To these ends" means "for the purpose of accomplishing these goals." In order to accomplish the goal of spurring entrepreneurship, the organization provided loans and training to women.
14. **C.** An example transition is needed because the second sentence gives examples of ways to improve vocabulary.
15. **B.** A comparison transition is needed to show that both ranchers and people in the timber industry were similarly affected negatively by the drought.

Key

Week 12B: Bonus Passage 7
1. **B.** The paragraph establishes Quixote's obsession with literature about knights.
2. **D.** Quote D shows how Quixote was able to overcome a deficiency in his materials and craft a mask using paper and iron.
3. **B**. Panza accepted Quixote's offer to be his squire out of a desire for material gain, as Quixote promised him land to govern.
4. **C.** Quixote fixed up a helmet that belong to his ancestors and made the visor out of loose pieces of iron and paper.
5. **C.** Quixote initially believed the windmills were giants. After Quixote's attack on the windmill failed, he rationalized (made an excuse for) what happened by claiming that an evil enchanter turned the giants into windmills. Thus, he never admitted his initial impression of the windmills was wrong.
6. **A.** Quote A makes clear that the stories Quixote read caused him to have a break from reality.
7. **B.** The quote shows that Quixote feels compelled to battle the windmills, which he perceives as thirty giants he is meant to battle.
8. **A.** "Your worship" is an address of respect.
9. **C.** The paragraph explains how various people, including Sancho Panza and the general public, react to Don Quixote's adventures.
10. **B.** That Panza tries "frantically" (anxiously) to get Quixote to see things as they really are shows Panza is worried about him and wants to ground him in reality.

Key

Week 13

Drill 1

1. **D.** Only "frequently" is needed. The other choices contain redundancy errors.
2. **C.** Only "have" is needed. The other choices are repetitive. They contain words with the same meaning as "in addition," which is stated earlier.
3. **B.** The sentence has a redundancy error. "Problems" and "flaws" have the same meaning. "And flaws" should be deleted.
4. **B.** The sentence has a redundancy error. "Famous" and "renowned" have the same meaning. "And renowned" should be deleted.
5. **B.** It is redundant to say "written works" (the other items listed are clearly examples of written works).
6. **A.** "Reach" is the most concise choice.
7. **C.** "Modified" is the most concise choice.
8. **A.** The other choices use casual phrases that are more appropriate for informal conversations.
9. **B.** The other choices use casual phrases that are more appropriate for informal conversations.
10. **B.** Choices A, C, and D use too many casual phrases ("big things behind," "letting go of," "major reasons leading up to," "giving off of," "huge deal").
11. **A.** Choices B, C, and D use too many casual phrases ("everything you learn," "things," "whatever they need to learn").
12. **C.** Choices A, B, and D use too many casual phrases ("hooted and hollered," "went on and on," "said a lot of bad things").
13. **C.** Weeding and mulching are the specific kinds of work performed.
14. **C.** Choice C makes clearest which people (flavorists) manufacture (produce) artificial flavors that rival (are similar to) natural flavors. The other choices include vague or more imprecise language (*entities, fake, put together, real ones, are like real, workers, products*).
15. **C.** Choice C clarifies the specific activity (reading over the summer) that is being examined.
16. **B.** Choice B clarifies that the property tax was discussed and that it was criticized. Though Choice C mentions the property tax, it does not make clear the journalist's stance on the issue.
17. **A.** Choice A makes it clear that the four highest paid actors will be on the talk show. It also clarifies that they will be guests and not merely in attendance.
18. **A.** Choice A provides the most specific information about the number of calls and the percent increase from the day before.

Key

19. **B.** Choice B makes clear which types of skills (crisp writing skills) are valued and why they are valued (people are perceived as more intelligent to coworkers and clients). The other choices use vague or more imprecise language (*are aware, may appear better, people they deal with, diverse workplace acquaintances, related to the act of good writing, positive reputation, many kinds of people*).
20. **A.** Choice A makes it clear what type of painting (a mural-sized oil painting) the *Guernica* is and provides the clearest description of it and its effect (violent imagery that criticized war). The other choices use vague or more imprecise language (*kind of artwork, visual features, large painting, drawn pictures, strong artistic choices*).
21. **A.** Choice A makes clear that artifacts were discovered during a dig by archaeologists. The other choices use vague or more imprecise language (*group of people, remainders, team of experts, things, ecosystem, locale*).

Key

Week 13B: Mixed Review

1. **D.** The singular subject is "classification," so the singular verb "has" is needed.
2. **B.** The original sentence is a run-on. Changing the comma after "tomorrow" to a semicolon to separate the independent clauses corrects the error.
3. **C.** The original sentence is a run-on. Changing the comma after "donations" to a semicolon to separate the independent clauses corrects the error.
4. **C.** Choice C appropriately uses "since" to show the cause-and-effect relationship between the two original sentences. Brandon was not seated as a result of the formal dress code. A and B illogically use contrast transitions. D is awkwardly worded and uses a semicolon to separate an independent clause from a phrase.
5. **A.** A correctly uses the relative pronoun "who" to define the activists. B is a run-on sentence. C and D illogically use contrast transitions.
6. **C.** The past tense verb "meant" is needed to be consistent with the other verbs in the sentence ("said" and "had").
7. **D.** D gives the clearest indication of the type of activity Ryan performed.
8. **C.** The nonessential appositive phrase "an acclaimed writer and philosopher" should be set off by commas. The sentence is otherwise correct and complete when this phrase is ignored.
9. **A.** Commas should separate cities from countries.
10. **B.** The original sentence suggests that the bill rather than the governor intended to restore the damaged wetland. B arranges the ideas in the clearest order to show that the bill was signed last year by the governor as part of an effort to protect the wetlands. A contains a dangling modifier (the governor, not the procedures, was trying to protect the wetland). C is awkwardly worded and suggests that the water was cleaned last year, rather than that the bill was signed last year. D is awkward and suggests that the phrase between commas is unimportant to the sentence. It also separates "last year" from "signed" by too many words.
11. **C.** Changing "gave" to "would give" clarifies the speech occurred after Sadie's boss asked her to give it. "Gave" illogically suggests that the boss talked to Sadie after the speech, but "the following December" makes clear that the speech was to occur later.
12. **B.** Choice B highlights the cause-and-effect relationship between the clauses (the spike in applications resulted from the investment in stipends). A and D illogically include contrast transitions. A is also wordy. B is wordy and illogically suggests an addition relationship.
13. **C.** A chemistry kit is the precise item that Desha bought.
14. **C.** The parenthetical comment "according to some critics" should be set off by commas. The sentence is otherwise complete when this phrase is ignored.
15. **B.** The singular subject "way" requires the singular verb "is."
16. **B.** Choice B most specifically addresses what the students learn and with whom they can better interact.

17. **C.** The singular subject "ability" requires the singular verb "has."
18. **B.** The sentence takes place in the present tense, so "had their" should be "have their."
19. **D.** Choice D clearly uses a nonessential appositive phrase to describe cassowaries. Choice A inappropriately uses the contrast transition "although." Choice B inappropriately uses the cause- and -effect transition "because." Choice C is wordy and illogically uses the cause-and-effect transition "by."
20. **A.** The original sentence contains a dangling modifier (it suggests that millions of people are known for its climbing routes and sequoia trees). A arranges the ideas in the clearest order. It makes clear when millions of people visit (spring and summer months). It uses a relative clause beginning with "which" that clarifies what Yosemite Park is known for. Choice B inappropriately suggests that "each year" is known for its climbing routes and sequoia trees. Choice C inappropriately suggests that the months are known for their climbing routes and sequoia trees. Since Choice D does not use a comma after "trees," it inappropriately suggests that Yosemite Park only has climbing routes and sequoia trees during the spring and summer months.
21. **B.** A comma should separate "capable" and "resourceful" since the order of the adjectives can be switched.
22. **B.** A comma should follow "lithographer" since "Milton Bradley" is a nonessential appositive (the sentence is correct and complete when the name is ignored).
23. **C.** Choice C appropriately uses an introductory participial phrase describing Agatha Christie, followed by an independent clause. Choice A is a run-on. Choice B is awkwardly constructed and has a dangling modifier ("real archaeologists" were not inspired). Choice D incorrectly uses the present participle "inspiring," which cannot logically describe Agatha Christie (she was "inspired" by her visits: she herself did not inspire them).
24. **D.** Choice D appropriately uses a relative clause to explain a feature of political action committees. Choices A and C illogically suggest a contrast relationship. B confusingly uses "which" to suggests that campaigns, rather than political action committees, date back to 1943.
25. **D.** Choice D is the most concise. The original sentence contains a redundancy. Since "depiction" and "representation" have the same meaning, "and representation" should be deleted. The other choices use repetitive language.
26. **C.** The singular subject "Delicate Arch" requires the singular verb "has."
27. **C.** The original sentence contains a dangling modifier and inappropriately suggests that $5,000 reviewed the arguments rather than the judge. C corrects the dangling modifier and appropriately shows that the judge reviewed the arguments. The other choices are awkward and inappropriately suggest that the plaintiff reviewed the arguments.
28. **D.** Choice D gives the clearest indication of the exact number.
29. **B.** The singular subject "investigation" requires the singular verb "has."
30. **D.** No comma is needed between the compound objects connected by "and."
31. **A.** No comma is needed between the subject "newspaper" and the main verb "featured."

Key

32. **C.** C clarifies which people used the washing machine (the previous owners). The other choices are too vague.
33. **D.** The present tense "contains" is consistent with the present tense "is decorated."
34. **B.** A comma is needed between each task performed. Thus, a comma should separate "cleaning the office" and "answering phones."
35. **A.** A shows the contrast relationship between the fact that the two fruits have similar appearances and the fact that they are eaten differently. B uses "although" (meaning "even though") in the incorrect place (it should be used before the clause that indicates the similarity between bananas and plantains in order to signal the surprising contrast that they are eaten differently). C incorrectly uses the cause-and-effect transition "since." D repetitively uses two contrast transitions and lacks an independent clause.
36. **B.** A comma should separate the adjectives "dedicated" and "talented" since their order can be reversed.
37. **D.** "It enables" agrees with the singular noun "investment."
38. **C.** The contrast transition "while" is unnecessary because "although" is already present. The sentence is also a fragment lacking an independent clause. The sentence now contains an independent clause when "while" is removed ("this fact...both mammals).
39. **A.** The comma after "various" should be deleted since its order cannot be switched with the adjective following it.
40. **C.** C gives the clearest indication of the exact revenue and percent increase in revenue.
41. **A.** A clarifies the exact problem without any redundancies. B and C are too vague about the precise problems facing the community. D is repetitive ("lack" and "shortage" have roughly the same meaning).
42. **C.** An example transition is needed to signal examples of specific health benefits.
43. **B.** A comma should follow "strong" since the order of the adjectives can be reversed.

Week 14

Drill 1

1. **A.** The passage explains how computer use helps develop some types of cognitive skills while harming others.
2. **C.** The experiment provides evidence for how playing computer games can improve visual-spatial skills.
3. **B.** Sentence 7 states that video games can increase people's interest in a subject. The added sentence illustrates how playing a video game related to history led to students' being interested in history and getting better grades.
4. **B.** Choice B shows that computer games do not necessarily enhance cognitive skills: they actually can harm certain types of skills, such as those requiring deep thinking.
5. **B.** The passage focuses on the cognitive impact of computer use, not whether or not it should be regulated more stringently.
6. **D.** The paragraph focuses on ways that computer use either does not help or even hurts cognitive abilities. A sentence about the causes of computer addiction is not directly related to this topic.
7. **B.** This sentence supports the idea that there are financial concerns associated with funding public libraries. The money might better be spent on more essential services, such as education and healthcare.
8. **A.** The passage as a whole describes the importance of librarians in modern times. The other choices mention smaller details about the importance of libraries.
9. **C.** An example of how librarians help people prepare for the workforce is assisting them with job searches and resume development.
10. **D.** The passage is primarily about libraries and the role of librarians, not teachers.
11. **C.** Sentence 9 states that librarians must keep up with the latest trends. Sentence 12, which identifies these trends, should follow this sentence.
12. **D.** The added sentence gives an example of how librarians help researchers showcase their work, so it should follow sentence 11.
13. **D.** Line 18 mentions that libraries offer services to family. The added sentence elaborates on this by clarifying that librarians' education better situates them to offer these services.
14. **B.** Line 20 discusses how libraries provide space for students to work on projects and their studies. Line 25 expands on this by explaining how libraries assist students with their schoolwork.
15. **C.** Although some libraries face budget cuts and shutdowns, the author makes clear that librarians will remain relevant in the 21st century. Specifically, they will take on additional tasks associated with electronic information.

Key

16. **A.** The fact that fair trade products had increased sales would support the idea that shoppers were not deterred from purchasing them despite their expense.
17. **D.** The sentence about Adam Smith interrupts the discussion of fair trade products.
18. **A.** Sentence 6 discusses how fair trade products benefit workers. The new sentence elaborates on this discussion. By sentence 7, the focus has shifted to the effect of fair trade on communities more broadly.
19. **A.** Though sentence 8 mentions types of fair trade food products, it interrupts the discussion of fair trade's benefits.
20. **B.** Sentence 7 states that fair trade products benefit local communities. Sentence 13 gives examples of how communities benefit.
21. **A.** The paragraph describes "selfish" reasons to support fair trade: the products often taste better and are of higher quality. C is too extreme. The paragraph does indicate many benefits of fair trade products, but it never suggests that all the benefits must be analyzed (examined) in order for it to remain profitable.
22. **C.** Sentence 11 introduces crop rotation and sentence 12 indicates a positive result of this process. The sentence that is added between them should describe what crop rotation is so that the benefits of crop rotation are better understood.
23. **C.** The author would agree that the fair trade movement illustrates that people can make ethical economic choices despite cheaper purchasing options.
24. **B.** The author discusses how the idea of traveling to Mars is exciting and how a mission to Mars could potentially benefit humankind. The author also acknowledges that there are many reasons why going to Mars is not a good idea (it is dangerous and expensive). Thus, the author would think we should pause for consideration before pursuing such an ambitious plan.
25. **D.** Sentence 7 builds on sentence 6 by giving the first practical advantage of the mission (knowledge gained during the mission can benefit humans). The new sentence elaborates on sentence 7 by giving a second advantage, thus building on sentence 7 (that the technology used in the mission itself can be applied to Earth in various fields, such as in addressing environmental challenges). Sentence 8 further elaborates on how technology can address environmental challenges on Earth.
26. **B.** Choice B explains why the United States has political incentives to travel to Mars: to be a political and economic leader in the world. Note that Choice D, while political, deals with the past instead of the future.
27. **D.** Sentence 17 states that a source of breathable oxygen is needed. Sentence 11 clarifies why one method of obtaining it may not be possible.
28. **C.** The paragraph discusses the challenges of obtaining breathable oxygen on Mars. The fact that high levels of oxygen can cause health problems is irrelevant (the main concern is low levels of oxygen).

Week 14B: TEI

1. Which of the following choices represent actions performed by cool roofs that directly serve to keep buildings cool **AND** that are directly illustrated by the drawing of the cool roof in Figure 1?
   Select all answers that apply.
   - ☐ Some light that strikes the roofs enters the building as solar and heat energy.
   - ☐ Some heat trapped in the interior building exits through the cool roof.
   - ☒ **Some heat absorbed by the roof surface is radiated into the atmosphere.**
   - ☒ **Some solar energy that strikes the roof is returned to the atmosphere.**
   - ☐ The cool roof permanently traps excessive heat in the roofing material itself.

   Explanation:
   1) While the first choice is shown in the figure, it exemplifies how the building is heated rather than cooled (because sun enters the building as heat).
   2) The second choice is not shown in the figure.
   3) The third choice is shown by "thermal emittance" and contributes to the cooling of the building.
   4) The fourth choice is shown by "solar reflectance" and contributes to the cooling of the building.
   5) The fifth choice is not shown in the figure.

2. Based on the text, which attributes are relevant to each type of roof product? You may select more than one answer for each row.

Attribute	Low-slope Cool Roof Products	Steep-slope Cool Roof Products
Generally not used for personal homes.	☒	☐
Include asphalt-based products.	☒	☒
Include light- and cool-colored pigments.	☒	☒
May offer heat reduction savings comparable to cool walls.	☒	☒
Often include shingles.	☐	☒
Especially prone to regular maintenance costs.	☒	☐

   Explanation:

   1) The passage states that low-slope roofs are typically in commercial buildings while steep-slope roofs are usually used for residencies (paragraph 5), so low-slope cool roofs are NOT generally used for personal homes.
   2) Figure 2 shows that both roof types include asphalt-based products (first bullet point each roof type).
   3) Figure 2 shows that both roof types include materials with light and cool colors (second bullet point each roof type).
   4) The passage states that cool roofs in general offer services comparable to cool walls in terms of heat savings (paragraph 8).
   5) In the figure, steep-slope roof products include shingles (bullets 1,4,5,6).

6) The passage states low-slope roofs are especially prone to high maintenance costs (paragraph 7).

3. Reread the section below. Underline the two sentences that give quantitative evidence for the benefits of cool roofs.

Cool roofs provide a number of benefits beyond urban heat island mitigation, including:

- *Reduced energy use:* A cool roof lowers the amount of heat transferred to the building, which allows it to stay cooler and use less energy for air conditioning. <u>In air-conditioned residential buildings, solar reflectance from a cool roof can reduce peak cooling demand by 11–27%.</u>
- *Reduced air pollution and greenhouse gas emissions:* By lowering energy use, cool roofs decrease the associated air pollution and greenhouse gas emissions. When applied at a scale large enough to affect ambient temperatures, cool roofs could reduce the formation of ground-level ozone (which is heat-dependent) and reduce cooling energy use across a city.
- *Improved human health and comfort:* Cool roofs can help reduce the adverse health impacts of heat islands, such as heat exhaustion, respiratory difficulties, dizziness and cramps, and heat-induced death. <u>One United Kingdom study showed that cool roofs, when implemented across a city, could offset 18% of heat-related mortality associated with the heat island effect.</u>

Explanation: These sentences use quantitative evidence (numerical data) to show benefits of cool roofs in terms of saving costs and lives.

Because cool roofs reflect sunlight and reduce solar heat gain into a building, they may increase energy use in buildings during winter months in cold climates. <u>However, this so-called "heating penalty" is typically offset by summer cooling energy savings.</u> Several factors can limit or reduce the heating penalty of cool roofs in winter. The sun's angle in winter is lower and days are shorter than in summer, reducing the effect of cool roofs on wintertime energy use. Effective insulation and energy-efficient design can also reduce impacts. Buildings in areas with heavy and long-lasting snow cover would have the lowest heating penalty from cool roofs, since the roofs will be covered with reflective snow for most of the winter. To maximize the energy savings and heat island benefits of cool roofs, building owners should consider implementing energy efficiency improvements such as insulation and air sealing.

4. For the paragraph above, underline the sentence where the author most directly introduces the idea that a concern about cool roofs is overstated.

Explanation: If the "heating penalty" is offset (counterbalanced) by summer cooling energy savings, then the summer cooling savings make up for the heating penalty. The use of the term "so-called" further suggests the concern mentioned in the first sentence (cool roofs increase energy use in winter months) is overstated (exaggerated).

5. What does the author state or imply about cool roofs in this paragraph? Select all answers that apply.
   - ☒ **Geographic factors can worsen the heating penalty of cool roofs.**
   - ☒ **Cool roofs may increase demand for heating during the winter months.**
   - ☐ Energy-efficient design choices typically fully eliminate the heating penalty.
   - ☒ **Conventional roofs may be less subject to a heating penalty because more sunlight striking the roofs warms the building.**
   - ☐ Areas with shorter days during the winter see less of a heating penalty with cool roofs because the lower angle of the sun's rays prevents them from being reflected by the roofs.
   - ☒ **Areas with more snowfall have a lower heating penalty for cool roofs because conventional roofs behave more similarly to cool roofs under such conditions.**

   Explanation:
   1) The first choice is true and implied by the fact that areas with long-lasting snow cover (a geographic factor) have a lower heating penalty, suggesting geographic factors can strengthen or lessen the heating penalty.
   2) The second choice is true and indicated by the first sentence.
   3) The third sentence is not true. While the text indicates that design choices can reduce impacts of the heating penalty, it does not state that it fully eliminates it.
   4) The fourth choice is implied by the first sentence. If cool roofs present a heating penalty because they reflect light, this suggests conventional roofs allow more heat into the buildings, reducing energy use for heating.
   5) The fifth choice is not true. While shorter days are associated with a lower heating penalty and a lower angle of the sun, cool roofs can still reflect light. Rather, the heating penalty is implied to be reduced because conventional roofs receive less sunlight if the days are shorter, decreasing the advantage of conventional roofs (they do not benefit as much from the heat of sunlight entering the buildings).
   6) The sixth choice is true because conventional roofs covered in snow similarly reflect light (by acting more like cool roofs).

6. Based on the descriptions in the text, identify the numbers of the figures (1,2, or 3) that correspond to each method in the table.

Method	Figure Number
Transit Method	2
Wobble Method	1
Direct Imaging	3

   Explanation:

   1) Figure 2 shows the brightness of a star changing as a planet crosses in front of it, which exemplifies the transit method.
   2) Figure 1 shows changes in a star's spectra as a star wobbles, which exemplifies the wobble method.
   3) Figure 3 shows a direct image of four planets orbiting a star.

One of the most famous exoplanet detection methods is the **transit method**, used by Kepler and other observatories. When a planet crosses in front of its host star, the light from the star dips slightly in brightness. Scientists can confirm a planet orbits its host star by repeatedly detecting these incredibly tiny dips in brightness using sensitive instruments. <u>If you can imagine trying to detect the dip in light from a massive searchlight when an ant crosses in front of it, at a distance of tens of miles away, you can begin to see how difficult it can be to spot a planet from light-years away!</u> Another drawback to the transit method is that the distant solar system must be at a favorable angle to our point of view here on Earth – if the distant system's angle is just slightly askew, there will be no transits. Even in our solar system, a transit is very rare. For example, there were two transits of Venus visible across our Sun from Earth in this century. But the next time Venus transits the Sun as seen from Earth will be in the year 2117 – more than a century from the 2012 transit, even though Venus will have completed nearly 150 orbits around the Sun by then!

7. Underline the sentence that uses an analogy to shed insight into a scientific process.
   Explanation: The underlined sentence gives an analogy (comparison). It compares the difficulty of measuring a dip in light in stars caused by planets from many light-years away to the difficulty of measuring a dip in a searchlight when a tiny ant passes in front of it.

8. Based on the text, which of the following is true about transits and/or the transit method? Select all answers that apply.
   ☐ It takes advantage of the fact that a planet's brightness increases and dips as it orbits its host star.
   ☒ **Its utility is as a method of planet identification is limited in part by its position relative to Earth.**
   ☐ Transits are rarely detected by this method in our own solar system because of limitations in the sensitivity of instruments.
   ☒ **Not every orbit of a planet around its star produces a transit visible from Earth.**

Explanation:

1) **The first choice is incorrect because the transit method looks at dips in the brightness of stars, not planets.**
2) **The second choice is correct because the text states one drawback of the transit method is that the solar system must be at a favorable angle to our view on Earth. It also discusses how it is difficult to detect transits from far away.**
3) **The third choice is incorrect because while the text does suggest transits of Venus are rare (a planet in our own solar system), it does not say that this is because of a lack of sensitivity in instruments. In fact, the passage emphasizes how highly sensitive instruments are.**
4) **The fourth sentence is supported by the last sentence of paragraph 2. Venus will do over 150 orbits between two of its transits, showing not every orbit results in a transit.**

9. Based on the text, which of the following is true about the wobble method? Select all answers that apply.

☐ It exploits the fact that planets wobble at regular intervals as they orbit a star.

☒ **The extent of the shift in a star's spectra allows scientists to use this method to determine if a companion to a star is a planet or another celestial body.**

☐ Scientists use this method to determine a planet's rotation rate as it orbits a star at regular intervals.

☒ **It was employed successfully to identify an exoplanet orbiting a star before the transit method or direct imaging were.**

Explanation:

1) The first choice is incorrect because the method takes advantage of the fact that stars, not planets, wobble.
2) The second choice is correct because the text states astronomers measure a star's spectra to determine the size of the object pulling on the host star and learn if the companion is a planet.
3) The third choice is incorrect because the text states that scientists can determine the time it takes a planet to orbit a star, not a planet's rotation rate.
4) The fourth choice is true because the first exoplanet orbiting a star that was detected (Pegasi 51b) was detected using this method.

10. Based on the text, which statements are true for each method? You may select more than one answer for each row.

Attribute	Transit Method	Wobble Method
An indirect way of detecting exoplanets.	☒	☒
Takes advantage of properties of planets occurring at predictable intervals.	☒	☒
Detection method directly attributable to the motion of stars.	☐	☒
Detection method directly attributable to shifts in light's brightness.	☒	☐
Provides information about orbital periods.	☒	☒

Explanation:
1) The first choice is correct for both methods because the exoplanets are detected indirectly by measuring changes in stars rather than by direct imaging of planets.
2) The second choice is correct for both methods. The text suggests that transits can occur at regular intervals (scientists repeatedly detect dips in brightness of stars to confirm a planet orbits a star). The text also suggests that the wobble method takes advantage of periodic shifts in spectra and that this method can be used to detect orbital periods.
3) The third choice is correct for the wobble method because it takes advantage of the fact that stars wobble (move).
4) The fourth choice is true for the transit method because it measures changes in stars' brightness.
5) The fifth choice is correct for both methods. Scientists determine a planet orbits its star with the transit method by repeatedly detecting shifts in brightness as a planet passes in front of its host star. Scientists use the wobble method to determine the amount of time it takes a planet to orbit its star.

11. Review the five events listed below. Place the following events in chronological order by filling in the table. For example, the event that happened first should be placed into the row labeled "Event 1," and the event that happened last should be placed into the row labeled "Event 5."

DDT is banned in the United States.	The bald eagle is officially considered to no longer be in danger of extinction.	2,300 breeding pairs of Kirtland's warblers are estimated to exist in the wild.	The estimated number of peregrine falcons in the wild was 3,875.	The American alligator is listed as an endangered species under the Endangered Species Preservation Act.

Event 1	The estimated number of peregrine falcons in the wild was 3,875.
Event 2	The American alligator is listed as an endangered species under the Endangered Species Preservation Act.
Event 3	DDT is banned in the United States.

Event 4	The bald eagle is officially considered to no longer be in danger of extinction.
Event 5	2,300 breeding pairs of Kirtland's warblers are estimated to exist in the wild.

Explanation:

1) The estimated number of peregrine falcons in the wild was 3,875 prior to the 1940s.
2) The American alligator was listed as an endangered species under the Endangered Species Preservation Act in 1967.
3) DDT was banned after 1967 (when the bald eagle was listed as endangered) and helped to conserve the eagle's habitat.
4) The bald eagle was officially unlisted as endangered in 2007.
5) 2,300 breeding pairs of Kirtland's warblers were estimated in 2019.

12. Based on the text, which statements are true for each species? You may select more than one answer for each row.

Attribute	Peregrine Falcon	Bald Eagle	Kirtland's Warbler
Faced threats to its natural habitat.	☒	☒	☒
Chemicals used by humans were largely responsible for declines in its populations.	☒	☒	☐
Was removed from the endangered species list within 30 years of first being listed.	☒	☐	☐
Hunting from humans was a major reason it was listed as endangered.	☐	☒	☐
Parasitic threats were a key danger for this species.	☐	☐	☒
Initially listed as endangered under a predecessor to the ESA.	☒	☒	☐

Explanation:

1) The peregrine falcon faced threats of pesticides in its natural habitat. The bald eagle faced habitat destruction and degradation. The Kirtland's warbler faced habitat threats.
2) The peregrine falcon was threatened by pesticides. The bald eagle was threatened by the insecticide DDT.
3) The peregrine falcon was listed as endangered in 1970 and delisted in 1999, a period of less than 30 years. The other birds were delisted more than 30 years after being listed (the bald eagle was listed in 1967 and delisted in 2007; the Kirtland's warbler was listed in 1973 and delisted in 2019).
4) The bald eagle was threatened by illegal shooting.
5) The Kirtland's warbler was threatened by parasitism.
6) The peregrine falcon and bald eagle were listed as endangered prior to the ESA of 1973.

13. Which of the following species is no longer listed as endangered? Select all answers that apply.
- ☒ **Bald eagle**
- ☒ **Kirtland's warbler**
- ☒ **Peregrine falcon**
- ☐ Whooping crane
- ☒ **American alligator**

Explanation:

The passage states that all of the listed organisms except the whooping crane were unlisted as endangered, though the whooping crane is making progress towards recovery.

14. Reread the paragraph below. Underline the sentence that most directly identifies the aim of the ESA.

The ESA was enacted in 1973 as a response to the declining populations of many species of animals and plants. **The Act was designed to protect and recover species at risk of extinction and to promote the conservation of ecosystems and habitats necessary for the survival of those species.** Each of these species is a part of the web of life, each with a unique cultural and biological community, performing services that are essential to our combined well-being. By conserving them, guided by the best-available science, we help protect healthy air, land, and water for everyone.

Explanation:

The second sentence directly states what the act was designed to do (its aim, or goal). The first sentence explains the impetus for the act. The last two sentences explain the importance of the act.

15. Based on the text, which of the following is true about the ESA? Select all answers that apply.
    - ☐ Its impact is limited to species that have been officially listed as endangered.
    - ☒ **The act is credited with saving the majority of species listed under it.**
    - ☒ **The act has been employed to save both plants and animals.**
    - ☒ **Humans themselves benefit from the impact of the ESA.**
    - ☒ **Its success in saving certain species may hinge on cooperation from multiple entities.**

Explanation:

1) The first choice is not true because paragraph 3 says the ESA prevented some species from needing protecting from the act, implying it helped save them in advance.
2) The second choice is correct because paragraph 4 says the ESA is credited with saving 99% of the species listed under it.
3) The third choice is correct because paragraph 1 states that the act has saved plants and animals.
4) The fourth choice is correct because the passage makes clear humans benefit from the act, as it helps provide healthy water and air for everyone and performs services for "our combined well-being."
5) The fifth choice is correct because the passage makes clear that multiple partners have played a role in protecting species, such as in paragraph 3 and in paragraph 6.

16. The table below gives several steps in a sequence of events Kegerreis's team proposed. Put the events in chronological order by labeling them a whole number from "1" to "5" such that "1" is the first event and "5" is the last.

Event	Step in Hypothesized Sequence
A disk formed around Mars as a result of the products of multiple collisions.	4
The gravitational pull of Mars disrupted an asteroid passing by it.	1
Material from the disk clumped together to form moons.	5
Asteroid pieces that remain in Mars' orbit collided, grinding each other down over a long period of time.	3
Some rocky fragments from the disrupted asteroid were strewn outside of Mars' orbit, and others stayed in its orbit.	2

Explanation:

Paragraphs 3 and 4 show the sequence of events proposed. First, the gravitational pull of Mars disrupted (broke up) an asteroid, leading some rocky fragments to stay in Mars' orbit and others to get strewn outside of it. Over a long period of time, the asteroid pieces that remained collided, grinding each other down. The chunks resulting from these collisions formed a disk. The materials from the disk clumped together to form the moons.

17. Which of the following identifies an aspect of Kegerreis's team's hypothesis that is SIMILAR to an attribute of one of the two leading hypotheses discussed in paragraphs 8 and 9? Select all answers that apply.

    ☒ **Debris formed a disk that formed the moons.**
    ☐ The debris that formed the moons included material originating from the Martian surface.
    ☒ **Mars' moons contain at least some material deriving from asteroids.**
    ☐ Tidal forces disrupted an asteroid passing by Mars.
    ☐ Celestial bodies captured by Mars' gravity remained intact.

    Explanation:

    1) **The first statement applies to Kegerreis's team's hypothesis and the giant impact hypothesis.**
    2) **The second statement only applies to the giant impact hypothesis.**
    3) **The third statement applies to Kegerreis's team's hypothesis and the capture hypothesis.**
    4) **The fourth statement only applies to Kegerreis's team's hypothesis.**
    5) **The fifth statement only applies to the capture hypothesis.**

18. Underline the sentence that identifies an expectation that would need to be met to make the giant impact hypothesis more convincing.

[8] Two hypotheses for the formation of the Martian moons have led the pack. One proposes that passing asteroids were captured whole by Mars' gravity, which could explain the moons' somewhat asteroid-like appearance. The other says that a giant impact on the planet blasted out enough material – a mix of Mars and impactor debris – to form a disk and, ultimately, the moons. Scientists believe a similar process formed Earth's Moon.

[9] The latter explanation better accounts for the paths the moons travel today – in near-circular orbits that closely align with Mars' equator. <u>However, a giant impact ejects material into a disk that, mostly, stays close to the planet</u>. And Mars' moons, especially Deimos, sit quite far away from the planet and probably formed out there, too.

[10] "Our idea allows for a more efficient distribution of moon-making material to the outer regions of the disk," said Jack Lissauer, a research scientist at Ames and co-author on the paper. "That means a much smaller 'parent' asteroid could still deliver enough material to send the moons' building blocks to the right place."

Explanation: This statement identifies what would be expected if the giant impact hypothesis were true (the disk should stay close to the planet).

19. Underline the sentence that identifies an advantage that one of the leading hypotheses has over the other.

[8] Two hypotheses for the formation of the Martian moons have led the pack. One proposes that passing asteroids were captured whole by Mars' gravity, which could explain the moons' somewhat asteroid-like appearance. The other says that a giant impact on the planet blasted out enough material – a mix of Mars and impactor debris – to form a disk and, ultimately, the moons. Scientists believe a similar process formed Earth's Moon.

[9] <u>The latter explanation better accounts for the paths the moons travel today – in near-circular orbits that closely align with Mars' equator.</u> However, a giant impact ejects material into a disk that, mostly, stays close to the planet. And Mars' moons, especially Deimos, sit quite far away from the planet and probably formed out there, too.

[10] "Our idea allows for a more efficient distribution of moon-making material to the outer regions of the disk," said Jack Lissauer, a research scientist at Ames and co-author on the paper. "That means a much smaller 'parent' asteroid could still deliver enough material to send the moons' building blocks to the right place."

Explanation: The bolded sentence states an advantage of the giant impact hypothesis over the capture hypothesis (it better explains the moons' paths).

20. According to the text, which of the following is true about the MMX mission? Select all answers that apply.
    ☒ **Its main objective is to examine hypotheses for how Mars' moons formed.**
    ☐ The mission itself will use a supercomputer to determine if it is possible for Martian material to have formed the moons.
    ☐ Samples from Phobos and Deimos will be collected for chemical analysis.
    ☐ The mission will be developed and spearheaded by NASA.
    ☒ **Kegerreis's team will attempt to make predictions about what the mission can find through further studies.**

Explanation:

1) **The first choice is true because the first sentence of paragraph 11 indicates the main goal of the mission is to test ideas for how Mars' moons formed.**
2) **The second choice is incorrect because the mission itself is a sample collection mission (though Kegerreis's team will likely do this).**
3) **The third choice is incorrect because only samples from Phobos will be collected.**
4) **The fourth choice is incorrect because the Japan Aerospace Exploration Agency will lead the mission.**

5) The fifth choice is true because paragraph 13 indicates Kegerreis's team will attempt to make predictions about what the MMX mission could find.

21. In the first paragraph, the narrator employs which of the following techniques? Select all answers that apply.
    ☐ Extended metaphors.
    ☒ **Repetitive constructions.**
    ☒ **Personal confession.**
    ☐ Personification of inanimate objects.
    ☐ Detailed imagery.

Explanation:

1) The first choice is incorrect because no metaphors are given in the first paragraph.
2) The second choice is correct. We see the repetition of "John is," "what is one to do?" and "personally, I."
3) The third choice is correct, as the narrator confesses her true feelings about her situation, such as how she feels about her condition and her treatment plan. She also confesses to writing in secret.
4) The fourth and fifth choices occur later in the passage when the narrator describes the yellow wallpaper but not in the first paragraph.

22. Read the paragraph below. Underline the sentence that most directly reveals that the narrator has deceived her loved ones.

John laughs at me, of course, but one expects that in marriage. John is practical in the extreme. He has no patience with faith, an intense horror of superstition, and he scoffs openly at any talk of things not to be felt and seen and put down in figures. John is a physician. You see he does not believe I am sick! And what can one do? If a physician of high standing, and one's own husband, assures friends and relatives that there is really nothing the matter with one but temporary nervous depression—a slight hysterical tendency—what is one to do? My brother is also a physician, and also of high standing, and he says the same thing. So I take phosphates or phosphites—whichever it is, and tonics, and journeys, and air, and exercise, and am absolutely forbidden to "work" until I am well again. Personally, I disagree with their ideas. Personally, I believe that congenial work, with excitement and change, would do me good. But what is one to do? <u>I did write for a while in spite of them; but it DOES exhaust me a good deal—having to be so sly about it, or else meet with heavy opposition.</u> I sometimes fancy that in my condition if I had less opposition and more society and stimulus—but John says the very worst thing I can do is to think about my condition, and I confess it always makes me feel bad.

Explanation: The choice reveals that the narrator lied about writing (she wrote in secret).

23. Consider the themes below.

The restorative power of intellectual outlets.
Gender discrimination in professional settings.
The subordination of women in marriage.
The destructive effects of isolation on personal happiness.
The power of an unrestrained imagination.

In the table below, identify which theme is most directly related to the corresponding quote. One theme will not be used.

Quote	
"And what can one do? If a physician of high standing, and one's own husband, assures friends and relatives that there is really nothing the matter with one but temporary nervous depression—a slight hysterical tendency—what is one to do?"	The subordination of women in marriage.
"The front pattern *does* move—and no wonder! The woman behind shakes it! Sometimes I think there are a great many women behind, and sometimes only one, and she crawls around fast, and her crawling shakes it all over."	The power of an unrestrained imagination.
"Personally, I believe that congenial work, with excitement and change, would do me good."	The restorative power of intellectual outlets.
"The color is repellent, almost revolting; a smoldering unclean yellow, strangely faded by the slow-turning sunlight. John does not know how much I really suffer."	The destructive effects of isolation on personal happiness.

Explanation:

1) The first quote illustrates the power the narrator's husband has over her, thus illustrating the subordination of women in marriage.
2) The second quote illustrates the power of the narrator's imagination, as she sees things in the wallpaper that are not really there.
3) The third quote illustrates the narrator's belief in the importance of intellectual outlets (such as work) to be restorative (do her some good).
4) The fourth quote reveals the narrator's suffering as she is locked away in her room, showing the destructive effects of isolation on personal happiness.

24. Select which attributes the narrator states or implies about each character. Select all answers that apply.

Attribute	John	John's sister	The narrator's brother
Has a high social status.	☒	☐	☒
Complicit in the narrator's treatment plan.	☒	☒	☒
Believes the narrator should avoid writing.	☒	☒	☒
Works as a physician.	☒	☐	☒
Oversees the narrator's prescriptions.	☒	☐	☐

Explanation:

1) We are told John is a physician of high standing. Since the narrator's brother is also a physician, it is implied he too has high social status. John's sister works as a housekeeper, so she likely does not have high social status.
2) All three characters are complicit in the narrator's treatment plan. While John oversees it, the narrator's brother agrees with his ideas. It is also suggested John's sister agrees, as the narrator believes John's sister would be upset if she caught the narrator writing.
3) John believes the narrator should not write, and the narrator's brother agrees with John's ideas. John's sister is described as believing writing makes the narrator sick.
4) John and the narrator's brother are physicians.
5) John controls the narrator's prescriptions, as indicated in paragraph 2.

25. Select the best answer for both blanks.

"He is very careful and loving and hardly lets me stir without special direction."

In the context of the passage as a whole, the statement above can primarily be characterized as (i) _____ and suggests John's attentiveness _____

Blank i	Blank ii
ironic	is a reflection of his deep expertise in mental health conditions.
mendacious	removes the narrator's doubts about the efficacy of her treatment plan.
adulatory	is a mere façade to keep up appearances as a doting husband.
recriminatory	**may reflect his controlling nature.**

Explanation: The statement is ironic and shows the contradiction between the seemingly good intentions of John and the destructive impact of his treatment on the narrator (as revealed elsewhere in the passage). It also presents a contradictory image of John as both loving (a positive quality) and controlling (a negative quality). John's attentiveness (he is described as "careful") may be show his controlling nature: he does not let the narrator stir without special direction. While this could be taken to mean he looks out for her safety, it can also mean he exhibits excessive control over her freedom.

26. The passage above has 13 sentences labeled from 1 to 13. In the blanks below, write in the numbers corresponding to the three sentences that should be deleted from the passage for the sake of logic and cohesion.

Sentence 3
Sentence 11
Sentence 13

Explanation:

1) Sentence 3 about the age of individual birds interrupts the discussion of banding studies (which study the habits of birds).
2) Sentence 11 interrupts the discussion of why hummingbirds migrate with a loosely connected point about migration that goes unexplained.

3) Sentence 13 introduces a new point about migration without further explanation that is not directly related to the discussion about why hummingbirds migrate.

27. Without adjusting the capitalization, insert a comma or colon to fix the sentence.
*For example, the ruby-throated hummingbird shows a high degree of **fidelity:** approximately one fifth of birds return to the same site year after year.*

Explanation: A colon should follow the independent clause to illustrate how ruby-throated hummingbirds show a high degree of fidelity (loyalty).

28. Without adjusting the capitalization, insert a comma, semicolon, or colon to fix the sentence.
*In the United States, hummingbirds typically migrate to the North during the spring and to the South during the **winter;** however, the precise reasons why they migrate are not completely understood.*

Explanation: A semicolon is needed after "winter" to avoid a run-on. "However" should follow the semicolon since it introduces a contrasting independent clause to the one before the semicolon.

29. Underline the word in this sentence that either has an unnecessary comma after it OR is missing a comma that should be present after it.

In banding studies, individual hummingbirds are <u>trapped,</u> and given identification numbers, which are written on aluminum foil and wrapped around their legs.

Explanation: The two coordinate descriptions of hummingbirds in the predicate connected by "and" do not need a comma between them since there are only two of them (if three details about hummingbirds were given, a comma would be needed). There is also no independent clause on both sides of "and" (there is just one before it), so no comma is needed.

30. Underline the word that produces a grammatical error in the sentence below.

Evidence from various studies <u>suggest</u> that many birds follow a set route each year, demonstrating loyalty to particular sites.

Explanation: The singular subject "evidence" requires the singular verb "suggests."

31. Underline ONE word that should be deleted from this sentence to eliminate the redundancy error.
In the beginning, the camper was <u>initially</u> concerned about hiking along the trail, but his worries quickly subsided once he saw the beautiful scenery.

Explanation: "Initially" is implied by "in the beginning."

32. Underline TWO words in the sentence below that result in a redundancy error.
As a result of assimilation programs, many Native American groups have lost aspects of their cultures, such as widespread use of their native languages. Yet efforts by Indian and Alaskan native elders to teach their native languages to younger generations <u>raised</u> and <u>lifted</u> these languages from obscurity.

Explanation: The underlined words have the same meaning (to "elevate").

33. Underline the word in the sentence below that is grammatically incorrect.
The mantis shrimp is one of the strongest animals in the world on a pound for pound basis. This crustacean, using clubs at the ends of <u>their</u> forelegs, produces quick and powerful strikes to its prey.

Explanation: The singular possessive determiner "its" is needed instead of "their," since the forelegs belong to the singular subject "crustacean."

34. Add missing punctuation that is needed to make this sentence grammatically correct.
*Male tanagers can consume carotenoids to make their feathers darker, an honest signal of fitness to potential mates. The ability of some tanagers to manipulate light to give their feathers a darker appearance without actually having to consume the carotenoids**, though,** can serve as a dishonest signal of fitness.*

Explanation: The conjunctive adverb "though" is nonessential in the sentence and adds a pause for effect. It shows a contrast relationship to the sentence before (while tanagers can consume carotenoids.

35. Add missing punctuation that is needed to make this sentence grammatically correct.
*Consistent with the vision of its **founders**, the nonprofit serves to promote a **nurturing,** inclusive environment for students to develop their artistic skills.*

Explanation: A comma is needed after the optional opening phrase ending in "founders." A comma should separate the coordinate adjectives "nurturing" and "inclusive."

36. Underline the word in the sentence below that is grammatically incorrect.

Throughout her career, Jane Addams, founder of the Hull House, sought to improve education for children, <u>documenting</u> social illnesses, and promote feminist values.

Explanation: "Documenting" creates a parallelism error. For the list to use consistent verb forms, "document" is needed.

37. Select the best answers for each of the three blanks

Managed care networks seek to promote disease management and preventative care. The ability of managed care networks to meet these goals (i)_____ integral to lowering costs. Many companies hire representatives to regularly contact clients to make sure that (ii) _____ are engaging in healthful behaviors. They will often encourage at-risk patients to seek medical care during times when they are experiencing minor health issues. (iii)_____ precludes more catastrophic health disasters that would be costlier for companies to cover.

Blank i	Blank ii	Blank iii
is	he or she	That
are	them	**This practice**
being	**they**	Doing it
to be	whom	It

Explanation:
1) **Blank 1: The singular subject "ability" requires the singular verb "is."**
2) **Blank 2: The plural pronoun "they" refers to the "clients." The subjective form "they" should precede "are" since "they" perform the action**
3) **Blank 3: "This practice" uses the most precise language, avoiding an ambiguous pronoun error.**

38. Select the best answers for each of the three blanks.

Some social psychologists question if there is such thing as a genuinely altruistic good deed and instead argue that seemingly generous actions have (i)_____. For example, students may engage in community service to be more "competitive" for admission to selective colleges. A rider on the bus may give (ii)_____ seat to an elderly person to avoid negative social judgement by observers. By definition, altruistic acts are done to help others without expectation of any benefit in return. The empathy-altruism hypothesis argues that evidence from both psychological experiments and neuroimaging suggests that people high in empathy may help others out of genuine concern for their welfare, (iii)_____those lower in empathy may engage in helping behaviors for more selfish reasons.

Blank i	Blank ii	Blank iii
selfish motivations?	their	which
selfish motivations.	our	**while**
selfish, motivations?	**his or her**	instead,
selfish, motivations.	whose	however,

Explanation:

1) **Blank 1: No comma should separate the adjective "selfish" from the modified noun "motivations." The indirect question should end in a period.**
2) **Blank 2: The singular possessive determiner "his or her" is needed because the seat belongs to "a rider."**
3) **Blank 3: The subordinating conjunction "while" is needed after the comma to avoid a comma splice. "Instead" and "however" cause comma splices. A contrast transition is needed to show the difference between people with high and low empathy, so "which" does not make sense.**

39. Select the best answers for each of the three blanks.

Mohammad Yunus, the Founder of the Grameen Bank in Bangladesh, is a pioneer in the concept of microcredit. Since Yunus perceived traditional banks as profit-seeking entities primarily serving the wealthy, he established the Grameen Bank to serve disadvantaged populations. Under the microcredit model, the bank gives small loans to individuals (i) _____ are too poor to qualify for (ii) _____. Each time a borrower repays the loan, he or she is entitled to an even larger loan. Due to the success of the Grameen Bank, microfinance institutions (iii)_____ now a global phenomenon.

Blank i	Blank ii	Blank iii
whom	**traditional bank loans**	will be
which	traditional bank loans owing to a lack of funds	has become
who	traditional bank loans due to a dearth of income	**are**
they	traditional bank loans in an impoverished state	is

Explanation:

1) Blank 1: The subjective "who" is needed before the verb "are" to create a relative clause defining the individuals. "Whom" cannot be used before a verb. "Which" cannot refer to people. "They" would result in a comma splice (two independent clauses improperly combined).
2) Blank 2: The other choices are redundant, repeating information about the individuals being in poverty.
3) Blank 3: The plural verb "are" agrees with the plural subject "microfinance institutions." The sentence takes place in the present (as indicated by "now'").

40. Select the best answers for each of the three blanks.

Both the *Harry Potter* series and the *Hunger Games* trilogy portray young protagonists who experience what is often (i)_____ a "hero's journey." In *Harry Potter*, the titular character is a valiant wizard who takes on supernatural forces of evil. (ii)_____ in *The Hunger Games*, Katniss Everdeen becomes a somewhat reluctant hero against an oppressive regime. In both cases, the characters rely on the help of their friends and (iii)_____ all while navigating ordinary challenges associated with being teenagers. Both characters came from humble beginnings before assuming heroic roles with humility and courage.

Blank i	Blank ii	Blank iii
dubbed	Nevertheless,	allies;
dubbed,	Specifically,	allies
dubbed:	**Similarly,**	**allies,**
dubbed—	For instance,	allies and

Explanation:
1) **Blank 1: No punctuation should separate the verb from its object.**
2) **Blank 2: A comparison is made between how the protagonists in the series take on forces of evil.**
3) **Blank 3: A comma should separate the independent clause from the supplementary phrase.**

41. Select the best answers for each of the three blanks.

The Mycenaean civilization flourished in Greece from 1650 to 1200 B.C. The Mycenaeans were the first people to speak the Greek language and were influenced by the culture of the Minoans, who resided in Crete. While later Greeks often told stories about this (i)_____Homer in *Iliad* and *Odyssey*, there was no evidence that the Myceneans actually existed until (ii) _____Heinrich Schliemann made a discovery in 1876. He found artifacts from this lost civilization high in the mountains of (iii)_____ golden masks, bronze weapons, and palaces that illustrated the wealth of Mycenaean rulers.

Blank i	Blank ii	Blank iii
group they included	**archaeologist**	Mycenae, such as:
group, they included	archaeologist:	**Mycenae:**
group, including	archaeologist	Mycenae,
group such as,	archaeologist;	Mycenae

Explanation

1) Blank 1: The nonessential example should be set off by commas in the middle of a sentence. "Including" is a conventional participle that can start this phrase. The second option is wrong because the optional phrase between commas itself cannot be a full sentence.
2) Blank 2: No punctuation should separate the professional title "archaeologist" from the essential name.
3) Blank 3: A colon should follow the complete sentence to introduce the list.

42. Select the best answers for each of the three blanks.

Many marine mammals rely heavily on (i)_____ a process whereby they use sound waves to locate objects and gain information about their surroundings. By emitting sound waves and interpreting their reverberations off of objects, marine mammals can get a sense of these (ii) _____ shapes and positions. (iii)_____ echolocation essentially functions as a means by which these animals "see the world." This is especially important in areas where water is dark or murky.

Blank i	Blank ii	Blank iii
echolocation	objects	**Therefore,**
echolocation,	object's	On the other hand,
echolocation;	**objects'**	For example,
echolocation, this is	objects':	Nonetheless,

Explanation:

1) Blank 1: A comma should separate the independent clause from the nonessential appositive.
2) Blank 2: The plural possessive form "objects'" is needed since the shapes and positions belong to multiple objects. No colon is needed since there is no complete thought before the colon.
3) Blank 3: The cause-and-effect transition is needed because the sentence before clarifies how echolocation is a means by which some mammals can "see" the world (they can learn detailed information about objects).

Colorado-based artist Gregg _____ to use his work to share his perspective as both an Indigenous person and human being, believes in using his craft to produce accurate portrayals of Indigenous experiences and shatter stereotypes.

43. Which of the following best completes the text so that it conforms to the conventions of Standard English? Select all answers that apply.
   - ☒ **Deal, seeking**
   - ☐ Deal, whom seeks
   - ☐ Deal, that seeks
   - ☒ **Deal, who seeks**
   - ☐ Deal, he seeks
   - ☐ Deal seeks

Explanation:

1) The first choice correctly creates a nonessential participial phrase to describe Deal.
2) The second choice incorrectly uses "whom" before a verb.
3) The third choice incorrectly uses the essential relative pronoun "that" after a comma.
4) The fourth choice correctly creates a nonessential relative clause to describe Deal. "Who" can precede a verb.
5) The fifth choice incorrectly places a complete sentence in between commas as if it is an optional phrase.
6) The sixth choice fails to set off the optional information by commas on both sides, resulting into two main verbs ("seeks" and "believes") improperly combined.

A California sea lion who achieved fame in 2013 for her ability to bob her head to a rhythm reentered the <u>limelight she appeared</u> in a new study that showed her synchronization matched or surpassed that of humans.

44. Which of the following corrects the underlined portion? Select all answers that apply.
   - ☒ **limelight; she appeared**
   - ☒ **limelight, appearing**
   - ☒ **limelight. She appeared**
   - ☐ limelight appeared
   - ☐ limelight; appearing
   - ☒ **limelight when she appeared**

Explanation:

1) The first choice correctly uses a semicolon to separate independent clauses.
2) The second choice correctly uses a comma to separate an independent clause from a nonessential present participial phrase.
3) The third choice correctly uses a period between two complete sentences.
4) The fourth choice has two main predicate verbs ("reentered" and "appeared") improperly combined.
5) The fifth choice incorrectly uses a semicolon to separate an independent clause from a nonessential present participial phrase.
6) The sixth choice correctly adds a subordinating conjunction to create a complex sentence, connecting an independent clause to a dependent clause beginning with "when."

One of the most popular items traded along the Silk Road, a network of ancient trade routes connecting the East and the West, was jade,_____ for its appearance, rarity, durability, and spiritual significance.

    45. Which of the following best completes the text so that it conforms to the conventions of Standard English? Select all answers that apply.
- ☐ it was highly prized
- ☐ it is highly prized
- ☒ **highly prized**
- ☒ **which was highly prized**
- ☐ prizing

Explanation:

1) The first blank creates a comma splice, separating independent clauses by a comma.
2) The second blank creates a comma splice, separating independent clauses by a comma. It also has a verb tense error.
3) The third blank correctly results in a comma between an independent clause and a nonessential past participial phrase.
4) The fourth blank correctly results in a comma between an independent clause and a nonessential relative clause defining "jade."
5) The fifth blank is confusing and unidiomatic, suggesting jade itself prized something.

Made in the USA
Middletown, DE
31 May 2025

76244868R10256